AMBITIOUS HE

Writing, Friendship, Love –
The Jewsbury Sisters, Felicia Hemans,
and Jane Welsh Carlyle

Norma Clarke

ROUTLEDGE

London and New York

First published 1990
by Routledge
11 New Fetter Lane, London EC4P 4EE

Simultaneously published in the USA and Canada
by Routledge
a division of Routledge, Chapman and Hall, Inc.
29 West 35th Street, New York, NY 10001

Printed in Great Britain
by Butler & Tanner Ltd, Frome, Somerset

British Library Cataloguing in Publication Data
Clarke, Norma
Ambitious Heights: writing, friendship, love: the
Jewsbury sisters, Felicia Hemans, and Jane Welsh Carlyle.
1. English literature. Women writers, 1775–1886 – Critical
studies
I. Title
820.9′9287
ISBN 0–415–00051–3
ISBN 0–415–00052–1 pbk

Library of Congress Cataloging in Publication Data
Clarke, Norma
Ambitious Heights: writing, friendship, love: the Jewsbury
sisters, Felicia Hemans, and Jane Welsh Carlyle/Norma Clarke.
p. cm.
Includes bibliographical references.
1. Women and literature–Great Britain–History–19th century.
2. English literature–19th century–History and criticism.
3. English literature–Women authors–History and criticism.
4. Women authors, English–19th century–Biography. 5. Hemans,
Felicia Dorothea Browne, 1794–1835. 6. Carlyle, Jane Welsh,
1801–66. 7. Jewsbury, Geraldine Endsor, 1812–80. 8. Jewsbury,
Maria Jane, 1800–33. I. Title.
PR115.C54 1990
820.9′9287–dc20   89–24205

FOR MY MOTHER AND FATHER

Felicia Hemans, born 1794, died 1835.
Maria Jane Jewsbury, born 1800, died 1833.
Jane Welsh Carlyle, born 1801, died 1866.
Geraldine Jewsbury, born 1812, died 1880.

I saw ambition's heights arise,
Fame's pathway o'er it spread sublime ...

Unwearied up the steep I prest,
And vainly deemed my home would be
'Mid the bright bowers where crowned ones rest,
Amid the glorious and the free.

But soon came on a darker mood,
Fame's lingering sunbeam ceased to glow,
The heights grew barren where I stood,
And death's wide Ocean roared below.

Maria Jane Jewsbury, 'A Summer Eve's Vision',
Lays of Leisure Hours (1829), p. 152

if I might write my own biography from
beginning to end – without reservation or false
colouring – it would be an invaluable document
for my countrywomen in more than one
particular, but *'decency forbids!'*

Jane Welsh Carlyle, Letters to her Family 1839–63,
ed. Leonard Huxley, p. 77

CONTENTS

LIST OF ILLUSTRATIONS

ACKNOWLEDGEMENTS

I have been helped by many people while writing this book and it is a pleasure to be able to put my thanks on record. As a student on the Women's Studies M.A. at the University of Kent from 1983 to 1985, I benefited from the energy, scepticism, and stimulus of feminist scholars working in a variety of disciplines. I should especially like to thank Clare Ungerson who first suggested the course to me; the members of the Feminist Aesthetics seminar, in particular Iris Dove, Wilma Fraser, Kate McLuskie, and Jan Montefiore; and Mireille Belloni, Maddy Paxman, and Wendy Lee.

The librarians at the British Library have been unfailingly helpful. I am also grateful to the British Library international interlibrary loan service which made it possible for me to study on microfiche copies of Geraldine Jewsbury's letters to Walter Mantell, over five hundred of which are in the possession of the National Library of New Zealand, to whom thanks are also due. Glenise A. Matheson, Keeper of Manuscripts at the John Rylands University Library of Manchester, made the Jewsbury papers available to me, as did staff at the Manchester Central Library. Staff at the Liverpool Record Office made available papers relating to Felicia Hemans's early life. Richard Woof, Director of the Wordsworth Trust, Centre for British Romanticism at Dove Cottage, Grasmere, gave permission to consult the Wordsworth Library holdings of Maria Jane Jewsbury's letters to Dora Wordsworth. I should like to thank both him and Jeff Cowton for their help. I am grateful to the Duke of Northampton for permission to consult Carlyle material among the Northampton papers at Compton Winyates. Permission to reproduce pictures in their keeping was granted by: Tamworth Library; The Wordsworth Trust; Carlyle House; and the University of Columbia, for the pictures of Maria Jane Jewsbury; Felicia Hemans; Thomas Carlyle and *The Chelsea Interior*; and Geraldine Jewsbury and Jane Carlyle respectively. The National Trust supplied the prints of Thomas Carlyle and *The Chelsea Interior*.

Early parts of this book were drafted during a six-month stay in California where I was able to draw on the magnificent resources of the University of California at Davis. For special services in this regard I have to thank Cynthia Brantley. I should also like to thank the librarians of the Norman and Charlotte Strouse collection at the University of California at Santa Cruz for their assistance.

Nancy Bramberg and Dick Curley did much to make our stay a happy one, and certain regular Wednesday lunches on campus with Donna Reed were a lifeline.

The London Feminist History Group gave me the opportunity to speak about Geraldine Jewsbury and Jane Carlyle when I was beginning my research; and History Workshop conference provided a chance to talk about the Jewsbury sisters. I should like to thank both organizations for being there. WEA classes, over many years, have forced me to sharpen my ideas.

Cora Kaplan gave encouragement at an early stage. Jenny Uglow made time in an exceedingly busy life to read the manuscript and meet to talk about it. I am deeply grateful to her, not only for her scholarly advice but also for her enthusiasm and warmth. Isobel Clark has been a good friend, fine critic, and industrious helper. Lynette Willoughby took the children up mountains and over moors and still had energy left to talk. Jane Armstrong believed in the project and in a very real sense made it possible.

As always, however, it is those closest to home to whom the deepest debts are due. John Tosh has lived with the book almost as long as I have. I thank him for his continuing support which has always been solidly practical as well as intellectual and moral. Thanks, too, to Nick and William Tosh for their patience and humour; they are probably right in supposing that they know more about the Jewsbury sisters than any other children in *the whole world*.

INTRODUCTION

Sometime in the mid-1970s, browsing in a bookshop, I came across a worn, yellowish, fraying edition of the *Letters and Memorials of Jane Welsh Carlyle*, edited by J.A. Froude. It was three volumes packed into one, stumpy and ugly, and some of the pages were already falling out. But I had a curiosity about Jane Carlyle. Her name popped up here and there with epithets like 'brilliant' and 'incomparable' attached, and somebody had certainly said she was one of the greatest letter writers these islands had produced. So I bought the unprepossessing volume and took it home. Thus began what was to become a long, not always obviously purposeful, often frustrating, fascinating journey into some of the more remote regions of nineteenth-century literary studies.

Jane Carlyle herself, of course, was neither remote nor obscure. For over thirty years she lived at the centre of London literary and intellectual life; beginning in 1834, when she settled at 5 Cheyne Row, Chelsea, with her husband Thomas Carlyle, and ending with her sudden death, while out riding in her carriage, in 1866. She numbered amongst her friends and acquaintances the great names of nineteenth-century literature: Tennyson, Dickens, Mill, Browning, Forster. These men, who came in the first instance to hear Thomas Carlyle – his fame as a speaker having preceded him from Scotland to London – discovered a wife whose loquacity and individuality were no less striking than those of her husband. She expressed herself vividly and forcefully, in speech and in writing. Too forcefully for some, as she realized: 'All the men take fright sooner or later at my violence – *tant mieux!*'[1] But for others, the energy of self she manifested was her most compelling and intriguing quality.

To these men of letters, it was something of a mystery that Mrs Carlyle, with all her obvious talents and proven eloquence, did not write books. Every other literate woman seemed to be doing so. Women writers had made the novel their own. Since the 1840s, the novel had taken the place of poetry and essays as the leading literary genre. G.H. Lewes spoke with barbed ambivalence for all ambitious male writers when he observed, in 1850, that women had begun to 'carry all before them' in the field; women were defining an area in which men were at a disadvantage. 'How many of us can write novels like Currer Bell, Mrs Gaskell, Geraldine Jewsbury, Mrs Marsh, Mrs Crowe and fifty others, with their shrewd and delicate observation of life?'[2] Lewes asked with genuine respect, although his 'and fifty others' would not have sounded out of place at Cheyne Row, indeed probably took its authority from some of Thomas Carlyle's influential growlings against novel writing in general and female novel writing in particular. The expressed culture of the Carlyle household was antagonistic towards the sentimental and romantic fiction popular in early Victorian Britain, which, rightly or wrongly, was associated with women's increasing participation in literary production. This did not stop them reading novels, nor did it stop their friends from suspecting that Jane Carlyle was a secret writer of them. When *Shirley* appeared in 1849, under what was known to be a pseudonym, Jane Carlyle was keen to get hold of it, for as she explained to her cousin Jeannie Welsh, 'I get the credit with certain *critics in style* of writing these Jane Eyre books myself – and I was curious to see whether the new one was up to my reputation!'[3] Ten years later, another book that was published pseudonymously, *Adam Bede*, was also thought, by some, to have been written by Mrs Carlyle.

The fact was that she never published in her lifetime and never sought to publish. No long lost manuscript will be found under a Chelsea floorboard or in a Scottish peat bog. She burnt many of her journals and private papers. The collection of letters that would have had most to tell us of her private self, those she wrote to Geraldine Jewsbury, were destroyed by Geraldine on her deathbed in 1880. For this demanding task, Geraldine enlisted the aid of her friend, the historian Mrs Everett Green; together, the two women fulfilled the promise Geraldine had made to Jane: that what she wrote in privacy would remain private. One can have little doubt that Jane's shade must have smiled benevolently and gratefully down on the scene.

While almost nothing that Jane Carlyle wrote to Geraldine Jewsbury escaped the diligence of Geraldine and Mrs Everett Green, thousands of letters written to family, friends, and acquaintances have survived. These letters have been published, continue to be published, in different volumes and by different editors. Not one of them was intended for publication, or prepared or arranged in any way by its author. Jane Carlyle's control over the product which has served very largely to form the known picture of her ended the moment she sealed the envelope and put it into the post. Each letter might tell her story in her own words, but each collection of letters was at the same time a story told by others. This is true of any letters published posthumously; but as a brief consideration of the publishing history of Jane Carlyle's letters will show, the story told by others often had very specific purposes to fulfil.

When Jane Carlyle died, Thomas Carlyle was grief stricken. Sorting through her letters, he was pierced by the 'electric shower of all-illuminating brilliancy, penetration, recognition, wise discernment, just enthusiasm, humour, grace, patience, courage, love' that he found there. Carlyle was an experienced editor and critic and spoke with professional authority when he observed, 'As to "talent", epistolary and other, these *Letters*, I perceive, equal and surpass whatever of best I know to exist in that kind.' And although Jane Carlyle never wrote a novel, it was to novelists, the acknowledged greatest women novelists, that Carlyle compared her, in a characteristically backhanded way: 'Not all the *Sands* and *Eliots* and babbling *cohue* of "celebrated scribbling women" that have strutted over the world in my time could, it seems to me, if all boiled down and distilled to essence, make one such woman.'[4]

As well as a woman of outstanding but unpublicized literary talent, Thomas Carlyle discovered afresh in Jane Carlyle's letters the bitterly unhappy woman his wife had been. He was filled with remorse for what he saw as his failures as a husband. With hindsight and in grief, he judged himself to have been selfish, egotistical, guilty, neglectful, and blind. These feelings centred on issues that had to do with writing and formulated themselves into a specific guilt: that in his pursuit of his own ends he had crushed a brilliant literary talent. In expiation, he collected and annotated as many of her letters as he could get hold of, with a view to publishing them after his own death. His annotations were the reverse of self-justifying: where she found cause for blame he found more, and he poured out his guilt and remorse. The eleven months' work was, he wrote, 'sad and strange as a pilgrimage through Hades'. And in his journal he reflected, 'Perhaps this mournful, but pious, and ever interesting task, escorted by such miseries, night after night, and month after month – perhaps all this may be wholesome punishment, purification, and monition.'[5]

The collection and annotation completed, Thomas Carlyle handed the bulky manuscript over to his literary executor and disciple, J.A. Froude, in 1871. Carlyle died in 1881. Froude was already at work on his biography of Carlyle. In 1883 he published *Letters and Memorials of Jane Welsh Carlyle* complete with Thomas Carlyle's breast-beating annotations and his own editorial interventions; and followed it up with the first two volumes of his mammoth *Life of Carlyle*. These publications, together with Carlyle's *Reminiscences*, which had also been mostly written in the sad, self-reproachful months after April 1866 but not published until 1881 (almost before the ink was dry on the long and respectful obituaries), created a literary storm that raged for decades.

Between them, Thomas Carlyle and J.A. Froude tenderly and sympathetically constructed a picture of Jane Carlyle that represented her as a martyr to duty and self-denial. She had suffered enormously, but she had never ceased to be a perfect wife. The victim of an inhumanly selfish genius, she had sacrificed herself in all her potential brilliance. And, with the perfect timing of tragedy, it was only after her death, when it was too late, that her grieving husband, the beneficiary of so much sacrifice, was able to appreciate the worth of what he had used, abused, and lost.

In the controversy that ensued, it was Thomas not Jane Carlyle who was the subject of fiercest debate. Froude was attacked as an indiscreet and treacherous biographer whose unseemly curiosity or unconscious jealousy had led him to speak about aspects of a great man's life which should have remained private. Froude suggested that Carlyle was impotent. Mrs Carlyle had been 'the victim of Carlyle's neglect' in a profound and disturbing way. Much ink was spilled and much titillating speculation given its head on whether, when, and how often the Carlyles had sexual intercourse; whether Mrs Carlyle was *virgo intacta*; whether her depressed middle years were evidence of a disease women were distressingly liable to catch: 'climacteric insanity'. Commentators took up positions for him or for her. Most vociferous were those who were for him.[6]

Saving Thomas Carlyle's reputation mattered more because the Victorian public had more invested in Thomas Carlyle; he, after all, was their hero and sage. Reading the books Froude laid before them, which seemed to tell in vivid, articulate prose the inside story of a desperately unhappy marriage, nobody denied that Jane Carlyle had had a difficult job to do. It was agreed that he had been monstrous; it was agreed that she had been a victim. The question of impotence was fundamental for it called into question the institution of marriage itself. If Thomas Carlyle was impotent, then he had not fulfilled his part of the marriage agreement: he had not been the husband his wife and society had a right to expect. Apart from its important symbolic overtones in a patriarchal society, male impotence undermined the very fabric of the power relations between the sexes: a husband who was not a husband in the full sense of the word could not expect a wife to be a perfect wife. Wifely duties did not exist in a vacuum; they called forth husbandly responsibilities.

The dreadful prospect Froude and Carlyle – aided by Jane Carlyle – opened up was of male failure. A reluctant reading public had forced upon it a human being rather than a hero. Unable to bear this reality, they dropped Carlyle like a stone; his reputation never recovered. The fact that it was the public – not Carlyle, not Froude, and not Jane Carlyle – who could not contemplate male failure was buried along with his reputation.

Female failure, however, presented no such psychic difficulties. Blame of every kind engulfed the acknowledged victim. The furore over Jane's conduct as a wife was determined by the shape Thomas had devised in his annotations to her letters. He had blamed himself for her failure to develop as a writer; the public took this failure on trust and turned the blame around: instead of blaming him they blamed her, and they blamed her failure as a writer for the failure of her marriage. This quickly became an orthodoxy. In its crude form it is well expressed by an anecdote related by Ella Hepworth Dixon in her book, *As I Knew Them: Sketches of People I have Met on the Way*. The story was told to her by the De Morgan family who were neighbours of the Carlyles in Chelsea:

> I remember the De Morgans telling me one day Mme Bodichon had rushed into their house exclaiming: 'I have just seen Mrs Carlyle. She has one of her headaches and is in a terrible temper. She told me she had just thrown the sherry decanter at Carlyle!' ... If that incomparable letter writer, Jane Carlyle, had applied her talents to serious literary work, her marriage might have turned out differently. As it was, she was a brilliant, embittered woman. With money, she could have run a salon, given dinner parties, and shone as she ought.[7]

The banality of Ella Hepworth Dixon's remarks may obscure their oddity. For odd they are. What does she mean by 'serious literary work'? And in what sense could 'serious literary work' ever save a marriage? No literary work could have been more seriously pursued than Thomas Carlyle's, and Jane Carlyle, for one, thought it the chief cause of her marital unhappiness. And what is the relation between 'serious literary work' and shining at dinner parties? What was the relation between marriage and money, marriage and writing, marriage and head-ache, marriage, money, salons, temper and talents, women and men in literary production? Since 'serious literary work' implied serious literary ambition and its pursuit, how did that square with wifely duties? Could a woman be a wife and a writer in the same way that a man could be a husband and a writer?

Ella Hepworth Dixon knew many writers, women as well as men, but her common-place remarks about Jane Carlyle show no special insight. Indeed, they uncomfortably endorse the double standard while seeming to promote the virtues of female independence. Assumptions about wifely satisfactions or standard wifely frustrations, blending with comic traditions of the shrewish bad-tempered wife, take precedence over any positive image of Jane as a serious literary worker.

Though trivial as a commentary, Ella Hepworth Dixon's reminiscences never-theless proved useful, for they illuminated the structure that was typical of comments about Jane Carlyle: her brilliance was acknowledged but her serious-ness as a writer was not. Credited with a great deal of writing, she was accorded no identity as a writer. All her identity was as a wife. She was a wife who happened to write, not a writer who happened to become a wife.

This foregrounding of the wife over the writer extended to the published collections of her own writings, all of which were first made available to the public by male editors. After Froude, Alexander Carlyle entered the fray. He published a collection of letters in 1892, with the specific object of salvaging his brother's reputation. The letters antedated those published by Froude, and they were by both Thomas and Jane. They were letters written from the time the couple first met in 1821 until their marriage in 1826, a period during which they did not meet very often (and when they did meet, invariably quarrelled) but cultivated a relationship through correspondence.

Jane presented herself to Thomas in these letters as an ambitious writer. She emphatically rejected his tendency to place her as the object of his intentions, insistently remaining the subject of her own projected life. That life was to be the life of a writer; and even if she had not said so, it would be plain from the self-conscious artistry of the letters themselves. Highly crafted, polished productions, her letters were the chosen vehicle for conveying her fullest artistic self.

Their fate, in the collection published by Alexander Carlyle under the title *The Love Letters of Thomas Carlyle and Jane Welsh*, was to be almost the exact reverse of their original intention. Far from expressing Jane's full self, they were employed to demonstrate her proper and willing surrender of self.

Alexander Carlyle's formulation of the letters as love letters had far more to do with the attacks on Carlyle's virility in the 1880s than with any romance in the letters of 1821–6 themselves. Even a later biographer who could say in passing that 'Woman, like ivy, naturally clings', had to concede, in discussing this collection of letters, that 'The love-letters of the Carlyles differ from most of their kind by the unromantic tone that pervades many of them.'[8] The collection as a whole had a specific ideological purpose: it was designed to show Thomas Carlyle, stonemason's son, Anandale peasant, as the hero who through true love and natural genius overcame a young woman's haughty manner and her mother's selfish social snobbery. In the course of her epistolary courtship, the young woman learned to give up all for the young man's genius and gained her reward in love. The conventions of the romantic novel worked at different levels within the text, even though the text was a collection of letters, and drove to the happy-ever-after of marriage as completion – of text and life.

To complete the text, which was the hero's story, the woman had to become incomplete. In the inappositely entitled *Love Letters*, what the reader actually witnesses is a battle to the death. These are bulletins from the front line. The corpse of the loser has, however, been rendered invisible: the writing self in process of formation is never acknowledged as such. A high-spirited, highly intelligent, independent-minded, voluble and witty young woman is reduced, in the course of this specific text, to silence and extreme emotional dependency on an exceptionally egotistical and controlling young man and the process is naturalized as the necessary prelude to marriage.

The disappearance of Jane's identity as a writer went largely unchallenged in the critical and biographical studies that subsequently appeared, as well as in further collections of letters. Even the splendid and scholarly *Collected Letters of Thomas and Jane Welsh Carlyle*, which began to appear in 1970, occasionally operated a double standard in its editorial comments. Jane was liable to be corrected for her faults, a liberty that was never taken with Thomas. Footnoted comments such as 'her blame of him [is] somewhat exaggerated'; 'Jane's mockery suggests some ill feeling'; 'Jane greatly magnifies her mother's faults here . . . and . . . greatly magnifies Carlyle's in her later life' sprinkled the text.[9] They suggested a more literal approach to her writing than its evident artistry properly demanded.

*

Feminist literary criticism in recent years has demonstrated some of the many processes by which the identity of writer, the authorial position, has been defined as the property of the male sex.[10] This is not to say that women did not write: quite patently they did, and in very large numbers – far more so than it has been convenient to admit. But the cultural meaning attached to writing is not a single meaning that women or men participate in by the act of becoming writers; and in the early nineteenth century especially, women with ambitions to become writers faced a complex mixture of permission and prohibition, deriving from their sex, which men were spared.

In writing about Jane Carlyle, I found that my task required a sort of archaeology. I had to dig behind the woman who wrote letters about her life as the wife of a famous man, to find the writer who might have written about anything else. I had, in the first place, to separate her from Thomas Carlyle (if only to put her back together with him later). I wanted to see her in other contexts, and particularly in the context of other women writers. It would have been possible to do this historically, by approaching her work through an examination of the genre of letter writing as a recognized female form. She would certainly occupy a prominent place in any such history. But to assert and demonstrate her achievement in such a way, while satisfying in itself, did not begin to tackle the underlying questions that Jane's life and work so troublingly posed. These were questions to do with the relation of the work to the life: specifically, the relation of the female work to the female life.

That life included marriage, but it also included friendship, and above all a friendship with a woman who was a professional writer. Jane's friendship with Geraldine Jewsbury, novelist, reviewer, and publisher's reader, extended for twenty-five years, from the early 1840s until 1866 when she died. It was the longest lasting and most significant friendship in her life. It was crossed by stormy differences and bitter quarrels, errors of what were called 'bad taste' on Geraldine's part and patches of unforgiving coldness on Jane's. The two women were an unlikely combination, and the closer one looked the more unlikely they became. If Lillian Faderman's description of their relationship in *Surpassing the Love of Men* as a 'passionate attachment' could be accepted, it was only on the understanding that such passions as anger and resentment and jealousy and impatience formed a part of the definition.

However, viewed as a relationship between a woman whose identity as a writer became ever stronger as her career progressed, and a woman whose writing identity had been repressed and whose writing self had been squeezed into narrowed channels by the demands of her married life, the friendship was an illuminating one. The points of stress related to the questions I was asking about Jane, questions to do with the writing self, the relation of female life to female work, marriage and money, the selection of particular genres and the varying potential for development within those genres. Geraldine's life offered a counter-point and comparison. But Geraldine's life was also significantly affected by her relationship with Jane. This interweaving of influence, one upon the other, demanded attention both for its personal impact and for its literary implications.

*

Virginia Woolf wrote about the two women in her evocative essay, 'Geraldine and Jane'. Like Geraldine's biographer, Susanne Howe, who published her life of Jewsbury in 1935, Virginia Woolf had a respect for Geraldine, and for the relationship she formed with Jane, that was often sorely lacking in the comments made about her by writers on Thomas Carlyle.[11] Geraldine's energy, her intellect, her warm enthusiasms, her willingness to make mistakes, her impatience and her certainties, above all, her commitment to passion as an aspect of women's lives –

the very qualities that make her such an attractive and resonant figure for our own times – aroused ambivalent reactions, not least in Jane Carlyle.

She was a working woman writer whose productivity was phenomenal. Jeanne Rosenmayer, in 'Geraldine Jewsbury: novelist and publisher's reader', has an index listing 1600 reviews written for the *Athenaeum* alone. She wrote for a variety of other periodicals, including the *Westminster Review* and *Household Words*, as well as writing six novels and two long children's stories between 1845 and 1859. In 1858 she worked with Lady Morgan, helping to edit her *Memoirs*; and she wrote an introduction to a *Memoir of Caroline Herschel* in 1876.

Geraldine Jewsbury created all her own opportunities in a long professional life, including the opportunity to sit with her feet on the fender at Cheyne Row. Given the mixed messages women writers encountered, I wanted to know, in the first instance for purposes of comparison with Jane, the extent to which the forces of permission and prohibition had operated on her. Evidently permission had triumphed, for she became a well-known professional woman of letters. On the other hand, she began as a novelist of enormous vigour, but her novels became increasingly less challenging as her position as a writer became more secure. In 1859 she gave up novel writing altogether in favour of the influence she could exert, and the regular income she could expect, as a publisher's reader.

Without exaggerating the similarity, there seemed to me some parallel here with Jane's decision to confine herself to private letter writing. And, again without asking it to carry too much weight, it was also the case that 1859 was a significant date in Geraldine's life, and one which could be compared to 1826 in Jane's life, the year that she married Thomas. 1859 marked the end of Geraldine's hopes of marriage. More specifically, it marked the moment when she accepted that she could not and would not give up her fully realized self for the sake of marriage; and that none of the men she had loved, the most serious of whom was the last, Walter Mantell, would take her on any other terms.

Marriage, the heterosexual drama which defined woman always and entirely in relation to man, and writing, which for women in the nineteenth century was potentially a means of expressing a self on the same terms available to men, existed uneasily together. The one did not exclude the other, but the broad impact of the social demand that women be wives had a profound influence on the thinking and writing of women who made their way into print. Geraldine never married; nevertheless, the issue of self for her, as she represented it in her fiction, was shaped in the main by male demands. An acute observer of other people's marriages, she noted particularly the regularity with which marriage increased men's comforts while decreasing women's. Her eye for the woman's side in every question never faltered, which is another way of saying that she could not agree to ignore the question of the female self, even within the institution of marriage. A single woman and a writer, the social territory she herself occupied was ill-defined, but it was a territory, as will be seen, which she had unusual knowledge of.

Geraldine's friendship with Jane was a by-product of her attempt to launch herself as a writer. In 1840 she was 28 and had been, for eight years, keeping house in Manchester for her father and younger brother. Intellectual, ambitious, with the freedom and time to read as widely as she wished, she was frustrated with the limitations of her life as a dutiful daughter. She wanted the opportunities that being a writer seemed to offer. In pursuit of openings, she wrote a long letter to Thomas Carlyle, signing it only with her initials. The letter mentioned nothing about being a writer, and expressed her frustrations and impatience with duty in terms of religious doubt. She was suffering, she told him, from 'the paralyzing influence of *Materialism*', a subject Carlyle had written eloquently about himself. Approaching him thus in terms of his own definitions – which were relevant –. rather than more specifically as a dissatisfied woman, she elicited a detailed and positive reply.[12] A correspondence developed, in which Carlyle's emotional interest in her was as evident and as unspoken as her excitement at having succeeded, through the power of her words, in interesting him in her future. He thought her 'one of the most interesting young women I have seen for years; clear, delicate sense and courage looking out of her small sylph-like figure'.[13]

More interesting still was the sequel. Carlyle had not wanted his wife to know about the correspondence, but when, in March 1841, Geraldine took the opportunity of a trip to London with her brother and was invited to Cheyne Row, she transferred her attentions to Mrs Carlyle and began a heated correspondence with her which progressed from 'Dearest Jane' to 'My Darling Jane' within a matter of months. Looking at these letters, it is hard to believe that they were written by the same person who had been writing to Thomas. The polite questioning, the deferential desire for answers, and the flattering implication that she had come to the authoritative source are gone. When Geraldine wrote to Jane she wrote not vaguely about duty and God, but specifically and trenchantly about women and men. She was not mysteriously anxious and depressed, but flatly and energetically angry.[14]

She asked Jane, not Thomas, why it was that 'the sufferings of any individual woman, however great, seem to be absorbed in that of her sex, and the sufferings of women seem not to be altogether recognised as the legitimate evils of life'. Was it true that women were born to suffer? Were women really perfected through suffering? Were women made to be made miserable by men since 'a woman's trials are appointed through her affections'?[15] The logic of that, if it were true, was not only that women were doomed to suffer in their relations with men but that such suffering was the right and proper route to self-realization. Giving up the self was woman's means of finding the self; marriage being the institutional form of self-surrender. There was, she observed, 'a great deal that wants saying about matrimony. Who dare say it? ... I wish I might say my say about matrimony.'[16]

It was to Jane, not Thomas, that she presented herself as a writer, speaking of her plans and involving Jane in her projects. Given Thomas Carlyle's generally venomous comments on women writers, that was only sensible, but Geraldine also had a precedent in her own life for following the path she took towards establishing herself on the literary scene.

*

When Geraldine wrote her fan letter disguised as a plea for spiritual guidance in 1840, she did not mention that she was employing a strategy used with remarkable success by her sister in 1825. Geraldine's sister, Maria Jane Jewsbury, anxious to launch herself in literary circles, wrote to William Wordsworth. The result was that she was invited into his household, became a friend of the family, and formed a close attachment not with the great man himself but with a woman dependent: Dora Wordsworth, the poet's daughter.

Maria Jane already had a book in her name in 1825 – unlike Geraldine in 1840 – and she presented herself unequivocally as a writer. For Geraldine, as a young woman and a developing writer, her sister had been an extraordinary model: independent woman, celebrated figure, a thinker, a feminist polemicist, an active journalist, essayist, poet, fiction writer, and literary critic.[17] And she was more than a sister, for Maria Jane had also, effectively, been Geraldine's mother. Their mother died in 1818, when Geraldine was 6 and Maria Jane 18. There were three boys between them in age and a newborn baby, Frank. Maria Jane took over the care of this large family.

Maria Jane Jewsbury had determined to be a writer from a very young age. She was avowedly ambitious and eager for fame. Burdened by responsibility for her father's children at a time when she was just beginning to break into print in local newspapers, she nevertheless continued to write and strive to get her work published. By 1825 she was a local celebrity: her first book, *Phantasmagoria*, a collection of satirical sketches, stories, and poems, had been commissioned and published to favourable notices. Embarked on a literary career, she worked extremely hard, wrote prolifically, cultivated friendships with other writers, travelled within England from her base in Manchester, and continued to take care of the family. Among the many and varied demands her siblings made on her time and energy, it was Geraldine's potential, Geraldine's propensities, and Geraldine's desire to be a writer that most concerned her sister. Maria Jane's preoccupation with Geraldine's dreams of fame, which were by no means entirely encouraging, even found their way into print in a collection of letters addressed to her and published in 1828 under the title, *Letters to the Young*.

Not many women writers had been mothered by a woman who was a writer as well as a sister. Not many had been involved (albeit indirectly) in a published debate with that sister about the benefits and drawbacks of literature as a career for women. Geraldine brought this unusual experience to her relationship with Jane. In many ways, her formative years with the first Jane (as Maria Jane was generally known) structured her friendship with the second. The two Janes were in any case remarkably alike in significant ways. Exact contemporaries, both were intellectual women of outgoing not retiring dispositions. Both were satirical and sharp; both had characteristics others labelled 'masculine'. They shared a love of truth, a dislike of hypocrisy, and a deflating sense of humour. In both cases, their energy and assurance of self led to them being regarded as 'unfeminine'.

And there was another connection too. Noting the similarities between the two Janes, and recognizing some of the ways in which Geraldine's assumptions about Jane derived from expectations set up by Maria Jane, I found a haunting link in their literary destinies. If Jane Carlyle was a woman of genius silenced by marriage to a towering man of genius, Jane Jewsbury, who never stopped writing, was just as effectively silenced by marriage to the rather humdrum Revd William K. Fletcher.

Fletcher took Maria Jane to India immediately after their marriage in 1832. She died there, of cholera, thirteen months later in October 1833. She was at the height of her career as a journalist when she left England, and, like a true professional, she had taken clippings of all her published pieces with her. These had been published anonymously, as was the custom of the time, and they had appeared in a wide variety of publications. Not even Geraldine knew all that her sister had written. When Maria Jane died, Fletcher did not inform the family. Their information came patchily, from newspaper reports. He answered none of their letters. He returned none of her possessions.

Encouraged by Maria Jane's literary friends, Geraldine was keen to assemble a memorial volume of her sister's best pieces. But without Fletcher's co-operation, the task was too difficult. Having none of the papers her sister had taken out to India, Geraldine abandoned the project. Maria Jane was remembered, by those who remembered her at all, for her earlier, named work rather than for her later, more mature, anonymously published writings. An extraordinarily successful woman, she was seen, ironically, as one who had failed to fulfil her promise.

This, too, was in keeping with judgements made about Jane Carlyle. The popular poet Felicia Hemans set the tone in her comment on her friend, when she heard the news of Maria Jane's death:

How much deeper power seemed to lie coiled up, as it were, in the recesses of her mind, than was ever manifested to the world in her writings! Strange and sad does it seem that only the broken music of such a spirit should have been given to the earth – the full and finished harmony never drawn forth.[18]

Maria Jane certainly had more in her yet to give; but to describe what she had already achieved, polished and powerful as it was, as 'broken music' was astonishingly inappropriate. Worse, a mental slide from the work to the woman is invited by the phrasing: the 'broken music' slips easily into the 'broken ... spirit' that produced it. Sadness, strangeness, failure, and loss emerge from this description as qualities possessed by Maria Jane Jewsbury. Nothing could be further from the truth. Felicia Hemans was Maria Jane's most intimate literary friend. Her opinion was to be most influential. She recorded her loss in terms which denied her friend's actual achievements; instead of pointing proudly to what had been, she sadly indicated what might have been.

11

The damaging theme of unfulfilled promise was to linger, even more surprisingly, over Felicia Hemans's own name. Mrs L.B. Walford in *Twelve English Authoresses* (1843) damned with faint praise: 'Whatever may be thought of the mass of her writings,' she wrote, 'it is incontrovertible that she possessed the *spirit* of poesy, and drew inspiration from sources unknown to ordinary mortals.'[19] The implication, that the spirit never quite managed to shape itself into a body of worthwhile poetry, was taken up by Henry Chorley, Mrs Hemans's friend and biographer, who thought her life one of 'misfortune and false influence' which between them had hindered the development of her gifts.[20]

*

The relationship Geraldine formed with Jane owed something to the friendship Maria Jane established with Felicia Hemans. Geraldine had a vision of 'the strength of sisterhood', which, though it did not translate itself into support for women's rights activity, was nevertheless a guiding principle of her life. As a professional writer, Maria Jane had demonstrated the value of community with other practising women writers; Geraldine tried, unsuccessfully, to establish some such sense of professional community with Jane.

The model Geraldine had to draw on was an immensely productive one. The two writers did not meet often but they corresponded, and during the summer of 1828 Maria Jane Jewsbury went to live for several months with her sister and two of her brothers in a rented cottage in rural Wales, expressly so that she could spend time with Felicia Hemans. 16 years old, Geraldine was included in the daily interchange between two profoundly committed female writers; included, too, was Harriett Hughes, Felicia's younger sister, whose appearance in print predated even Felicia's. Felicia Hemans's first collection of poems was published in 1808, when she was 13; Harriett Hughes produced *The Infantile Pleasures of Willow-dale* in 1807 when she was 8 years old – both girls publishing under their maiden name of Browne. Harriett subsequently turned her creative attentions to music, often setting her sister's verses to music which the family group would then play and sing.[21]

The long holiday in Wales was a working holiday: Maria Jane came away with a collection of verses, which she published as *Lays of Leisure Hours*, and the material for her most important full-length work, *The Three Histories*, which she began on her return to Manchester. Felicia Hemans sustained her accustomed high rate of productivity. Geraldine never forgot the summer. Years later, unexpectedly bumping into one of Mrs Hemans's sons at a gathering in London, she recalled the special quality of that time and the special place it had always held in her memory.

Maria Jane's early death deprived Geraldine of an important literary foremother, guide, and intermediary. Jane Carlyle, who knew editors and publishers, and who had had long experience of the business of transforming manuscripts into books, took her place. Geraldine made practical use of Jane's social position and literary skills. But it was also important to her to draw Jane into the realm

12

of public writing by encouraging her to write fiction. Only thus could Geraldine fulfil the vision early instilled in her: of the satisfactions to be gained from working within a female literary ambience, and of the possibilities of working within a literary tradition that was recognizably female. Geraldine's urgings and Jane's demurrals form a leitmotif to their correspondence. Significantly, however, Geraldine subordinated the positive (and radical) aspect of her vision to more negative, and safer, ways of expressing it. Geraldine posed writing as an employment just a little more stimulating than the sewing Jane spent so much of her time on. Writing, she explained,

> will really employ your energy. Writing, as an occupation, has most excellent properties; it not only blunts one's *amour propre* – or, as we politely term it, our sensibilities – so that we not only feel less acutely things that would otherwise irritate beyond endurance, but these things are transformed for us into artistic studies, instructions, experiences, and this goes a long way towards softening their intensely personal application to ourselves. Besides which, one's work is an 'ark of refuge', into which one flings oneself on all occasions of provocation.[22]

This was written in 1851, just one year after G.H. Lewes announced that women writers were carrying all before them. Women writers at the time were considered to be very numerous and well established on the literary scene. However, in encouraging Jane to join their ranks, Geraldine offered only negative advantages: a place of refuge, a form of defence, a means of generalizing horribly personal and painful experiences, and, most peculiar of all for a creative artist, a reliable method of blunting the sensibilities.

If this was the way writing functioned for her, perhaps this provides a partial explanation for what Virginia Woolf observed when leafing through the old, out-of-print volumes of Geraldine's novels in the British Museum: that not even Geraldine would have expected anybody to spend much time on them. They were work, and work that was preferable to mending old clothes. But much more importantly, they were a safety valve for aspects of female experience that threatened to engulf. Work was an ark of refuge; and, since the best defence is attack, that refuge was not a place for passive cowering. One flung oneself into it as a way of diffusing or diminishing unpleasant experiences, and in the energy of transformation, some purposeful strength was born.

Writing, in another words, might function as a form of comfort. It was a way of saving the sherry decanter and softening the impact of 'things that would otherwise irritate beyond endurance'. The lower Jane's self-esteem fell, the more Geraldine proposed writing as a means of propping it up. At the same time she urged her to be less of a good wife, her exasperation with Jane's conduct occasionally boiling over at the feats of self-abnegation she witnessed. Patience and endurance, Geraldine observed, were virtues that could kill.

But writing was also, as she went on to say, a means of passing on information from woman to woman. Casting herself as daughter to Jane as mother, Geraldine pressed Jane to distil her life's experiences in a work which would 'say both strengthening and comforting things to other women'; her experiences having been so 'singular', Geraldine argued, she ought to have 'enough maternal feeling, sisterly affection, esprit de corps, or what you will, to wish to help other women in their very complicated duties and difficulties'. She should certainly not expect help in this enterprise from her husband: 'Do not go to Mr Carlyle for sympathy, do not let him dash you with cold water.' She was to turn to Geraldine, work with her on a 'mutual tale' and direct the effort towards the wider community of women. Like mothers passing on knowledge and skills to their daughters, women, in their writing, could ensure a continuity of spoken female experience.

Unfortunately, this was not a vision that Jane shared. She did not think that she lacked engrossing employment; nor did she think that the writing of novels was intrinsically more worthwhile than the domestic activities she spent her time on; least of all did she want the responsibility of being mother to 'an amusing but ill regulated young woman'.[23]

*

Beginning with Jane Carlyle and the fact that she did not pursue a professional writing career, my researches led me to Geraldine Jewsbury, from her to Maria Jane Jewsbury, and finally to Felicia Hemans, whose name in her own time was a byword for professional female writer.

Jane Carlyle and Felicia Hemans had no personal acquaintance. Between the acid-tongued, fiercely subservient, notoriously unhappy wife of Thomas Carlyle and the popular poet of domestic harmony, there were few obvious points of similarity. But both occupied prominent positions in nineteenth-century literary culture, though of very different kinds and in significantly distinct historical eras. The accident of friendship with the Jewsbury sisters, which brought them into indirect connection, made it possible to see suggestive similarities in their lives which a conventional biographic or critical study of either individual was unlikely to raise. For Felicia Hemans and Jane Carlyle, personally and artistically so different, yet shared an over-arching structural reality: life shaped itself, for each woman, along an axis determined by the incompatibility of literary ambition and wifely duty. Their destinies differed, as did their choices and the way each described her life to herself and others, but the crucial underlying dynamics were not different and may be traced along that axis.

In the study that follows, it is this underlying dynamic – broadly speaking, the incompatibility of literary ambition and wifely duty – that I have tried to follow in relation to the lives, writing, and relationships with each other of the four women. Women's relations with men are part of the material reality of their lives, along with houses, and children, and money, and health, which significantly influence the art they produce. They also bear on the friendships they are able to form with other women. Jane's friendship with Geraldine could not, in the end, be considered in isolation from Jane's marriage to Thomas; similarly, Geraldine's attempt to form a lasting attachment with Walter Mantell, while it disrupted her friendship with Jane, also illuminated some of the essential conditions of that friendship. Maria Jane's marriage effectively terminated her career as a writer as well as separating her from her writing associates; while Felicia Hemans's writing was a chief cause of the failure of her marriage, which itself led her to value the friendship and support offered by Maria Jane Jewsbury.

Finally, Jane Carlyle, Geraldine Jewsbury, Felicia Hemans, and Maria Jane Jewsbury share one further characteristic: they have all been consigned to obscurity or marginality by the judgement of literary history. Each of them deserves more scholarly attention than she has hitherto received. Not one of them can be done full justice by the scope of this study. But in bringing them to attention, I hope that others will go on to write fuller accounts of the individual women and their work, and that they will, like me, take as their text a few wise words of Geraldine. Writing to Jane in 1849, she assured her that she had already burnt those of Jane's letters 'which could be misunderstood', and added:

> Oh, my dear, if you and I are drowned, or die, what would become of us if any 'superior person' were to go and write our 'life and errors'? What a precious mess a 'truthful person' would go and make of us, and how very different to what we really are or were![24]

What a revolting contrast there is in England between the extreme servitude of women and the intellectual superiority of women authors! There is no evil, suffering, disorder, injustice or misery arising from the prejudices of society, from its organisation and its laws, that has escaped their observation. The writings of the English women who cast such a brilliant light upon the intellectual scene are a dazzling phenomenon − especially when one considers the absurd education they have had to undergo and the brutalising influence of the environment in which they have lived.

One has only to live in England for a few months to be struck by the intelligence and sensibility of the women.... Isolation gives English ladies a propensity for observation and reflection, and a great number of them are moved to become writers ... many of these ladies contribute to the reviews and journals, but it grieves me deeply to observe that as yet not one of them has dared to embrace the cause of women's liberty, that liberty without which all other freedoms are short-lived and for which it is so peculiarly fitting that women authors should fight.

Flora Tristan, 'English women',
The London Journal of Flora Tristan, 1842, pp. 244–61

1

CONTRARY TO CUSTOM

Those who try to make their lot contrary to custom, are always broken in
the attempt.

Geraldine Jewsbury[1]

Women born at the turn of the nineteenth century in Britain were born into a
culture increasingly anxious to insist on their subordination and inferiority.
The intensity of this insistence indicates an unease about gender roles. The
subordination of women being a political, legal, economic, and social fact; the
power of men over women was one of the core realities around which nineteenth-
century society was organized. Nevertheless, the forcefulness and power of
women were equally facts and they could not be denied.

According to the dominant ideology, men's strength protected women's weakness; men's knowledge provided for women's ignorance; men's substantiality
buttressed women's flimsiness. In individual cases, such an account was as likely
to be true as untrue, but the significance of the formulation, as with all cultural
myths, was the use to which it could be put. Women writers who wished to
establish themselves in the mainstream cultural world, who desired to earn an
income and lead satisfying lives, participated in sustaining the cultural myths
which defined woman as weak and man as strong. How far individual women
consciously colluded, how far they covertly resisted, is a matter for individual
study; but the climate in which all women writers operated in the first half of
the nineteenth century was increasingly antipathetic to shows of strength from
women.

Though fraught with contradictions, weakness and its collaterals – sickness,
incapacity, self-doubt – were at the heart of the bourgeois womanly ideal. The
more sick and foolish a woman was, the more she showed her understanding of
her need for male strength and care. The less energy she possessed, the more
accountable was her love of home and fireside to which, both actually and
symbolically, she was ideally attached. In the symbolic representation of home
and fireside, these are places of stillness: the repose of the interior contrasted with
the clamour of the market-place outside. As such they exist and are created for
men, women approximating to a detail of the picture busy men may contemplate

19

at the end of a hard day. Ideally, women were to be as still as the objects by which, in their cluttered Victorian interiors, they were surrounded. Hannah More, writing in 1799, used the analogy of the picture to illustrate the symbolic immobility demanded of mobile women in relation to men:

> if a man select a picture for himself from among all its exhibited competitors, and bring it to his own house, the picture being passive, he is able to *fix* it there: while the wife, picked up at a public place, and accustomed to incessant display, will not, it is probable, when brought home, stick so quietly to the spot where he fixes her, but will escape to the exhibition-room again, and continue to be displayed at every subsequent exhibition, just as if she were not become private property and had never been definitely disposed of.[2]

Becoming 'private property', being 'definitely disposed of', meant learning how to be a picture for one man's eyes only. It did not come naturally, it had to be learnt. Hannah More's description is in the passive mode throughout, except for one active verb: 'escape'. Escaping to the exhibition room, women fail to meet the challenge of stillness, but they remain objects, in Roland Barthes's terms, 'entirely constituted by the gaze of man'.[3]

The cultural acceptance of the validity of this gaze, by men and by women, is the necessary context for understanding women's writing in the first half of the nineteenth century. Having the power of law, men also had considerable control over the powers of definition. Max Weber's dictum about culture, that man is an animal suspended in webs of significance he himself has spun, cannot be extended uncritically to include women: some of the webs women were suspended in were spun by men, designed according to the laws of those fictions which insisted on women's inferiority in order to underwrite the laws of fact which ensured their continuing subordination. Suspended and spinning from the moment of birth, women were taught the shape of the grand design and encouraged to view it from the perspective of men. Discouraged from understanding it as a cultural construct, women learned, on the whole, that their primary task was one of accommodation. Since the grand design was not amenable to being written upon and defined by writing women, many of them settled for writing and re-writing themselves according to its image.

The period which lies between 1792, when Mary Wollstonecraft's *A Vindication of the Rights of Women* appeared, and 1869, when John Stuart Mill and Harriet Taylor together produced *On the Subjection of Women*, saw the beginnings of organized feminist activity at home and abroad. Women of all classes were active on many fronts. Those who were engaged with other women and sympathetic men in political activity, whether Owenite, Saint-Simonian, anti-slavery, or abolitionist, had a better chance of resisting the psychological impact of debilitating cultural expectations than women who, generally alone, often isolated, chose to work as writers. Groups like the Unitarians did not fully subscribe to the prevailing views about women's place, arguing instead from concepts of natural rights, freedom, and toleration which encompassed daughters as well as sons. Women writers active in Unitarian circles, among the most well known of whom were Harriet Martineau, Elizabeth Gaskell, and George Eliot, had access to significant networks of support. By the 1860s, as Jane Rendall observes in *The Origins of Modern Feminism*, there did exist 'a public awareness of the question of women's rights' but, as she is careful to add, it 'has to be stressed that the numbers of women involved were very small, and their ideas still regarded as extreme and isolated'.[4] The fact that they were so regarded influenced the behaviour of even the most assertively feminist women. Harriet Martineau, thoroughly dissatisfied with 'the condition of my own sex; under the law and custom of my own country', nevertheless took care not to become too closely identified with other feminist women including those like the Langham Place women who looked to her as an inspiration.[5]

The conservative reaction to the revolutionary decade of the 1790s produced a flood of literature whose intention was to reinforce doctrines of female sub-ordination, and whose effects were to be felt certainly until the 1840s. An expanding female readership sustained an enormous expansion of reading material which flowed from the pens of female as well as male writers. Books, periodicals, sermons, guides to conduct, manuals of instruction for the education of daughters, poems, and even novels all reiterated the core reality: woman's subjection to man was natural, ordained by God, and good. Equally natural was male authority: in the market-place, in the home, and on the printed page.

To challenge male authority was to perpetrate forms of deviance. A woman who suggested that men – the natural order – might adapt to women, merely proved herself unnatural and in need of adaptation. The argument was always carried to women, for the natural order was – the natural order. Women who wrote and published their work exposed themselves to more than everyday risks of deviance. Writing women transgressed male authority in the three most significant areas: they used the home to write in, they occupied the printed page with words which might attain to the power of definition, and they competed with male writers in the market-place, earning money and potentially acquiring economic independence. Considering the enormity of these crimes it should not be surprising that they endeavoured to show themselves as being utterly conformist. The typical image projected by women writers during this period showed them as dutiful, home-loving, modest, reluctant self-publicists, whose writings went from the privacy of the home into the glare of the world only by the agency of parental admiration, or financial distress, or the desire to do good for others. Ambition, the aggressive and wilful reaching out for the forbidden fruits of worldly success, was of all things abjured. Actively seeking the status of public recognition was to trespass on male territory, which was, in turn, to be proved unnatural. The law could not prevent it, but custom could certainly hinder.

Women writers who achieved public recognition in the early part of the nineteenth century confronted the full weight of a cultural opposition in the process of codification. Authority, including cultural authority, was defined as intrinsically male, and deference to authority was defined as intrinsically female. A hierarchically minded society found it natural that the head should rule the heart since it was located in a higher sphere – and had little difficulty in accepting the axiom that the mind was masculine and the heart feminine. The heart should obey the head just as the woman should obey the man. Women who found themselves using their heads, and thus inevitably challenging male possession of that organ, endangered not male possession but their own femininity. They did not unsettle the definition of masculinity, nor the positioning of heads and hearts; they unsettled themselves and made their own cultural existence precarious.

This was a dilemma that faced all women writers of the period. No woman writer could escape it, and all, in trying to evade its impact on their own lives and careers, contributed in some degree to its perpetuation. It was to have baleful, far-reaching consequences. Women who wrote needed more security than those who kept their thoughts to themselves. That security might take the form of fathers or husbands or brothers who spoke for them, managing their affairs and interpreting their strange actions to the world. The significant male stood between the woman writer and her public as the assurance of her continued womanliness. Security might take the form of writing in code: constructing texts around hidden meanings, too subversive to be spoken, too powerfully felt to be repressed. This is an area of women's writing which has been well served by feminist scholarship.[6] The need for security certainly influenced the genres in which women elected to write, and the style as well as the content of that writing. It cut deeply into their expressive lives, influencing not only what they put down on the printed page but also what they said and wrote to each other. It is painful but necessary to recognize the extent to which women's support of each other, their friendship networks (which have received relatively little study as yet) might function to reinforce the iron laws of subordination and inferiority. A classic example is the literary friendship between Elizabeth Barrett and Mary Russell Mitford, two women whose fathers blighted their lives: their correspondence is filled with loving enquiries into the health of each other's loving and loved parent, a solicitude which never strikes the ear as forced. Not surprisingly, when Elizabeth Barrett married Robert Browning and ran away from her father, Mary Russell Mitford, her most intimate correspondent, was not among those who were party to the secret. Rather, she was among those who had to be appeased after the event. Elizabeth Barrett Browning managed to retain the friendship of Mary Russell Mitford, but it was in spite of, not because of, the blow she had dealt to her father.[7]

Fathers occupied an especially significant position in women's lives, both actually and symbolically. All men ideally approximated to the condition of fathers; all women were thereby relegated to the childlike position of daughters. Just as the daughter should never seek to know more than the father, so the woman was inhibited from knowing more than the man. Ambitious women put curbs upon their growth in order not to outgrow their personal and social roles as dutiful daughters. Childlike behaviour was commended in mature women. Mary Russell Mitford was an accomplished practitioner of the art of the childlike life, as was Elizabeth Barrett. Even women who did not, like these two, have vampirish fathers, lived as if under eternal paternal restraint, for that was the appropriate and therefore respectable cultural stance.

Knowledge by itself was acceptable (Elizabeth Barrett Browning and Mary Russell Mitford were models of erudition), but knowledge together with ambition spelled trouble. Sydney Owenson, Lady Morgan, early in what was to be an enormously successful writing career, took pains to assure an older woman acquaintance – Alicia Lefanu, sister of Richard Brinsley Sheridan – that her pursuit of knowledge was properly unconnected with her literary ambitions. Knowledge in women need not upset the natural order of things so long as women themselves knew how to order it. Sydney Owenson, writing in 1803 to a woman who, through personal qualities and family connections, had an established place in the literary circles of her time, carefully demonstrated that, though young, eager, and unknown, she was not about to break ranks. 'I entirely agree with you', the future Lady Morgan wrote,

> that *some women*, in attaining that intellectual acquisition which excites admiration and reverence, forfeit their (oh! how much more valuable) claims on the affections of the *heart* ... I am *ambitious*, far, far beyond the line of laudable *emulation*, perhaps beyond the power of being happy. Yet the strongest point of my ambition is to be *every inch a woman*. Delighted with the pages of *La Voisier*, I dropped the study of chemistry, though urged to it by a favourite friend and preceptor, lest I should be less the *woman*. Seduced by taste, and a thousand arguments, to Greek and Latin, I resisted, lest I should not be a *very woman*. And I have studied music rather as a sentiment than a science, and *drawing* as an amusement rather than an *art*, lest I should have become a musical *pedant* or a *masculine artist*. And let me assure you, that if I admire you for any one thing more than another, it is that, with all your talent and information, you are 'a woman still'.[8]

Assurances like these, from one woman to another, are commonplaces of nineteenth-century correspondence. Estimating their real weight in the lives of women writers is no easy task. Sydney Owenson's words are heavily tinged with irony; and people do not, after all, think quite the same things that they write. This is just as true of private correspondence as it is of public forms of discourse. The private letter is an artefact, just as the novel or the poem or the play is an artefact. Each is constructed according to its own laws, draws on its own traditions, and transmits its own truths. These traditions and truths overlap: the historical interplay between the development of the novel, especially, and the private letter are well known. And, as Ruth Perry warns in *Women, Letters and the Novel*, 'Letters were the perfect vehicle for women's highly developed art of pleasing, for in writing letters it is possible to tailor a self on paper to suit the expectations and desires of the audience.'[9]

The tailored self, in both private letters and published writings, aimed to please. Since cultural authority was male, women who assumed cultural authority (of however meagre a sort) by pitching their voices into the hubbub lost, or risked losing, or might be accused of having lost, their womanliness, ceased to be 'a *very woman*'. Sydney Owenson was certainly careful at all times to cultivate her 'womanliness', with the predictable consequence that reviewers – who savagely attacked her all her working life – castigated her for her 'womanly' licentiousness, vanity, and absurdity rather than for her radical political views. But she was unusual in that she gained a European-wide celebrity and made no secret of her enjoyment of it. Her career as a writer brought her social success: she began adult life as a poor governess and ended it as Lady Morgan. It brought her considerable financial reward. She also acquired intellectual status: not for her novels, which were, to use her own description, 'tissues of woven air', but for her travel writings and reflections on culture and life in France and Italy, and for her innovative biography of the painter Salvatore Rosa. More unusual still was the fact that she was happily married, to a doctor with literary leanings, and that there seems to have been little or no conflict between the demands of literature and the demands of marriage in their life. Both of them enjoyed the somewhat riotous existence Lady Morgan's fame and sociable temperament led them into.[10]

At the end of her long life, Lady Morgan decided to compile her memoirs. To help her sort the mass of letters and papers she had carefully hoarded over so many years, she enlisted the aid of another woman who had had her own way to make in the world: Geraldine Jewsbury. Lady Morgan died in 1859, before the manuscript had been completed. Geraldine, 'glad of the opportunity of working out in some degree her ideas of Lady Morgan's character and work', was left with the task of writing a connecting narrative for half of volume one and the whole of volume two. In these memoirs she constructed a picture of Lady Morgan quite unlike any other record of her, emphasizing the sober, hard-working woman of letters in preference to the vain and gossiping party-goer:

> [the] indomitable energy and indefatigable industry which characterised her both as Sydney Owenson and Lady Morgan are even more remarkable than her genius, and gave her the coherence and persistence essential to success. Her tenacity of purpose through life was unrelaxing – whatever project she had in hand nothing turned her aside; with her, the idea of Work was the first object in life. All other things, whether they appertained to love, amusement, society, or whatever else, were all subordinate to her work. Intellectual labour was the one thing she thoroughly respected and reverenced. She never wasted a moment of time and wherever she went, and whatever she saw, she turned it to practical use in her profession.[11]

The contrast between this and the young Sydney Owenson's letter about herself to Alicia Lefanu is striking. No flaps about womanliness disturb the smooth, stern flow of tributes to a hard and dedicated worker. This is the writer as hero, streamlined, single-minded. It reflects the workings of ideology no less than Sydney Owenson's letter of 1803; and, like that letter, it reflects social changes that had begun to open up opportunities for women on the cultural scene. Geraldine's portrait of Lady Morgan was designed to please the reading public of the early 1860s quite as much as Sydney Owenson's letter was designed to please Alicia Lefanu and the literary circles she was prominent in at the turn of the century. And just as Sydney Owenson modelled herself on what she thought was Alicia Lefanu's image, so Geraldine modelled a Lady Morgan for a mid-century audience out of her own, idealized, writing self.

The first half of the nineteenth century was a period of remarkable female activity and progress in cultural terms. When the Brontë sisters, Mrs Gaskell, George Eliot, and the hosts of serious, popular, and widely read women authors whom we usually mean when we say 'nineteenth-century women writers', burst on to the literary scene in the 1840s and 1850s and began, as Lewes said, to 'carry all before them', they did not spring from nowhere. Their work built on the work of previous generations. Their audiences had been primed and conditioned by those who had gone before. Their openings, their very opportunities to speak, had been carved out for them by their foremothers. Male publishers and editors, who knew a market when they saw one, had in large part been taught to see by the women writers of that earlier generation. As Ellen Moers and Elaine Showalter (to name but two pioneers) have painstakingly demonstrated, women writers have a tradition, draw on their traditions, and have had a habit of losing sight of their traditions. Elaine Showalter, describing the 'holes and hiatuses' in the history of women's writing, the tendency for each generation of writers to find itself 'without a history', speaks further of a 'self-hatred that has alienated women writers from a sense of collective identity'.[12] She might have had in mind George Eliot's remark in 1853: 'How women have the courage to write and publishers the spirit to buy at a high price the false and feeble representations of life and character that most feminine novels give, is a constant marvel to me.' And George Eliot might well have had in mind the novels of Lady Morgan.[13]

But in their different ways, George Eliot, Lady Morgan, and Geraldine Jewsbury all survived and succeeded because of one broad understanding which they shared. This was that the problem for women writers lay in the outer world rather than in the inner world, in what they had to deal with rather than in who they were. Those who were able to get the measure of what they were up against stood a better chance of survival than those who did not. The vigorous ability to take the argument to the other side is perhaps a more useful way of structuring women's literary development than the more traditional chronological one. The self-hatred which Showalter finds among women writers, while obviously a characteristic of enormous significance, was not universal. And it is not quite true to say, as she does, that 'almost no sense of communality and self-awareness is apparent among women writers before the 1840s'.[14] It would be truer to say that for the period from the turn of the century to the 1840s, the work on which any such judgement can fairly be based has yet to be done. Solid, scholarly attention has been directed for decades at the big names of the mid-century; and generalizations have been drawn from the study of their writings and their lives that may not be widely applicable to an earlier generation.

When George Eliot declared in 'Silly novels by lady novelists', written in 1856, that 'the average intellect of women is unfairly represented by the mass of feminine literature', she would have been staunchly seconded by a sizeable chunk of the female reading and writing public, including many of those who themselves wrote pap for a feminine market.[15] However, far from being seen as a female call to arms (a gesture of communality) and a recouping of a lost female tradition of rationality and intellect, this witty essay has been frequently understood as an attack on women writers *per se*. It has been seen as the proper and necessary prelude by a real writer who happened, alas, to be a woman, to separate herself from tainted associations. In a similar way, Jane Austen's avid reading of novels by women writers – her enthusiasm for Mary Brunton, for example – embarrassed those who decided that she was, though female, admissible to the canon of high literature. No doubt there would have been widespread relief in the groves of academe if only Jane Austen, too, had written a 'Silly novels by lady novelists', as well as *Northanger Abbey*.

The history of women's writing is a history of social, cultural, and personal interaction far more complex than any history drawn from the trajectories of men's lives can possibly convey. Whatever else men had to encounter in the uncertain world of literary endeavour, they did not have to defend their fundamental entitlement to speak and write. By the 1850s, as Inga-Stina Ewbank observes in *Their Proper Sphere*, it was fully accepted that women would write, and that they would probably write novels. The 'floodgates of female novel-writing' fully opened and with it came a flood of commentary, some of it serious, much of it salacious, malicious, and envious.[16] Under the barrage of often misogynist attention, women devised strategies for survival, the best known of which is, of course, the adoption of the male pseudonym. What the male pseudonym says is very plain: it says that male is acceptable and female is bad. Like clothing, it provides a respectable covering. In one way or another, whether they adopted a male pseudonym or not, all women writers had to clothe themselves in a respectable, recognizably male, covering. Geraldine Jewsbury's version of Lady Morgan is quite as outrageous as that lady was, in other ways, herself: camouflaging her in the genderless cloak of work, she endeavoured to draw her into a masculine scale of values and give to her life a dignity and purpose Lady Morgan's detractors had never granted her.

Neither Lady Morgan nor Geraldine Jewsbury suffered from self-hatred and they shared a strong sense of communality and self-awareness. Geraldine's trenchant defence of Lady Morgan itself represents a triumph over what must be one of the most sustained character attacks in the history of English literature. Even Byron (motivated, admittedly, by jealousy) was moved to protest to John Murray, publisher of the *Quarterly*, over that journal's deplorable treatment of her: 'What cruel work you make of Lady Morgan! ... It is perhaps as bitter a critique as ever was written.' He went on to add, 'I think it a pity so much good invective should have been laid out upon her, when there is such a fine field of us Jacobin gentlemen for you to work upon.'[17] The *Quarterly*'s rattling, rouged, ridiculous, hump-backed little woman with a squint is significantly absent from Geraldine Jewsbury's account of Lady Morgan. Or, if present, only in the accepting and unpatronizing way Lady Morgan saw herself when she said of her passion for parties at the age of 90: 'My life may be deemed a frivolity for one of my age, but no, it is a philosophy, founded upon the wisdom of the principle, to *do* and enjoy all the good I *can*.'[18] Instead of joining in the laughter, Geraldine Jewsbury insisted on the 'steady kindness' Lady Morgan had showed to her when she first came to London in 1853 to live an independent, single life. Geraldine gave Lady Morgan the credit for helping her to find her way in a community that was not above being snobbish towards provincials. As an Irish woman, Lady Morgan knew the score. She was, said Geraldine, 'the source of all my introductions and acquaintances, helped me to the knowledge of manners and customs of the entirely new to me society and circumstances, is always *good* to me'.[19] This goodness was a quality Geraldine unhesitatingly ascribed to the fellow feeling of one writer for another. Such feelings were undoubtedly one source of her own loyalty to Lady Morgan. When Lady Morgan died in February 1859, she left Geraldine Jewsbury a legacy in a codicil to her will, which the younger woman was touched by and interpreted as the evidence of solidarity and support: 'I think she did it from a feeling for a woman in the position she had occupied herself, earning her living by literature.'[20]

That the life of a woman 'earning her living by literature' was a specially difficult one was something Geraldine had known almost from the time she could begin to think. Maria Jane's steady progress through occasional verse in local newspapers, satirical sketches, published books (four in all before she reached the age of 30), friendship with prominent authors, and finally to the astonishing position of leading writer for the *Athenaeum*, had occupied the years of Geraldine's childhood and adolescence. Geraldine had seen her sister achieve celebrity in Manchester in the mid-1820s, where,

> the announcement of her name, at a party ... always set the room in commotion. There was a 'Hush! – silence! – hush!' as she entered; the music would cease, and the conversation come to a dead pause; and even the old steady whist-players would lay down their cards and look up; and young ladies would cease to twitter and rustle, and young men would stand erect, with their heads drawn back, and their arms straight down, as if in bodily fear; while, with a feeling of exalted condescension, the fair 'lioness' would advance, look benignly round, smile, and request that everything should go on as if she were not present.[21]

This description of Maria Jane at the mercy of 'provincial arrangements ... caught and caged in a close, low-ceilinged, over furnished apartment' was written by an old Manchester associate of the Jewsburys, Anna Maria Hall, who published under her married name, Mrs S.C. Hall. Through her husband, the editor Samuel Carter Hall, Mrs Hall had access to all the leading literary names. Though a novelist of some vigour, she was more comfortable in the role of literary hostess, chalking up triumphs in the form of lions bagged. The party at which she recalled Maria Jane Jewsbury's provincial ordeals took place at her house in Sloane St in 1830. Mrs Hall had the satisfaction at that party – according to her account in her novel, *A Woman's Story*, which she published in 1857 – of seeing Sir Walter Scott, William Wordsworth, Mary Russell Mitford, and numerous other of the literati all wandering under her roof, rapturously gazed upon by such hopefuls as Maria Jane Jewsbury and her sister Geraldine.

Mrs Hall was not among the women writers with whom Maria Jane Jewsbury attempted to establish a close and nourishing friendship. Anyone who reads *A Woman's Story* will quickly understand why. The portrait of Maria Jane herself is an unfriendly one: at the party she exhibits wounded vanity, bitterness of speech, a craving for flattery, and a fear of criticism – standing '*posed*, in a good attitude ... and evidently expecting homage, if not admiration, from all'. Whatever personal or actual truth there might be in this, it is also formulaic. The ambitious young writer, Maria Jane, according to Mrs Hall, suffered from a 'feminine weakness': namely that she had too great a love of admiration, too intense an involvement in her own literary achievements. This 'feminine weakness' prevented her from reaching feminine heights. Mrs Hall prescribed a season in London to bring her down a peg or two and make of her the 'graceful, delightful woman' she might otherwise be.[22]

Mrs Hall was, of course, watching her own back. She could patronize Maria Jane (who had not as yet found her place in London, as Anna Maria Hall – also a provincial, indeed doubly so for her origins were in Ireland not Manchester – already had) and she could relate jokes at Mary Mitford's expense, but she never suggests that Wordsworth or Scott was tiresomely involved in his own literary work. In *A Woman's Story* she tells the story of a woman writer. The dangerously autobiographical elements in such a tale propelled Mrs Hall into various defensive strategies. Her narrator, for example, is an unmarried, elderly, unassuming, and morally sound woman who goes by the illuminating name of NOBODY. This womanly NOBODY is our moral guide through a story of female literary ambition. Nobody-ness is shown to be preferable to Somebody-ness through the trials of young Helen Lyndsey, whose literary labours achieve for her a *Corinne*-like prominence and fame. But Helen is an angel and only writes because her father needs her to: having to write and be famous is Helen's tragedy. Life denied her her true fulfilment: the opportunity to be NOBODY.

Any description of a woman writer, in a book by a woman writer, should be treated with caution. The perspective of Nobody-ness was an organizing principle of the grand design and might be used consciously or unconsciously to shape the finished picture. Maria Jane Jewsbury took what she needed from Mrs Hall's London literary soirees – contact with editors like Charles Dilke, who invited her to write for the *Athenaeum* – and moved on. Her private opinion of Mrs Hall, as she expressed it to Dora Wordsworth, was that she was a 'clever absurdity' and prone to 'suspect exaggerations – in the literary way'.[23]

18 years old, and in London under her sister's charge in order to acquire a little extra educational polish before being launched on to a self-supporting life as a governess, Geraldine accompanied Maria Jane on her forays into literary life. She learned at first hand, and from a very early age, the extent to which women were active participants in creating culture at every level: writing poems, stories, essays, plays; producing travel books and translations, literature for children and parents, journalism and literary criticism; editing volumes of each others' work; and all the time, meeting, tea-drinking, discussing. Even if she did not go with Maria Jane to visit the venerable Joanna Baillie at Hampstead, she would have been given a report of the visit; as also she would have heard all about her sister's stay with those other Hampstead residents and active literary pair, Sara and Henry Coleridge, daughter and son-in-law of the poet. The early years of the nineteenth century had marked a change in literary life, at once an expansion – on a huge scale – and an increased coherence. The heavyweight literary periodicals founded at that time, the *Quarterly*, the *Edinburgh Review*, *Blackwood's*, the *Athenaeum*, concentrated and disseminated more widely than ever before the current opinions and orthodoxies. The pulse of literary life beat in the periodicals. It fed and drew sustenance from the buzz of discussion it itself created. The unprecedented openings into the club of literature thus offered, were seized on by women and men alike. The presence of women on the literary scene in large numbers was inevitably experienced as a threat; and one simple and convenient way for a woman to survive was to join in the chorus of anti-female, anti-woman-writer abuse. This was a literary device: a stage female was brought into being rather like the stage villain of melodrama. Women who resorted to the stage female could wrap a cloak of masculinity around themselves and achieve respectability. In practical terms, however, they not only knew the work that other women were doing, but took it very seriously.

The existence of the stage female was one reason why the life of a woman 'earning her living by literature' was difficult. The relentless insistence on its difficulty, which had brought it by 1859 to the status of a truism, had the useful function, for men, of warning women off and reducing competition. But women, too, contributed their fair share of lament. In a sense, bemoaning the difficulty of the life of a woman writer was required ritual: it was a version of claiming to be weak at the very moment of strength, a way of disclaiming the autonomy the printed book revealed. By presenting themselves as helpless and therefore in need of assistance, women reasserted a 'womanliness' that had been placed at risk. Like the assurances women gave each other about how little driven they were by ambition, their gestures of helplessness were a way of conforming to self-protective stereotypes. One of the reasons Lady Morgan was so viciously attacked was that she never played the card of helplessness. Nor did the Jewsbury sisters. Life dealt them a hand which made independence and a battling spirit prerequisites for survival and – if at times reluctantly – they played it for all it was worth. In her adult life Geraldine, who felt she had had an unhappy childhood, admitted, 'I used to cry to be carried, indeed I have had a great taste for it all my life, but I have been made to find my own feet.'[24] Candid and sturdy, Geraldine walked a path as a professional woman of letters from the 1840s to the 1870s that had been partly marked out for her by Maria Jane in the 1820s and 1830s. Their consecutive careers offer an unusual, perhaps unique opportunity to observe both the continuities and changes in women's experience as writers in the nineteenth century.

By 1880, when Geraldine Jewsbury died, the life of a woman 'earning her living by literature' was no less complicated than it had been in the early 1830s when Maria Jane Jewsbury died. The ground had shifted but the terrain was much the same. Such a life was still, as Geraldine said and Maria Jane knew, 'contrary to custom'. Custom, by 1880, still dictated that women should be weak and self-effacing. Most women, like most men, desire to live in peace within the culture which has formed them and of which they make up a part. Few people actively choose to live uncomfortable lives. If custom and cultural law insisted that women were weak and self-effacing, then women who were strong and self-assertive found themselves in a vulnerable position: their strength and self-assertion existed not as virtues but as pathologies. For the most part, Maria Jane and Geraldine each managed to resist the tendency of their culture to pathologize their best energies. But it was not easy. Living 'contrary to custom', the struggle of resistance consumed a vast amount of energy. All the more so since they did not adopt a politics of resistance, seeking rather to work, as far as possible, within the dominant conventions of their times. The feminist principles each espoused were not linked with political activity of any sort. Geraldine Jewsbury, like Florence Nightingale and George Eliot and other prominent women, did not align herself with the women campaigning as a body for women's rights in the 1850s. She did not wish to sign the petition in support of the right of married women to control their own earnings which was a major issue for middle-class women in 1857; worse, she made fun of the young woman who came knocking on her door hoping for a signature.[25]

Intellectual and forceful, pursuing careers in journalism and achieving the ambition of being able to 'move in the world of letters as a man, a good comrade', both the Jewsbury sisters had bestowed on them the epithet, 'masculine'. They lived what they themselves, as well as others, recognized as 'masculine' lives. Before 1880 such a description did not suggest sexual deviance, and it did not mean that they were supposed to be lesbian. On the contrary, what the word 'masculine' gave them was a sort of respectability. It indicated approval and achievement in a way that the word 'feminine', applied outside the home, could not do. Women's rights women, knocking on the door and holding petitions, made that respectable cloak of masculinity a suddenly flimsy garment. The times were not ready for women to stand forward in the full freedom of their female selves. Geraldine knew this; a lifetime of working in a man's world had taught her caution. But she looked forward to a time when women would be 'very different to what they have ever been yet'. The difference she envisaged was one which would be determined by the removal of men's power over women. Men's power over women functioned not only through external controls – legal, economic, institutional – but also by working within women through the influence of cultural practice. The result was that women did not, in Geraldine's opinion, lead 'normal' lives. A man's life was the 'normal' life, masculinity was the norm. Women were drawn to men and became dependent on them not only because they sought economic and social support, but also because men and masculinity occupied the centre and held the power of definition. Men were the channel through which women were required to find themselves. Geraldine, in 1849, looked to a better future for subsequent generations of women:

> I believe we are touching upon better days when women will have a genuine, normal life of their own to lead. There, perhaps, will not be so many marriages, and women will be taught not to feel their destiny *manqué* if they remain single. They will be able to be friends and companions in a way they cannot be now. All the strength of their feelings and thoughts will not run into love; they will be able to associate with men, and make friends of them, without being reduced by their position to see them as lovers or husbands. Instead of having appearances to attend to, they will be allowed to have their virtues, in any measure which it may please God to send ... in short, they will make themselves women as men are allowed to make themselves men.[26]

The desire to be true to herself as a woman, as a man could be true to himself as a man, dominated Geraldine's life. She held fast to the conviction that truth to the self was 'the first condition on which we live'.[27] Individualistic, she was also a passionate comforter and supporter of other women. While enjoying close friendships with many leading men of her time, and suffering unfulfilled love affairs with several others, she had a low opinion of men generally, especially as husbands. After witnessing an episode in which she was granted a 'loathsome insight into the position women stand in', she vowed to get her own back in the one way open to her:

> I'll be hanged if I don't ease my mind in the next book I write! I have not felt so indignant in my life, and I wish I were a man for five minutes to kick them – *ma foi, ma foi!* I will have a little bit of 'settling' yet; if I cannot do that I can preach a gospel – a set of lying, hypocritical beggars! Well, it's no good swearing – only, I am angry, and it eases my mind.[28]

Unfortunately, men could not be kicked by women in the nineteenth century; the boot was on the other foot, actually and metaphorically. The most that an indignant woman could do was to ease her mind. Giving other women comfort and support often meant encouraging them to ease their minds, or find ways of feeling better about circumstances which naturally provoked great indignation. Strong women striving hard to be weak; voluble women maintaining silence;

active women agreeing to be passive; ambitious women struggling to curb their ambitions and accept as natural the lack of professional opportunities; energetic women trying to be graceful, available and learning how to sit still in order to be looked at; women with strong drives and strong desires working to convince themselves that they had none; women with a will to self-assertion and an impulse towards self-direction, who would be the subjects of their own lives standing squarely in the centre, who daily argued themselves into being good objects fitly occupying discreet positions on the margins of men's lives – all experienced their moments of demoralization. All looked to other women, similarly placed, to help them ease their minds and feel better about things. Women looked to women for the strength they needed to live out their 'unnatural' lives.

Geraldine's friendship with Jane Carlyle offers an insight into the workings of these dynamics. So, too, does Maria Jane's shorter, but no less passionate involvement with Felicia Hemans, which began in the latter half of the 1820s and effectively came to an end in 1832 when Maria Jane married William Fletcher. These were friendships between writing women, women for whom personal experience invariably found its way into public expression of some kind. The interplay between life and art was subtle and continuous. For each one of the four, close friendship with another woman had artistic as well as personal significance.

For Maria Jane, involvement with Felicia Hemans was an encounter with the potentially devastating effects of the cultural construction of ideal femininity on a woman artist. Felicia Hemans, like her contemporary, Lady Morgan, earned large sums of money and efficiently managed an extraordinarily successful literary career. Unlike Lady Morgan, she also managed a family of five sons while at the same time projecting helplessness all her life. Rivalling Byron in popularity in her own time and throughout the nineteenth century, she arguably formed the poetic taste of the Victorian period. Her work was never out of print and was enormously widely read, both in Britain and in America. Cheryl Walker, in her classic analysis of nineteenth-century American women poets, *The Nightingale's Burden*, describing the influence of Felicia Heman's work, rightly reminds us that, 'we can no longer imagine the way her name was cherished and her work admired by women on both sides of the Atlantic.... She was looked upon as a kind of sacrosanct model and eulogized.'[29]

Critics loved Felicia Hemans with no less fervour. The *Edinburgh Monthly Review*, in a notice of her long poem, *The Sceptic*, which appeared in 1820, set the tone:

> The verses of Mrs Hemans appear the spontaneous offspring of intense and noble feeling, governed by a clear understanding, and fashioned into elegance by an exquisite delicacy and precision of taste. With more than the force of many of her masculine competitors, she never ceases to be strictly *feminine* in the whole current of her thought and feeling, nor approaches by any chance the verge of that free and intrepid course of

speculation, of which the boldness is more conspicuous than the wisdom, but into which some of the most remarkable among the female literati of our times have freely and fearlessly plunged.[30]

It was agreed that Felicia Hemans's poems 'could not have been written by a man'. H.F. Chorley, in his *Memorials of Mrs Hemans*, which he published in 1836, a year after her death from tuberculosis and heart disease at the age of 40, elaborated on this: 'Their love is without selfishness – their passion pure from sensual coarseness – their high heroism . . . unsullied by any base alloy of ambition. In their religion, too, she is essentially womanly – fervent, trustful, unquestioning.' Turning from the poems to the woman, Chorley described her as 'self-distrustful, open, with a child-like gratitude, to words of kindness and encouragement – seeking rather sympathy than praise'.[31]

The awkward truth was conveniently ignored: the writing of poems, the earning of money, the seeing of books through the press – almost a volume a year for twenty years – were work, and supremely self-directed work. In ignoring this aspect of Felicia Hemans's real life, critics demonstrated their loyalty to her and to the values which her poems upheld. The invisibility of the work involved in writing poems was a crucial determinant of their 'womanliness'. By 1847, writing in *Tait's*, George Gilfillan managed to remove the element of work altogether, so much so that the poem barely seems to need to move through consciousness to get itself born:

> Mrs Hemans's poems are strictly effusions. And not a little of their charm springs from their unstudied and extempore character. This, too, is in fine keeping with the sex of the writer. You are saved the ludicrous image of a double-dyed Blue, in papers and morning wrapper, sweating at some stupendous treatise or tragedy from morn to noon, and from noon to dewy eve – you see a graceful and gifted woman, passing from the cares of her family, and the enjoyments of society, to inscribe on her tablets some fine thought or feeling, which had throughout the day existed as the still sunshine upon her countenance, or perhaps as a quiet unshed tear in her eye. In this case, the transition is so natural and graceful, from the duties or delights of the day to the employments of her desk, that there is little pedantry in writing a poem as in writing a letter.[32]

In *Tait's* in 1847, even more forcefully than in the *Edinburgh Monthly Review* in 1820, commendation of Mrs Hemans for her ethereal womanliness was used as a stick to beat other women writers. In the praise lay the warning. For those women who endeavoured to live it out as fact, the fiction that women's writing happened as spontaneously as a tear dribbling down a cheek, must have been a significant factor in their experience of that widely reported phenomenon, 'the pains and penalties of female authorship'.

In Felicia Hemans's life there was a tension between the facts of her existence as a professional woman writer and the fictional ideal of the poetess according to which she was constructed. The fame which she undoubtedly pursued she also suffered from. Giving the public what it wanted meant – in the 1820s, that period of mass production – giving them herself in the image they desired. But to be given, to be public, was the exact antithesis of the womanly ideal which Felicia Hemans was herself busily shaping. Fame was a burden because fame was unwomanly. In opposition to fame – the glare of publicity – Felicia Hemans posed, in poem after poem, the attractions of the subdued light of the fireside. Domesticity and, by a natural progression, a place of subordination to a male figure in the shadows of whose activity the female could be properly passive, represented the ideal which she articulated in both private and public speech and writing. Her words were accorded an authority that significantly helped weave the cultural patterns, the webs, in which she and other women struggled to live. Up and down the country women confined to the home read Mrs Hemans's poems and were comforted. They read 'Woman and Fame', for example:

> Thou hast a charmed cup, O Fame!
>   A draught that mantles high,
> And seems to lift this earthly frame
>   Above mortality.
> Away! to me – a woman – bring
> Sweet waters from affection's spring.
>
> Thou hast green laurel leaves, that twine
>   Into so proud a wreath;
> For that resplendent gift of thine,
>   Heroes have smiled in death:
> Give *me* from some kind hand a flower,
> The record of one happy hour!
>
> Thou hast a voice, whose thrilling tone
>   Can bid the life-pulse beat
> As when the trumpet's note hath blown,
>   Calling the brave to meet:
> But mine, let mine – a woman's breast,
> By words of home-born love be bless'd.
>
> A hollow sound is in thy song,
>   A mockery in thine eye,
> To the sick heart that doth but long
>   For aid, for sympathy –
> For kindly looks to cheer it on,
> For tender accents that are gone.
>
> Fame, Fame! thou canst not be the stay
>   Unto the drooping reed,
> The cool fresh fountain in the day

Of the soul's feverish need:
Where must the lone one turn or flee? –
Not unto thee – oh! not to thee!

Or they read 'Evening Prayer at a Girls' School', in which the innocent happiness of the young girls is tragically contrasted with the misery that lies ahead for them when they grow to maturity and take on the sorrows and woes of woman's lot. They are full of hope and sunshine now, but a woman's destiny will find them out:

Her lot is on you – silent tears to weep,
    And patient smiles to wear through suffering's hour,
And sumless riches, from affection's deep,
    To pour on broken reeds – a wasted shower!
And to make idols, and to find them clay,
And to bewail that worship – therefore pray!

Her lot is on you – to be found untired,
    Watching the stars out by the bed of pain,
With a pale cheek, and yet a brow inspired,
    And a true heart of hope, though hope be vain;
Meekly to bear with wrong, to cheer decay,
And, oh! to love through all things – therefore pray![33]

The underlying ambivalence in these lines may be more striking to modern eyes than their idealism – well might the girls be exhorted to pray since there seemed to be no other resource for them.

Mrs Hemans's 'essentially feminine' verse, with its depiction of 'the whole sweet circle of the domestic affections – the hallowed ministries of woman, at the cradle, the hearthstone, and the death bed', has been as unpopular since the end of the nineteenth century as it was popular and culturally significant throughout the century. No full-length biography of her has ever been written, apart from Chorley's *Memorials* and a memoir, written partly in response to Chorley, by Harriett Hughes. Both appeared in the years immediately following her death. Few literary professionals know anything about her work or her life, and so absolutely has she been identified with pre-Victorian and Victorian ideal woman-hood, with all its renunciation, suffering, and 'self-devoting affection', that even feminist scholars have shown little interest in recouping her for the revised tradition.[34]

This represents a serious omission. Felicia Hemans established a position in her own lifetime which no woman had held before. She wrote as a woman for women, putting women's experiences at the centre of her poems. Her popularity with women readers testifies to the centrality of 'the cradle, the hearthstone, and the death bed' in women's lives, and to their desire for literary representation of

35

those experiences. The fact that Felicia Hemans's poetry confirmed and validated lives lived within the confines of the cradle, hearth, and deathbed should not of itself be a reason for consigning her to oblivion.

Barbara Welter in her essay, 'The cult of true womanhood', defined the four cardinal virtues on which the womanly ideal which evolved in the nineteenth century rested as: piety, purity, submission, and domesticity.[35] Although speaking of America, her words are as valid for British women. It is important to recognize that the effort to conform to this ideal engaged the energies of almost all women to some degree during at least some parts and possibly all of their lives. It constitutes a female tradition. Even women who supported women's rights movements subscribed to some or all of these values. As a tradition it is fraught with paradox – most apparent in the lives of those who were most visible – but it was also weighted with comforts. The real experiences of women have always been accorded only muted voices within the dominant culture. The reality of close familial and friendship bonds, of childbirth and the raising of children, of tending the sick and supervising the deathbed, made up the substance of life for most women. The ideals of piety and purity, submission and domesticity, represented *inspiration*. The tendency of our own time to see them as restriction alone introduces a blind spot. Felicia Hemans's expression of those ideals, in the context of women's experiences glorified, was a source of comfort to her readers.

The friendship between Felicia Hemans and Maria Jane Jewsbury was recorded by all who observed it as a meeting of opposites, opposites drawn along gendered lines. The 'masculine' Maria Jane and the 'feminine' Felicia Hemans found that a 'warm interest and thorough understanding' existed between their 'two minds so rarely gifted'. Harriett Hughes, close to both of them, commented on the contrast in her memoir of her sister:

> it was scarcely possible to imagine two individual natures more strikingly contrasted; the one so intensely feminine, so susceptible and imaginative, so devoted to the tender and the beautiful; the other endowed with masculine energies, with a spirit that seemed born for ascendancy, with strong powers of reasoning, fathomless profundity of thought.[36]

'Masculine' and 'feminine' here are synonymous with thought and feeling, head and heart. Maria Jane was an intellectual with a sharp, satirical mind that moved so fast that William Wordsworth, for one, said no individual of his acquaintance had ever equalled it. This 'quickness in the motions of her mind' was matched by a facility with words.[37] One nod from a willing editor, and Maria Jane could knock off a moving or funny or stirring set of verses. Her favourite subject, the one which she made her own and upon which she was often hilarious, was literary ambition and the literary life, with all its vanities, grandiosities, and envies. In *Phantasmagoria*, which she wrote while still unknown, the literary type set up to be mocked was male. Women barely featured at all; the book was published only under the initials 'MJJ', and the narrative voice Maria Jane adopted was designed to be read as a male voice. By 1830, when she published her fourth book, *The*

Three Histories, the personal and literary impact of friendship with Felicia Hemans was clear. *The Three Histories* contains a direct portrait of Felicia Hemans. But more than that: the subject matter and theme – the incompatibility of womanliness and writing – were learned from Felicia Hemans, the woman all the critics agreed had succeeded in being both a woman and a poet.[38]

Felicia Hemans's life did not correspond with the ideals she promulgated in her poetry. She was not quite what she was loved for being, but those who loved her, like Maria Jane, kept the clouds of an idealizing smokescreen billowing protectively before her. Felicia Hemans had not succeeded in combining womanliness and poetry. She had failed. Her marriage, every bit as unhappy as that of the Carlyles, was a failure. Her life stood as a stark and terrible warning to an ambitious, young woman writer. Maria Jane knew Felicia intimately. Felicia confirmed her knowledge of her: 'she has loved me sincerely and understood me as no other being has ever done.' And further: 'there was a strong chain of interest between us, that spell of mind on mind, which once formed can never be broken. I felt, too, that my whole nature was understood and appreciated by her; and this is a happiness which I consider the most rare in all earthly affection.'[39]

Maria Jane Jewsbury, she whose spirit seemed 'born for ascendancy', saw in Felicia Hemans's womanliness her vulnerability. Exploring this in *The Three Histories*, she was able to articulate for herself the dangers she needed to avoid. *The Three Histories* had its origins in the urgent necessity to confront the cultural incompatibility of being a woman and being a writer. What makes it important is less the conclusions Maria Jane gave public expression to within it, than its liberating impact on her life. Her subsequent writings tell the really interesting tale.

Liberated by friendship and knowledge, she went on to develop an authoritative, feminist, and decidedly 'unfeminine' voice which under cover of anonymity enlivened the pages of the *Athenaeum* for several years. Her vigorous critical style is unmistakable. She wrote mostly on poetry, fiction, and women's issues. As the *Athenaeum*'s lead reviewer, her preoccupation with the situation of the woman writer brought a serious consideration of women's issues to the front pages of that influential new journal. Well thought of, highly successful, moving 'in the world of letters as a man, a good comrade', Maria Jane was profoundly aware of men's cultural power and women's exclusion from it. She was not afraid to say that in a culture which authorized public speech for men and prescribed silence for women, women's cultural productions (or the lack of them) had to be approached with an awareness that women's writing was rooted in 'a paralyzing fear of man'. Anticipating modern feminist critics, she saw how fictional forms were attractive to women because they offered effective coverings for the naked female voice. Fiction, by its indirectness, its disguises, made possible a degree of freedom otherwise not readily available. The woman writing fiction, she observed, 'fancies herself veiled, and often enunciates important truths; the fear of man somewhat departs from her mind, and she becomes (by comparison) free, natural and unconventional'.[40]

Maria Jane Jewsbury's acute understanding of men's cultural power and its pervasive effects on women's writing – even under cover of fiction, the fear of man only 'somewhat' departs from women's minds, and their writing is only 'by comparison' free and natural – marks her out in this period of literary history when there were few other voices willing or able to speak out so clearly. Her own veil was anonymity and the assumption on the part of readers (which she deliberately helped along) that they were reading words penned by a man. The world of the periodicals was a tweedy world of deadlines and debate, a far cry from the well-ordered interiors damp-eyed ideal women writers were supposed to grace. It also had high prestige. In the first few decades of the nineteenth century, ambitious male writers looked to the elegant literary essay as the way of establishing their names. An essay placed in the *Edinburgh Review*, for example, such as Thomas Carlyle's essay on Schiller, accepted by Francis Jeffrey (to Carlyle's great relief) in 1825, opened the doors to literary society. Writing for the respected periodicals lent an authority to a writer which novel writing – still an uncertain genre in the 1820s, partly because it was associated with women – did not give. For a woman like Maria Jane, it offered a way out of tightly bound, gender-structured limitations. It brought her from the margins into the centre, took the edge off insecurities, and made possible experiences which were both maturing and demystifying. She was able to maintain her position without feeling the need to attack other women. From this position of strength, she was able to set an example which her younger sister learnt from: an example of undeviating loyalty to women as women, over and above all other categories of definition. But she was only able to do this by acting like a man.

*

Power was a male possession. In *Zoe*, Geraldine Jewsbury's first novel, which she published in 1845, she asserted bluntly: 'Weakness is the only state for which there is no hope, either for this world or the world to come.'[41] If weakness was womanly, then womanly was hopeless, and Geraldine, inspired by Maria Jane, embraced the strengths inherent in the masculine. She was, in any case, the antithesis of the nineteenth-century womanly ideal. To be pious, pure, submissive, and good did not come easily to her (though she was enough a woman of her time to keep on trying). She was ambitious, contentious, adventurous, emotional. Like her sister, she was quick witted, and with an intellect that liked to burrow behind the surfaces of things. She smoked cigars and used strong language. She had a predisposition to be frank in analysing and expressing her feelings. At a time when all the highest ideals for women tended towards the obliteration of the self, she not only pursued truth to the self for her own benefit but recommended it to others, urging Jane Carlyle to 'patronise the pronoun *I* as much as I do myself!'[42] At a time when women were most applauded for their capacity to swallow insult and wrong with quiet forbearance, she protested that holding her tongue was 'a horrid *smouldering* process ... bad for everybody'.[43] She never married, but it was not for want of interest: she proposed marriage to at least three men, not one of whom could quite overcome the shock of being asked. She, for her part, was undaunted by refusals; she picked herself up, dusted herself off, and carried on as before. Jane Carlyle was astonished at Geraldine's capacity to recover her emotional equilibrium after episodes of high emotional drama, such as those she was herself drawn into when staying with Geraldine at the house of her friends, Mr and Mrs Paulet, at Seaforth near Liverpool. Geraldine's passion for Jane got the better of her. She was 'jealous as a Turk' and 'jealous as a tiger', embodying her own conviction that 'when one loves either a man or woman it rouses all the ferocity that was calmly slumbering till then in the profound depths of indifference'.[44] During her stay with the Paulets, Jane Carlyle suggested that she might alter her plans to stay with Geraldine alone in Manchester afterwards, since they were, in any case, spending time together at Seaforth. Geraldine was furious and Jane was shocked: 'Such mad, *lover-like* jealousy on the part of one woman towards another, it had never entered my heart to conceive.'

> Mrs Jordan in *The Jealous Wife* acted no more astounding vagaries than Geraldine has been treating us to here for the last twenty-four hours. *Thank God* my temper happened to be in an *unusually* placid state – and the thing has been got *put down* without any poisonings or suicides, though not without great annoyance to Mrs Paulet and the whole household.[45]

This was the triumph of rationality over emotion. As such it was also Jane Carlyle's bid for the position of power in the relationship. She did not let herself be carried away by emotion, and if she had done so she would not have recovered with the ease Geraldine was able to command. Jane Carlyle agreed to go home via Manchester after all, and Geraldine 'with her hair all dishevelled and her face all bewept, ... thereupon sat down at my feet and – smoked a cigarette!! With all the placidity in life!'[46]

Geraldine was used to being told to control her emotions: Maria Jane had lectured her about it all her life. Jane Carlyle was used to being the calm and rational centre, pillar of sanity and reliability in a world where humans were horribly liable to hysterical collapse. She had built herself an identity around that vision of herself. Like Maria Jane, she was intellectual and had a wit that was, in the opinion of some, unwholesomely satirical. Her sharp wit grated on her friends, the elder Mr and Mrs Sterling, when she spent an uncomfortable short holiday with them in 1837. Jane Carlyle reported to her husband 'a fair specimen of our talk at Malvern from dewy morn to balmy eve'; it was Mr Sterling's observation, 'Do you know, Mrs Carlyle, you would be a vast deal more amiable, if you were not so damnably clever!'[47] Damnably clever (and damnably funny), however, she was, in all but one significant area: the management of her own life.

Reading the records of Jane Carlyle's life is, in spite of her wit, a sad and dispiriting affair. The humour which lights it is too often gallows humour. The progress from the clarities of a bright and sociable childhood to an adulthood in which bafflement, bitterness, darkness, solitude, sickness, and despair are the key motifs is painful to follow. All the more so since her life was viewed by many as illustrating to perfection the ideal of womanliness in its most significant function, the one which concerned men most: that of being a wife. She was 'Jane Welsh Carlyle, truest of true women; than which said, there can be no more to say'.[48]

On the contrary, there is a great deal more to say. The business of being a wife was not, as it has been convenient to assume, a set of simple and known procedures engaged in by simple beings. Wives of famous men are wives twice over: they serve the man who serves society, and any failure in serving the man is a failure to the service of society. Any criticism of the man is a criticism of society. Even more than most wives (for their men are more than most men), wives of famous men will be expected to exhibit less of everything than their husbands: less ego, less drive, less desire, less talent. Powers behind the throne, their very nearness to the throne makes any manifestation of their personal abilities suspect: they would be well placed to seize the throne. Wives in literary history are often an embarrassment. Just as contemporary visitors to famous writers did not want to be stuck, conversationally speaking, with the wife – few literary men went out of their way to engage in debate with Mary Wordsworth – so literary historians acknowledge the wife's existence and pass on. Dimly visible in the shadows, she may be noble, powerful, and true; she may suffer, have babies, complain of neglect, and die. What she will not do, unless she positively courts opprobrium, is give any sign of considering herself the social or intellectual or artistic equal of her husband.

This is a social fact of far more importance than any individual exploration of the relative talents of particular men and women. Its significance in nineteenth-century Britain was profound, for the womanly ideal found its ultimate expression in concepts of wifeliness that extended to cover the whole community of women, not confining itself to those who were legally wives but drawing all women into the definition. The defining quality of a wife was subordination of the self in service to one who existed on a higher plane. Even if, in real terms, given the existence of the so-called surplus women, not all women could be wives, certainly all women should be. Failing a husband, resourceful women could find a father, a brother, an uncle, a cousin, or an ailing godfather to whom they could perform all the wifely services except one. The comfort of others, Geraldine Jewsbury assured Thomas Carlyle, was that one of women's duties with which 'we have no right to trifle'.[49] Geraldine was at the time keeping a comfortable house for her father and brothers. The comforts of others meant the comforts of men. Subordinating the self to men was represented as a means of finding the self, just as subordinating the self to God was the route to the real self. As is well known, and as Leonore Davidoff and Catherine Hall reaffirmed in their study, *Family Fortunes*, religion, especially the upsurge of evangelical religion at the beginning of the nineteenth century, powerfully legitimized men's superior status. God the father looked for obedience in all his children, but set his sons on earth in authority over women, having first made them (but not women) in his image. Much of the difficulty for women in the nineteenth century was the agony of conscience that followed any lapse from patriarchal law, since to disobey man on earth was to disobey God for whom man was the chosen representative. A woman's self that did not acknowledge the God-ordained superiority of man was a self that most women recoiled from in horror. Even women like Geraldine Jewsbury and Jane Carlyle, who had thrown over religious doctrine, did not throw over the belief that men were born to rule. Observation and experience merely provided to them that most males were incapable of fulfilling their own destinies. Mrs S.C. Hall, responding to what she called the 'monstrous project' of electoral reform in the 1850s – the attempts to reform the laws concerning married women's right to their own earnings which led to the petition which neither Geraldine nor Jane signed – put the relation of marriage and religion as it affected women (i.e. husbands and Gods) as concisely as it may be put. 'It is Christianity that places woman in her true position', she wrote. 'A woman without an Altar is even more degraded than a woman without a hearth.'[50] Hearths and altars were alike places of worship, and the deity was always male. A woman without a deity was not only sad but bad.

Like God, man was ideally immovable. Masculinity, like religion, was about absolutes and certainties. The more religion came under attack in the nineteenth century, the more concepts of masculinity were looked to to stand fast and hold the wobbling line. Thomas Carlyle, one of the spiritual architects of the Victorian era, was influential in popularizing a philosophy derived from German Romanticism, which placed man in the position of God's representative on earth and woman in the position of God's intermediary, standing between God and man, closer to God, more spiritual, speaking for man to God and from God to man in order to enable man to be more God-like. Curiously, this responsible role did not give women any direct power; they acted merely as agents. More curious still, women had to achieve their ends while deferring to the authority of the men they were attempting to influence. When Jane Welsh married Thomas Carlyle in 1826, Thomas made it clear to her that he believed that the absolute authority of the husband over the wife was part of the natural order of things:

> the man should bear rule in the house and not the woman.... I must not and I cannot live in a house of which I am not the head.... It is the nature of man that if he be controlled by anything but his own reason, he feels himself degraded.... It is the nature of woman again (for she is essentially *passive* not *active*) to cling to the man for support and direction; to comply with his humours, and feel pleasure in doing so, simply because they are his; to reverence while she loves him, to conquer him not by her force but by her weakness, and perhaps (the cunning gypsy!) after all to command him by obeying him.[51]

This is an early statement of what was to become, by the mid-century, a series of cliches. The absolute authority of husband over wife was a test of manliness which Thomas Carlyle, obedient son but inexperienced lover, hoped to be able to pass. Insecure in his manliness – his nature showed alarming tendencies towards irrationality and passivity – Carlyle looked to his future wife to cultivate an ideal womanliness that would define his masculinity. Wifely self-subordination and service included the requirement that for his sake she should embrace irrationality. She was to agree that words had different meanings according to whether they were applied to men or women: for women, weakness was to be understood as a conquering strength; obedience to be recognized as a form of command. Her reward for playing this silly game would be his approval and the success of her marriage. In other words, respectability instead of degradation.

Success on these terms was, however, also failure. Feelings of failure and worthlessness consumed much of the second half of Jane Carlyle's life. They took the form of mental depression and insomnia – sometimes so severe that she would be unable to sleep for weeks on end – and appallingly debilitating physical collapse. The symptoms might include vomiting or simply retching – with 'spasmodic writhing, that would last from twenty-four to sixty hours'[52] – fainting, influenzas, headaches, and irregular and heavy menstrual bleeding. However, no organic disease was ever diagnosed. Temperamentally, morally, and by training committed to valuing what was rational, practical, and concrete, the inexplicability of her feelings led her to fear madness. In all seriousness, she wrote, 'my most constant and pressing anxiety is to keep out of Bedlam!' In the depths of sickness, it was not her bodily health that preoccupied her but that of her mind: 'I fear not for my life but for my reason.' The fear of madness was linked to the fear of doing wrong, and the protection against madness lay in penitence and the attempt to be better: 'Submission! Acknowledgement that my sufferings have been no greater than I deserved is just the most that I am up to.'[53]

Failure, ill-health, self-blame and a stoic refusal to seek excuses outside the self, marked the married life of Jane Welsh Carlyle. Like most women, but with more remorseless logic than most, she knew what marriage meant when she entered upon it: it meant that she agreed to put herself in her husband's power. Marriage, in the early nineteenth century, meant civil death for a woman. Like lunatics, married women ceased, legally, to exist; they became dead in the law. The dead person had access to life only through the agency of a living husband. Accepting a proposal of marriage meant accepting the terms of the agreement. A woman might hope her husband would prove 'kind' or 'good' once she became legally his, but she would not waste time supposing that he would dispute laws enshrined by Acts of Parliament and enforced by cultural practice. While there was little cultural or social approval of the obviously tyrannical or selfish husband – men who took advantage of the freedoms the law gave them to beat their wives, turn them out of the house, seize their property, and deny them access to their children – codes of privacy based on the all-importance of idealizing daily life ensured that their behaviour would not figure largely in drawing-room conversation. Many people knew many men who were cads, but it was almost as degrading to speak of them as it was to be the victim of one. Moreover, the presumption of blame would always attach to the woman.

The reason for this lay not only in knee-jerk anti-woman attitudes. Marrying and becoming subject to the power of a strange man (a man who was neither father nor brother and who therefore did not necessarily have family interest at heart), learning to obey him, and ceasing to assert herself were widely recognized as demanding challenges for a woman. It was understood that the woman's part of self-subjugation was far more difficult than the man's part of authority and command. In consequence of this, failures to reach the ideal of pure harmony and domestic bliss were commonly seen as originating in the woman's inadequate adjustment to the requirements of marriage. The burden of happy marriage lay on the woman's shoulders. Quarrels and disagreements, unhappinesses of every kind, could always, in the end, be attributed to her failure to submit, her continuing inability to obey her husband utterly, or her inability to submit to God's will.

How this might operate in daily life may be indicated by an example from the autobiography of Mary Smith. Mary Smith was a governess who began a correspondence with Jane Carlyle in the 1850s (hoping for an entry into literary life as an amanuensis to a literary lady). Mary Smith's life, as she told it in her autobiography, was one of heart-breaking hard work and poverty which eventually taught her a truth she would never forget: that 'the inequality of the sexes in privilege and power, was a great cause of the dreadful hardships which women, especially in the lower classes, had to suffer'. One of Mary Smith's positions as a governess was with a Quaker family. She described the perfect marriage of the Quaker couple as follows:

> There was no scolding; no storms of any kind between husband and wife. His wishes were studied and observed from morning to night. 'William likes it so', was continually on his wife's lips in arranging for the day, and in giving orders to the servants. She was, in fact, a model wife, exerting herself continually to do whatever he required.

This was the ideal, both in its workings – womanly obedience, male command – and in the payoff: harmony. Mary Smith was adamant that she wanted nothing of the sort for herself: 'I did not want matrimony,' she stoutly wrote, 'it was congenial labour I wanted.... I often thought that my plainness and poverty were my best safeguard.'[54]

Mary Smith had no doubts that being a wife, especially a model wife, was labour. Marriages which did not achieve the perfection of the Quaker couple were more likely to be seen as failures of effort than as failures of nature. There was not a wide assumption that women were naturally inclined towards obedience; rather, the assumption was that a properly conditioned woman would work at it. The woman whose marriage did not work for her was not working hard enough. Like all professions, the profession of marriage was one in which training and experience, together with application, could be expected to lead to a generally high level of expertise. Thomas Carlyle, it has to be said in his favour, did not expect his wife to be a model wife overnight, but he did expect her to keep on trying.

2

THE PRIDE OF LITERATURE

'Oh Woman! but in weakness, strong,
In suffering, only, brave! –
            Maria Jane Jewsbury[1]

If 'to be weak is miserable' ... to exercise any kind of power, or have any
kind of strength, is so far an abatement of misery.

                                                    Sara Coleridge[2]

Felicia Hemans, Maria Jane Jewsbury, Geraldine Jewsbury, and Jane Carlyle all
lived lives in which the business of literary production was an organizing principle.
Even Jane Carlyle who, once married to Thomas Carlyle, relinquished the
ambitions she had had as a young woman to achieve literary fame, wrote her life
as well as lived it. Her private letters to family and friends, when published,
established Jane Carlyle at once – for those who didn't already know it – as a
writer of brilliance. Social historians and literary historians have mined these
letters for their vivid accounts of daily life and for their thumbnail portraits of
nineteenth-century figures, most of whom seem, at one time or another, to have
passed through Cheyne Row. As a shrewd observer and sharp commentator,
well placed to have prominent subjects under her unsparing eye, Jane Carlyle's
usefulness to historians has never been in doubt. Nor has the intrinsic quality of
her writing been denied. But in literary history she has been accorded no place
at all except as the wife of Thomas Carlyle.

Literary history is equally dismissive of Felicia Hemans, Maria Jane Jewsbury,
and Geraldine Jewsbury. Felicia Hemans's hymns, homes, and battles hold little
appeal for an anti-imperialistic, anti-heroic, and anti-religious age still struggling
to throw off the effects of nineteenth-century domestic ideology. Probably her
two most famous lines – 'The boy stood on the burning deck / Whence all but
he had fled' – are known only in one of the many corrupt versions: 'The boy
stood on the burning deck / Picking his nose like mad'; 'The boy stood on the
burning deck / Whence all but he had fled. *Twit*'. The significant fact, that a
poem about filial obedience *in extremis*, literally to the death, achieved enormous
popularity, is lost. The lack of biographical or critical studies (surely unpre-

cedented in a poet of such widespread popularity, the undisputed representative poet of Victorian imperial and domestic ideology) has meant that the relation of the poet's personal experiences to her public expression has remained unexplored. During the nineteenth-century this was due in part to the family's reluctance to expose themselves, and her memory, to casual gossip about painful events. The crucial biographical detail, which was not a secret, may be simply told: in 1818, after six years of marriage, Felicia Hemans's husband, Captain Alfred Hemans, left his wife. They had four baby sons and she was very shortly to give birth to a fifth. Captain Hemans, apparently for reasons of health, went to live in Italy and Felicia Hemans never saw him again.

The poet of domesticity, of hearth and home, had skeletons rattling by the fireside. As a wife, which meant also as a woman, she had failed. The failure of her marriage came to preoccupy her, and she returned to it obscurely but obsessively in her mature poetry. Her most autobiographical collection, *Records of Woman*, which appeared in 1828, reflects a psyche troubled by questions to do with gendered expectations and gendered roles. For the modern reader, the conjunction in Felicia Heman's life of success as a poet and failure as a woman, insofar as poetic success may be judged by prizes and popularity and womanly failure by a husband's desertion, is a key conjunction. It unlocks the fastness of her mature work, allowing access to the more interesting meanings that the heroisms and nobilities and nostalgias of its surface have obscured.

Equally important, however, and as interesting, were the strategies devised by Felicia Hemans and her family, friends, and fans to hide the truth. A certain amount of tittle-tattle following her death in 1835 made it inevitable that Harriett Hughes should refer to the separation when she came to write her memoir of her sister. She made the best of a bad job: she elevated the writing of poetry into a religious sacrament. Felicia Hemans and Maria Jane Jewsbury, according to Harriett Hughes, were both 'intent upon consecrating their gifts to the highest and holiest purposes'. With poetry viewed in the light of a religious offering, the poet answered to God alone, not his representative on earth. Thus Harriett Hughes was able to say baldly that 'literary pursuits' along with 'the education of children' made it 'more eligible for her to remain under the maternal roof, than to accompany her husband to Italy', and get away with it.[3] Even Evangelical religion sanctioned the activity of writing for women so long as both the woman and her readers believed she did it as a service to God. Writing, as duty and service – as in the writing of moral tracts, religious pamphlets and poems, or educational materials – could be presented as an extension of the duties and service women performed within the home, from which the business of writing need not remove them. Indeed, it kept them – like housework, which, in its drudgery, writing also resembles – ever more firmly tied. In privacy and retirement, the door closed and the shades drawn, women might take up both book and pen, and by improving their minds benefit themselves and their families. So long as God was present, man might be dispensed with. Thus religion, so powerful a medium for transmitting messages of self-sacrifice and self-denial to

1. Felicia Hemans, by Thomson (after the bust by Angus Fletcher) (July 1835), reproduced by kind permission of the Dove Cottage Museum.

women, could also be used to legitimate desires that were anything but self-denying.

The crucial decision in Felicia Hemans's life was not the decision to be a poet, nor the decision to marry, at the age of 18, a man who for most of his few years as a husband had no career, no prospects, and no money, but the decision to place her literary career in precedence over her marriage. When Captain Hemans (discharged) left for Italy, his wife apparently gave little thought to any notion of going with him. She was comfortably settled in her own childhood home, with her mother and brothers and sisters, a home she had gratefully returned to after one year of married life alone with Captain Hemans. In this close family network in Wales, Felicia Hemans's much-loved mother provided her with 'the old home feeling of shelter and security', and her siblings were on hand to share in the care of the children. Beautiful, talented, and precocious, Felicia had always been the family darling, encouraged, loved, and cherished for what she was and what she wrote. Living in the family home, 'as a member and not as its head', she was able to concentrate on her art. She was 'excused ... from many of those small cares of domestic life, which might have ... fretted away her day-dreams'. Although little is known of what the departure of her husband on the eve of the birth of a fifth child meant to her, what is clear is that the moment of the past which ever after glowed with a special light was precisely those years in the early 1820s when she had her mother, her children, and her work, but no husband:

> How I look back upon the comparative peace and repose of Bronwylfa and Rhyllon – a walk in the hay-field – the children playing round me – my dear mother coming to call me in from the dew. . . . How have these things passed away from me, and how much more was I formed for their quiet happiness, than for the weary part of *femme celebre* which I am now enacting![4]

The emotional satisfactions she drew from her children appear to have contributed to her productivity, not hindered it. The children shared in her triumphs and disasters as a writer. When her play, *The Vespers at Palermo*, failed in 1823 at Covent Garden, it was having to break the news to the children which hurt her most:

> The boys had worked themselves up to an uncontrollable state of excitement, and were all lying awake 'to hear about mamma's play'; and perhaps her bitterest moment of mortification was when she went up to their bedsides, which she nerved herself to do almost immediately, to announce that all their bright visions were dashed to the ground, and that the play had ended in all but failure.[5]

In the same way, triumphs involved the whole family. In June 1821 the Royal Society of Literature awarded Felicia Hemans its annual prize for her poem, *Dartmoor*. She wrote, in a letter to a friend:

> I wish you had but seen the children, when the prize was announced to them yesterday. Arthur, you know, had so set his heart upon it, that he was quite troublesome with his constant inquiries on the subject. He sprang up from his Latin exercise and shouted aloud, 'Now I am sure Mamma is a better poet than Lord Byron!'[6]

Living 'under the maternal roof' and having a childlike status in the home, Felicia could play and work at her art in much the same way that the children played and worked at their Latin exercises, fishing, and sketching. Descriptions of her emphasize her childlikeness: she had an 'engaging playfulness'; a 'childlike abandon' with friends; 'very old gentlemen', we are told, found her 'winning and filial manner' especially endearing. Although the mother of five children, she considered herself to be 'in feeling . . . more of a child than any of them'. Childlike satisfactions, in life and art, did not seem to her to be strange ones for mature women to pursue. In a letter she wrote to the unmarried Mary Mitford, whose *Our Village* had a huge success, she said: 'I often think of you, and of the happiness you must feel in being able to run to your father and mother with all the praises you receive.'[7] The image is striking in its almost toddler-like innocence, its suggestion of a child upwardly looking into the faces of the adults who conveniently mediate between the self and the world. Mary Mitford was over 40 at the time.

While there is no reason to suppose that Felicia Hemans did not genuinely feel the childlike emotions she said she felt, the association of childlikeness and ideal femininity played an important part in her popular image and undoubtedly contributed to her success. Meanwhile, the cultural construction of the feminine as essentially childlike fed into Felicia's understanding of and projection of herself, and existed comfortably alongside notions of the poet as one poorly equipped to deal with the workaday world. What it most emphatically did not exist comfortably with was the fact that she was a woman whose marriage had failed and whose husband had left her. Her childlikeness needs to be considered in the context of that reality and everybody's desire to obscure it. Furthermore, and related to her childlikeness, Felicia's idealization of her mother (and her idealizing of Mary Mitford's parents) should be understood in terms of another family skeleton about which little is known: like her husband, Captain Hemans, Felicia's father, sometime in the early 1800s, abandoned his wife and family and took ship for Quebec to make his fortune. Harriett Hughes tells us nothing about her father, nor of the impact of his departure on the family, but the words she uses to describe Mrs Hemans apply with equal force to Mrs Browne, her mother; she was in 'a position so painful, as must ever be that of a woman for whom the most sacred of ties is thus virtually broken'.

In the only modern study of Felicia Heman's life and work, an unpublished doctoral thesis completed in 1943 by M.I. Leslie, the author concludes that Felicia's mother was crucially important in enabling her to devote herself to her writing. Her loyal mother, Leslie writes, 'stood as a bulwark between her daughter's writing and the impact of the world's facts'. The salient fact in this case was the worldly expectation that a wife would subordinate her interests and desires to her specifically wifely obligations. It does not appear that Felicia ever even contemplated doing that. She was a compulsive reader as well as a prolific writer, and in her ordering of priorities, serving others barely entered the lists. Mrs Elwood, in *Memoirs of the Literary Ladies of England*, published in 1843, certainly found no room for it in her description of Felicia Hemans:

> Mrs Hemans's eagerness for knowledge continued to be intense.... She loved to be surrounded by books of all sorts and languages, and on every variety of topic, turning from one to another. And this course, it is said, she pursued at all times – in season and out of season – by night and day – on her chair, her sofa and bed – at home and abroad – invalid, convalescent and in perfect health – in rambles, journeys and visits – in company with her husband, and when her children were around her – at hours usually devoted to domestic claims, as well as in the solitude of the study and bower.[8]

Allowing a little for hyperbole, as well, perhaps, for Mrs Elwood's self-defensive construction of Mrs Hemans as not quite mortal in her dedication to literature, the picture remains one of extraordinary single-mindedness. While the precise reasons for the breakdown of the marriage may never be known, it can with confidence be said that Captain Hemans's wishes were rarely 'studied and observed from morning to night' like those of Mary Smith's Quaker employer. Or, as M.I.

Leslie puts it, concluding that financial and temperamental disagreements were at the base of the estrangement but that what effectively separated the two was the incompatibility in their lives of literature and marriage, the inescapable and absolute fact was that 'Felicia was far more the possession of poetry than of Alfred'.[9]

It was the death of her mother in 1827, not the departure of her husband, which brought about devastating changes in Felicia Hemans's life, including a change in the way she regarded her husband's desertion. At first, having lost her mother – 'How hollow sounds the voice of fame to an orphan!' – she continued to live in the family home, under the household management and supervision of a brother and sister. But in 1828, the year she published *Records of Woman* and the year she came to know Maria Jane Jewsbury intimately, two unwelcomed developments occurred. Felicia's brother received an appointment in Ireland and made plans to move there, and her sister decided to marry. Her brother's removal made her feel helpless; she was acutely aware of how little she had learned to negotiate an adult path. Thrown 'exclusively upon her own resources', she was 'compelled ... to make acquaintance with an "eating, drinking, buying, bargaining" world, with which from her dispositions and habits she was ill-fitted to cope'. Her sister's marriage plans, meanwhile, made her utterly depressed. Indeed, marriage seems to have suggested distance, finality, and absolute loss only a little short of physical death:

> I am to lose this, my only sister – indeed I may almost say my only companion – very shortly. She is about to change her name and home and remove very far from me. O how many deaths there are in the world for the affections![10]

The summer of 1828, when Maria Jane came to stay, had a special quality because it was the last summer before Felicia and her brothers and sisters went their separate ways. She had already found a house for herself and her boys in the village of Wavertree, not far from Liverpool. Though it broke her heart to leave her beloved Wales, she had friends in the vicinity of Wavertree whose protectiveness was an inducement to come. There is some evidence that she wrote to her husband asking if she could come out to Italy and settle with him among the expatriate community in Rome. If she did, he must have declined to have her. But the two eldest boys did go out and from that time on lived with their father. These 'nightmare' partings from sons, brother, and sister, so soon after her mother's death, induced a 'constant depression'. She was ill with inflammatory attacks and palpitations, 'suffering much', as she put it,

> from the dispersion of a little band of brothers and sisters among whom I lived, and who are now all scattered; and, strange as it may seem to say, I am now, for the first time in my life, holding the reins of government, independent, managing a household myself; and I never liked anything less.[11]

In describing the 'painful' background to Felicia's lifelong separation from her husband, Harriett Hughes referred to the increasing fame that her sister experienced throughout the 1820s. Far from providing consolation for the loss of family security, this fame exacerbated the feelings of isolation Felicia was already suffering from. Readers, American readers in particular, were relentless in pursuit of her. She had an extensive correspondence to manage. Demand for her lyrics was insatiable. Feeling 'conspicuous', 'unprotected', and in 'constant want of protection and domestic support', she lived and worked in a 'constant excitement, homage' which made her profoundly uneasy. The terms in which she described this unease are revealing:

> Fear not any danger for me in the adulation which surrounds me.... Of all things, never may I become that despicable thing, a woman living upon admiration! The village matron, *tidying up* for her husband and children at evening, is far, far more enviable and respectable.[12]

This letter was written to Mary Mitford, who had had her own share of public attention to deal with. But unlike Miss Mitford, whose literary achievements could be construed as only one more way a dutiful daughter might please her parents (thus contributing to domestic happiness), Mrs Hemans, in her domestic isolation, felt endangered. Her life having become 'troubled and storm-beaten' in the particular shape her troubles took – which she claimed not to be able to understand – the 'despicable' and the 'respectable', instead of holding firm, threatened to leap from their moorings.

To enjoy the rewards of fame might suggest that she had set out expressly to achieve it. Such an objective was in flat contradiction to the message which her readers took from her poetry and for which she was venerated. The more attention she received, the more troubled she became:

> one might as well hope for peace in the character of a shadowless man as of a literary woman.... Do you know the song – 'Where shall be bury our *shame?*' Change the last word into *fame*, and it will express all my present perplexities.[13]

One source of Felicia's perplexity must have been the thought that by her own actions – publishing her poetry and setting her foot irrevocably on to 'life's tumultuous road' – she had wilfully caused her own expulsion from the refuge of home: 'Home, where pure affection glows, / That shrine of bliss! asylum of repose!' Certainly she was more than willing to believe that the unhappiness of other unhappily married celebrated female poets had its origins in their own weak craving for celebrity. Of Mary Tighe, an Irish poet who was much admired by Keats, especially for her long poem, *Psyche*, on which he drew heavily, Felicia wrote to her intimate correspondent, Robert Graves, the following:

> I heard much of her unhappiness was caused by her own excessive love of admiration and desire to shine in society, which quite withdrew her from

Hearth and Home and all their holy enjoyments, and that her mother, standing by her deathbed passionately exclaimed – 'My Mary, my Mary, the pride of literature has destroyed you.'[14]

This lurid vision of the depths to which the pursuit of literature might lead a woman expresses a central motif: like so much else in women's lives, the answer to external 'danger' was perceived to lie within – in this instance, not in the outer world of literature, but in the inner world of a woman's capacity to control its impact on her. In short, in self-control. The familiar interior of the home, 'Hearth and home and all their holy enjoyments', shrank at times to an even smaller interior with which it became almost synonymous: the woman's body. Cast out by circumstances from the family home, Felicia Hemans felt with full bodily force the indecency of fame.

*

Ambitious women who succeeded in worldly terms, by writing books, by achieving public recognition, placed themselves on a narrow and precipitous path from which they might at any moment plunge into failure as women. The propensity to mental and physical collapse characteristic of so many women writers in the nineteenth century, the failure of bodily health following, with grim regularity, on the completion or success of a piece of work (a projection of an assertive self, no matter how self-effacingly dressed up) reflect the workings of this reversal of success and failure in women's lives. By the time she began her correspondence with Felicia Hemans, Maria Jane Jewsbury had experienced in full measure, on her own body, how the success of a book could turn into the failure of health. Unlike Felicia, Maria Jane was blunt about her ambitions. She had always wanted to be a writer, and not merely for activity or diversion. She wanted fame:

The passion for literary distinction consumed me from nine years old. . . . The ambition of writing a book, being praised publicly, and associating with authors, seized me as a vague longing. As I grew older it took permanence and led to effort. I sat up at nights, dreamed dreams, and schemed schemes.

In 1818 when her mother died, Maria Jane became 'mother, nurse and governess', as well as full-time housekeeper and companion to her father. The family was not rich. They had recently moved from Measham in Derbyshire, where Maria Jane had grown up and where her father had been a mill owner. It is likely that the move to Manchester followed financial difficulties and that there was little money to spare as Thomas Jewsbury set himself up as a cotton and insurance agent in the city. Having received what she described as only 'common-place instruction' as a child, Maria Jane's immersion in the cares of housekeeping coincided with a powerful impulse towards self-education. Already a writer, and, in a small way, a published one, she became, at the age of 21, a reader: 'seized upon by a blended passion for knowledge and truth'. Under the circumstances it was a passion far from easy to satisfy: 'My life after eighteen became so painfully, laboriously domestic, that it was an absolute duty to crush intellectual tastes. . . . I could neither read nor write legitimately till the day was over.'[15]

If crushing intellectual tastes was 'an absolute duty', then it was a duty Maria Jane shirked. But the practical obstacles were severe, as all women who have had charge of small children know. Dorothy Wordsworth (who also knew about looking after small children not her own) described to her friend Catherine Clarkson the very demanding circumstances under which Maria Jane's first book, *Phantasmagoria*, had had to be written:

> she has had a sickly infant to nurse and has bestowed this care upon the rest of her brothers and sisters. . . . most of the things in those two volumes were written in ill-health – Booksellers urgent – Children sickly so that she wrote in a sick room, and often sat up till three or four o'clock to enable her to do so.[16]

In spite of the obvious difficulties of such a life, it did offer some paradoxical advantages. Maria Jane's 'spinster matronhood' gave her the responsibilities of motherhood, with all the maturing experiences that implies, along with a measure of independence and authority. Whereas Felicia Hemans 'never liked anything less' than having to be responsible for her household, Maria Jane Jewsbury, practical, competent, energetic, and forceful, took hold of 'the reins of government' with a firm and capable hand. She was warmly admired for her abilities in the domestic sphere. Her father was irascible and demanding, but not in a position to oversee her every action: she thus escaped the insistent scrutiny that might otherwise have been her lot as a young woman of marriageable age (though Thomas Jewsbury, as a point of principle, did not allow unmarried young men into the house). She also escaped, since she was a mother but not a wife, the controlling influence of a husband. Relatively unconstrained, she was able to be self-regulating; and if her time and energy were conscripted, at least her freedom to think was not. In this respect her position was the exact reverse of that of many young women of the middle classes in the early nineteenth century, for whom enforced leisure made time hang heavily and whose minds were carefully filled with dross.

Maria Jane's domestic situation did not prevent her mind from ranging or her pen from scribbling. The early 1820s were, for her, 'the days when facility and audacity went hand in hand', and they produced, in *Phantasmagoria*, a startling first work by any standards. The qualities she showed in her domestic life – above all, the ability to take command – were reflected in her writing: it was authoritative, accomplished, outspoken, deeply serious, and irreverent.

Like most first books, *Phantasmagoria* was impelled by an autobiographical impulse. Its unifying subject was the meaning of literary ambition as it is generally understood: as men experience it. Maria Jane Jewsbury assumed the male pronoun and an implicit or explicit male persona for much the same reason that later writers like Charlotte Brontë, Marian Evans and Madame Dudevant were to

2. Maria Jane Jewsbury, by G. Freeman, engraved by J. Cochran (1832), reproduced by kind permission of Tamworth Library.

adopt male pseudonyms: for the textual freedoms it licensed. With this freedom she was able to explore the follies and conventions of a literary life she longed to be part of, mocking the vanities of young men, the crustiness of old men, the delusions and spites of literary ambition, the absurdities of novels in which 'the hero and heroine soliloquize, quote poetry and make love in a thunderstorm', and even, in an audacious parody of a typical review by the poet laureate Robert Southey − notorious for his habit of riding hobby-horses on the back of some hapless author's book − criticizing the power of the critic.[17]

The brilliance and success of *Phantasmagoria* transformed its author from an unknown young woman into a local celebrity. It also, as a natural consequence, blew her cover. Within months her health had broken down. By June 1826 there was said to be 'little hope' of her ever recovering. Describing her illness to a new friend, Dora Wordsworth, daughter of the poet, Maria Jane made it plain that no organic disease had been diagnosed, and that emotional upset was strongly indicated: 'I am still unable to sit up ... my stomach is a regular rebel ... there is nothing seriously wrong ... months will probably elapse before I am fit for anything.'[18] A letter to Geraldine (at school in Tamworth) was even more suggestive: 'talking *disagrees* with my stomach, as much as it accords with my inclinations'.[19] It took some stomach for a young woman to make her literary debut with the fireworks of *Phantasmagoria*. Such an aggressive and high-spirited work, such bold slapdash effects and biting wit – reminiscent, for a modern reader, of the critical essays of Virginia Woolf (who also knew the reversals of success and failure in the dialectic of bodily health and printed page) – claimed their apology in the form of a retreat to ideal female passivity and silence.

What *Phantasmagoria* was *not* is in some ways as interesting as what it is, and points to the highly self-conscious awareness its author had of her position as a woman writer, both as a public construction and in terms of her private and individual experience of it. It is not, for example, a novel. More specifically, it is not a novel with love at its centre. In 1824, when Maria Jane Jewsbury was intensively writing new material to fill the second volume, Mrs Alaric Watts suggested she should write a love story. There was a demand for such material, and an assumption that it would come from the pens of women. Maria Jane distanced herself from this expectation. She wrote to Mrs Watts:

> A love tale I shall never write. The moment I begin to cogitate over the proper materials I feel an irresistible inclination to laugh. With one or two exceptions, I never have read a love-tale without seeing its ludicrous side. ...
> If you had any compassion you might make me a present of a love-tale; I would be very grateful, and honest too, and acknowledge in a note that I was indebted for it to a married friend of great experience. But I know how it is; you are on your sofa in a state of enviable serenity of body and mind, and from that sofa and that serenity no elocution of mine will stir you. How different is my condition at present! Three dear children are catechizing me at the rate of ten questions in every five minutes. I am within hearing of one servant stoning a kitchen floor; and of another practising a hymn; and of a very turbulent child and unsympathetic nurse next door. I think I could make a decent paper of the miseries of combining literary tastes with domestic duties.[20]

Such a paper was, alas, never written. For although Maria Jane wrote at that time with – as she expressed it – a 'simplicity which neither dreaded criticism nor knew fear', she did not then project her female self and her female experiences into her published writings. But those words, 'dreaded criticism' and 'knew fear', are ominous, and *Phantasmagoria* has plenty of evidence that fear and dread were already working.[21]

Along with the 'facility and audacity' manifest on every page, runs an undercurrent of appeasement. Aware of being young and gifted, the author is at pains to lampoon the pretensions of the young and gifted. Aware of being female, she trails some diversionary disparagement of women. Aware of being ambitious, she is anxious to hide the fact: she presents herself as 'only' a manufacturer of 'literary small wares', one of the 'sketch and scrap' or 'shred and patch school of writing'. These elaborate apologies act as a shield to deflect criticism and also provide protection for some covert explorations. Aware of home and hearth as a bustling, noisy place of distraction where 'holy enjoyments' came only in the form of children's catechizings and a servant's hymn-singing, Maria Jane Jewsbury was not inclined, like Felicia Hemans, to idealize woman's place in it. Few readers could have found *Phantasmagoria* a 'woman's' book in any of the many meanings such a description might imply: with a few important exceptions, women do not feature in it. However, by means of such simple shifts as reading through the pronoun 'he' to the female author whose experiences are recast and shaped for public consumption, it will be seen that *Phantasmagoria* emerges as a significant text in the history of women's relation to literary production in the early part of the nineteenth century.

*

The longest item in *Phantasmagoria* is a story which deals directly with the subject of literary ambition. 'The Miseries of Mediocrity', subtitled 'Confessions of a Disappointed Author', tells in autobiographical, confessional form the cautionary tale of a male literary aspirant who at last, after much self-delusion and vain ambition, recognizes the folly of trying to pursue a literary career for which he is really not fitted. His story is one of early success and lavish praise which between them encourage 'visions of literary glory'. The young man imagines 'Generous patrons! Liberal publishers! admiring readers hailing me on all sides! celebrated poets acknowledging me as a brother!' But sad to say, criticism, neglect, bad sales, and poverty follow. He finds himself neither the 'star of drawing rooms' nor the 'pet of periodicals'. At last he treads the path from folly to good sense by tearing up his manuscripts and abandoning hopes that have made him ridiculous and unhappy. The few shafts of good sense he has left enable him to recognize his personal mediocrity and repent of his 'folly, in having obstinately pursued a profession for which nature had denied me the talent necessary to command success'. He ends his story convinced of 'the melancholy truth, that I was intended for a reader not a writer ... [to] follow ... but must never hope for the honour of being followed.'[22]

The moral of the story exactly reproduces the accepted view of the place women should occupy in cultural life generally and in literary production specifically: they should be readers not writers, followers not leaders. It is indeed a melancholy truth that women were to be told, but were not to expect to do the telling; and that the most important lesson energetic, ambitious women had to learn was to accept this state of affairs as something originating from their natural unsuitability. The tale, 'The Miseries of the Mediocrity: Confessions of a Disappointed Author', read as a woman's tale, may be seen as a placatory confession of a woman's unfitness, by gender rather than by lack of genius, for the place of telling. At the same time it is a victory over that unfitness, for she tells the tale.

Throughout *Phantasmagoria*, unfitness, looking on from the outside, an exclusion from the place of telling that has its origins in socio-sexual arrangements are expressed in the traditional language of literary criticism: genius versus mediocrity. Genius enables its possessor to construct rules beyond the social dictates by which lesser mortals live. Should a woman be a proven genius, then, and only then, might she carve out her life, work, and relationships in the world of affairs, setting her own standards without being expected to defer to those set for her. She might be autonomous. Only by possessing genius might a woman be autonomous. A woman who wrote – which, in its self-assertiveness, is a bid for autonomy – was a woman claiming to be a genius. Maria Jane's later work, *The Three Histories*, was to be a full-length exploration of the woman-genius-autonomy triangle, but in *Phantasmagoria* too it can already be seen at work. For one thing, a profound awareness of its linkages lies behind the author's eagerness to disclaim pretensions of any sort. The privileges of authorship were such that it attracted vast numbers of hopeful women (as well as men) pushing and jostling for a foothold in what was becoming a rapidly expanding industry. With virtually all other avenues closed to them, authorship presented itself to women as the obvious (often the only) channel for their energies and self-expression. All implicitly laid claim to genius, for it was the only way of surmounting gender exclusions. Genius has no sex, that was agreed. But genius is also rare. In *Phantasmagoria* genius is possessed by Milton, Shakespeare, and Madame de Staël. One notable characteristic that distinguishes the truly great is that they do not engage in the endless and ever popular disputes about the quality of women's minds: only the 'small occupiers of intellectual territory' concern themselves with *that* debate. Shakespeare and Madame de Staël, in Maria Jane's account, recognize one another as equals.[23]

The consideration of literary ambition raises questions that have to do not only with the nature of literary greatness but also with the literary tradition. That tradition is one from which women have been systematically excluded. In 'A Vision of Poets' Maria Jane addressed the subject of the literary tradition and, using the device of a dream, created a resonant image of female exclusion. A sleeping person dreams that former generations of writers, 'the Shades of the departed British poets', have come back to earth in ghostly form to hear what is being said about them. Hoping to find themselves appreciated by 'a grateful and admiring' posterity, they eavesdrop on living writers and readers. With the exception of the truly great, who are utterly indifferent to their reputation, all concerned reveal their quarrelsomeness, vanity, and prejudices. Dead and living alike carp, grumble, and object to whatever is said about them, be it praise or be it criticism. In the midst of so much partiality and contradictoriness, the dreamer becomes, even in sleep, 'perfectly worn out with vexation and fatigue'. But at last all the ghostly forefathers gather around the leading living poets, and putting malice and envy and petulance aside, they begin to talk. They talk as 'kindred spirits'. They are united by the earnestness of a shared endeavour. In this atmosphere the living writers are able to acknowledge the greatness of those who have gone before, and to learn from their talk. The dreamer is no longer vexed, but none the less cannot participate in the charmed, almost magical circle that these kindred spirits form for their 'earnest yet respectful discussion':

> I felt my heart beat and burn with celestial ardour ... [at] the living and disembodied met together, though they knew it not, in the bond of love and brotherhood.... I was in the presence of wisdom and wit, and pure fancy, and mighty reason – all the varied and combined force of intellect of every kind, and of every age – and I felt, though asleep, warm tears trickling down my cheeks, because I knew myself unworthy to be in such an assembly of giants.[24]

Though no sex is specified, the dreamer is surely female. She is a non-participant observer, floating on the coat-tails of active men. She looks in from the outside, invisible and silent. Hours of observation have sharpened her perceptions and developed her ability to discriminate between the true and the false to a high pitch. She recognizes and reverences superior gifts, gifts that are, and are seen to be, in male possession. She longs to draw on the wisdom they have to offer, to sit at the feet of the masters and grow. But this opportunity is not available to her, even in her dreams. In a properly female way she understands her exclusion from the 'brotherhood' in terms of her own inadequacy and unfitness. Only at the most exalted level, between Shakespeare and Madame de Staël, is gender-free literary companionship possible, and to aspire to such heights is surely to be riding for a fall. The assembly of giants is male, the literary tradition is male, and there is no direct access to it for a woman who is not a genius. The penalty for the woman who has the presumption to want to belong is tears and self-blame.

'Town and Country', a dialogue between a poet and a poetess, offers a postscript to 'A Vision of Poets' and an alternative to tears. In this dialogue (the only piece in which a woman's voice speaks out unmediated by any male narrator) poet and poetess argue the relative merits of town life and country life for the development of poetic genius. The poetess, conventionally, favours country solitude; the poet argues for 'the crowded street'. Overlaying a traditional debate about the place of action and reflection in the literary life, and the virtues of country retirement with all its supposed spiritual purity against the corruption of the town, is an explicit gender dimension: in the literary life as the poet describes it, there is no place for a woman. Further, the poet eulogizes town life in words which suggest his hostility to women's increasing participation in literature. Town life, the 'hum of men', he insists, has always given nourishment to writers. He calls in the aid of tradition to support his view. The older poets, he tells the poetess, always lived in cities, they did not stand aloof from the multitude, but participated in their business and interests, their wild revelries and sports and sometimes wilder strifes. There was no sickly fastidiousness in their habits of life, and we see no . . . elegant weakness in their compositions.

By this stage the poetess has already begun to withdraw from the argument – with what looks suspiciously like boredom or contempt. Her response to the poet's highly virile account of the literary life, with its insinuations of emasculating femininity creeping like a disease among his contemporaries, is a cold, 'Have you not finished?' There are no tears and no self-blame, only a refusal to participate further in a pointless discussion.[25]

The poetess's voice is easily silenced, but her withdrawal from the discussion has a dignity that indicates strength. A few other female voices are present in *Phantasmagoria*, all mediated by ghostly narrators who undercut their authority and invite the reader's amusement. The female voice, like the voice of the young writer who 'had the misfortune . . . to discover that he was a genius', is there to be made fun of. This fun runs easily along certain familiar lines. A young lady with a '*taste* . . . for polite literature, for scenery, for satire, for sentiment . . . for everything elegant and intellectual' and a capacity to 'appreciate' and be '*dreadfully* affected' by everything she sees on a trip to Paris, is satirically contrasted to an old bachelor who has an equally undiscriminating dislike of everything. Six young ladies feature in 'A Rural Excursion', a tale about a day's outing 'in quest of the sublime and beautiful'. These young ladies are entirely mute; the account of their trip is narrated by a young bachelor who finds himself, to his horror, accompanying them. While the women are 'obstinately enchanted' with everything, this man's mind is fixed on food. In the hamper he hears no cheerily clinking bottles to suggest wine, finds no gravy: 'all was dry, silent, light'. Unpacking the basket is a depressing experience: 'let not the civic pasty, the baronial ham, the regal sirloin haunt your fancy', he bemoans, for the catering has been pitched at the level deemed appropriate for women's bodies not men's. Whereas Virginia Woolf, in 1928, could protest openly about the disparity in the food given to men in Oxbridge colleges and the food given to women, Maria Jane Jewsbury, in 1825, was more circumspect. It is her male narrator who cries out, 'I would have given the whole range of the blue sky for a beefsteak.' But it is the female author who has thought it, written a whole tale around it, and in uttering it casts a doubt on the silence and gastronomic quiescence of her six young ladies.[26]

Similarly, it is the male narrator in 'The Young Author', he who 'found it very easy' to write six sonnets in imitation of Milton between one meal and the next, who declares: 'perfectly infamous for a woman to write, and write well; ought to be satisfied with reading what men write. Shall make a point of abusing every clever book written by a woman.' Through mockery of the young man, the female author mocks misogynist attitudes that uphold social realities bearing directly on her experience as a clever woman who writes, and writes well, and whose books are liable to be abused by critics because she is a woman.[27]

Critical abuse comes in many forms. In 1838 Mrs Ellis, taking her place among the ranks of women writers who found a market in guiding other women down womanly paths, published an obituary notice of Maria Jane Jewsbury in the *Christian Keepsake*. In this notice she observed:

> It is a well-known truth, that genius is a fearful, and sometimes fatal gift; and genius of that particular kind which distinguished the character of Miss Jewsbury is perhaps the most to be feared in connexion with the happiness or misery of its possessor. The author of 'The Enthusiast' has, in that story, bequeathed to the world a striking and most melancholy picture of the ceaseless conflict, the insatiable thirst for what is unattainable, and the final wretchedness necessarily attendant upon the ungoverned ambition of superior intellect, when associated with the weakness, natural dependence and susceptibility of woman.[28]

This critical response is sufficient by itself to explain why Maria Jane did not explore her experiences as a woman writer in direct form until, with increased confidence and maturity, she wrote *The Three Histories*, of which 'The Enthusiast' is the first and longest tale. In the mid 1820s 'weakness, natural dependence and susceptibility' were already the defining characteristics of women. What meaning, then, could be given to strength, independence, and power? One meaning which Maria Jane resorted to was a meaning which arose naturally out of attempts at self-control. Having strength, independence, and power in abundance, and being a woman, she gave direct, literary expression to those qualities only in situations where they could be shown serving the purposes of heroic self-sacrifice. In poems on Roman themes the heroic strain came naturally. Thus Roman history provided a convenient vehicle for expressions of woman's strength, courage, and power. This strength and power was invariably located in woman's capacity to love, and its heroic quality was shown in woman's willingness to die in a higher cause. What fuels both the power and the willingness to die (the willingness to give up the power) is energy. Clearly, a delicate balance had to be maintained between the energy required to be heroic and energy which merely made a woman powerful: showing women using their energy in willingness to die was a way of celebrating the energy without drawing down wrath on the heads of either the women or the writer. Death was another apology, the ultimate 'susceptibility'. In a poem in *Phantasmagoria*, 'The Women of Suli', the balance between energy and heroic self-sacrifice falls strongly on the side of energy, celebrated for its own sake. The women of Suli respond to the sacking of their town by clasping hands and flinging themselves round and round in a thrilling dance on the edge of the cliff. All the power and force of the poem are in the liberated glee of the women, in their relish of the opportunity for action, their combined strength, banded together as they are to escape the rapacious invading army. But the final action is self-sacrifice: the dance culminates in a group suicide as they throw themselves over the cliff. Thus the poem dutifully illustrates the dependency – weakness – susceptibility conjunction explicitly expressed in the poem, 'Woman's Love':

Oh Woman! but in weakness, strong,
In suffering, only, brave! –
Watching, and tears, to thee belong, –
And silence, – and the Grave! –

So long as there is suffering, silence, tears, and the grave to act as a frame, then there can also be the expression, within that frame, of energy.[29]

Maria Jane Jewsbury was far from blind to the dilemmas this gave rise to, even before she had had the advantage of studying its effects on her poetic mentor, Felicia Hemans. In 'The Lonely Grave', a melodramatic and at first sight rather ludicrous tale, a woman's energy is shown leading her to a most unheroic abyss, to 'the delirium and danger of intense passion!' The tale is, however, a tale about the failure of self-control, and interestingly, the twin evils of sex and ambition are linked. The description of the woman – who in the end remorsefully poisons herself and dies – is set within a corrective analysis of the relation between women's expected demeanour and their real feelings. A woman's life, the author explains, is supposed to be 'sameness and serenity ... unperturbed', while her 'habitual thoughts and feelings seem to preserve a like noiseless tenour'. Given the universality of this death-in-life outward appearance, 'few suppose that the anxieties of ambition, the stirrings of passion, or the fierce tumults of pride, disappointment and despair can possibly exist beneath so quiet a surface'. But they do. Furthermore, women are said to be 'constitutionally trifling' but this is because 'from education, necessity and habit, they are continually placed in contact with trifles'. The woman in the story, Ellen, has a 'reflective, passionate and proud' nature which is offered no scope for action. Hence she is ripe for falling. She is judged to have deserved her fate because she failed to 'appreciate the true distinction which should be sought by women'. This 'true distinction' is, of course, heroic self-sacrifice which can give the meaning Ellen so sorely lacks to her strength and passion.

Ellen's tale is told from the point of view of her sorrowing father. In following her passion, Ellen moves from the unselfish (self-sacrificing) love she can offer her father, and into the selfish (self-assertive) 'love of mere lovers'; out of what Maria Jane in another essay calls the 'relative' roles, and into the realm of 'personal will and pleasure'. This is represented in the tale as carnal love for a man, but phrases like 'the anxieties of ambition' as well as the homilies on education which fit uneasily into a melodramatic love tale, suggest other kinds of 'personal will and pleasure'. (As well as confirming Maria Jane's own critical acumen in declaring that the love story was not her *forte*.) Indeed, the whole tale makes more sense read as a dramatization of the anxieties occasioned in a young woman on the verge of publishing her first book. Far from giving herself to a man in a delirium, what she proposes is coolly to challenge them, Far from going into 'silence, – and the Grave! –' she intends to use her voice and her pen vigorously and to be a living presence in the world of literature. These gratifications of personal will and pleasure conflict with the 'devotedness', 'sacrifice', 'patience', etc. which were to be a true woman's proper inspiration. The presence of her father in the story makes the veiled autobiographical explorations and anxieties more explicit when we take into account the fact that during the writing of *Phantasmagoria*, Maria Jane was in the very relative and self-denying, potentially heroically self-sacrificing role of mother to her father's children; and even if literary success did not remove her from that place, it certainly contained within it new possibilities and – for the family – the danger of unwelcomed changes in their domestic arrangements which depended so heavily on Maria Jane's readiness to hold the reins of government within the household.[30]

*

One of the indices and rewards of fame has always been contact with the already famous. *Phantasmagoria* made very plain how passionately Maria Jane wanted to be admitted into personal communication with those she judged to be the leading literary spirits of her time. She wanted to be inside the circle, not dreamily and tearfully looking on from outside. But the circle, as *Phantasmagoria* also made plain, was a male circle. It was a 'brotherhood'. In the few short months between the publication of *Phantasmagoria* and her complete physical collapse, Maria Jane learned that it was possible for to take up a place in that circle but that she would do so on female entry terms only.

To say that she learned it then is not strictly true, of course, since she knew it already; like *Phantasmagoria*, the steps she took towards her place were characterized by a more or less equal mixture of 'facility and audacity' on the one hand, and 'fear and dread' on the other. With great audacity, she dedicated her first book to the man who in her essays she had singled out as the only living poet to approach the stature of Milton and Shakespeare: William Wordsworth. Her work, she said, was intended to be a 'public tribute' to him. He was her 'spirit's father' and she, studying his works every day, his humble 'pupil'. Receiving an early copy of the first volume in the summer of 1825, Maria Jane rushed to sent it to William Wordsworth, with an accompanying letter full of modest deprecation of her own writing and warm, worshipful gratitude for his.

The results of this self-marketing strategy were stunning. Wordsworth wrote back at once and within a few days the hitherto unknown young woman had travelled to the Lake District, been admitted as an intimate into the poet's family, succeeded in making herself popular with all, and had been invited to join the Wordsworths on their annual holiday at Kent's Bank, near Morecambe, later that summer. She was undeniably inside the circle: through William Wordsworth she had access to the literary tradition whose exclusion of her beats like a muffled drum through the pages of *Phantasmagoria*. How had she done it, and what did it mean? She had done it by serving Wordsworth's needs in trying to meet her own, and it meant that she could have access to him, and to the literary tradition through him, on the same terms that his wife, his sister, and his daughter did.

William Wordsworth's self-absorption was great, even by the standards set by male poets. Maria Jane's reverential letter of appreciation came at a time when he felt in need of encouragement. He had been feeling, he told her, that he had 'lived and labored to little purpose'.[31] Her worship of him, her energy and enthusiasm, her eloquent appreciation of his writings, lifted a mood of despondency and restored his confidence in himself. They enabled him, in other words, not to see her more clearly, but to see himself in a better light. Serving him thus, Maria Jane took her place among a household of working women who all worked directly for William Wordsworth. The household at Rydal Mount consisted of the poet's wife, Mary; Mary's sister, Sara Hutchinson; William's sister, Dorothy; and the Wordsworth children, of whom Dora was increasingly being looked to as the poet's personal assistant. As Dorothy retreated into mental disorder, Dora's life began to shape itself into the career her father favoured: that of being a daughter to a great poet. Between them these women ran the poet's household, educated his children, fair-copied his verse, wrote letters to publishers and editors, and entertained literary visitors. Wordsworth's use of them was absolute and unquestioned. Dora's excuses for not writing to her friends, even to Maria Jane during the period in the late 1820s when they were 'deeply attached', invariably turned on her busyness: 'I have been at my desk for Father since the instant I swallowed my breakfast and now tea is ordered'; or,

> We shall have *all Blackwood* to breakfast to-morrow Sir Walter Scott, Wilson and Lockhart ... such a whirl! No peace! ... up every day before six to take an hour's ride and back to make breakfast for 12.... I am turned out of my own room, and have but $\frac{1}{2}$ of my Aunt's bed – and as for thinking of writing in the day – flying to the moon would be quite as practicable.[32]

Such a life was premised on female self-denial willingly embraced. The morality at the heart of it was a morality of willing service. The poet, the poet's work, the poet's admirers, the poet's children, the poet's clothes, the poet's food, all the constituents of the poet's day were the business of four women. Wordsworth's achievement in making wives of four unusual and gifted women remains quite a remarkable one.

Maria Jane Jewsbury's feelings of reverence for William Wordsworth, as a man and as a poet, were sincere. The fatherly figure served by the women in his household, the undisputed source of wisdom and authority, was a figure she was accustomed to. She served her own father unprotestingly. Without a doubt, her willing and practical efficiency in the domestic sphere played a part in her rapid acceptance at Rydal Mount equal in importance to (and possibly more important than) the brilliance of her writing. But though Wordsworth was her 'spirit's father', it was not another father she was looking for. Her restless and ambitious strivings were the strivings of a co-worker, a writer not a reader, and far removed from the gratified contentment of the devotee. Maria Jane did not go to Rydal Mount for purposes of worship only. Her professional ambitions took her there, and brought her to something of a full stop. Young, unmarried, unknown, the daughter of a failed mill owner, self-educated, and self-launched, it would have been difficult under any circumstances for her to establish a close professional relationship with William Wordsworth, no matter how proper and pure her intentions. But it might not have been impossible. As it was, she did not do so, turning her attentions instead to Wordsworth's daughter, Dora. This was a second best choice, and it had less to do with propriety than with the fact that Wordsworth, in full accord with his times, assumed that women, by nature, existed to serve men.

Maria Jane Jewsbury never became intimate with William Wordsworth. Friendship with his sister and intimacy with his daughter aligned her instead with a group of talented women who had seen the superior virtue of suppressing their own literary talents. Dorothy Wordsworth, as her most recent and most interesting biographer, Susan M. Levin, insists, was typical rather than untypical of women writers of her time in that she constantly denigrated herself and her talent 'in a manner that goes far beyond common protestations of modesty'. Dorothy Wordsworth's writing was writing 'characterized by refusal', writing that evinced 'a positive will not to put itself forward'.[33] In this she was supported by Mary Wordsworth, Dora Wordsworth, and Sara Hutchinson, all women who wrote well enough to have their letters, verses, and diaries saved and published after their deaths. The literary culture among the women of the household was a female literary culture. It was marked by passivity or hostility towards female self-projection. Dora Wordsworth published, in her early forties, a two-volume account of her travels in Portugal (where she had gone in a vain attempt to regain some health). Mary Wordsworth's response to this was mixed. It was observed by Sara Coleridge, daughter of Samuel Taylor Coleridge, and a woman who had grown up with Dora but who did not share the female literary values espoused in the Wordsworth household. Sara Coleridge wrote about Dora's publication and her mother's reaction to it:

> Mrs Wordsworth insists so that the only motive for publishing the tour
> was pecuniary gain.... Mrs Wordsworth has all her life wished her daughter
> to be above both marriage & authorship, & finds it hard to submit to these
> vulgarities on her behalf in this stage of her life career.[34]

Sara Coleridge, a published author herself, understood the dynamics that lay behind Mrs Wordsworth's ambivalence and stress on 'pecuniary gain': a publication done for money was not done for self-inflation; it did not mean that Dora was putting herself up to be admired, claiming to be a woman of genius, wanting flattery, and running the risk of having her head turned and being utterly destroyed by vanity.

Women, because 'naturally' vain and impressionable, required to have such tendencies checked. Mary Wordsworth's doubts were the doubts of a good mother. To understand something of the literary circle Maria Jane was welcomed into when she knocked on the door of Rydal Mount, one need only look at the reception given to Mrs Hemans a few years later in 1830. She certainly did not bring all Blackwood with her, but her visit was none the less a source of disturbance. She stayed 'two *long* weeks'. A mature writer at the height of her career, Mrs Hemans was accustomed to occupying the centre and being listened to. Mrs Hemans therefore talked. It will never be known exactly how much she talked, but however much it was, it was felt to be too much. Sara Hutchinson and Dora certainly disliked her and probably their feelings were shared by the other women. According to Sara, Mrs Hemans was 'spoilt by the adulation of "the world"... her affectation is perfectly unendurable'. Instead of listening to Mrs Hemans, Sara made a point of sitting in the same room and writing a letter to Edward Quillinan, the family friend and neighbour who was soon to marry Dora: 'What bad taste in me', she gloated, 'to have been writing to you rather than attending to Mrs Hemans's "brilliant" conversation – for she is always, or would be, brilliant.'[35]

William Wordsworth himself seems not to have objected too much to this talk, perhaps because it contained sufficient acknowledgement of his genius. Mrs Hemans's comment on her stay makes it clear that she served up more than meagre portions of praise: 'Oh! what relief, what blessing there is in the feeling of admiration when it can be freely poured forth.'[36] While this and a somewhat flighty, giddy manner worked for the poet, it did not go down well with the women. Sara Hutchinson observed acidly, 'Mr Wordsworth *pretends* to like her very much – but I believe it is only because we do not – for she is the very opposite, her good nature excepted, of anything he ever admired before either in *theory or practice*.'[37] Presumably, since no woman poet of comparable stature had ever stayed in the house before, Mr Wordsworth had only had the opportunity of admiring such a woman in theory. But Sara Hutchinson knew what Wordsworth liked and wanted. In interpreting Mrs Hemans's talking as a demand for endless flattery (of which, poor woman, she 'found a scanty supply here') she reflected, just as she lived out in her daily life at Rydal Mount, Wordsworth's deeply held convictions.

Obedient listening to men's speech, in the particular and in the general, was a basic female duty thoroughly internalized by all but the most exceptional women. The American, Margaret Fuller, a woman of public visibility for whom self-expression as both talker and writer came naturally and forcefully and who was accustomed to occupying the centre of a circle of listeners, was unusual in finding it strange that she was not listened to when she attempted to have a conversation with Thomas Carlyle. 'To interrupt him', she complained, 'is a physical impossibility. If you get a chance to remonstrate for a moment, he raises his voice and bears you down.'[38] Admittedly, men, too, found it difficult to interrupt Carlyle, but the listening of women to men's speech has a cultural specificity. In the meeting of Margaret Fuller and Thomas Carlyle, just as in the meeting of Felicia Hemans and William Wordsworth, there was more than a merely accidental collision of volubilities. Both women transgressed the code expressed in the final year of the eighteenth century by Hannah More – a woman who, like the women in Wordsworth's household, had a great deal of her own to say – as follows:

The animated silence of sparkling intelligence with an occasional modest question which indicated rational curiosity and becoming diffidence is in many cases as large a share of the conversation as it is decorous for feminine delicacy to take.[39]

Sara Hutchinson certainly thought Felicia Hemans would have been better off '*tidying up* for her husband and children' than talking and reading and writing and publishing poetry. Wordsworth, too, observed that Mrs Hemans's education had been 'most unfortunate. She was totally ignorant of housewifery, and could as easily have managed the spear of Minerva as her needle.'[40] The male hand was made for the pen as it was made for the spear; the female hand was made for the needle. Mrs Hemans would have been more acceptable had she been like Dorothy Wordsworth, whose journal entries appear to make no value judgement between the activities of sewing and writing, as in: 'He completely finished his poems, I finished Derwent's frocks.'[41] The mystifying process of equalizing writing and sewing was brought to perfection by Thomas Carlyle, but Wordsworth, the 'true *Poet of Home*, and of all the lofty feelings which have their root in the soil of home affections', laid some of the ground.[42] The Wordsworth women listened to men, and, because they were intelligent, heard their vanities and weaknesses as well as their strengths; they became rather superior to the shifts and stratagems of literary gentlemen. Sewing was undeniably more useful than much of what the men they knew produced. It had far more worth than the average literary product. It was not difficult to regard sewing as a higher achievement than writing, nor the needle as a more valued adjunct than the spear of Minerva. What was harder was to notice how these values came from the mouths of those whose shirts had to be sewn by hand and at home.

Talking instead of sewing convicted Felicia Hemans of being 'that despicable thing, a woman living upon admiration!' It was not Wordsworth, however, but his friend Robert Southey who gave the key expression to cultural misogyny. When applied to by the unknown Charlotte Brontë for his opinion of an early manuscript, Robert Southey was blunt:

> The day dreams in which you habitually indulge are likely to induce a distempered state of mind; and in proportion as all the ordinary uses of the world seem to you flat and unprofitable, you will be unfitted for them without becoming fitted for anything else. Literature cannot be the business of a woman's life, and it ought not to be.[43]

Southey's daughter, Edith, was, until Maria Jane Jewsbury came along, Dora Wordsworth's most passionate and most intimate friend, a young woman whose marriage left Dora distraught. William Wordsworth's style was less direct, but his fundamental attitude agreed with Southey's. He used women for his vital nourishment. Surrounded as he was by a solid, supportive female presence, his poetry projected that consciousness into a celebration of the nourishing qualities of Nature – the female principle. But, as Susan M. Levin points out in writing about Dorothy Wordsworth, it is the tranquil, nurturing domestic scene which is in reality more vital than Wordsworth's nature. Nature doesn't keep people going, families do; and within families, women. What it meant for Maria Jane to be admitted into Wordsworth's household as a friend of the family was the exact opposite of what she sought. It meant agreeing to remain on the margins of the circle. As she said to Dora: 'how much better to have strong domestic affections than great brilliancy of intellect!'[44] The guardians of the domestic affections were women. Wordsworth's female dependants provided the soil out of which his lofty feelings arose into verse, and it was a soil enriched by their life blood. This sacrifice was perhaps not a consciously painful one until another woman, like Felicia Hemans, tried to draw on it.

Maria Jane Jewsbury did not. Her record on female self-denial was in any case double-edged. She could claim full credit for her services to her father and siblings; but her literary ambitions precluded her from identifying wholeheartedly with a life premised on service to another. Her friendship with Dora was a second best choice not because Dora was 'only' a woman, but because she was not a practising, professional writer. Maria Jane's intimacy with Dora was a real intimacy, based on heart to heart exchanges in the garden, long talks, and letters in which they each expressed longings to be with one another and confessed miseries for days after partings. There is no doubt that the women gained a great deal from the friendship, with its pleasurable romantic flourishes. Dora especially, dutiful and home-bound, found something in the energy of the eager, vagabond-ish, Manchester woman which sustained her in her very different life. But it was not a relationship that could grow. The position each occupied in her literary life made growth impossible. They were divided by opposing responses to the most powerful commitments of their emotional lives: to their fathers and to their own selves. This was a political divide so profound and sensitive that it could not even be spoken. Maria Jane had already shown that she put her writing before her service to her own father: her relationship with Dora could not grow unless Maria Jane was willing to remain a daughterly 'pupil' to her 'spirit's father', her cultural father, William Wordsworth. In the end, she was not prepared to do that; but she was willing to go a long way.

Maria Jane Jewsbury blended, in a way Felicia Hemans did not blend, with the conventions of the Wordsworth household. She possessed those very feminine qualities of adaptability and the capacity to listen actively, having 'a peculiar faculty for identifying herself with the tastes and predilections of those she loved; and ... a singular talent for eliciting thoughts from others'.[45] She deferred to the teasing of her as a 'vagabond'; she accepted that Dora would always put her father's demands for her services before any claim that a female friend might have on her; she applauded Dora's submission to her domestic and literary tasks. When Dora was depressed and sick, Maria Jane did not suggest that her confined life had anything to do with it. Dora, it should be remembered, had grown up not only under her father's shadow but in the midst of a whole community of male poets: Samuel Taylor Coleridge, Robert Southey, Hartley Coleridge. The values upon which domestic life, including the subordination of women, rested, were not challenged by these men, all of whom placed at least a theoretical value on home affections. Maria Jane agreed that home affections were best sustained though the very homely tasks of sewing, sweeping, and dusting.

'Christopher North', who recorded Maria Jane Jewsbury's stay with Wordsworth in *Blackwood's* magazine in 1825, was satisfied that she had conducted herself as a young woman should. His pen portrait appeared in a facetious piece, purporting to be a serious 'conversation' on the subject of male and female genius. The columnist allowed that Miss Jewsbury would certainly quality for a place at the table when male and female genius sat down to banquet. Having registered her genius, he moved swiftly on to the more important consideration of whether she was 'bonny':

> I do not pretend to be positive on that point, for the only time I ever had the pleasure of seeing Miss Jewsbury it was but a momentary glance among the mountains. Mounted on a pretty pony, in a pretty rural straw hat, a pretty rural riding habit, with the sunshine of a cloudless heaven blended in her countenance with that of her own cloudless soul, the young author of *Phantasmagoria* rode smilingly along a beautiful vale, with the illustrious Wordsworth, whom she venerates, at her side, and pouring out poetry in that glorious recitative of his, till the vale was overflowing with the sound. Wha Jamie, wouldna ha' looked bonny in sic a predicament?[46]

The characteristics of the acceptable female genius may be inferred from this ambrosial description: she will be pretty, smiling, and ready to listen.

If Maria Jane's soul was 'cloudless' when she arrived at Rydal Mount in the full flush of her first success, it did not long remain so. Judging the balance between brilliance, which gained her her initial entry, and the appropriate feminine behaviour which would assure a continued welcome, can never have been easy. Essentially it demanded a choice. Two letters written after her return home at the end of July show Maria Jane's understanding of that choice. They sound a note only too familiar in the history of women's writing: dissatisfaction, guilt, and renunciation. She was, she told Wordsworth, 'proud and happy, when I only knew and appreciated you as a poet. What then are my feelings, now that I am emboldened to look up to you as a friend!' In the first instance, and with regard to her own work, her feelings were feelings of embarrassment. She was 'heartily ashamed' of the second volume of *Phantasmagoria*, now ready to be sent if only its author still possessed the confidence she had had when she launched the first volume into the world. She was 'ashamed and angry with myself'. Looking up to Wordsworth as a friend caused her to look down on her own artistic productions with the eyes of an enemy. A third letter, written in October, contained a poem, 'A Farewell to the Muse'. In this poem Maria Jane bid goodbye to high poetic aspiration. Poetry had always been a comfort, but she realized that she was not one of the elect whom the Muses had charged with celestial fire. It had not been given to her to be among the poetic great. She was still outside, anxious to show that she knew her place. This poem of renunciation is one in which she claims to be happy to give up old ambitions; sensibly, calmly, and matter-of-factly recognizing the simple truth that Wordsworth had helped her see: she was not chosen.[47]

As in *Phantasmagoria*, the distinction between the celestially touched and the unchosen is represented as a distinction between genius and mediocrity. But Maria Jane was also required to agree to it as a gendered division. Listening in animated silence and taking 'a share' of the conversation literally meant that men must determine its shape, and into that shape they projected their views of women. The hallowed air of Rydal Mount was as liable to be clogged by the circulation of negative stereotypes of women as were less exalted interiors. Maria Jane, representing 'you ladies', was told by Wordsworth: 'Your hearts very often resemble looking-glasses, not in their capability of being broken, but in that of receiving every impression and retaining none.' This sort of gallantry, which women grew up on, could be dismissed with a tinkling laugh. But other observations bit more deeply. Right at the very hearth-side of the leading male poet of domesticity, Maria Jane learned to repeat the lessons of her exclusion. In 1829 she wrote to Dora:

> You cannot think how often and how fondly I look back to Kent's Bank and your father's conversations there – when in Wales I repeated some of his opinions on the pains and penalties of female authorship, and Mrs Hemans agreed to them, in the sober sadness that I do. Her fame has gilded *her* chain, but it has not lost its clank. I cannot conceive how, unless a necessity be laid upon her, any woman of acute sensibility, and refined imagination can brook the fever strife of authorship. Do you remember your father's simile about women and flowers – growing in their native bed and transplanted to a drawing room chimney place? I wish I could forget it.[48]

This is a good example of the sympathetic male as the woman's worst enemy. Wordsworth's sympathy forces the choice: woman or author. It is not possible to be both. By 1829 Maria Jane had published three books, was working on her fourth, and was producing a steady flow of verses for a wide variety of publications. The trite phrases in her letter to Dora could have been lifted from the pages of *Phantasmagoria*. But there is no edge of satire here. Alone with Mrs Hemans, she apparently repeated the orthodox opinions of the influential poet, approvingly passing on, as one woman writer to another, words which negated her own and Mrs Hemans's entire enterprise. She might well wish that she could forget them. One is confronted by the spectacle of two successful and enormously productive women assuring each other in 'sober sadness' (and privacy) that they do not know how they possibly can do what they do. While the reviews agreed that Mrs Hemans showed it was possible to be a poet and a lady, Mr Wordsworth, as Miss Jewsbury heard him and reported back to his daughter, seemed to think writing and femaleness a regrettable combination.

3

DRAGOON KINDS OF WOMEN

'And what good would fame do you, – a woman?'
'It would make amends for being a woman – I should not pass away and perish.'

Maria Jane Jewsbury[1]

Within a few months of visiting Wordsworth, Maria Jane collapsed. She was disabled by guilt, tormented by a fear of death, and painfully anxious to agree that her writings had been motivated by a love of self and self-aggrandisement. From early 1826 until the summer of 1828 she was more or less continuously an invalid. Part of that time was spent convalescing at Leamington Spa. Though sick, she was far from idle. Released from the demands of domestic life, removed from what had become the oppressiveness of her local celebrity in Manchester, she read, wrote, maintained a flow of correspondence, and, above all, reflected with some anguish on the meaning of her experiences.

Success brought two years of wretchedness, manifesting itself in physical debility and intellectual retreat. Maria Jane spoke of herself as a 'misguided being' whose ambition had led her astray. In October 1826 she wrote Dora a long letter of religious reflection, writing it, she explained, 'as a duty' at a time when it was generally thought that she was dying. In the letter, which was about her own experiences but which she wrote in the third person, she explained the misery her success had brought her: 'it was not in the hour of disappointment and of chagrin – it was always in the moment of full unalloyed success that she was most wretched'. And she directed Dora's attention to Herbert's poem, 'Teach Me My God and King', that essential text for housewives with its inspiring lines:

> A servant with this clause
> Makes drudgery divine
> Who sweeps a room as for Thy sake
> Makes that and the action fine.

Her strongest desire, she said, was to keep just 'well enough to fulfill my home *duties*'.[2]

In this subdued and self-castigating mood, Maria Jane produced her second book. This was the edited version of letters written mostly to Geraldine, published in 1828 as 'a real and not a fictitious correspondence ... the fruit of a protracted recovery from long illness'.[3] That was perfectly true, but the book was also a bid for a recognizable market. Both the form – real, not fictitious, letters – and the framing – female illness unto but not quite as far as expiration – had great popularity. Real letters, even those made up by hacks in garretts, had been popular ever since the seventeenth century, as Ruth Perry has shown.[4] In 1828 female illness was enjoying a vogue in the wake of the success of Anna Jameson's *Diary of an Ennuyée* which appeared in 1826.[5] The heroine of *Diary of an Ennuyée* is poorly throughout a short but remarkably active life. In between bouts on the sofa and before dying of a broken heart, she manages to travel the length of Italy, climbing Mt Etna (during an eruption) and exploring every nook and cranny of the Vatican museum like the energetic art professional Anna Jameson herself became. Such activity and independence were legitimized by images of passivity made credible by illness. Even illness that was a fact could be useful as a fiction. This, however, led (still leads) to confusion: people who met Anna Jameson after reading her book felt cheated. She was an extremely robust woman. Fanny Kemble, meeting her at a party, remarked: 'The Ennuyée, one is given to understand, dies; and it was a little vexatious to behold her sitting on a sofa, in a very becoming state of blooming *plumptitude*.' But Fanny Kemble, like many another young woman of the time, had had her imagination fired by Anna Jameson's images of a young woman walking alone in Italian streets, observing the life around her, and thinking her own thoughts.[6]

Maria Jane Jewsbury's *Letters to the Young* was addressed to Geraldine, then in her 16th year. Its general tone may be indicated by Maria Jane's birthday message to Geraldine in 1827, when she was 15: 'The wreath of fame is often a fiery crown, burning the brows that wear it – I do my dear love wish you all *good* things on your birthday – and amongst them moderated expectations of life.'[7] *Letters to the Young* was a plea for moderated expectations. Claiming to be real, it denied the freedoms of fictional creation; claiming to have evolved from sickness, it denied the bodily health which might imply ambition. It was a woman's book. It is probably the only book of its kind, one in which a sister/mother warns her sister/daughter of the dangers of literary ambition. The message of *Letters to the Young* was that success in literature, fame, would bring not happiness but its reverse: unhappiness. Happiness for women was to be found in religion, with its counsels of self-restraint and its consolations of an afterlife where 'Fame's trumpet will be silent'. Women's lives demanded unfaltering self-control; this could only be achieved through religion, but sickness helped. The retirement of sickness enabled women to regain the self-control which a worldly existence eternally threatened. In retirement, Maria Jane, experienced older woman, explained through Geraldine to all young aspiring women, we 'learn ourselves, that book of many pages, that text of many meanings!' And what we learn is how better to control it. For the problem with books and open pages is that some of their meanings are inscribed upon them by others:

> I can deeply feel for anyone thrown ... into close and constant intercourse with the world, because such an individual has this book closed against him. ... In the noise and glare of a worldy life, how many false motives, how many erroneous opinions, may steal in and out of the heart unnoticed; and shape themselves into action, and express themselves in words ... with an influence so silent and unobtrusive, that the individual is not aware of the deadening process going on within.[8]

It is a familiar reversal: the 'deadening process' is really the enlivening one, the fuller, richer life. The life women are encouraged to seek is really a dead one, a life of sickness and stillness. The experience of worldly distinction is shown as synonymous with the loss of self-knowledge and true judgement which are the basis, in a woman, of self-control, itself the basis of her definitive womanliness. Without self-control, the woman's best powers are her worst enemies: 'the stirrings of internal power; the longings after intellectual distinction; the seductions of literature' all contain within them the seeds of womanly death, for they exist on 'prohibited ground, that on which the tree of life may not grow'. Life, for women, according to *Letters to the Young*, was best expressed through the imitation death of sickness and withdrawal; it was a modest, Wordsworthian affair of 'graceful and good-humoured attention to inferior employments, homely duties and ordinary associations'.[9] The self-control needed to tolerate such a life was the passport to happiness here on earth and eternal bliss beyond for it assured the existence of the woman.

Unfortunately for Geraldine, as she was depicted in *Letters to the Young*, her 'natural character', like that of her elder sister, exposed her to the likelihood of unhappiness. She possessed the same 'premature energy and ambition' that Maria Jane possessed. She already showed an 'ardent, ambitious temper' and a 'love of pre-eminence'. She showed little sign of possessing the vital ingredient of self-control which *might*, under certain highly conscribed circumstances, make a literary career possible for a woman. It was hard for Geraldine to contain her energies and aspirations within the shrunken frame of woman's sphere. Her tendency was to expand and grow, to reach out perilously for a realm of action in which woman's place was at best ill-defined, at worst a glaring and unacceptable contradiction; a realm in which, for a woman, the word 'fame' rhymed with 'shame'. Maria Jane asked Geraldine:

> Ardent, ambitious, impatient of control, consumed even now by romantic fancies, tell me how you can be happy without that principle which, by regulating your mind, would reconcile you to life as it is really constituted; not the life you now picture, nor that depicted in a novel, but the life of common occupations relieved only by common pleasures? I admit you have a resource in your excellent abilities and taste for mental cultivation; but

so long as your present feelings continue, and you consider them merely available for ambitious purposes, you will derive more disappointment than comfort from the possession of them.[10]

There are several exhortations of this sort in *Letters to the Young*, culminating in the cry of parents through the ages: 'Are you determined . . . to learn by no one's experience but your own?'

The picture of Geraldine that emerges from *Letters to the Young* is a remarkably lurid one. Though still an untried schoolgirl of 15, she is described as a 'wild and wayward spirit' for whom even images of storm, fire, volcano, and whirlwind are inadequate to convey her 'unholy tumult of heart'. She suffers, it appears, from a 'hidden world of hopes and desires, affections and fancies, restless as a troubled sea, unstable as the flitting clouds'. She deems happiness to consist in 'constant excitement'. She is 'a being whose "events are emotions"; whose principles are impulses; whose feelings are passions; whose changes are contradictions; to whose whole moral existence enthusiasm is a never setting sun'. In consequence of all which, her sister instructs her: 'you, more than any other human being I know, should unite vigilance and self-distrust'. It should be her daily object to subdue emotion, that 'delicious but dangerous influence', and ensure that 'regulated feeling' be put in its place. By the aid of 'self-denial' and 'holy resolution', as well as devotional study of the Scriptures, she may attain to a 'calm and sober . . . lofty temperament'.[11]

This was a fictional Geraldine. The real Geraldine, home from school for the summer holidays in 1827, was, in Maria Jane's report on her to Felicia Hemans, 'a sweet girl, with a wonderful turn for composition, but practical and very modest'. She was affectionate and dutiful, and Maria Jane was glad to have her at home since she was able to 'make breakfast for poor father, and read to him at night, and so make amends for my lack of service'.[12] The contrast between this and the figure so remorselessly hectored in *Letters to the Young* is striking. But the language of tumult in that work, directed at Geraldine, belongs properly to Maria Jane. Geraldine, a younger woman, a sister, and a daughter, was a convenient autobiographical projection, a means of speaking in the third person just as Maria Jane wrote of her own experiences to Dora in the third person. It was a way of not patronizing the pronoun I, one more symptom of self-suppression. *Letters to the Young* dramatizes the mental struggles of a successful author and ambitious woman to find a way of living and understanding her life that did not destroy her. By protesting disillusion with earthly success − 'life now wears another aspect. . . . I perceive that neither the goal nor the crown belong to this world' − by remaining anxious, like a true woman, to 'unite vigilance with self-distrust', she attempted to present an image of herself (and to some extent for herself) that accorded more closely with prevailing notions of ideal womanhood such as Dora, Dorothy, Sara, and Mary lived by under the shadow of the poet Maria Jane still revered above all others.

The retirement of sickness aided this project in a practical sense too: it ensured the time in which reflection, reading, and writing – the day-to-day business of a writer's life – could go forward. *Letters to the Young* did not proceed, as did much of *Phantasmagoria*, from snatched moments by the bedsides of sick children. Being a patient afforded uninterrupted time in a way that efficiently holding the reins of household government did not. Throughout the years of her collapse, Maria Jane continued to contribute verses to the Annuals, those lavishly produced illustrated albums with titles like *Forget-Me-Not*, *Friendship's Offering*, *Literary Souvenir*, and *Winter's Wreath*. Taking her career as a whole, she was one of the most prolific contributors of all, her ubiquity exceeding even Felicia Hemans and L.E.L. (Laetitia Landon). Editors of Annuals competed to attract big names and they offered good money even to the smaller fry. Though the quality of writing was rarely high, the Annuals sold well and for a writer like Maria Jane were a useful source of regular income. The importance of this can hardly be overstated. Considered from Geraldine's point of view, Maria Jane's ability to gain an income (and independence) for herself was a powerful counter to all the arguments of *Letters to the Young*.

Geraldine understood that she was being educated to provide for herself, and that conquering her ambitious temper was more than a merely moral objective: it was a part of the necessary training for what was likely to be her career, that of a governess or teacher. While her sister reminded her that literature was morally dangerous and materially unpredictable – success, as Maria Jane said, being unlikely 'on the ground of probabilities' alone, 'which in regard to women are as one to ten thousand against' – she also, and at the same time, offered a living example of that one in ten thousand who *could* make it work.[13] Beyond all the lecturing, fictioneering, and ambivalence, what Geraldine had before her as she grew to maturity was an increasingly successful, rigorously professional woman writer. One, too, in whom the advantages of her chosen path clearly outweighed the disadvantages, not least because she was able to put those disadvantages into literary form and reap the benefits in hard cash, prestige, and even popularity. These truths were not lost on Geraldine. *Letters to the Young*, which failed in its avowed purposes for both writer and recipient, since neither Maria Jane nor Geraldine heeded its advice to stop writing, succeeded marvellously as a saleable piece of literature. Didactic, in the tradition of writing for young people, mixing the voice of the teacher with the popular autobiographical tones of the penitent who has learnt from painful experience the error of her ways, it was a very well received volume at the time (going rapidly into three editions) and was still 'cherished', according to Francis Espinasse in *Lancashire Worthies*, by a certain class of reader as late as 1877.[14]

Just as the poem, 'A Farewell to the Muse', was the immediate literary result of Maria Jane Jewsbury's acquaintance with William Wordsworth, so *Letters to the Young*, with its passionate prohibitions flung out at the ambitious writing woman its author was and her sister seemed set on becoming, testifies to Wordsworth's influence. Albeit unintentionally, it none the less emphatically demonstrates the extent to which he, and the literary tradition within which he occupied a secure place, had let Maria Jane down. Whether she was a genius or not, Maria Jane certainly had a sex and she was not to be allowed to forget it. Wordsworth might have been the poet of home, but he was not expected to contribute towards home affections through the divine drudgery of sweeping and cleaning. Nor was he expected to claim to want to remain obscure. Sara Hutchinson's defensively disdainful remark about Maria Jane, 'write she *will* and fancies she *must*', or of Felicia Hemans, that a Miss Hamilton wrote 'ten times better poetry than Mrs Hemans but would be shocked if she thought *the world* should ever know she had written a line', simply could not have been said about Wordsworth, for reasons that have nothing to do with the quality of work produced.[15] These are comments about womanliness not writing. No male poet of proven ability would be warned to curtail his genius and in its place 'study mildness of deportment'. Unlike his female counterpart, he would probably not be told, as Geraldine was told in *Letters to the Young*, that 'Genius is not Grace', or that 'Splendid ideas are good but a humble heart is better.... In all disputes suppose yourself worthy of blame.'[16] Even to imagine Wordsworth speaking thus fraternally to Coleridge, or Byron to Shelley, makes the blood rush dizzily to the head. But women writers regaled each other with injunctions to be little, cautious, restrained, and self-denying, and to persist enduringly in narrowed lives. What they did not share, what was virtually a taboo subject, was their experience of men. Unable to voice criticisms of men, they could not speak the occasions when they were let down by men. Just as biological fathers were beyond reproach, so too were spiritual fathers. All that was left was to blame themselves and look ever more deeply within for improvements.

*

Throughout 1827, Maria Jane held out the hope that she might travel to Wales to visit Felicia Hemans (the possibility of Mrs Hemans travelling to Leamington or Manchester seems never to have been raised). By the spring of 1828, though still an invalid, she had determined on it. Harriett Hughes found the cottage for them, just half a mile from Rhyllon. It was tiny and too close to the road, but it had a little garden with roses and greenery and fresh country air which contrasted dramatically with the smogs of industrial Manchester. When Maria Jane had gone to stay with the Wordsworth's at Kent's Bank in 1825, she had arrived full of energy and virtually empty-handed having lost her luggage on the way. She had only the image-creating accessories of a coffee pot and writing desk. The arrival in Wales was more sedate and domestic. According to Harriett who was there to meet her, Maria Jane 'came into Wales ... completely as an invalid'. But she was an invalid who recovered remarkably quickly under the influences by which she was presently surrounded. By the time Mrs Hemans arrived from Wavertree for her last summer in Wales, Maria Jane was well established in her new surroundings. Practical as ever, she had erected a tent in the front garden of the cottage to give herself more living space. Her two brothers were absorbed into the outdoor activities of the five Hemans boys, and she herself was sufficiently strengthened to go for long rides on a donkey with Geraldine and 'a troop of juvenile knights-errant' in attendance.[17]

Visiting Wordsworth, Maria Jane had been more than willing to repay in homage what she received in hospitality, and so too, she went to Wales fully prepared to adore Mrs Hemans. She described her to Dora:

> She is almost deeply interesting, more painfully so than any one I ever saw, just a being to put in your heart in a place by herself. Her circumstances are so sad – and her alterations from child-like glee to the most profound melancholy make your heart ache. She possesses wonderful information – and her memory is very strong. . . . [She] never went to school – taught herself everything – was in childhood a regular romp – at seven years old used to climb into an apple tree to read Shakespeare.[18]

The women spent their days roaming the countryside, reading, talking, and resting in dingle and nook while the children ranged more widely. In the evenings there was more talking, more reading, and music, usually provided by Harriett Hughes and Felicia Hemans. The two families were in each other's company every day. Though covering similar subjects to those covered at Rydal Mount, 'the converse of those bright hours at Rhyllon' was imbued with a singular charm which Rydal Mount lacked: the circle into which Maria Jane gained admission at Rhyllon, was a circle within which she was unambivalently welcomed as a woman writer. It was a circle of which a woman writer was the centre. No one at Rhyllon, no one indeed in the entire neighbourhood, lamented Mrs Hemans's insufficiency with the needle, and neither did anybody suggest that she talked too much (just as nobody at Rydal Mount suggested Wordsworth demanded too much attention).

The intimacy which developed between the two women during a short summer of walks and talks and evenings by the fireside, had its roots in the absolute priority each gave to literary work and literary ambition in her life, which she was free both to reveal in herself and recognize in the other. This was the knowledge Felicia Hemans testified that Maria Jane Jewsbury had of her. Mrs Hemans was, by the late 1820s, an item on the cultural tourism map, 'sought out in her retreat by every species of literary homage'. Few who sought her out had anything to offer. They came to stare at a poetess and to request autographs. Maria Jane offered the understanding friendship of an emerging writer who, like the mass of Mrs Hemans's fans, had a curiosity about the woman which derived from her reading of the poetry, but which also drew on the intense personal resonance of their shared experiences as women occupying a literary ground well trodden by women like themselves but marked out, shaped, defined, and possessed by men. It was an apposite time for the women to meet. Each had recently completed a work in which she gave some expression to her experience of being let down by men: Maria Jane's *Letters to the Young* and Felicia Hemans's *Records of Woman*.[19]

The pages of *Records of Woman* are filled with heroic suffering women and eloquently empty of adequate men. The promise held out to women as the reward of marriage, that of being looked after, protected by manly strength as parents protect a child, was a promise Felicia Hemans's marriage had not fulfilled; but the lack of protection was not something she had felt acutely until her mother's death in 1827. This event propelled her into the specific adult, unprotected world made for her by her own achievements. Unlike childhood and marriage – which, for women, in its ideal form was essentially childlike – worldly success was an adult affair and therefore synonymous with masculinity. Felicia identified her unhappiness at this stage of her life in terms which opposed her essential 'femininity' to the hazards of a 'masculine' public life. In doing so she exploited the images of femininity – passivity, helplessness, suffering, the desire for privacy and retreat from the world – as a defence against a personal unhappiness which had significant general implications. For the isolation Felicia Hemans experienced was as much the isolation of the artistic woman who stood at the pinnacle of her profession, as it was the isolation of the abandoned wife and child. Unfortunately (for other women artists), while she could say she felt the need of worldly protection, she could not say she equally felt the need of artistic support. If, as a woman, her work took its justification from the spontaneity of the impulse, the natural, unstoppable nature of the emission, to assert a need for support or community among other like-minded individuals was unthinkable. She could speak out her unhappiness as a woman but she could not speak it out as a poet. No more than Maria Jane could she publicly encourage a young woman of talent, for example Geraldine, to follow her down the road she had travelled.

The difficulty of her position may be seen in *Records of Woman*. Three poems in that collection address the experience of the woman who reaches out to a public. In 'Joan of Arc, in Rheims', the warrior Joan is pictured in the cathedral 'mantled with victorious power', 'Daughter of victory!' receiving the whole nation's approval and praise: 'What a power to bid the quick heart bound'. But at once a doubt intervenes: 'Is there indeed such power? – far deeper dwells / In one kind household voice, to reach the cells / Whence happiness flows forth!' Joan catches sight of her father and brothers in the crowd and is at once transported in memory and love to her childhood. She takes off her helmet and begs to be taken back with them, 'To the still cabin and the beechen-tree / Let me return!' No such return is possible. Joan has to pay the price of her fame:

> Oh! never did thine eye
> Thro' the green haunts of happy infancy
> Wander again, Joanne! – too much of fame
> Had shed its radiance on thy peasant-name;
> And bought alone by gifts beyond all price,
> The trusting heart's repose, the paradise
> Of home with all its loves, doth fate allow
> The crown of glory unto woman's brow.

The self-assertiveness of the woman warrior, like the self-assertiveness of the woman writer, is in direct contradiction to the 'trusting heart's repose' of ideal homely happiness. The woman warrior is a woman in a man's world, but so too is the woman artist. The most important poem in *Records of Woman*, 'Properzia Rossi', tells the story of Properzia Rossi, the celebrated female sculptor of the Renaissance. Properzia Rossi was not only a sculptor, she was also a poet, and a woman of intense musical susceptibility (like Felicia Hemans). Her story was one of unrequited love leading to death. Felicia Hemans presents her as a woman attempting to attach to herself the man she loves through the one activity which is the expression of her deepest self: her art. She fails. Her failure implies the inescapable conflict in gifted women between their passion for art – their true selves – and their acceptability as women. Properzia Rossi values the power she has for its own sake: 'It comes, – the power / Within me born, flows back; my fruitless dower / That could not win me love. Yet once again / I greet it proudly, with its rushing train / Of glorious images.' Like Felicia Hemans, Properzia Rossi creates her 'own life's history' through her artistic production. She knows the pleasure of self-creation: 'line by line, / I fix my thought, heart, soul, to burn, to shine'. But when she thinks about posterity, the ultimate judge of her artistic achievements, she looks to it to prove her as a woman: she wants posterity, by applauding her work, to win for her, posthumously, the love of the man she desires and has failed to win in life. Posterity, however, cannot give her womanly love; it can only award her fame:

> Thou shalt have fame! Oh mockery! give the reed
> From storms a shelter, – give the drooping vine
> Something round which its tendrils may entwine, –
> Give the parched flower a raindrop, and the meed
> Of love's kind words to woman! Worthless fame!
> That in his bosom wins not for my name
> Th'abiding place it ask'd! Yet how my heart
> In its own fairy world of song and art
> Once beat for praise!

Properzia Rossi is typical of female artists in that her work falls short of what she might have achieved. She knows this. The power was within, but external circumstances denied her the nourishment and enrichment that might have enabled her to give it the fullest utterance. The desire for praise (invariably a source of guilt) is in part a desire for that placing of each other which peers provide, for the constructive comments and criticisms available to men who were able to know themselves as part of a community of writers and readers, and to grow from that knowledge:

> I might have given
> Birth to creations of far nobler thought,

I might have kindled, with the fire of heaven,
Things not of such as die! But I have been
Too much alone; a heart whereon to lean,
With all these deep affections, that o'erflow
My aching soul, and find no shore below;
An eye to be my star, a voice to bring
Hope o'er my path, like sounds that breathe of spring,
– These are denied me – dreamt of still in vain, –
Therefore my brief aspirings from the chain,
Are ever but as some wild fitful song,
Rising triumphantly, to die ere long
In dirge-like echoes.

As an explanation for Felicia Hemans's well-known melancholy, which darkened the last years of her life, this rings true. In the poem, the 'heart whereon to lean' is an individual male heart, but in the context of the whole collection and its depiction of the failure of men's hearts to sustain women (even the women whose love is requited are left alone) it suggests broader meanings: a loneliness that is more than personal and thus a failure that is also more than personal.

Records of Woman opens with the poem 'Arabella Stuart', a reconstruction of the thoughts and feelings of the imprisoned descendent of Henry VII whose closeness to the throne 'shut her out from the enjoyment of that domestic happiness which her heart appears to have so fervently desired'. Locked up because she married William Seymour, Arabella spends the rest of her life in prison. At first she is determined to maintain hope, 'feeling still my woman's spirit strong'. But after a failed escape attempt in which Seymour gets away but she is recaptured, she begins to be haunted by images of the life she imagines him leading. He has the freedom of the sky, the wind, the rain, the flowers, 'the green, the free / The full of all sweet sound, – the shut from me!' Her rancour growing as the time passes and she is still not rescued, she pictures him feasting and dancing 'where the red wine free and high is pour'd' and rails at him: 'What dost *thou* amidst the bright and fair, / Whispering light words, and mocking my despair?' Vengefully she reminds him that she can kill herself and find freedom that way:

Wherefore not spread free wings – Heaven, Heaven control
These thoughts – they rush – I look into my soul
As down a gulf, and tremble at th'array
Of fierce forms crowding it!

The madness passes, leaving her weak, dying, but with still just enough strength to repent of her harsh words and nobly assure him – imprisoned woman speaking to freed man – of his freedom from her:

> but now take back
> From dying hands, thy freedom, and re-track
> (After a few kind tears for her whose days
> Went out in dreams of thee) the sunny ways
> Of hope, and find thou happiness!

Throughout *Records of Woman*, marriage followed by death, 'To die for what we love', is woman's portion. Marriage involves separation from the mother, a kind of death in itself. It marks the probable entry into motherhood and the increased vulnerability love for children brings. It is, literally, a bloody affair, and *Records of Woman* is awash with blood. Eudora, the bride in 'The Bride of the Greek Isle', desperately reluctant to leave home, at last goes with her new husband to their idyllic dwelling in the woods; but the wedding feast is interrupted by pirates, the banquet becomes a battle, blood flows everywhere. 'Imelda' reworks *Romeo and Juliet*, with Imelda's lover stabbed by her brother because of family feuding. Edith, in 'Edith, A Tale of the Woods', is covered with the blood of her dead husband as she sits all alone in a field of the slain, 'pale and silent on the bloody ground'. In 'The Indian City' it is a Moslem boy beaten to death by Hindus whose blood 'rush'd like a river' while his mother kneeled in it trying vainly to staunch the flow.

Leading as it does to death, marriage offers the opportunity for female heroism in the form of heroic self-sacrifice. Eudora, in 'The Bride of the Greek Isle', captured by the pirates who have slain her husband, revenges his death and brings about her own by setting fire to the ship. The weeping, pensive, clinging child of the first part of the poem is transformed into a heroic woman with

> a brand
> Blazing up high in her lifted hand!
> And her veil flung back, and her free dark hair
> Sway'd by the flames as they rock and flare;
> And her fragile form to its loftiest height
> Dilated, as if by the spirit's might,
> And her eye with an eagle-gladness fraught, –
> Oh! could this work be of woman wrought?

Eudora is setting fire to a ship, but the images evoke heroic creativity, free, grand, and larger than life – especially woman's life. Like the women of Suli in Maria Jane Jewsbury's poem, such energy is only permissible as a prelude to heroic self-destruction. Gertrude, in 'Gertrude, or Fidelity Till Death', 'with the most heroic devotedness' stays the long night with her husband who has been bound alive on the wheel. She 'had her meed – one smile in death –'. Juana, in 'Juana', mother of the emperor Charles V, convinced that her husband Philip, who had treated her with 'uniform neglect', was not really dead but would revive under her care, had his body laid out in magnificent dress on a bed of state and sat by him through the night. Her thoughts as she watches are forgiving and confident: 'humble, patient love *must* win back love at last!' When he wakes she is sure she will find that 'years of hope deferr'd were paid by one fond glance of thine!' Too soon she discovers that hoping for happiness from a dead husband is even more fruitless than expecting it from him living, and she is left to her despair as the corpse is carried away. Another maltreated wife, the Indian woman in 'Indian Woman's Death-Song', is energized by her anger at a husband who has deserted her. Taking to the river with her female baby at her breast, dauntless and proud, with 'a strange gladness', even triumph, she determines to go at once to the better world. Death is preferable to life for a daughter, 'born, like me, for woman's weary lot'.

Woman must devote herself, but man will always disappoint. Physical death terminates what has, in the best woman, been a heroic battle against the spiritual death of man's inadequacy – by faithlessness or death in battle (a form of abandonment). There are no satisfactory husbands in *Records of Woman*: all are dead or dying or untrue. Equally, there are no happy women, the chief cause of women's unhappiness being: unsatisfactory men. The only exceptions to this are the husband and wife in 'The Switzer's Wife'. In this poem the husband is depressed because he wants to go off and fight the oppressing Austrians, but feels his first duty is to stay with his wife and child. She, when she realizes this, immediately reveals her 'free Alpine spirit' and emerges from the timid 'meek thoughtfulness and quiet smile' of the perfect wife she has been into an uncompromising champion of the cause of national liberty. She eloquently sends him off to rouse the people. Both husband and wife are made happy, and glorified, by her willingness to do without him in a higher cause. Even good husbands are elsewhere.

Through all her Imeldas, Ediths, and Eudoras, and bloody battles, heroic fidelities, and solitary endurings, Felicia Hemans returned to and reworked the central event in her life as a woman artist: her husband's desertion of her (failure as a woman) and her continuing literary fame (success as a poet). The combined impact of her mother's marital experiences and her own similar destiny fuse in the images of heroic suffering women which fill the pages of *Records of Woman*. But her mother was not a poet, and Felicia's life differed from her mother's in the public fame her poetry brought her. While Felicia recognized that her life posed itself around the struggle to reconcile a womanly self with unwomanly gifts, she also implied, through this fusion of the non-poet mother with the poet daughter, that the qualities revealed in her poetry were latent in all women. By cultivating an aesthetics of heroism and suffering, she drew all women into the sphere of its possibilities. Women's strength and capacities were forces for good, and should thus be developed. Nowhere in *Records of Woman* does she suggest women should stop whatever it is they are doing, but she does conclude that some activities and some gifts claim a price in bitter personal unhappiness. The final poem in the collection, not accidentally placed, is 'The Grave of a Poetess'. In this poem Felicia travelled in imagination to the grave of Mary Tighe. She

pictured herself, a living woman poet, standing over the grave of the dead poet –
killed, in her mother's view, by literary ambition. Reflection on the sadness of
Mary Tighe's death is succeeded by a 'nobler thought': that though death has
removed the poet from the beauties as well as the miseries of this world, it does
offer one telling advantage over life. Beyond the grave lies a world where the
woman and the poet may be reconciled and live as one:

> Thou hast left sorrow in thy song,
> A voice not loud but deep!
> The glorious bowers of earth among –
> How often didst thou weep?
>
> Where couldst thou fix on mortal ground
> Thy tender thoughts and high?
> Now peace the woman's heart hath found,
> And joy the poet's eye.

It is only in death that the woman's heart and the poet's eye may both, at once,
find satisfaction.

The broad cultural uncertainty about the place of the woman poet – even a
lengthy and serious consideration of Felicia Hemans's work by Francis Jeffrey in
the *Edinburgh Review* in 1829 turned on the nature of the beast: woman poet – did
not lead Felicia to doubt her own gifts, but it had a predictably demoralizing
effect.[20] Writers benefit from a healthy climate in which their virtues and failings
alike are treated to informed critical scrutiny. For all women of the first half of
the nineteenth century, it was their virtues and failings as women which determined the scope of the discussion of their virtues and failings as writers. What
this meant in practice was that women writers lived and worked under a sustained
barrage of fundamental doubt about the validity of the exercise. Such doubt
revealed itself both in the serious critical review by men like Jeffrey and in the
adoring uncritical gush that flowed from less elevated pens. When Felicia Hemans
lamented that it was not easy to find *'friends* who will love me and enter into my
pursuits', she identified a professional need as well as a personal one. In the search
for such friends, she had looked to other women occupying similar positions to
her own. Mary Mitford was one, and in their correspondence some tentative
gropings towards mutual supportiveness can be seen. But the support women
writers could offer each other was ill-defined in their own eyes; and, as has already
been argued, most women writers, Mary Mitford included, had too much invested
in loyalty to fathers of every kind (biological, spiritual, cultural) and in denying
that what they did was work at all, to go looking for support in their difficulties.
Like so much else, the need for support was a need that could not be spoken.

In Maria Jane Jewsbury, Felicia Hemans found the friend who would love her
and enter into her pursuits.

*

Maria Jane Jewsbury's tribute to the emotional and artistic importance of her friendship with Felicia Hemans may be found in the volume of poems, *Lays of Leisure Hours*, and in *The Three Histories*. Of these, by far the more significant is *The Three Histories*. It consists of three tales: 'The History of an Enthusiast'; 'The History of a Nonchalant'; and 'The History of a Realist'. In 'The History of an Enthusiast' Maria Jane told her own story; and in 'The History of a Nonchalant' she told Felicia Hemans's story and the story of Mrs Hemans's impact on herself. All three tales were written out of the deepened understanding that intimacy with Felicia had given Maria Jane of the private and public dimensions of a woman writer's life.

The nonchalant young man who tells the story of 'The History of a Nonchalant' is a man stunned by sudden love for a goddess. Through the voice of the man, Maria Jane described her own reactions to Mrs Hemans who in this tale she modelled on the mythological Roman nymph of the fountain, Egeria. (Egeria, it should be noted, inspired and instructed Numa Pompilius, the legendary king of Rome, supposed to have followed Romulus, in the forms of religious worship he established during his long and peaceful reign.) The young man falls in love with Egeria whilst on tour in Italy:

> Egeria was totally different from any other woman I had ever seen.... She did not dazzle; she subdued me. Other women might be more commanding, more versatile, more acute; but I never saw one so exquisitely feminine. She was lovely without being beautiful; her movements were features; and if a blind man had been privileged to pass his hand over the silken length of hair, that when unbraided flowed round her like a veil, he would have been justified in expecting softness and a love of softness, beauty and a perception of beauty, to be distinctive traits of her mind. Nor would he have been deceived. Her birth, her education, but, above all, the genius with which she was gifted, combined to inspire a passion for the ethereal, the tender, the imaginative, the heroic – in one word, the beautiful. It was in her a faculty divine, and yet of daily life; – it touched all things, but, like a sunbeam, touched them with a golden finger....
>
> Her gladness was like a burst of sunlight; and if in her depression she resembled night, it was night wearing her stars. I might describe, and describe for ever, but I should never succeed in portraying Egeria; she was a muse, a grace, a variable child, a dependant woman – the Italy of human beings.[21]

Harriett Hughes confirmed that the story of 'The History of a Nonchalant' and this portrait, while requiring allowance for 'a certain degree of idealization', were drawn with 'truth' and 'delicacy'. She knew, for she had been a constant member of the day and evening gatherings in Wales, that Felicia had spoken frankly to Maria Jane about her life. As H.F. Chorley put it, emotional openness was an essential for her nature: 'It was necessary for her happiness ... to find those to whom she could constantly open "all that was in her heart".'[22] Opening her heart meant, in Felicia's case, revealing how badly she had been let down by her husband. In using the word 'delicacy', Harriett Hughes was probably thinking gratefully of the way that the story Maria Jane told about Felicia managed to transform the marriage of Captain Hemans to young Felicia Browne into a doomed romance blasted by disapproving parents.

The nonchalant's father, disapproving of the connection, cuts him off without a penny. The tragic story of the nonchalant is made to turn on his horror at the thought of Egeria using her great talents to earn money on which they might both live. Considering that Felicia might have been a dependent woman in many ways but one way in which she was not dependent, certainly was not on her husband, was economically, this is a detail which suggests a complex 'truth', and possibly one overcome by 'delicacy'. The nonchalant's response to Egeria's modest proposal to earn a little is a shriek:

> live upon the money earned by a woman – that woman my wife – and that
> wife Egeria! – I could far sooner have died than permitted such a reversal
> of the order of nature, such a desecration of my dignity and her softness.[23]

So threatening is this possibility that Egeria is killed off – in scenes of full-blown eroticization of death. If earning money is a desecration of softness, then the softness of a woman who earns money is endangered and must be defended by the rigidities of death. The delicate hint in this account, that Captain Hemans could not tolerate living with a wife who earned more than he did in a society which judged such an arrangement as 'a reversal of the order of nature', is revealing. In representing the situation fictionally, Maria Jane resolved the problem by making the woman die, not the man. She is the one in need of examination and change, not him. The man's position cannot be questioned.

Physical death marks the limits of possibility, but death comes in many forms. The living death of restricted growth is a key to the lives of women in the early nineteenth century: accepting restricted growth was womanly and womanly credit attached to it. 'The History of an Enthusiast' takes up where *Letters to the Young* left off. The central figure in this story, Julia, is a composite of Felicia Hemans and Maria Jane Jewsbury out of Madame de Staël's *Corinne*. Julia is an artist who, in spite of many warnings – 'Genius [is] the smallpox of the soul'; 'Notoriety is not distinction; praise is not fame; ... Come home ... study – think – feel ... but let all be done quietly and at home' – refuses to accept restricted growth. She develops her talents to their fullest. She is driven on by 'the burning hope of self-emancipation', by her longing to have 'a more brilliant sphere' and to be 'placed there by her own mental efforts!' She is bored with the small world of home: 'I pine for living intercourse with the great, the gay and the gifted ... oh this dull, dreary and most virtuous domestic life'. She writes a book which gives her all the fame she could ever dream of. At 22 Julia is her own mistress, 'Wealthy, distinguished, ambitious'. She is also, it therefore follows, 'environed with brilliant perils, the more brilliant and the more perilous because her own energy was the only oracle she ever consulted'. Julia leaves home and goes to London.

Having plenty of both money and wit, she is socially successful and happy. 'Energy was her leading characteristic.... Her mind had wings and she made it use them.' The author's judgement on Julia at this stage is as follows: 'Intellectually that energy had guided her aright; whether it would now do the same morally, remained to be proved.' In other words, expanding the mind was not in itself wrong: a mind with wings should spread them; but the world into which she might fly was a world of great danger, and the solution to this danger was not to change that world but to change herself. Unless she made proper womanly choices – 'Come home ... let all be done quietly and at home' – she would inevitably suffer either the unhappiness of inner conflict or the complete disaster of moral fall. She is advised to pinion her wings, to put a brake on her energy. Julia does not heed this advice. Creating a 'studious solitude' around herself, she grows out of sympathetic communion with her friends; her time is spent communing with 'the illustrious dead', asking them to teach her

> how to tread the path that leads to fame! ... Fame! what energy dwells in that one word.... I long for it.... I pay it an idolatry – I feel that for it I could surrender ease, health, happiness, friends, fortune.... O fame! let me not pass away unknown, a hidden rill in the world's mighty forest.[24]

Following where energy leads is to court death. After six years of glittering life in London, Julia is visited by a young man who might have considered marrying her, Cecil Percy. Cecil finds Julia 'withered at the root ... with energies that only kindled their own funeral pile'. Cecil had feared that the adulation Julia had received would have spoiled her, but that is not her problem; she is 'safe in the citadel'. Her problem, as she explains it to him, is her inability to find sources of secure belief. Her mind has become 'a source of evil and blight and sorrow'. Following her considerable mental energies where they led has resulted in 'a dark and universal habit of doubt, a restless and universal desire of change'. This potentially productive and regenerative condition is pathologized, for in a woman doubt, like energy, must lead to sickness since it cannot lead to change.

Cecil explains to Julia why neither he nor any other man would want to marry her now, even if she is still 'safe in the citadel':

> I should not like a lioness for a wife, Miss Osborne.... She who is brilliant in mind, and gifted with the perilous gifts of genius, may receive the homage of saloons, may be courted as a companion, and worshipped as a goddess; but for his help-meet, man chooses far otherwise.... Man does not secretly dread and dislike high intellect in women, for the main reason generally supposed – because it may tend to obscure his own regal honours; but because it interferes with his implanted and imbibed ideas of domestic life and womanly duty.[25]

It is given to Cecil to say the words which reverse the usual terms of the discussion. Cecil admits that there are very few men 'able and willing to do the justice of the heart (a very different thing from the justice of the head) to women distinguished by talent'. This is perhaps as near as one will get to an admission, in the literature of this period, that men fail women rather than the assumption that women (in failing themselves) fail men.

Julia's genius shuts her out from the ideal womanly life represented in 'The History of an Enthusiast' by Julia's married friend Annette. Julia may be 'one of the most distinguished women of this or any day', but Annette, living in 'elegant, quiet domestic happiness' at Myrtle Cottage, where there are daily 'witty good sense in man, and delicate vivacity in woman', and charming children charmingly romping on the green grass, has true happiness. Annette's life epitomizes what Julia understands to be the ideal: that a woman should *be* poetry, not write it. Annette swims in the stream of common life, a life Julia feels severed from by her energetic mind, that 'curse'. In Annette's home Julia feels 'degraded' (feels the shame of her fame) and her state of mind is one 'bordering on phrensy'. She wishes she could be like Annette, who in her affections resembled 'a little skiff moored ever in the same creek, venturing at the farthest but a little way from land, and then merely for the use or pleasure of her owner'.[26] This image of the skiff recalls Hannah More's analogy of the picture on the wall, both intended to indicate the amount of movement considered desirable in wives. A skiff, unlike a picture, implies some movement, will indeed move with the current unless tied down. Maria Jane Jewsbury used a similar image in much the same context in a poem entitled 'To My Own Heart', in which she tried to explain to herself why she was such a 'self-torturer':

> within thee burned th'enthusiast's fire
> Wild love of freedom, longings for the lyre; –
> And ardent visions of romantic youth
> Too fair for time, and oh! too frail for truth!
> Aspirings nursed by solitude and pride,
> Worlds to the dreamer, dreams to all beside;
> Bright vague imaginings of bliss to be,
> None ever saw, yet none despaired to see,
> And aimless energies that bade the mind
> Launch like a ship and leave the world behind.[27]

For all the self-castigation of the poem as a whole, the image of the mind as a ship that can launch itself away from the restraining ropes of convention and navigate its own path on the high sea of life, has a certain excitement and promise. The rub is that the splendid isolation of such a mind is enforced; the quiet gardens of Myrtle Cottage cannot accommodate it. Further, if energy is what makes the mind want to launch like a ship, what quality will convince it instead to be a little skiff 'moored ever in the same creek'? Presumably the opposite of energy, which is debility of one sort or another. Julia's energy is her real enemy. She would have more chance of being at peace with herself, and her society, if she were weak and miserable.

The moral of 'The History of an Enthusiast' is the familiar one: a woman who develops her gifts is doomed to a life of isolation and unhappiness commensurate with the brilliance of those gifts. That said, Maria Jane introduced a significant variation into what was already beginning to harden into formula. Unlike Anna Jameson in *Diary of an Ennuyée*, she did not give her readers the satisfaction of the ultimate punishment – death. Julia decides to go away, to go alone to Europe, and she decides to go without undue depression; indeed she goes vigorously, without a hint of sickness. Recognizing that domestic bliss is not to be her portion, she accepts the fact. She leaves not as the victim of failed love looking to Europe to bind the wounds in her heart, but as a woman caught between opposing life styles that cannot be reconciled. Challenged by her friends, 'What possible enjoyment can you have in wandering about, like a woman belonging to nobody?' she replies, 'How else would you have me wander? I *am* a woman belonging to nobody.'[28] The defiance in this is underlined by an indecorous farewell poem left for her society friends and, further, by a final quotation from Shelley – 'one with whom in many things I can sympathise too well' –

> O lift me as a wave, a leaf, a cloud
> I fall upon the thorns of life – I bleed;
> A heavy weight of hours has chained and bowed
> One too like thee, tameless, and swift, and proud.

A woman quoting Shelley in 1830 was assuredly fixing her colours to the mast and launching out upon perilous waters. Like the Shelleyan hero, Julia accepts alienation. Instead of retreating to sickness, retirement, domesticity, and death, she goes forward into an unknown, uncharted new life. Instead of succumbing to a defeatist philosophy that placed death at the centre of life – with an afterlife as consolation for irresolvable conflicts here below – she asserts her determination to live a life of some sort on the basis of her real self. In selecting this destiny for her heroine, Maria Jane Jewsbury put a distance between herself and that school of women's writing which provided literary consolation for narrowed lives lived only just this side of the grave. She was, however, an accomplished enough professional to cover her tracks. Julia's story, which was also Maria Jane's story, was read in the way its readers wanted to read it. Mrs Ellis of the *Christian Keepsake* was not the only reader who read in it only a dire and dreadful warning to young women of genius to beware their best impulses. Blaming the woman was so well established as a habit of mind that a woman who momentarily did not wholeheartedly blame herself, who for a moment relaxed her eternal compulsion to 'unite vigilance with self-distrust' and chose instead to be 'tameless, and swift, and proud', was simply not heard. Or if heard, heard only for her suffering (weakness), not for her exhilaration (strength).

*

In an otherwise irreproachable essay on Felicia Hemans in the *Athenaeum* in 1831, containing such precepts as 'a poetess ought to be feminine', and such assurances as 'Mrs Hemans throws herself into her poetry, and the said self is an English gentlewoman', Maria Jane, writing anonymously, teased her readers a little. 'If', she wrote,

> after sighing away your soul over some poetic effusion of female genius, a personal introduction took place, and you found the fair author a dashing, dragoon-kind of woman — one who could with ease rid her house of a couple of robbers — would you not be startled?[29]

Nobody could suggest that Felicia Hemans was a 'dragoon-kind of woman', but Maria Jane's personal introduction to her was an introduction to the sometimes startling workings of gender expectations and fabrications among the famous. Entering Mrs Hemans's 'feminine' ambience, she put away her own 'masculine' intellectuality and smoothed down her shafts of satire. From Mrs Hemans she learned to admire intellect in 'an imaginative state' rather than as the 'raw material' she was accustomed to getting from her intellectually active Manchester friends. The 'softening effect' which the company of Felicia induced, and for which Maria Jane thanked her, was seen by the women themselves as a move away from masculine tendencies and towards feminine ones. From her stay in Wales in 1828, and subsequent shorter visits to Wavertree, Maria Jane acquired, she told Mrs Hemans, 'a habit I do not wish to lose — the habit of looking for beauty'.[30] Finding beauty 'even among the harshest realities of life' — and there were few better opportunities to observe life's harsh realities than by living in Manchester in the 1820s and 1830s — is the essence of sentimentality; and, while certainly not confined to women (Dickens was to build a literary career on it), sentimentality was achieving definitive status as the quintessential feminine form of feeling.

Maria Jane Jewsbury had an eye for humbug; particularly, as *Phantasmagoria* revealed, the humbug of writers. She also had an instinct for a market, and was well placed to perceive how commercial elements played their part in shaping the end product, be it poem or novel or moral tract. The reading public had always liked to read about women. Novel readers, from the time of Samuel Richardson's *Pamela* onwards, read novels at least in part for the pleasure of contemplating women. Women on the printed page were objects of freely roaming attention and desire; a desire which can be seen at work as much in the thunderous pulpit denunciations of such novels as *Corinne* (a novel in which the reader's eyes, ears, and perhaps other organs too never cease attending to the heroine) as in the secret reading under the bedclothes such inflamed disapproval gave rise to. Desires roused by novels had to be hedged, not only for the protection of the avid reader but for the good of society as a whole. Compressing the throb of vicarious pleasure which they had themselves aroused was the duty of every writer, and it could not be left to hard covers alone. Death was the most effective full stop to flowing feelings. The more vividly a woman had functioned to arouse pleasurable feelings in a story, the more incumbent it was upon her author to kill her off. The creepy necrophilia of much nineteenth-century literature may thus be understood as not only a response to a high level of mortality, making the death-bed scene a feature of domestic life, but as a by-product of literary conventions. Poetry and novels structured the feelings. The residual pleasures of sex carried over to that fine and quiet place the grave where, if people did not actually embrace, they could nevertheless feel as if they might – which is precisely what the experience of reading is itself about. When the second edition of *Diary of an Ennuyée* came out, Anna Jameson apologized in a preface for the fact that her heroine's death was not 'true' in the sense that her heroine's author was still very much alive. She had, she confessed, 'cheated some gentle readers out of much superfluous sympathy'. The desire for the author to die along with her heroine was a gruesome variant on the theme that a woman should be poetry not write it; womanliness collapsed the distinction between making and being. In making work invisible, it also erased intention. Felicia Hemans's ability to fuse her poetry with images of the poet that were desired, was the source of her popularity and, in turn, of her regular income. She knew well the processes by which her sensitivity to pain and sorrow, her female suffering, could be converted into funds. She was the most popular writer of funerary verse, accepting commissions to write moving lines to be engraved on the tombstones of children, husbands, wives, mothers, and fathers throughout the land. One of the reasons why death was so willingly embraced – imaginatively – was that it was a money-spinner, though it required the sort of 'blooming plumptitude' of an Anna Jameson not to become a victim of one's own imagery.

In 'The Three Histories' Maria Jane gave the reading public what it wanted in the shape of women to contemplate, admire, desire, and moralize over, while at the same time exploring issues that were vital to her own development. It was a watershed in her career. She had been the dynamic between author and public, subject and self, laid bare in Felicia Hemans's life in a particularly destructive way. Maria Jane's own version of Felicia, as Egeria, statuesque and noble, presented her in the frozen stillness of the muse rather than as a living individual. The transition from life to death of such a figure need only be nominal. But Maria Jane herself was far from being either a statue or a skiff, and she could certainly not stay still long enough to be a picture. The success of 'The Three Histories' gave her an opening into mainstream journalism at just the moment when her mind was ready to launch into the deep waters of critical commentary.

While 'The History of an Enthusiast' stands, like *Diary of an Ennuyée*, in the tradition of female autonomy established by *Corinne*, Maria Jane Jewsbury's real homage to Madame de Staël is to be found in the tone and substance of her writing for the *Athenaeum*. Few women in the early nineteenth century were allowed the opportunity publicly to lecture men as Corinne knowledgeably lectures Oswald Nelvil on his tour round the monuments of Italy. The voice of authority, in life and letters, was perceived to be a male voice. Partly this was because only male voices were neutral: female voices, like female bodies, were stamped with sex. A woman who could avoid being identified as a woman could avoid the contortions that literary conventions increasingly demanded of women. The ease with which Maria Jane entered on her career as a journalist suggests that there was not so much prejudice against women themselves – in the late 1820s and 1830s numerous women were earning a living from journalistic work of various kinds – as against a perception of women; a prejudice which condemned them, like female Atlases, to carry the moral weight of the universe on their supposedly frail shoulders. On the whole, money and power accrue to those who perpetuate the prevailing myths of any culture rather than to those who oppose them; it should not be surprising that women writers found their audiences and their incomes amongst those who wanted their social myths, including the myth of the inferiority of women, confirmed. By acceding to such myths, consciously or not, cynically or otherwise, women writers lent them powerful weight. In direct or indirect ways, women writers of the early nineteenth century helped to develop and maintain the cultural climate which made it impossible to speak with neutral authority as a woman. The textual voice used by Hannah More or Mary Wollstonecraft in the 1790s was no longer available to women in the 1830s.

The anonymity of the periodical press, however, and its specific maleness of tone, allowed Maria Jane to grow as a critic and thinker. She had the freedom to speak as a man, and she used that freedom to write increasingly feminist articles about women. She wrote about men too: a long article took the public to task for preferring Byron to Shelley; a front-page review quarrelled with Robert Southey over his definition of the working-class writers of 'Corn-Law rhymes' as 'uneducated poets', arguing with passionate identification that all 'who really deserve the name of poets . . . educate themselves'. They are 'men and women of *dis*advantages; – men and women who worked for themselves, fagged out their own diplomas, and fought their own way to estimation'.[31] She knew what she was talking about. Having had to fag out her own diplomas and work her own way to estimation, Maria Jane was remarkably well educated; she also possessed the courageous individuality of view which at its best distinguishes the self-educated of any age. On the subject of poetry, a lifetime's hard practice had given her firm views. By 1831 she was 'sick of horrors, tired of sorrows, and ready to throw sentiment into the sea'. She was in no mood to be tolerant of the 'kisses and blisses, sylphs, zephyrs, odours, sounds, dreams, dews, blushes, flushes, gushes' served up by one R.C. Campbell in a volume entitled *Lays from the East*. Whether these *Lays from the East* were really so much more awful than her own *Lays of Leisure Hours*, or than some of the more routine productions of Mrs Hemans's pen, is a moot point. In any case, Maria Jane took the opportunity to lay down some principles, observing that Mr Campbell's 'very fervid style of writing is a stain that sadly wants a sponge':

poetry, in its wildest flights of fancy, its most anguished eloquence of grief,
ought to be true to its own principles of interpretation: a metaphor may be

untrue as a moral statement, but it ought to be correct as an imaginative creation; – poetry should err perspicuously, and we cannot, for any appearance of grandeur, consent to the oblivion of grammar. Young minstrels and minstrellesses are apt to fancy that 'pouring out sorrows like a sea' in the first words that come to mind, constitutes poetry; that an accumulation of figures must, of necessity, ensure meaning; that the wild beatings of ungoverned sensibility, the tawdry descriptions of common-place tragicalities, the affixing of one kind of epithet to a directly opposite class of image, thus giving to their thoughts an air of amphibiousness; that forming compound words, and making substantives verbs, and adjectives adverbs; that all these, and a thousand similar absurdities, make POETRY. Errors of this nature have not been fallen into by Mr Campbell through ambition, or a wilful defiance of established modes of thinking and speaking, but from a want of intellectual knowledge, from over-estimating the poetical worth of mere emotion, and a consequent mistaking of vehemence for vigour.... Were we inclined for a good slaughtering article, and to play the gentle savage at Mr Campbell's expense, nothing would be easier.[32]

Nothing would be easier, so long as her name did not betray her. It is inconceivable that a woman, a young woman, an unmarried young woman, could have written with such aggressive superiority, laying down the law and exposing the deficiencies of a (presumably) well-educated man, complaining of his 'faults and follies' and lamenting his 'want of intellectual knowledge', if her identity had been known. Such writing was only possible on the assumption that she was male, a man speaking to his equal, another man.

Maria Jane Jewsbury saw the social construction of femininity in her own day as a straightforwardly damaging influence on women's writing. Comparing the women writers of her own time with those active thirty or forty years earlier, at and just prior to the turn of the century, she observed striking and not at all pleasing differences. The writings of her foremothers had displayed 'nerve, simplicity, vigour'; what she saw in her own time was 'accomplishment, grace, sentiment ... talent ... but not so much that can claim the name of genius':

> Our elder literary women were, in the spirit of their intellect, more essentially masculine; our younger ones are integrally feminine – women of fashionable as well as studious life, women generally, who not only write books but abound in elegant accomplishments.[33]

Women who, in other words, had put the pejorative implications of blue stockingism behind them but had paid a large price. Of the 'elder literary women', Maria Jane instanced Mary Wollstonecraft, Mrs Inchbald, Mrs Radcliffe, and Joanna Baillie, the subject of the review. Her sympathies were with these women whose intellects, as she saw it, had been allowed a masculine scope for development which by the 1830s was deemed unwomanly. 'Rational' was a word Maria Jane strove to reclaim. The definition of woman that had emerged in her lifetime, exemplified by the popular image of Felicia Hemans, emphasized the uncontrollable beat of the heart over the controllable march of intellect. For intellectual mentors, she had to look back to the late eighteenth century. Her moral guides were Mary Wollstonecraft and Hannah More, not such an unlikely coupling as might at first appear. For though Hannah More's evangelical pieties sit uncomfortably with Mary Wollstonecraft's radical politics, the women sound remarkably like one another when on the subject of women and women's education. Both Wollstonecraft and More were educationists impatient with an educational practice that sought to narrow women's intellectual sphere for the sake of the higher aim of making them more charming and more pleasing to men. By 1830, the tradition of intellectual women that Wollstonecraft and More unselfconsciously drew on was no longer available. Intellectuality (possibly even intelligence) and womanliness had become opposites. A woman who showed intellect, like Maria Jane Jewsbury, was automatically defined as 'masculine'. The word 'feminine' could no longer contain intellectual achievement.

The separation of 'feminine' heart and 'masculine' head served to justify ideologies of subordination. The huge appetite for literature which made sense of the rapid social changes of the time was served by women like Mrs J. Sandford who, in 1831, produced *Woman in her Social and Domestic Character*, a book which anticipated the best-sellers by Mrs Lewis and Mrs Ellis which appeared later in the decade: *Woman's Mission*, a translation from the French by Mrs Lewis; *The Women of England: Their Social Duties and Domestic Habits*; *The Mothers of England*; *The Wives of England*; *The Daughters of England*, all by Mrs Ellis. Reviewing Mrs Sandford on the front page of the *Athenaeum*, Maria Jane identified the worst of the 'many faults' in the book as Mrs Sandford's very low estimate of female intelligence. Mrs Sandford's depiction of women was timid compared with the more full-blooded version of women given currency during the 'reign of audacity among female moralists' which had held sway some forty years earlier. Not only timid but also temporizing: Maria Jane accused Mrs Sandford of not telling the truth about women because she was afraid of what men would say. Her purposes towards women were not directed towards what was best for them, but towards what would most please men. Consequently, although her book would be read by women, it would do them more harm than good. It would 'impede the progress of really rational treatment and education of women'. It would be positively damaging to their self-esteem; indeed, damage to women's self-esteem and the political advantage that would thereby accrue to men were implicit purposes of the morality she espoused. While the moralists of the eighteenth century had sought to enlarge women's possibilities, Mrs Sandford, Maria Jane warned, sought to contract them. In her book, as compared with what might have been available to women readers forty years before:

> the claim on behalf of female intellect is couched in a far humbler tone, the sphere of female duty is made far narrower, and the avowals of female inferiority and folly are ungracefully frequent and severe. We can hardly

recollect a virtue or accomplishment inculcated without some reference to the pleasure of man; that is not less set forth as rendering the possessor a more valuable possession: now, a woman, with all her social dependence, can never cease to be a separate and responsible intelligence; but Mrs Sandford's ultra doctrines of adaptation, amalgamation, and subordination, go far to make this forgotten. Mental culture is treated as a higher branch of cookery, and recommended as were diet-drinks and possets in antique books of pharmacy. It is possible to sensualize knowledge; and this is done when the main motive given for its pursuit is, *to please*.[34]

In her review, Maria Jane indicated that she intended to pursue the argument with Mrs Sandford (so similar to the debates about women's magazines, glossy and otherwise, of our own time) but in the meantime there were other destructive tendencies to nail. In 1831 also, Anna Jameson published *Memoirs of Celebrated Female Sovereigns*. In this book she made, in the opinion of her sister writer, 'two capital errors', and Maria Jane took her to task on them at considerable length. Mrs Jameson, writing for the market (she was the sole economic support of her mother and three sisters and had herself been abandoned by an alcoholic disaster of a husband), carefully judged the taste of her time. With a female readership mostly in mind, she advertised her intention to write the lives of the female sovereigns from 'a moral and picturesque point of view' rather than from anything so stringent as political analysis or historical understanding. She would dwell only on personalities, not on public affairs; on the 'passions and prejudices' of the sovereign in question, not on her relation to the times in which she governed. Further, should the sovereign's reign display facts of an unpleasant kind, Mrs Jameson did not intend to dwell on them for fear of causing her female reader pain. Thus both subject and reader were shifted out of the mainstream of human life, even though her subjects, queens, had occupied powerful positions within it. Mrs Jameson's 'Memoirs' were fictions: power, at the centre of the lives of sovereigns, was not allowed to figure in the picture. Maria Jane Jewsbury objected:

> the memoirs of sovereigns cannot be separated from history, any more than a large tree can be properly transplanted without a quantity of adhering earth. Unless we know something of their times, we are not likely to judge correctly of their lives. Amongst facts, the connexion of facts, and correct inferences from facts, lies the labour of the historian; facts taken 'in a moral and picturesque point of view' belong to the poet and the novelist. The writer who thus treats history, is sure to write like a partisan; and thus female critics and historians too often illustrate the remark, that women can rarely pass judgement without lifting a corner of the veil to ascertain the parties they are to praise or condemn.[35]

As a female critic and historian herself, already prohibited by partialities from functioning openly, Maria Jane Jewsbury saw how Mrs Jameson's contribution turned the prison screws tighter. By giving credence to the stereotype of woman as a being in need of intellectual cosseting, whose mental world should be thinner, lighter, nicer than that of men, she lent it authority and served purposes which in the broader social sense worked against her own advantage. But Mrs Jameson went even further in her second 'error'. This was her claim that women who *have* had the opportunity of political power have used it badly: they have been 'conspicuously unhappy or criminal'. Mrs Jameson allowed herself to conclude from this that women were intrinsically unfitted to hold power, and that 'the power which belongs to us, as a sex, is not properly, or naturally, that of the sceptre or the sword'. This innocently conventional view, which *Corinne*, *Diary of an Ennuyée*, and *The Three Histories* had all espoused in at least indirect form, aroused Maria Jane's indignant wrath. Her position on the subject of power for women indicates more than anything else how far she had come:

to the incompetency of queens, and their superiority in misrule, crime, or suffering, we must strongly object. We are surprised, too, not only by the assertion, but by the evidence brought to support it – experience. The question is not, have there been better or worse women than queens; but have queens been worse than kings? Have they originated *more* unjust wars? Have they squandered national resources with *greater* profusion? Have they disgraced themselves by *worse* favourites? Have their reigns been *less* marked by improvement? Have the laws been *more* arbitrary – the people *more* discontented? Were the pyramids built by a king or a queen? And was Nero a man or a woman? Had Mrs Jameson stated that females rarely acquire surreptitious power without abusing it, she would have been borne out by facts. The feminine instruments of political crime and disaster have not been queens gifted in their own right with supreme authority, but the mistresses, or intriguing wives and mothers of kings – the Pompadours, the Henriettas, the Catherines de Medici. France excludes women from the throne, England permits them to inherit it – and which history is more free from female influence wrongly obtained and madly exercised? In bestowing power, as in everything else, rational conduct meets its own reward: give a woman a definite portion, give it her as a right, and she will try to use it to the best of her judgement – lend it her as an indulgence, or let her obtain it by stratagem, and she will infallibly use it profligately. ... All who incline to be severe on female sovereigns should compare their annals and characters, not with any ideal of womanhood, but with the annals and characters of men. The madwoman of the North (Christina of Sweden) did her *country* less harm than the madman of the North (Charles XII). Maria Theresa, though no favourite of ours, may be brought forward in preference to her imbecile father and her impetuous son: Isabella of Spain surely loses nothing beside her husband; and the reign of Elizabeth, stern, imperious and subtle as she was, is not the reign for which Englishmen peculiarly blush. Power injures men no less than it injures women: when women are more rationally educated, they will make better queens; and when men are more rationally educated, they will make better kings; at present the balance is pretty equal – if anything it leans to the feminine side. Besides, if Mrs Jameson proves that women have no business to succeed to the sceptre, how will she prove that they have any right to wield the pen? Power is power; and the power of disseminating opinions is not much less valuable than that of holding a levee or opening parliament. There is sufficient prejudice undestroyed, without women, and women of mind helping its diffusion.[36]

What if, after reading this article and observing that it contained much sense, the average reader of the *Athenaeum* had a personal introduction to the author and found him to be a she, an intellectual 'dragoon-kind of woman'? Maria Jane Jewsbury, textually free to take all the masculine freedoms she chose, had the advantage over Anna Jameson in her use of women's lives as subject matter for her *Athenaeum* writings. In the 1830s few women could speak with such clarity, and it is an open question how far they could think it. Personally successful, but living in unpropitious times, Maria Jane revived the debate about woman's place in public life which had languished since the 1790s. Paradoxically, the passionate commitment of her writing was only possible because her audience assumed that she was male.

In February 1832 she launched a series of articles under the general title *On Modern Female Cultivation*. These articles represent the continuance of the debate with Mrs Sandford and Anna Jameson and the schools of thought on women's issues to which they lent their pens. At the heart of all dispute about the position of women was the question of power in society. The nature of education considered appropriate for women was a vital consideration because it determined the place women might occupy in public life. Decorative, undemanding accomplishments, such as were becoming the rule, were, Maria Jane argued, 'the intellectual shadow of an intellectual substance' only. So long as women were fobbed off with 'mental elegance' in place of real knowledge, their understanding would never develop and they would be fit only for decorative roles in society. In three crackling articles which appeared one after the other on the 4th, 11th, and 23rd of February, Maria Jane pointed the finger at men and accused them of having, throughout history, used women for their own purposes. Outlining the history of men's writing about women, she concluded, 'female cultivation will always accord with the masculine taste predominant for the time being'. Women, 'adored or stigmatized, flattered or libelled, despots or puppets', would never be treated or spoken of impartially. Men have reasons for saying the things they say about women, for creating the cultural climate in which women live, and those reasons have to do with men's needs. Men mould women in the image that suits themselves. Wise women, properly educated women able to think for themselves, would not be malleable women. Hence, women are not allowed to become wise:

subordination is the complexion of female life ... instruction which would nurture the faculties and encourage them to act vigorously for themselves is feared and disliked.... Amongst the highly finished young women who have spent eight or nine years as the recipients of tuition, how many shall we find who have thought out for themselves a single thought, or have any notion of the value of knowledge beyond the mere credit of possessing it?[37]

Very few, is the answer; but the fault lies not in themselves:

we cultivate our women to the highest pitch that can make them fascinating, with a careful abstinence from that which would make them wise.... We deprive the nightingale of sight, in order that it may sing us sweeter songs; we render the captive weak, and demand him to be strong as the free; we stimulate his feelings to madness, and expect from him the exercise of reason; we spread our treasures before him and mock if he ask to share them; we deprive him of liberty and bid him rejoice in his prison.

(Reading the above with a judicious substitution of the pronoun 'she' for 'he' – 'we stimulate her feelings to madness, and expect from her the exercise of reason' – brings the gender critique, with its Wollstonecraftian directness, more startlingly forward.)

Every woman, Maria Jane Jewsbury goes on to argue, is brought up to a conventional morality that keeps a veil 'between herself and the knowledge of her true position in society'. She lives a mystified life, one in which the powerlessness of ignorance is the true aim and end of the education she is offered. Under the guise of knowledge, she is really led to its reverse: ignorance. Apportioning blame for this state of affairs, Maria Jane singled out the poets and novelists, creators of images, aspirations, and models; depicters of modes and manners; custodians of social values; legislators of custom, who,

can effect more mischief in a few minutes than may be undone with long and weary toil. Women, and the influence of women, have been to them such fertile themes, that, if all their descriptions were fairly copied out we might cover the world with them; the globe would be an entire sheet of foolscap – the real 'Ladies Magazine'. But amidst all the bevies of angels they have drawn, how passing few of them have been rational creatures; their heroines have mainly become such personifications of tears, love, death, poetry, and helplessness, that an honest man, linked to such in real life, would surely be at his wits end before the end of the honeymoon.

The poets and novelists, she asserts, have 'mainly erected the standard of female excellence', and female excellence, according to their standard, lies in the performance of female duty. Female duty, according to the poets and novelists, is twofold: 'being beautiful and being devoted'. Women's 'two great occupations' deriving from their 'two great duties' are: 'loving and dying'. Women,

have received from poetry and fiction lip homage and knee reverence, adulation, incense, every concomitant of idol-worship, with *only* the absence of fervent rational respect. The process of degradation has taken the semblance of adoration; compliments to their love has veiled contempt of their understanding – for one female portrait that society would be benefitted by its having life, how many hundreds have we who would only be less intensely, etherially useless than the ghost of a rose or the phantasm of a lily. Earth is too gross for these essences of womanhood. This is only one point in which poetry and fiction may be arraigned on behalf of the female character: over against the land of sentiment lies the kingdom of heartlessness, and the topographers of this kingdom, otherwise fashionable novelists, have assuredly done *their* best to erect a low standard of womanly excellence.

The high standard of womanly excellence Maria Jane envisaged was one which did not have its origins in, and direct itself towards, the gratification of men. Being beautiful and loving, being devoted and dying, were all ways of representing women which reaffirmed the centrality of men in women's lives: beauty, love, devotion, and death were women's tributes to men's power over them. To insist that women had a right to be treated as rational creatures was not new: Mary Wollstonecraft had asked the same, as had Hannah More, Maria Edgeworth, and numerous other writers on the subject of women's education. What was new was the emphasis Maria Jane gave to cultural power, to the images of women shaped by men and consumed and reproduced by women.

And what was also new was a cultural climate in which the pieties of domestic ideology were rapidly hardening. Mrs S.C. Hall, for example, invoked merely the known and familiar in the mid-1850s when she asserted that 'the leading, guiding and controlling impulse of women is to render themselves agreeable and helpful to men'.[38] This is what Maria Jane, and those who shared her vision, meant by sensualizing knowledge. But Mrs Hall, like Mrs Sandford, Mrs Ellis, Mrs Lewis, and even Mrs Jameson in the 1830s, was intent on survival. By writing and publishing their dutiful adumbrations, they practised what they preached: they survived by pleasing men, by writing what was 'agreeable and helpful to men'. It should come as no surprise that they did so, but their writings need to be understood in the context of the broad cultural climate within which they worked.

Paradoxically, Maria Jane's support must have come in large part from the men in the *Athenaeum* circle: Charles Wentworth Dilke and, after Maria Jane's influence got him his position on the journal, Henry Chorley. In London the poet L.E.L. – Laetitia Landon – almost as prolific as Mrs Hemans, and a woman who supported herself by her writings, and whose ultimate fate was curiously similar to Maria Jane's, was a friend. She lived in digs and mingled in the literary circles Maria Jane frequented when she was in town.[39] Like Mrs Hemans, L.E.L. was 'feminine' in a way that Maria Jane was not; and perhaps the 'masculine' nature of Maria Jane's gifts enabled the men with whom she worked to put the same value on her professionalism that they gave each other – an advantage L.E.L. does not seem to have had. Maria Jane's 'masculinity' also allowed women to accept her as that oddity, a woman removed from women's sphere, condemned by her gifts to a life of suffering. Cultural factors might have been much to blame for that suffering, but the suffering itself could not be denied. Fiction was, after all, nothing like so effective a veil as writing for the periodical press, for fiction was a major route for the transmission of the values of domestic ideology. Women who wrote anonymously for the press might write as men. It would be interesting to know how many other women availed themselves of the freedoms it offered.

4

DIFFICULTIES AND DANGER

Were I sure that my idol Fame, however distant, however difficult, is *actually within my reach*, then indeed I would not care how I loitered on the way – but I am *not* sure, on the contrary I begin to believe myself the greatest ass in God's creation – what a destiny I have chosen! how full of difficulties, disquietude, and danger! and, perhaps, to end in disappointment! but I *cannot* turn back *now*.

Jane Welsh to Thomas Carlyle[1]

When she came to write *The Three Histories*, Maria Jane Jewsbury cast her impressions of Felicia Hemans and her feelings about her into the form of a heterosexual romance. This domestication of their relationship, bringing it into the realm of the bourgeois myth of love and marriage which had man at its centre (as husband and father), issued in a statuesque portrait that conformed in almost all points to the portrait that could be assembled from any contemporary or later Victorian accounts of her. Femininity was the keynote, and Felicia Hemans's poetic gifts an accidental, though integral, part of that femininity. For all her objections to men's use of women, Maria Jane did not take her argument from cultural affairs to the social institution which above all others ensured the subjection of the female to the male, and the use of the female by the male: marriage.

Nineteenth-century law did not recognize the existence of a woman's self beyond the altar. Upon marriage, the woman was legally incorporated into the man; he spoke for both of them. This is a fact that quite properly arouses indignation now, as it aroused the indignation of many women (and men) in the nineteenth century. Nevertheless, for even greater numbers of women and men, such an arrangement seemed not only the way things were and therefore inevitable, but a desirable state of affairs. The primacy of the male and woman's secondary role as helpmeet had biblical authority and was reinforced weekly in churches throughout the land. Even for those who had doubts about it, or who failed to meet its challenges, it might still retain its position in their minds as an ideal to aspire to.

No cultural or social historian nowadays would dream of writing about the legal position of women in the nineteenth century in approving terms. However, it is worth pausing a moment to try to understand the attractions of a system which reduced women to the same legal status as children and lunatics. For it was not only attractive to men, it was also attractive to women. Women worked hard to make themselves what law and custom decreed they should be as wives: as close to a reflection of the man they married as they could possibly make themselves. Like religion, marriage offered women the promise of daily happiness and ultimate fulfilment through the loss of self; by losing the self women might find the self, and in doing so find the cure for misery below and the key to bliss above. Unlike religion, however, in which the loss of self was the route to God – between whom and his petitioner no intermediary need come – in marriage women lost a self in order to take on another self: the husband's self.

The promise of marriage was the promise of a better self: a masculine self. The masculine self was the respectable social self, the self through which the woman pursued her social identity. Through this masculine self she achieved her economic position and social status. The masculine self in the form of individual husbands promised support, protection, care, concern, and a socially visible existence not available to the average unmarried woman. Thomas Carlyle endorsed this view of marriage when he told his wife, who told Geraldine, who indignantly reported it to her (as she hoped) prospective lover, Walter Mantell, that 'a woman's natural object in the world is to *go out* and find herself some sort of *man her superior* – & obey him loyally and lovingly & make herself as much as possible into *a beautiful reflex* of *him*!' Geraldine's indignation did not quite prevent her from briefly trying to do precisely that, in the hopes that by so doing she might win Mantell's love. She did not succeed, possibly because she lacked conviction.[2]

Failure was not part of the project of this superior masculine self, and women and men together strove to ensure that it should not be so. Even legislative changes which improved the legal position of married women in the latter half of the nineteenth century, making it possible (if still difficult and expensive) for women to remove themselves from bad marriages, indirectly served men's interests; by reducing the volume of complaint, they diverted attention from the objects of women's dissatisfaction, and by focusing on the woman's part, and seeking solutions which altered the woman's position, they ensured that the subject continued to be seen as a woman's issue. Probably this was inevitable anyway, and the changes in the divorce law and the Married Women's Property Act (introduced in 1856 but not consolidated until nearly thirty years later in 1882) were unqualified gains. But it is less certain that they reflected or led to major changes in the way marriage was viewed. What they offered was legitimate escape for discontented women; a means, at bottom, of keeping unruly (because dissatisfied), turbulent (because unhappy), noisy (because embittered) women quiet.

Just as the burden of happy marriage lay on the woman's shoulders, so too did the resolution of unhappy marriage. And just as, in earlier decades, social ostracism affected women more keenly than men where marriages broke down in acrimony – Lord Byron, in spite of everything, continued to be socially desirable in a way that Lady Byron did not – so too the woman released from marriage by due process of the law at the end of the century faced harsher social and economic conditions than her ex-husband. The men who governed the country and ran the judiciary did not see it as their function to smooth the path of a woman who chose to make her lot contrary to custom – as they saw it. Those who sought to improve conditions for women and those who sought to blame women in different ways agreed that attention should be directed at women not men.

The fact was – and many women, married and unmarried alike, knew it – that the promise of marriage was pitched well beyond what most men had it in them to produce. Ideal versions of womanliness called for ideal versions of manliness which were often quite as problematic for men as the womanly ideal was for women. The crucial difference was that woman's part was spoken, was a part of public discourse, and a very popular part, while man's was not. Geraldine Jewsbury was unusual in expressing dissatisfaction with men, but she was careful to buttress it about. She claimed to agree with Thomas Carlyle's version of marriage in principle, only observing, from her own experience as well as her knowledge of other women's lives, that it did not always work in practice:

> True enough, the difficulty is to find a man who *can* be our master. We desire nothing better than to obey one wiser & stronger than ourselves – we set up an idol and hope it will rule us like a true god but when it can not & does not – we fling it down & break it to pieces to mend the road withal. It is not women who fail in docility but the men who are not high enough to rule.[3]

This is a response which hovers closely, in spite of the final sentence, on the borders of self-blame. Men failed women, according to Geraldine, women did not fail men, but it is easy to see how the failure to find a man strong enough to be master might eventually be seen as the fault of the woman; Geraldine was certainly capable of blaming herself for being too assertive and strong.

Geraldine's leading impulse was very far from being to render herself agreeable and helpful to men, but even she did not fully say her say about matrimony. She observed the demands husbands made on their wives, and peppered her private letters with her disgust, but she did not portray such men in her fiction: her fictional villains were not selfish husbands but sexually predatory unmarried men. Fictionally, she gave no expression whatsoever to attitudes like the following which may be found in her letters:

> I have indulged in a matrimonial scheme, but the gentleman is so dreadfully in love with himself that I have not patience, energy, hope, or inclination enough to persevere. Indeed, these things are not much in my way; it was only the eligibility that put it into my head.[4]

The approved public tone for speaking about men as husbands was a respectful tone modelled on the tone of respect appropriate to fathers. Felicia Hemans's reversion to a childlike status within her family was aided by the similarity of tone generally accepted as fitting for both husbands and fathers, even bad ones.

It was not in her interest to draw attention to her position, even supposing she had been so inclined, by complaining about her husband; ostensibly, she continued to view all men in ideal terms as heroes while speaking vaguely about women's sufferings in marriage. The childlike status depended at some level on retaining a childlike psyche, which, projected in her verse, was taken up by readers as the dominant image and message her poetry purveyed. Victorian readers chose not to hear the undercurrent of strain and resistance which may be read in her work as a whole. But it was only in the last years of her life, sick, lonely, and dispirited, feeling 'the constant want of protection and domestic support', that she allowed herself the luxury of a little outspokenness. She laid the blame for the artistic inadequacy of her writing at the feet of the husband who had failed her:

> It has ever been one of my regrets that the constant necessity of providing sums of money to meet the exigencies of the boy's education, has obliged me to waste my mind in what I consider mere desultory effusions.... My wish ever was to concentrate all my mental energy in the production of some more noble and complete work ... which might permanently take its place as the work of a British poetess. I have always, hitherto, written in the breathing times of storms and billows ... a greater freedom from those cares, of which I have been obliged to bear up under the whole responsibility, may do much to restore me.... I feel the powers of my mind in full maturity.[5]

Five children, and only a pen and poetic inspiration to turn a penny with, had taken its toll. Choosing to put literary ambition before wifely aspirations had meant a heavy price in self-censorship. Felicia Hemans could not be specific about the 'storms and billows' in her life; she could explore her experience in only oblique and fragmentary ways. All the more so since her overriding commitment to her own poetic development had been undeviating, and even at the last she was uttering words which, in the early 1830s, were hard to square with the rather supine, childlike, self-devoting, and dependent ideal figure of woman she had helped create. *Powers*, *mind*, and *maturity* were not words that were supposed to issue from the mouth of a true woman. Far more acceptable were their opposites: debilities, emotions, and childishness. Enforced independence, much as she hated it, brought her personal and poetic maturity. Her last poems, the sonnet sequences 'Records of the Spring of 1834', 'Records of the Autumn of 1834', 'Thoughts During Sickness' and the poem 'Despondency and Aspiration', are the strongest she produced. Taken together, they represent a sustained meditation on the meaning of her life. Deeply religious, personal, and direct, they reaffirm the centrality of poetry as her calling. God, after all, not only approved of poetry, he positively demanded it of those he first entrusted with the gift. Poetry and religion together gave access to an ideal world in whose clear light the confusing and perplexing struggles of daily life could be shaped into meaning. By going directly to God, by leaping the hearth and heading straight for the altar, Felicia Hemans, poet of the fireside, resolved what were both personal and artistic inhibitions. God could be praised unreservedly. Praising God was a way of asserting with renewed vigour, amidst all the sadness and isolation of her last years, the 'liberty and light' which poetic composition had always been to her and symbolized for her. Through dependency on God rather than God's representative, the childlike supplicant, confessedly weak and ignorant but striving to be good, might issue out into the world of perfect truth and knowledge where all would be made whole. Profound religious conviction, such as Felicia enjoyed, opened up an illuminated path from the home to heaven.[6]

Like Maria Jane Jewsbury, Felicia Hemans died before the onslaught of religious doubt in the 1840s. The doubts that shadowed God in the mid-century, by threatening to make man's place unstable too, contributed to the hardening of domestic ideology: if the altars were going to be torn down, then the hearths had better be built up. Man, the guardian of the hearth, took the place of God, but without any of God's advantages to the artistic woman: the path from home to heaven in men's arms merely led back to home. Domestic ideology meant domestic life, and domestic life did not include the 'liberty and light' of poetry. The servitude of domestic life, as Felicia Hemans well knew, was in fundamental conflict with the freedoms of poetry. Addressing herself directly to God, she could speak out the thoughts that were in her mind. Feelings of failure, given to God, were forgivable and transfigurable; they did not lead her to raise her voice against her husband.

If a woman's voice raised in complaint is an unlovely sound, unlovelier still is a woman's voice raised against her husband. Disaffected wives, no matter how innocent or abused, cease to be victims and start to become villains when they speak out on their own behalf. Felicia Hemans was left after six years of marriage and, her pain and outrage muted in the cause of self-protection, wrote poems about the beauty of domestic happiness. Jane Carlyle, who served Geraldine Jewsbury as a model, an inspiration, and a warning in much the same way that Felicia Hemans served Maria Jane Jewsbury, was, like Felicia, a woman bitterly disappointed in her marriage but prohibited by social custom, cultural convention, and personal decisions from giving full expression to that disappointment. Not an acknowledged professional artist, she had neither the 'liberty' nor the 'light' that Felicia was able to draw on for sustenance. She lived beside Thomas Carlyle for forty years, subordinated her desires to his in observation of the strictest wifely codes, and uttered some of the bitterest, most sardonic comments about marriage to be found in the whole of nineteenth-century literature. Jane Carlyle did not merely complain about her husband; she raised complaint to the status of art. What she lacked, and still largely lacks, was a sufficiently informed audience.

Serving her husband with a punctiliousness that verged on parody, Jane Carlyle played the part of a wife as if it were a dramatic creation. Charlotte Cushman, the actress, at tea with the Carlyles, described the performance. Thomas Carlyle, she wrote,

had a method of talking on and on and on with a curious rising and falling

102

inflection of voice, catching his breath now and then on a lower key, and then going on again in the higher, in the broadest Scotch accent, and ever and anon giving out peals of the heartiest laughter at his own extraordinary pictures.... Meanwhile his wife, quiet and silent, assiduously renewed his cup of tea, or by an occasional word, struck just at the right moment, kept him going, as if she wielded the mighty imagination at her pleasure, and evoked the thunder and sunshine at her will. When she was alone, and herself the entertainer, one became aware of all the self-abnegation she practised, for she was herself a remarkably brilliant talker, and the stories of quaint wit and wisdom she poured forth, the marvellous memory she displayed, were in the minds of many quite as remarkable and even more entertaining than the majestic utterances of her gifted husband. It was said that those who came to sit at his feet remained at hers.

Charlotte Cushman was fascinated by Jane Carlyle. After one long afternoon and evening which she spent with her alone, she wrote: 'such a day I have not known!' Mrs Carlyle was, 'Clever, witty, calm, cool, unsmiling, unsparing, a raconteur unparalleled'. She had 'a manner un-imitable, a behaviour scrupulous, and a power invincible', and, Charlotte Cushman concluded: 'a combination rare and strange exists in that plain, keen, unattractive, yet inescapable woman'.[7]

Everything about this description suggests a deliberate refusal to give in to soft womanly stereotypes. Jane Carlyle presented herself to Charlotte Cushman, proper wife to professional actress, in the strong light of dramatic contrast: she had none of the qualities of the conventional wife. She was calm not excitable, unsparing not indulgent, unsmiling not smiling, clever not stupid, a talker not a listener, powerful not weak. Finally, she was inescapable, which is only another way of saying that the essential, definitive quality of a wife was one she did not convey: she could not be easily put aside. She was comfortable occupying the centre of the stage. Like Maria Jane Jewsbury, Jane Carlyle experienced no fundamental, personal difficulty with the position of command.

*

The part Jane Welsh Carlyle played as the wife of Thomas Carlyle was worked out during the years 1821–6. In 1821, when Thomas Carlyle was first introduced to the young woman he decided to make into his wife, she was living, not very peaceably, with her mother, Grace Welsh, in the small Scottish town of Haddington, about eighteen miles from Edinburgh. Two years earlier, Jane's father, John Welsh, the leading doctor in the town, had died suddenly from typhus fever caught from a patient. Neither woman had recovered from the shock of his loss. To his daughter, Dr Welsh had been 'her divinity'. An only child, brilliant and precocious, she had shone and glowed in his eyes and desired at all times to please him. Quarrelling with her mother, she had modelled herself on her father. He was a man to whose authority everyone seemed willing to defer, and of whose character no one recorded a word of criticism. He was scholarly, precise, punctual, reliable, 'a man of strong and noble character, – very true and hating all that was false'. The benign approval showered on Dr Welsh is in marked contrast to the accounts that were left of Grace Welsh. She, it appears, displayed a fine assortment of female follies to match her husband's manly virtues. She was unpredictable, capricious, irrational, over-emotional. While her husband was 'decisive', she was 'imperious' – a distinction that surely has more to do with power and the expectation of success or failure than it has with personality, for both 'decisive' and 'imperious' bespeak a strong will. The only commendation Grace Welsh has ever received from biographers, beginning with her son-in-law, was for her good sense in agreeing to be managed by her husband and setting her daughter the example that his word was law, inside the house and outside.[8]

Jane did not find it difficult to obey her father since she aspired to be like him. From the time she begged to be allowed to 'be a boy' and learn Latin; through an intense Scottish schooling (including, for one year, four hours of private tuition in addition to the day's normal school timetable) during which her consistent, driving aim was to beat the boys in academic and physical pursuits; until, at the age of 16, she was sent to Edinburgh for some ladylike finish, Jane strove to reproduce in herself her father's qualities, the ones he taught her were universally desirable: scholarship, precision, punctuality, decisiveness, hard work, and, above all, truthfulness.

John Welsh's death devastated Jane. Only a few hours before he rode out to visit the patient from whom he caught typhus fever, Dr Welsh had had cause to remind his daughter that, home from Edinburgh with some frivolous ladylike habits (the ones she had been sent to Edinburgh to acquire), she had been falling short of his high standards. She had been neglecting her books. She had not been treating life as the serious and earnest pursuit which he, a professional man who had made his own way, knew it to be. Remorse at his death was mingled with intense guilt; she believed that he had died feeling that she had let him down. His death, in Thomas Carlyle's words, 'drowned the world for her in the very blackness of darkness. . . . A father so mourned and so loved I have never seen.' Losing her father brought about a catastrophic loss of feelings of security and purpose. The years immediately following his death were years of depression and loneliness: 'I had no counsellor that could direct me, no friend that understood me; the pole star of my life was lost and the world looked a dreary blank.' She lived, she said, 'without plan, hope or aim'.[9]

Alone with her mother, and with a feeling of responsibility for her, Jane was vulnerable to her mother's designs for her. Grace Welsh had concurred – because she obeyed her husband – but had never in her heart agreed with the fierce scholastic training Dr Welsh had deemed appropriate for his daughter. She did nothing, once he was dead, to encourage her further. Instead, she set herself to the task of maximizing her daughter's opportunities of securing for herself the best husband possible. There was nothing empty-headed or cynical about this: it was a responsible attempt, such as all responsible mothers with marriageable daughters concerned themselves with, to secure her daughter's future in a world where that future depended entirely on the choice of a husband. Such a state of affairs was but too obviously open to corruption; and the corruption of mothers who callously sold their daughters to the highest bidder was a theme Geraldine Jewsbury was later to take up with some passion. But Mrs Welsh was only enthusiastic, she was not corrupt. Jane's efforts to sit in her bedroom and study were undermined by a constant round of tea-parties and gentlemen callers.

Under protest, but with some attendant pleasures, Jane obeyed her mother and made herself available to the young men who, after establishing their credentials with Mrs Welsh, came to Haddington to assess her. The pleasures she found in the rituals of courtship were largely the pleasures of combat. She volleyed, feinted, teased, attacked, defeated, and despatched what one would call the enemy, except that, as opposition, the young men who offered themselves as suitors do not seem quite adequate to merit the term. Every victory triumph was recorded in a letter. And if Jane's letters about her suitors are to be taken at face value, it would appear that each and every young man who beat a path to the late Dr Welsh's home in pursuit of his daughter, had one predominating characteristic: he was a nincompoop.

Jane found the procedure of courtship vexatious and deplorable. On the one hand, she relished the opportunities it offered her, as the courted female, to exert her power. It is well known that the balance of power in courtship is traditionally the reverse of the balance of power in marriage: according to the rituals of courtship, the man must sue and the woman may accept or reject with as much exaction of worship or arbitrary exertion of her will as she desires. The courtship moment offered women a final fling with power before marriage took away all further right to determine their own future. Essentially, courtship, for a woman, was about having control and being willing to give it up; the erosion of the woman's position was a functional part of the progress from courtship to marriage. It is possible that Jane was specially ill-fated in being besieged by an army of imbeciles, but it is also possible that some at least of the gallery of fools that her victory letters celebrate had imbecility thrust upon them. A young woman who took pleasure in power might secure her pleasures by finding no suitor suitable. Add a talent for caricature, and narrative skill and dramatic flair, and the result was the courtship experience registered as a significant, symbolic episode in female life.

This was the predominating subject of Jane's letters in the period 1821–6; even her letters to Thomas Carlyle were full of her adventures with rival suitors. The exercise of power in life found its corollary on the page: she was indisputably at the centre. In drawing-room encounters she presented to her suitors as still a picture as Hannah More could wish, but the letters proved her mind was elsewhere. She scored a double victory, being doubly in charge. She was true to her father's desires for her while obeying her mother's wishes. She was 'wise, as well as good-looking and good'; and her satiric humour occupied itself in constructing alternative versions of the courtship story. No nineteenth-century novelist represented courtship in the way Jane Welsh presented it. The difference between her version of courtship and everybody else's lay in the way she reversed expectations about men and women. In Jane's letters it will be seen that the 'manly' qualities of sense, command, and truth are possessed by the female, herself; while the 'womanly' tendencies towards irrationality, foolishness, and hysteria are demonstrated by the men. It is the men who flap and faint, who run up enormous bills at their tailors out of the vain desire to impress by outward show, who cannot be trusted to command themselves let alone anybody else. It is the men who want to waste time in idleness which the woman would rather put to better purposes. It was the 'goosish man' who insisted that they had to

> walk, and play at battledoor, and talk inanities, about new novels, and new belles, and what had gone on at a splendid party the night before, where he had been (he told us) for half an hour *with his arm under his hat*; and then he corrected himself, and said, *with his head under his arm*! It was of very little consequence where his head was; it is not much worth.

And it was 'a most prosaic' young man,

> who intimated to me by post that tho' he had spent *five years* without beholding the light of my countenance, he could not exist any longer without seeing me always. I was under the necessity of delivering my opinion of this project: and that occupied more time than you [i.e. Thomas Carlyle, to whom this letter was sent] who are not plagued with those things, can imagine. And even after I had answered his ridiculous Letter, I could not learn my lessons; for I knew him to be a stubborn hot-headed blockhead; and there is a deep mill-pond within a minute's walk of his house. He has continued to pester me with Letters, in which he tells me it is my duty to run my head into a halter because 'the greatest woman in the world ever produced (Madame de Staël) was twice married!! ... This unanswerable argument has had no effect on me.[10]

Jane's explanation of the young man's motives was no less rational: 'He has got a house and some money lately, and he wants an agreeable young woman to look after the cooking of his victuals, and the strings and buttons on his waistcoats.'

In this young woman's accounts, the men, their judgement and balance over-turned by love play, lead the field in inanities while the observing and reporting woman occupies the firm ground of certainty. Her judgement is not disturbed by emotions. Her observation is unclouded by romantic or self-deceiving partialities. The part Jane cast for herself was one in which she displayed not power alone, and not coquettish or manipulative power, but power in the service of good judgement, the sort of power her father displayed. One story will illustrate it further. This was the drama precipitated by one Dugald Gilchrist who fell in love with Jane at the Musselbro' races in the summer of 1824. Once he had seen her he followed her everywhere; 'there was no escaping his ubiquity'. Mrs Welsh evidently favoured him, for she invited him to pursue his suit by coming to stay with them at Haddington, accompanied by his sister, 'a little smiling girl from an English boarding-school'. With very little delay, 'what I had foreseen and dreaded came to pass: the first time that I was left alone with him, out came a matrimonial proposition in due form.' Jane's refusal, which she found it difficult to give, not because she 'had the smallest disposition in the world to consent – oh dear no!' but because 'he has fair silky locks, the sweetest eyes in nature, a voice like music, and a heart so warm and true and so wholely, wholely mine!', threw the young man into a fit of hysterics:

> Poor youth he threw himself down on the sopha beside me, and wept and sobbed like a child . . . he would not be comforted: he lay in bed, and cried all the rest of the day; my Mother sat and cried beside him; and his Sister and I cried in another apartment.

By ten o'clock that evening, the 'poor Boy', having cried himself into a fever, was persuaded out for a walk in the cool evening air. Jane was instructed to walk with him, 'that he might say out what he had to say to me, and be done with it; my Mother and Catherine followed at a little distance'. But Dugald Gilchrist was locked into a miserable inarticulateness:

> We were on the way back, he had not spoken for several minutes, when all at once he gave a sort of cry, and fell down at my side; I shut my eyes and stood motionless; I could not stir to assist him; I thought he was dead. Fortunately my Mother had more presence of mind; she ran up to us when she saw him fall, and lifted him off his face. God! how he looked! He was as white as ashes and his eyes were wide open and fixed. He stirred and spoke at last; but he could not stand without supporting himself on my Mother, and what he said was quite incoherent.

Carried home by Mrs Welsh, Dugald was put to bed in a delirium and stayed there 'for three days and nights without sleep and almost without sustenance, tossing on his bed and crying his lovely eyes out'. Faced with this manifestation of masculine hysteria, Jane decided that it lay with her to bring him to his senses. Her strategy for doing so was modelled on her father's bedside manner with his patients. She went into his room, 'asked very gravely what ailed him', refused to be disconcerted when he responded by hiding his face in the bedclothes, and in about a week, 'by skilful treatment', brought him round – barring the odd tumble off a chair.[11]

Nineteenth-century literature is not rich in descriptions of male hysteria. In nineteenth-century novels the *sal volatile* on the mantlepiece was for helpless women, not helpless men. To find literary parallels one has to look to an earlier period, to Shakespeare's Andrew Aguecheek, for example, or, indeed, any number of his lovers who find that the chief pleasure of love is precisely its unmanning of them. The fluidity of gender distinctions in the Elizabethan period, for example, enabled dramatists and audience to enjoy the fun without feeling undercurrents of fear at the unsettling of prescribed roles. A man pretending to be a woman pretending to be a man could demonstrate power and good judgement, as Portia did, and win the day. Such power derived from the assurance of greater knowledge and deeper understanding, not from gender. Jane Welsh, telling the story to Thomas Carlyle, announced that it was an artefact, a dramatic piece: 'There has been such a tragedy performing here!' It was a tragedy that was to be understood according to the rules of dramatic art rather than the rules of everyday life; just as the letter which carried the tale was more than a literal transcription of events. Like the drama, the letter was highly conscious of its audience. It gained its effects partly by exaggerating the contrast between subject – foppish, hysterical young man – and recipient – dour, serious, potentially jealous, soon-to-be-husband. At the same time it was an idealized portrait of the writer. Jane placed herself authoritatively at the centre in such a way that Dugald's emotional flimsiness served to emphasize her emotional and moral solidity. She, by her calm, cool rationality, was able in the end (after a symbolic three days and nights) to introduce order into chaos. Aided by her mother and his sister – three women basically looking after one big baby of a man – she had no doubts about her capacity to do this, or of the importance of keeping her wits about her. Jane, sitting on Dugald's bed, was not just finding a way through one man's hysterical fit. She was a female protagonist who represented all young women in her position, women who were, like her, in constant danger of finding themselves subject to the complete control of a man who could not control himself.

The tragi-comedy of Dugald Gilchrist and Jane Welsh, because it was a courtship story, hinged on the unspoken but well-known, understood, shocking social fact which might have formed its denouement: that the sensible woman might become 'incorporated and consolidated' into, lose her legal existence to, the insensate young man. This social reality underpins the account, and partly explains why it forms part of a private letter and not a chapter in a novel or a scene in a play. Jane had literary ambitions. She had written a novel by the time she was 9 and a five-act tragedy of extreme bloodiness by the age of 14. Her literary talents as well as her intellectual abilities had been recognized, and Thomas Carlyle, for one, had assured her that in cultivating them she would find fame. He saw, he said, 'a niche in the Temple of Fame' for her. As a young woman, she had already become dissatisfied by her own attempts at the obvious literary genres: writing intellectual essays, such as the essay on friendship Carlyle suggested, or on Madame de Staël whom she admired, bored her, and as for writing novels:

> So many 'sunny mornings in the month of May', and 'stormy nights in the month of December', have shone and snowed at the commencement of works by ladies young and very young, that without committing plagiarism, I cannot avail myself, for a first line, of any one day of either Summer or Winter. Spring and Autumn have also been already appropriated.[12]

Escapist fictions by – or pitched at the level of – 'ladies young and very young' were the stuff of publishers' dreams. Few publishers would have been interested in fictions which represented a self-possessed, authoritative woman plagued by

imbecilic men. Even Emma Woodhouse, 'handsome, clever and rich' is introduced in order to be brought down a peg. *Emma's* Mr Knightley set the type for
sagacious males in the novels that followed. More father than lover, this man was
wiser, more emotionally mature, more knowledgeable, and more responsible than
the women who, typically, looked to him for leadership. As Judy Little puts it,
in *Comedy and the Woman Writer*, the adventurer and hero in our myths is always
male: 'Women had no life adventures considered worthy of being used as a
symbol for a divine adventure . . . hence no quest that might serve as a "paradigm"
for a "tradition" in literature.' Hence, also, no opportunity to act as guide, passing
on experience to the coming generations, for she herself had no experiences. She
was the source of the experiences that happened to others: 'The woman is catalyst,
landscape or "maternal depths" but not herself the adventurer.'[13]

Even if Jane had not been inclined to create men who were imbecilic nin-
compoops, the fact remained that women, in literature and in life, could not
comfortably occupy positions of knowledge and truth. To be a learned woman
was to be an anomaly and a threat; the term 'bluestocking' was already in use as
a derogatory term designed to warn women off. On a trip to the Highlands, Jane
told Thomas, she

> thought it adviseable to play the part of a lively, dashing goodhumoured,
> thoughtless blockhead of a girl – you cannot think how this character *took* –
> it won the hearts of all the women and turned the heads of all the men in
> the place.

She became so much a favourite of one couple that they agreed to continue their
friendship by correspondence. As soon as she got home, Jane wrote to them.
The couple were appalled and intimidated: the woman confessed 'her own
inferiority at the pen', while the man aggressively put the young woman in her
place for what Jane insisted had been nothing other than 'writing grammar': 'If
you choose to be a blue stocking,' his letter began, 'do you think or expect we
common people can answer you in the same style?'[14]

Choosing to be a bluestocking was choosing to be beyond the pale. It is one
of the many ironies in the history of women's lives that women who sought
fundamental truths through intellectual study were most likely to be accused of
artificiality and pretence. Or perhaps it would be fairer to say that they would be
no less likely to be accused of artificiality and pretence than other women. Whether
women sought the truth in their intellectual lives or in their emotional and social
lives, their efforts were liable to be interpreted as strivings after effect not
substance. Writers, of course, since they *do* strive after effects, were more suspect
than most. And among writers, comic writers: comedy, with its levelling tendencies, may be the most democratic of the arts but it is also the most subversive.
During the period 1821–6, Thomas Carlyle tried to help Jane Welsh make sense
of her talents so that she could establish herself as a writer and break free from
the narrowness of provincial life – Haddington was 'the pit of dullness' – and
achieve the fame she wanted. Fame meant, for her, understanding; communion

with people who would identify with her aspirations and not condemn them. Admiration, of which she had had a great deal in her life, was not enough: 'I feel clearly', she wrote, in a long letter that dealt very seriously with the subject of fame, 'that I wish to be loved as well as admired.'[15] As an intellectual woman of proven ability there was just a chance (a slim one) that she might manage to yoke admiration and love – gain that 'justice of the heart' which Maria Jane Jewsbury has Cecil admit, in *The Three Histories*, is hard for men to give to women of talent. But as a satirist, particularly one whose satirical shafts were aimed at men, it was highly unlikely. Thomas Carlyle himself, making exactly the distinction Jane had made between what was fully loveable and what was merely admirable (with all the ambivalence that suggests), bluntly observed that the satirical gifts she possessed, of which he had too often and too painfully been the target, were unloveable. He also, most significantly, recognized that they were a feature of strength and health; when she was sick, Jane was not satirical and for that reason Thomas gave thanks. Considering the part that sickness played in her married life, this early association of sickness and womanly goodness rings like a portent. Carlyle wrote to her:

> your sickness I have striven to make light of; I will not let myself believe that it is more than temporary; and the serious mood you partly owe to it, is that in which to me you are by far most interesting. Do not mock and laugh, however gracefully, when you can help it! But for your own sake, I had almost rather see you sad. It is the earnest, affectionate, warm-hearted, enthusiastic Jane that I *love*; the acute, sarcastic, clear-sighted, derisive Jane I can at best but *admire*. Is it not a pity you had such a turn that way?[16]

The path to true womanliness lay through sickness. By depressing health and strength, she might be sure of depressing her instincts towards satire and so achieve the higher goal of one man's love and applause. Jane's gifts were in direct conflict with womanliness: neither passive nor acquiescent and malleable, she was mocking, caustic, assured, and subversive. And her powers of judgement were cribbed and confined to one intense arena: the choice of a husband. Thomas thought her situation enviable: she had the freedom to read, write, talk to her mother, and look to him for tutorly guidance. She did not, like him, have to struggle for a position in the world of letters. Idealizing her life, envying what he idealized, he conveniently ignored the central issue of power and control. Jane, caught in it, could not: her life was 'a continual sacrificing of my inclinations and opinions for peace's sake; and there is no peace after all!' She was speaking of life with her mother, but it was true, too, of life with Carlyle, both then and later.[17]

Jane Welsh and Thomas Carlyle did not meet often during the five years of their courtship; when they did meet, they invariably quarrelled. The one time they did not quarrel, was when they spent a fortnight together with Carlyle's family shortly before marrying. Of this restful period Carlyle recorded, 'She and I went riding about; the weather dry and grey, – nothing ever going wrong with us; – my guidance taken as beyond criticism.'[18] Thomas encouraged Jane to criticize her mother's guidance (up to a point) but not his own. Communicating with him through the protective medium of the written word, she was able to give expression to inclinations and opinions which, face to face with a man who harboured desires to make a wife of her, were often explosive:

> These nonsensical people with their *Heirathsgedanken* [thoughts of marriage] and *Heirathsvorschlagen* [proposals of marriage] will assuredly drive me mad ... positively I cannot fall in love; and to sacrifice myself out of pity, is a degree of generosity of which I am not capable. Besides matrimony under any circumstances would interfere shockingly with my plans. The philosopher that used to thank the gods he was born a man and not a woman, must have had more sense than the generality of his calling. Truly our fate is very deplorable: as soon as a poor girl takes that decisive step called *coming out*, she is exposed to a host of vexations men know nothing of. ... What I would give to be a Prime Minister or a Commander-in-Chief! An old woman that boiled blankets in this town used to say when I was leaping the Mill-dam some dozen years ago, 'that Providence had stickit a fine callant' (stopped a fine *lad* in his career) She understood my character better than anybody I have had to do with since – '*The extreme enviableness of my condition*!' Oh dear me – I wish you had a trial of it for one twelve-month –[19]

Having all the instincts of a leader not a follower, unable to be either a prime minister or a commander-in-chief, denied the opportunity she would probably have taken had she been the son whose education she had largely been given, to study medicine and follow her father in his successful practice, the only alternative to 'marrying and making puddings' was literary achievement. Fame, being a woman of genius, would give coherence to her discontents. But despair and self-blame prevailed. She was 'a very worthless concern', with 'neither genius, taste nor common-sense ... no courage, no industry, no perseverance':

> I have not force of mind to struggle through. 'I have no genius' – I feel it – my ambition will be borne down by the difficulties that oppose its gratification – and when my ambition is no more what good reason will there be that I should occupy any room in our Creator's Universe – Lord have mercy upon me! When I cease to be ambitious I am a ruined woman![20]

Thomas Carlyle's letters were on hand to support her in her despair. He subtly turned the formulation around: when she ceased to be ambitious, she would become a proper woman. He wrote:

> I heartily rejoice that you *cannot* write a book at present! Had you succeeded in these enterprises, certain Milliners' apprentices might have adored you, and you would have had a rank among the Blues of this planet; but as a woman it would have proved your ruin. This is sure as fate. Gifts like yours are fit for something else than scribbling.[21]

What they were fit for was serving a man's gifts: his. He confided his dreams, a fantasy that might have sprung from the pages of *The Three Histories*:

> In hours of happy musing, I figure myself as the interpreter of truth and manly integrity and imaginative beauty to thousands of my fellow men; and Jane, my fair and pure Egeria, my inspiring Goddess of the Fountain, to originate, to perfect, adorn and recompense my labours![22]

The man who had predicted a niche in the temple of fame for his beloved, envisaged an altogether different type of temple for her once discontent and despair in her life as a dutiful daughter drove her to contemplate the possibilities of peace in becoming a wife. 'You have a deep, earnest, vehement spirit, and no earnest task has ever been assigned to it', Thomas assured Jane. He knew where her hopes of happiness lay:

> O that I saw you the mistress of a house; diffusing over human souls that loved you those clear faculties of order, judgement, elegance ... blessing living hearts with that enthusiastic love.... All this is in you, Jane! You have a heart and an intellect and a resolute decision which might make you the model of wives, however widely your thoughts and your experience have hitherto wandered from that highest destination of even the noblest woman.[23]

This was the offer of a form of command rooted in womanly love, not unwomanly satire and scorn.

Earlier in their relationship, the word 'noble' in Thomas's letters had attached itself to Jane's efforts at intellectual improvement. Carlyle heartily endorsed her contempt for the stupidities of elegant young men, apparently prepared to die for a sight of her eyes or ankles. Considerably inelegant himself, he saw only 'nobility' in her scorn for 'callers, tea-bibbers and suchlike hereditary encumbrances'. He applauded her desire to read books rather than be 'stuck up among imbecelles', giving her an encouragement that no one else, after her father's death, gave her. His influence over her came largely from the association in her mind of his values and qualities with those she had loved in her father. She told Carlyle:

> I had never heard the language of talent and genius but from my father's lips; I had thought that I should never hear it more. You spoke like him; your eloquence awoke in my soul the slumbering admirations and ambitions that *His* first kindled there. I wept to think the mind he had cultivated with such anxious, unremitting pains, was running to desolation; and I returned with renewed strength and vigour to the life that he had best destined me to lead. But in my studies I have neither the same pleasure, nor the same motives, as formerly: I am *alone*, and no one loves me better for my industry.[24]

Alone and wanting to be loved for her abilities, Jane looked to Thomas, who spoke like her father, to bestow a fatherly blessing on her unconventional instincts.

3. The Carlyles at Cheyne Row or The Chelsea Interior, by R. Tait (1858).

Contemptuous of genteel social forms himself, a romantic individualist, excited by intellectual possibilities rather than bourgeois aspirations – what the Carlyles later called 'Gigmanity' – Carlyle's earnestness and bohemianism offered a way through what was increasingly coming to seem an enclosed future. Marrying him was a move out of the enclosure. The hysterical and trivial young men who by their attentions pinned her within it, would no doubt develop into petty and conventional husbands. Thomas Carlyle possessed all the untold possibilities of genius. Married to him, there was a chance that she might be able to live her adult life in a way that was true to herself.

Truth, however, to the self or others, was a commodity which the complexities of female life made slippery. Thomas Carlyle valued truth; so did his father; so did Dr John Welsh. They knew what they meant by it and projected it as a universal value. But women who attempted to claim their place in the universe of truth discovered that other values, with the unadmitted connivance of men, took precedence. Manners, for example, were more important than truth for women, just as gracefulness was more important than intellect. At a surface level, Thomas understood and sympathized with the frustrations Jane expressed when she described to him some of her daily constraints:

The enemy is within doors – my uncle Robert and his cold, prosaic, beautiful, artificial Glasgow wife have been here a whole week; and God knows when we shall get rid of them! the one shoots and sleeps, the other yawns and dresses, all day long – they would *ennuyer* Job himself were he living at this day. But what is worst to bear I am compelled by etiquette –

eternal etiquette to take leave of Schiller, Alfieri and all my dear companions to listen in agonies of patience to their insipidities – To read, in my own house, before visitors, would be a breach of politeness never to be forgotten or forgiven.[25]

Good manners, 'eternal etiquette', required violations of will and truth; submerging her will to be elsewhere, she was required to be patient when she felt impatient and to show interest in and approval for a way of life that bored and disgusted her. The scope for violation of truth has always been wider for women, just as the scope for violation of custom has been wider for men. Both men and women are subject to codes of etiquette, but men are allowed to stumble more before they fall. Women are strapped by etiquette, men by truth. Truth is a manly quality. Women are not only allowed, they are often expected, to be devious. Jane Welsh, admiring her father and modelling herself on the Roman heroes her Latin studies introduced her to, made truth a virtue. But she learned from an early age that it would often have to be subordinated to other, more womanly characteristics. In her childhood she became friendly with a clever but very poor boy in her class. They pored over books together and he taught her everything he knew. Then one day,

> An aunt who came on a visit saw her standing by a stile with him, and a book between them. She was scolded and desired not to keep his company. This made her very sorry, for she knew how good he was to her; but she never had a notion of disobedience in any matter small or great. She did not know how to tell him or to explain; she thought it shame to tell him he was not thought good enough, so she determined he should imagine it a fit of caprice, and from that day she never spoke a word to him or took the least notice; she thought a sudden cessation would pain him less than a gradual coldness.[26]

The aunt – perhaps the same aunt whose life was dedicated to yawning and dressing – was concerned, like Grace Welsh and like Dr Welsh, that Jane's manners should not become too free or too rough. If they did it would damage her marriage prospects. To tell the boy the simple truth would have been hurtful, and so, in order to be obedient (and gain moral approval), the young Jane Welsh employed a deceit: morally repugnant, but for a female socially sanctioned. Women were expected to be capricious. Caprice, here, was a strategy in the service of heroism. Not only was it a typically female heroism in being silent and inward, secondary and unsung, it was also typically female in presenting in terms of its opposite: self-denial was at the heart of what must have looked to the boy – what it was intended should look to the boy – like incomprehensible self-indulgence. Only Jane knew what had really happened, and thus she took the blame of the broken friendship on herself and bore the burden of the boy's regret as well as her own. A tiny episode, it bothered her conscience for years. When she was a middle-aged woman she sought the man out in order to tell him, at last, what had happened.

J.A. Froude, who came to know Jane Carlyle in the latter part of her life, spoke about her devotion to truth. She was, he said, 'not an easy person to live with. She had a terrible habit of speaking out the exact truth, cut as clear as with a graving tool.'[27] For men, such a quality represented the highest virtue. For women, it made them difficult to live with. When Thomas Carlyle said of his own father, 'he was a man of rigid, even scrupulous veracity', he did not accompany the observation with any subtly critical riders.[28] When Jane Welsh married Thomas Carlyle, it was in the hope of clawing back some of the claims on truth which her father's values had seemed to promise. But genuine truthfulness did not feature in the array of idealistic categories Thomas laid down for his wife. Nobility, a far more manipulable concept, stood higher. *Noble* was applied with legislative force: it was synonymous with *womanly*, stretching as it did to cover any extreme of self-sacrifice including the sacrifice of truth. In marrying, she promised to obey. She promised to be 'meek-tempered'. She promised to be 'everything, anything you wish'. And for a little while she seems to have managed admirably. Thomas praised her to his mother:

> my good little wife is the best of all wives: I declare I am astonished at the affection she bears me, and the patience with which she listens to my doleful forebodings and turns them all into gay hopes. In *every*thing great and little she gives me entirely my own way.[29]

She also promised to prefer listening to speaking and kept her promise so well that after four months of marriage *his* talking and *her* listening had become an established routine. She, too, boasted to his mother:

> I am ... among the best listeners in the kingdom. And my Husband has always something interesting and instructive to say. . . . It is my Husband's worst fault to me that I will not, or rather *cannot* speak; often when he has talked for an hour without answer, he will beg for some sign of life on my part.[30]

This was learning to play dead with perfection, trying not merely to stop speaking but to lose the power of speech altogether. It was among the panoply of new skills and remarkably adroit manoeuvres that marriage demanded. Agreeing to conquer by weakness and command by obeying was to power and truth what 'imperious' was to 'decisive': they were the caprice code of honour, and the reverse of a position of strength. The effort of willingly eroding her own sources of power made Jane Welsh very miserable in the months that led up to her marriage just as it did for a sizeable portion of the rest of her life. Towards Thomas Carlyle she learned to become 'tractable and submissive' as required, in spite of being, as she reminded him, 'self-willed as a Mule with others'. The gay, mocking young woman disappeared, the woman whose wit had so alarmed Carlyle that he admitted, 'it seems as if I *dared* not to love you'; and in her place was someone out of touch with herself as well as others:

115

I know not how your spirit has gaind such a mastery over mine in spite of my pride and stubbornness. ... I never *can* talk when I have got anything to say ... at all times, I can be anything easier than myself. ... I have grown as difficult to come at as a snail in a shell; and what is worse, I cannot come out of my shell when I wish it.[31]

Perplexity, withdrawal, and weakness formed the soggy clay out of which a good wife might best be moulded. Self-dislike helped. Writing to Anna Jameson some years later, Jane declined Anna's request that she should write about herself: 'I dare not write on so sorry a subject – myself was never much in favour with me and less now than ever.'[32]

*

To go from talking to listening is to travel a gender specific path. Woman's domestic role, as Ellen Pollack convincingly demonstrates in her eighteenth-century study, *The Poetics of Sexual Myth: Gender and Ideology in the Verse of Swift and Pope*, was 'to fit herself to masculine desires'. Ceasing to assert and starting to obey demanded the willing renunciation of both failure and truth: women's lives as ideal wives were to be about perfection and dissimulation. In Pollack's words, woman was to be:

like ... the original incarnation of perfection – to rectify human lack by means of beautific suffering. By bearing the burden of all deficiency in herself, she would vindicate the sufficiency of men; should she experience subjection as a vicious impotence, it could only be by her 'ill managery' of the plenitude of his bounty to whom it was her duty to submit. ... As long as a woman subjected herself to social, legal and economic dependence on a man by becoming his wife ... conniving attempts on her part to gain advantage within the limits of that dependency were condoned. Dis-simulation on the part of women was not only permissible when it remained interior to a masculine desire, but was often necessary to sustain the desired relationships of power.[33]

Thus, an impatient woman ordered to become patient, a talkative woman ordered to become a listener, a disappointed woman ordered to be pleased, a woman of questioning mind ordered to be content with other people's answers, all went through processes of dissimulation for which they were commended. Jane Carlyle, listening in 'patience' to Thomas Carlyle's dreary 'forebodings' and turning them all into 'gay hopes', behaved in a way that – as far as one can tell – was unlike any way she had ever behaved before. No brisk retorts escaped from her lips, there was no deflating mockery in her glance. The persistent quarrelling that had been so much a feature of their years of courtship when they were physically together did not, in these early months, mar the perfection of the domestic scene. Jane had engaged herself to learn the skills of her new profession. But whereas wifely codes of practice entitled women, as Pollack says, to use dissimulation to gain advantage (so long as they remained, in their objectives, 'interior to a masculine desire'), Jane's personal commitment to truth made that womanly compensation a problematic one. Gaining advantage could only be done by acknowledging dissimulation; but rejecting the knowledge of dissimulation was crucial to maintaining the sense of her true self. Rather than advantage, Jane Carlyle sought to approximate to the ideal model of what Françoise Basch has called the 'wife–guide': to be her husband's helpmate and inspirer, soul of the home, 'collaborating with the man in his work, while serving him and inspiring him to seek the highest ends'.[34] In this capacity she could keep a hold on truth so long as her husband subscribed to it, which in his professional life as a writer he showed every sign of doing. Jane believed in Thomas's 'genius', which is another way of saying that she believed in his undeflectable commitment to the pursuit of truth. Attached through life to genius, she could live in the realm of truth.

In 1826 when Jane Welsh became Jane Carlyle, the picture of the glorified and dependent wife had yet to be fully drawn by such Carlylean enthusiasts as Charles Dickens. Thomas Carlyle's ideas on the subject were, like all philosophical convictions, developed in part from a conscious programme of specific reading and in part from the combustion of living. The 1820s were a bleak and despairing time for him. He had written nothing to make anyone pay him the attention he sought and he saw no clear path into the future. He was desperate to be recognized: 'ever since I have been able to form a wish – *the wish of being known* has been foremost'. Driven by that wish, idealistic and evasive, Thomas Carlyle looked to his wife to assure him by personal devotion and intellectual loyalty that the idealisms he persisted in were the fountainheads of truth. Her reception of his words was to be acquiescent; and further – the chief duty of dissimulation – she was to retire from the field, leaving only the male voice to utter what had previously been a mutual and equally heartfelt prayer: 'Grant me that with a heart of independence ... I may attain to literary fame.'[35]

Having chosen the writing of books as his life's work, Thomas struggled for inward assurance that books, working with words, constituted worthwhile activity. His conflicts shaped themselves around issues to do with masculinity which had implications for domestic life as it affected himself and his wife. The home-based, passive nature of the work of reading and writing, the invisibility of the work, and the diffuse impact and uncertain usefulness of the final product, all contributed to an unsettling of masculine identity. One could as well read Cromwell's despatches on a sofa as a French novel – that 'acme of human idleness'. Carlyle's model of a true man was his father, a man of profound Calvinistic principle, whose philosophy was 'that man was created to work, not to speculate, or feel, or dream'. James Carlyle built stone bridges and stone houses which people walked over and lived in; nothing speculative, nothing dream-like, only solid, long-lasting usefulness. However hard he tried, Thomas Carlyle, who had disappointed his father by not entering the church as his profession, could never quite believe that his own productions were equal in value to those of his father. Words poured from him in speech and writing, but they never gained his respect;

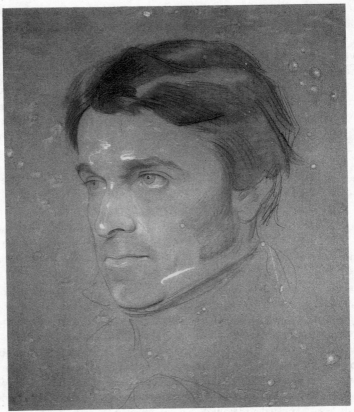

4.   Thomas Carlyle, *Head of Carlyle*, by Samuel Lawrence (1838), reproduced by kind permission of the National Trust.

indeed, he increasingly despised them for their capacity to deceive, as a stone bridge or a stone house could never deceive. His desire to be a man of action he projected on to the great men he wrote about: Cromwell, Frederick the Great – revealing in his tortured difficulties with both subjects his ambivalence about their freedom of movement compared with his confinement in the scholar's chair. And as his own half-formed projects for entering the world of affairs came one by one to nothing, so the disparity between words and action became more of a torment.

The less Carlyle's life resembled that of his father, the more absolute his father became for him as a model of manliness. He habitually placed the worlds of Edinburgh and London literary life, with their bohemian, sometimes effeminate, poets and painters, their aristocratic philosophers and politicians, against the background of his peasant upbringing in order to reassure himself that he still found them lacking. The famous Gospel of Work which he expounded and which became so influential, was a way of keeping faith with his father's life and values, and at the same time justifying his own work as a writer, work which had, to all appearances, taken him far from his father both intellectually and socially. It was the embodiment of what was in Carlyle's case the rather ironic conviction that 'Life was action, not talk':

> I call a man remarkable, who becomes a true Workman ... be his work that of Palace-building and Kingdom-founding, or only of delving and ditching, to me it is no matter, or *next* to none: *all* human work is transitory, small, in itself contemptible; only the worker thereof and the spirit that dwelt in him is significant.[36]

Such a view dealt at a stroke with doubt about his own work, the class status of his father, and the gender complications introduced by his wife's intellectuality and inescapable regard for truth. For no matter how hard she tried, Jane Carlyle could not lose that part of her self which revered truth. As she admitted: 'in spite of the honestest efforts to annihilate my *I-ety*, or merge it in what the world doubtless considers my better half, I still find myself a self-subsisting, and alas! self-seeking *me*.'[37] Instead of seeking advantage through dissimulation, Jane was able to find in her husband's philosophy something which suited them both better: a truthful way of being false to herself.

The right end of life, Carlyle taught, was not to ask questions but to do work. In *Sartor Resartus*, his spiritual autobiography, which he wrote during the early years of his marriage, this was compressed into seven simple words that reverberate through the Victorian era: 'Do the Duty which lies nearest thee.' This moral opportunism, only too obviously putting aside the pressing questions of value, was an essentially despairing philosophy, a desperate bulwark against anxiety and its consequent ill-health. A personal solution, it had far-reaching effects on Victorian society. Thomas Carlyle's formulation offered anguished Victorians a way through the ethical confusions of a rapidly changing, physically demanding world; and an alternative to the often paralysing doubts of religious scepticism and materialism. Duty was work, and all work had the same value: 'All work, if it be nobly done, is about alike: really so – one has no reward out of it except ... [the] spirit it was done in, that is blessed or that is accursed – that is all.'[38] Duty was always that which lay nearest to hand. The only profitable speculation was: 'What is to be done; and how is it to be done.' This suited the writer with doubts about the manliness of the activity, but it also suited the housewife brought up to value masculine aspirations and finding herself in an inferior, servicing role. Of all people, the housewife was never at a loss to know what was to be done, or, indeed, since the work was repetitive, how to go about doing it. The duty nearest at hand was always within hand's reach in the shape of cleaning, cooking, sewing, and generally organizing the household.

Thomas Carlyle's discovery that work could be a safeguard against temptation – in his case the temptation to perplexity and despair – was hardly original. When applied to women it combined with that specific tradition of thought which insisted that women were more prone to give way to bodily temptation. Carlyle put work in the place of religion as the answer to excess at both ends of the spectrum: misery and joy. In both cases it was more likely to be effective if it was constant. Just as no amount of drudgery was too much for a writer seeking truth in dusty old folios, so no amount of household drudgery could ever be considered too much for a woman attempting to live according to the teachings of Thomas Carlyle. In any case, success was not to be measured by contentment or happiness. *Sartor Resartus* was clear on that point: 'master the selfish desire for personal happiness and lead a life of dutiful labour'. No work had any worth, only the action of work had worth. Housework and writing were equal, along with stone-cutting and kingdom-founding. Nobody loved the young Jane Welsh any better for her 'industry' after her father died, but Thomas Carlyle did.

The Victorian period was an era when nearly everyone sought heroes, and they were, by definition, male. Carlyle came to be held in peculiar veneration as a man of rugged intellect offering new forms of certainties. His numerous male disciples paid tribute in their writings to the depth of his influence on them. Looking back from the present day, when Carlyle's work is of little interest to men and even less to women, it is easy to forget the fact that his writings, on German Romanticism, on the French Revolution, and, perhaps most importantly of all, the series of lectures on heroes which he delivered in 1840 and published in book form the following year, had a specially compelling appeal for women in the nineteenth century. The gospels of earnestness and work had a precise applicability to the lives of intelligent and literate middle-class women bred up to idleness. The very vagueness of Carlyle's philosophy enabled many meanings to be put upon it and many uses made of it. Like religion, it served as balm for confused emotions – first and foremost Carlyle's own. And like religion, it gave openings for energy at the very point that it seemed to be closing them.

The governess Mary Smith (though hardly a woman bred up to idleness) found 'Carlyle's gospel of Work and exposure of Shams, and his universal onslaught on the nothings and appearances of society' both intellectually liberating and self-affirming in her life as a woman.[39] Like other women, she found in his writings the highest legitimation of her desire to live to the limits of her true self. Carlyle seemed to offer heroic possibilities to all, men and women alike. With renunciation – *Entsagen* – at the heart of his doctrine, his books preached self-affirmation through self-renunciation – the essence of martyrdom, the essence of evangelical religion which taught that to lose the self was to gain the self. Domestic labour, performed not for the self but for others, and performed largely by women, easily occupied a central place in this philosophy. Staying at home, reading Thomas Carlyle, subjected from birth to domestic conditioning with its fears and timidities, women discovered that they too could have a heroic destiny: as housekeepers. Aspiring and energetic women might aspire to ever greater heights of domestic servitude, receiving social affirmation for their services to husbands, fathers, mothers, children, siblings, and friends. With Carlyle's words ringing in their ears, women could bustle about their kitchens and parlours as they had always done but with an inner sense of control and self-direction that was in harmony with cultural expectation. In practical terms nothing had changed: Carlyle reworked the values he retained from his Calvinistic upbringing for a religious but doctrinally sceptical age – renunciation, endurance (no matter how great the personal cost in suffering), and hard work. But women were able to feel differently about it.

Further, Carlyle's personal need to turn the writing of books into a heroic (masculine) struggle, met the needs of those women who were making their way into print in such large numbers in the 1840s and subsequent decades. By sacrificing himself to his writing, Carlyle threw a religious colouring over the activity, moving it away from its associations of personal ambition. The increasing feminization of culture, and the increasing popularity of literature which trivialized emotional experience into sentimentality and melodrama, were a threat to all serious artists and thinkers. Carlyle offered a sort of literary respectability to women: setting himself apart from sentiment but at the same time driven by emotion; intellectual but also incoherent; passionately dismissive of fiction and yet a (secret) reader and blatantly obvious writer of it; he was the masculine better self in the realm of writing that husbands provided in private life. He took away the shame of fame. His high seriousness was a cloak that women, too, could wrap themselves in.

Intellectual women were drawn to Carlyle. Jane Welsh was only the first in a long line of female disciples who were inspired by his thinking and found comfort in his assurance that the meaning of life and the resolution of difficulties had not been lost along with doctrine. As a first generation Carlylean female (Geraldine Jewsbury was to be among the second) who knew well that the word 'woman' contained 'weakness, timidity and bondage', she found strength, courage, and freedom through his teaching. The particular strength, courage, and freedom she found acted in ways which served to reinforce the status quo *vis-à-vis* men which had made 'woman' a word containing weakness, timidity, and bondage: that is to say, it changed nothing but appeared to enable her to feel better about things. Jane Carlyle explained how it worked in 1857 when she received a letter from Mary Smith. Mary had told Jane that she disliked intensely her current post as a governess. She felt a 'passionate inward protest' against it. But rather than leave her employer (and serve herself) she had chosen to take the harder, more heroic path of endurance. She intended to see it through (to serve him). Jane Carlyle responded by congratulating Mary Smith: finding ways to endure the uncongenial was the essence of Carlylean teaching. She reminded Mary Smith: 'it is not the greatness or littleness of "the duty nearest hand", but the spirit in which one does it, that makes one's doing noble or mean!' She then went on to recall the strategy by which she, too, had been given strength to put patience and endurance over passionate inward protests. It was by applying her husband's philosophy to the life she found herself living alongside him and in deference to his wishes. In 1828 the Carlyles had left Edinburgh, where they had settled upon marriage and where they were beginning to be very well established in literary circles, to go and live at Craigenputtock, a very remote moorland farm that belonged in the Welsh family. It was an irrational move, a 'savage place' as Jane described it, too isolated for any sane servant to want to live there, and so oppressively lonely that of the three women who had been Jane's predecessors, 'two ... had gone *mad*, and the third had taken to *drink*'. In these extreme circumstances, Jane experienced the full shock of what marriage meant:

> being an only child, and brought up to 'great prospects', I was sublimely ignorant of every branch of useful knowledge, though a capital Latin scholar and a very fair mathematician! It behoved me in these astonishing circumstances to learn – to sew! Husbands, I was shocked to find, wore their stockings into holes! and were always losing buttons! and *I* was expected to 'look to all that'. Also, it behoved me to learn *to cook*! No capable servant choosing to live at 'such an out of the way place', and my husband having 'bad digestion' which complicated my difficulties dreadfully. The *bread* above all, brought from Dumfries, 'soured on his stomach' (oh Heavens!); and it was plainly my duty as a Christian wife to bake at home! So I went for Cobbett's '*Cottage Economy*' and fell to work at a loaf of bread. But knowing nothing of the process of fermentation or the heat of ovens, it came to pass that my loaf got put into the oven at the time myself ought to have put into bed, and I remained the only person not asleep, in a house in the middle of a desert! One o'clock struck, and then two and then three; and still I was sitting there in an intense solitude, my whole body aching with weariness, my heart aching with a sense of forlorness and *degradation*. 'That I who had been so petted at home, whose comfort had been studied by everybody in the house, who had never been required to *do* anything but *cultivate my mind*, should have to pass all those hours of the night watching *a loaf of bread*! which mightn't turn out bread after all!'

But the 'degradation' of this humble womanly activity could be transformed by thought into the equal of that high heroic activity which it serviced. A 'germ of an idea' entering Jane's head, spread 'consolation' over that long night of the soul and many subsequent ones. 'Maddened' by her thoughts, Jane laid her head on the table,

> and sobbed aloud. It was then that somehow the idea of Benvenuto Cellini's sitting up all night watching his Perseus in the oven, came into my head; and suddenly I asked myself, 'After all, in the sight of the upper powers, what is the mighty difference between a statue of Perseus and a loaf of bread, so that each be the thing one's hand hath found to do? The man's determined will, his energy, his patience, his resource, were the really admirable things, of which the statue of Perseus was the mere chance expression. If he had been a woman living at Craigenputtock, with a dyspeptic husband, sixteen miles from the nearest baker, *and he a bad one*,

all these same qualities would have come out most fitting in a *good* loaf of bread!'[40]

This is fighting stuff, and the women in Wordsworth's household would have agreed with it. But it was fighting with both hands tied. In the sight of the upper powers there might have been no difference between bread and statues worked from bronze, but the lower world had always found big differences. Benvenuto Cellini's immense egotism, which his *Autobiography* rather charmingly reveals, was, like Thomas Carlyle's, sanctioned by the work he produced and by his masculinity, both of which fed on the self-suppressing bread-maker who in Carlyle's case was his wife. Bread might keep people going, but it did not give much scope to its maker for personal development. Some of the unspoken history of women's lives, transacted in drawing room, kitchen, and bedroom, is contained in this image of the young woman alone and miserably responsible for another's comfort in the dead of night, whose own comforts had to be found in feeling better rather than in thoughts of change. The prelude to the intellectual discovery, to the 'germ of an idea' which consoled her, was, as she told Mary Smith, that her life had driven her to the verge of madness. She was 'very near mad', suffering from 'fatigue and disgust', at the time of the bread-making episode. What had made her mad was the constriction of ambition and power that had been the specific conditions of marriage and that had characterized her married life. Finding out that the 'spirit in which one does' one's work was the most important thing provided a rationale for situations which led to madness:

I can't think how people who have any natural ambition, and any sense of power in them, escape going *mad* in a world like this, without the recognition of that! I know I was very near mad when I found out for myself.

'People' should surely be 'women'.

In situations which are designed to induce madness, the sensible response is to take steps to avoid going mad. Throughout her life, Jane Carlyle worked hard to convince herself that making bread was equal to making a statue of Perseus, that running a house was essentially the same as writing a book. This projection of her subjective experience on to a culture which quite clearly did not agree, took its logic from Thomas Carlyle's unique position and the dissemination of his ideas – which originated in the life he shared with Jane Carlyle – through that culture. The outward similarity of his life to hers, the uncomfortable congruences in writing and housekeeping, blurred important differences. Each had to find the means within to endure a deal of uncongeniality, but while his endurance answered to the meanings of existence (and took him outwards), hers answered to the dissimulations of domesticity (and drove her inward). Remaining 'interior to a masculine desire' included turning her own forebodings into gay hopes just as much as his. Interiority had to be felt as well as obeyed. An intelligent woman, she had to have an internal logic. Like a true woman, she had to be as well as do.

123

5

WORK

In England, work is considered degrading.
Flora Tristan, 1842[1]

Thomas Carlyle's Gospel of Work underwrote the appeal of heroic housekeeping and lent a masculine dignity to the intersection of bread-making and Benvenuto Cellini. Conceptually, work was in masculine possession. Ford Madox Brown's painting, *Work*, which shows Thomas Carlyle watching a group of workmen digging a tunnel in Hampstead, excludes women from the central definition. Felicia Hemans's poems were 'essentially feminine' because they appeared to be 'spontaneous effusions'. Femininity was synonymous with idleness: middle-class woman did not work because her true career was her sex. Long before Tennyson wrote his poem, *The Princess*, novelists from Richardson onwards had told literate women, in effect, that they were all princesses in disguise. The more distaste they had for work, the more ineptitude they showed when in the presence of it, the more proof they gave of royal womanliness. Feminine gentility, like aristocracy, consisted in doing nothing.

A training in idleness was, to some extent, the training Grace Welsh had sought to impose on her daughter by substituting shuttlecock for Schiller. In a life dedicated to triviality, the flower of pure femininity would bloom and achieve its reward: a husband. Such a version of femininity was one which Thomas Carlyle and Jane Carlyle agreed in despising. They saw it as a source of all that was negative in women, including the headaches and hysterias that Mrs Welsh suffered from. Thomas Carlyle, for instance, before he married Jane Welsh, observed of a Miss Merchant he knew in Kirkaldy that conditioning into her feminine role had deprived her of what were essentially human qualities:

> The more I know her and her *species* the more heartily I despise them. It is strange but it is true, that by a continuing and unvaried exercise of affectation, those creatures in the end entirely lose any kind of real feeling which they *might* originally have possessed. Ignorant, formal, conceited, their whole life is that of an *automaton* without sense and almost without – soul![2]

Thomas Carlyle despised the person less for what she was than for what had been

124

done to her in the name of femininity, itself directed towards what were considered masculine tastes. His own masculine taste, for one, did not lead him to want to spend his life with a senseless automaton.

Jane Carlyle was equally emphatic. 'If I have an antipathy for any class of people,' she wrote in 1832, 'it is for *fine ladies*.'[3] 'Fine ladies' were not in her view natural women, nor did they represent essential womanhood: they were the creation of artifice. In 1844, on a visit to her cousins, the Welsh family of Liverpool, she was shocked at the genteel idleness consuming the lives of the young women there. She declared herself 'heartily sorry for these girls, so good naturally, so gentle, and even intelligent'. Much as she loved her uncle, John Welsh, and the cousins, she found it a trial staying with them. Jeannie Welsh in particular ('Babbie'), who had been a modest and attentive sick nurse/companion at Cheyne Row in 1842, in the months of depression that had followed the shock of Grace Welsh's death, had become 'painfully indolent and young ladyish':

> [the] unwearying earnestness with which they all dress themselves three times a day, is a continual miracle for me, combined as it is with a total want of earnestness about everything else.... As for Babbie, she is sunk into the merest young lady of them all. Her indolence is absolutely transcendental.[4]

In this family, for these women, 'sufficient for the day is the marketing and eating and dressing thereof!'

> And a new satin dress can diffuse perfect beatitude through an immortal soul! The circulating library satisfies all their intellectual wants, and flirtation all the wants of their hearts; it is very convenient to be thus easily satisfied. One looks plump, digests without effort, and sleeps in spite of all the cats and cocks in the world.[5]

Over the years she became increasingly disgusted at the 'scene of waste, and fuss, and frivolity, and vanity, and vexation of spirit' that she was exposed to when with her cousins, and eventually she proved her antipathy by breaking with Babbie altogether. The final straw came in 1857 when Babbie had a baby – 'about three finger-lengths long' – and joined the family at Auchtertool in Scotland for an August holiday: 'Five packing cases came before them by the carrier, and as many portmanteaus and carpet-bags in the carriage with them.' That was not all. Babbie had also brought not one but '*two* six-feet-high nurses attending her about thro' a series of visits; such an affected, bedizened, caricature of a *fine-lady* I never came across. I could hardly keep my hands off her.'[6]

A femininity that was about fuss and affectation, indolence and emptiness, was not a femininity Jane Carlyle chose to identify with. It might enable sleep and digestion to go forward smoothly, as most conformity did, but: 'somehow "I as one solitary individual" would rather remain in Hell – the Hell I make for myself with my restless *digging* – than accept this drowsy placidity.' Digging, as Ford Madox Brown's painting showed, was quintessentially masculine, just as dressing was quintessentially feminine. Digging was work and dressing was leisure. Preferring to dig than to dress, Jane gave Thomas the credit for the more purposeful life she was able to live alongside him: 'How grateful I ought to be to you, dear, for having rescued me out of the young-lady sphere! It is a thing that I cannot contemplate with the proper toleration.'[7]

By working, Jane aspired to escape negative feminine definition and achieve positive masculine credit. The irony was that she merely fell in the feminine scale to the level of a servant – Froude specifically observed that she worked for Thomas Carlyle 'like a servant'. A lady who was no lady could only travel downwards; she might choose not to be a 'fine-lady', but she could not leave the feminine sphere. There was no category of positive recognition for a middle-class woman who lived according to a masculine scale of values organized around the work ethic. Women who respected hard work, ambition, and truth could not be encouraged to pursue them for they conflicted with womanliness. Within the domestic sphere, however, it seemed possible to put such values into the service of domestic ideology. Jane Carlyle, a morally scrupulous woman, saw in domestic labour a morally acceptable way through the negative definitions of bourgeois femininity which predominated in her time. Anyone who reads her accounts of her home life with Thomas must be struck by the volume of household labour she performed and the value she attached to it. She did everyday household work like sewing, sweeping, dusting, grate blackening and cleaning; and unexpected callers might find her looking 'like a little sweep on a Saturday night!'[8] This was not in itself particularly unusual; many middle-class housewives saw it as their role to work alongside servants in the shared task of running a home. But she also undertook schemes of home improvement that might make even a modern home-owner blench: schemes that involved putting in new floors and new walls, 'taking down a partition and instituting a fire-place where no fire-place could have been fancied capable of existing'; living in the din of bricklayers and plasterers and the commotion of carpenters, painters, and paper-hangers – many of whom had a habit of falling through the ceilings they were supposed to be building.[9]

These household 'earthquakes' were generally undertaken to suit Thomas's convenience or fancy. He himself played no further part in them: Jane negotiated with building contractors, dealt with any legal issues that arose, shifted furniture, placated neighbours, supervised the 'troop of incarnate demons, bricklayers, joiners, whitewashers & etc',[10] and, alone at night – because Thomas usually made himself scarce on these occasions – slept with pistols ready for any burglar tempted by the wide open windows. Household 'earthquakes' were housework on a grand scale, and they illuminate Jane's attempt to reach the moral masculine through the practical feminine. In supervising others, deploying skills of management and control in what was an essentially creative enterprise, she found an opportunity to be commander-in-chief. Always as comfortable in the position of command as she was uncomfortable in the position of obey, Jane found a fulfilment in the terrible upheavals of home improvement that can be measured

5.   Jane Carlyle and her dog, Nero (31 July 1854), reproduced by kind permission of
The Rare Book and Manuscript Collection, Columbia University, USA.

by the better health she mostly enjoyed while it was in progress. Housework, she
declared, was 'the only occupation that affords me the slightest self-satisfaction':
her existence would have been 'beggarly' without it.[11] Amidst a household
'earthquake', so long as Thomas was not at home and 'recognising it with his
overwhelming eloquence', she could become absorbed in a busy and assured
usefulness that was strangely restful; she could be 'not *thinking* of it at all but
living it very contentedly'.[12]

   This was a halcyon state of being, properly interior to a masculine desire whose
representative had fled. There is no evidence that Jane deliberately created
household chaos to give herself a rest from her husband, but she certainly
understood its uses with regard to her husband's brother. Dr John Carlyle had
all the indecisiveness, all the self-involved egotism of his elder brother without
any of the genius. He took it for granted that Cheyne Row was his home whenever
he chose to stay there, and that all its womanly services existed to be drawn on
as unthinkingly as if the house was 'like those charming palaces one reads of in

the fairy tales, where clothes are found hanging ready at the fire to be put on by the wearied traveller, and a table comes up through the floor all spread to appease his hunger'. Angered by John's complacent indifference to herself and the work she did in providing his comforts – 'oneself might be a thousand miles off, or like the enchanted princess of these establishments, might be running about in the shape of a little mouse without his contentment being disturbed' – Jane took drastic action on at least one occasion:

> I fairly *painted him out!* blessings on my powers of invention! There he was; waiting to 'see his way clearly' and never so much as wiping his spectacles – babbling and boring, and holding oyster-like to the external accom-modations of one's house – without a thought beyond! an element of confusion hindering all my efforts at order! But never let a living woman despair – I wielded the Earthquake in my small right hand, and one morning he awoke and found himself 'in his old lodging' – where there was no vestige of a reason why he should not have been all this while![13]

Between Jane Carlyle and John Carlyle there was an unspoken struggle over who had the right to call the other one idle: Jane did not recognize in his aimless movements from medicine to literature, from her house to his 'old lodging', a purposefulness at all comparable to her daily 'efforts at order'. He, on the other hand, judged her illnesses to be a manifestation of specifically female idleness. In 1833 she reported to her friend Eliza Stodart, 'He told me yesterday, "Could I give you some agreeable occupation to fill your whole mind, it would do more for you than all the medicine in existence".'[14] And in 1864, during the severest, most devastating of all her collapses, he offered much the same diagnosis, pro-voking a comparable fury:

> Fancy his telling me in my agony yesterday that if I had ever done anything in my life this would not have been: that no poor woman with work to mind had ever had such an ailment as this since the world began.[15]

Two years later, just four days before her death, she received an account from her husband of the suicide of a poor woman who lived in Scotsbrig, Thomas Carlyle's family home. She observed bitterly: 'What a deal of misery it must take to drive a working woman to make away with her life! What does Dr Carlyle make of such a case? No Idleness, no Luxury, nor novel reading to make it all plain.'[16]

John Carlyle's accusations carried the weight of cultural approval: novel reading (and novel writing) symbolized well-known, thoroughly condemned, womanly idleness. We might agree with his fundamental observation, that the origins of her psychosomatic illnesses lay in the mental frustrations of a woman of large abilities given small scope; but whereas, from a modern perspective, we might see hope in such a remark, she knew it contained only blame. Dr John Carlyle did not suggest his sister-in-law should join the women's movement as a cure. Nor did he cease littering her home with his papers and his presence. Her inability to be well in a life designed to make her ill remained her fault. Self-blame was fully reinforced by knowledge that the world blamed too: 'until I turn what health and strength I have to better account, I have no business to regret that I have not more.' Writing to Thomas in 1845 from Seaforth, near Liverpool, where she had been staying as the guest of Geraldine's friends, the Paulets, whose kindness and hospitality had helped her throw off a bad depression, the difficulty of her position became plain mid-paragraph. Her desire to have the purposes of a working woman was at odds with a culture which insisted that middle-class women did not work: such work as she did, which was housework, was lower-class women's work and as such culturally invisible. Thomas was no better than his brother at understanding that tables spread with food did not just come up through the floor. Jane wrote:

> There is plenty lying for me to do at home; and I cannot go on long in idleness, – however speculative and ornamental. You may say my life at home is vastly like *idleness*, so far as you can see into it; and in truth it might be busier, – at least busy to better purpose.[17]

No matter how much dust she raised around the house, her life was regarded as idle, for it was a middle-class woman's life – by definition removed from the definitive spheres of work and purpose. Thomas's struggles with his literary projects, the years during which he read and wrote but could not see clearly the direction or purpose of much of what he did, were never interpreted as idleness; John's vague disinclination to practise medicine, his preference for the soft world of travelling as private physician to a hypochondriac countess, and his subsequent decision to give it up in favour of literary work, were not judged idleness – though his indecision was a family joke. Neither the daily busyness nor the purposes of these men came under profound scrutiny. Nor were they subject to the mystifications that dogged female life. For example, in 1842 Thomas Carlyle wrote to his wife:

> My prayer is and always has been that you would rouse up the fine faculties that *are* yours into some course of real true work, which you felt to be worthy of them and you! Your life would not then be happy; but it would cease to be miserable.... I know well, none better, how difficult it all is, – how peculiar and original your lot looks to you and in many ways *is*. Nobody can find work *easily* ... all of us are in horrible difficulties.... But I will never give up the hope to see you adequately *busy* with your whole mind.[18]

Earlier still, during the Craigenputtock days – a place where, as Thomas informed his brother Alick, 'if a man did not work, he might so easily run mad' – his advice was more specific: 'I tell her many times there is *much* for her to do ... her whole sex to deliver from the bondage of frivolity, dollhood and imbecility, into the freedom and valour of womanhood'.[19]

There is no doubt that Thomas Carlyle genuinely wished for an end to the constructed insipidities of femininity. But his refusal to acknowledge men's part in it left him floundering in bafflement and mystery: it was a mystery that his wife was so clever and could find no adequate satisfaction for her mind; it was a mystery that she was so ill. His blindness to men's role in creating 'frivolity, dollhood and imbecility', also ensured that what began as fellow-feeling, sympathy, the voice of one human individual speaking to another human individual similarly placed, developed by degrees into criticism. Since she did not do the things he prescribed as needing to be done, she had only herself to blame.

Hard housework was Jane Carlyle's refuge from frivolity and dollhood; sooner than leave the doll's house, she tried to triumph within it. Her efforts were recorded in her letters. These letters tell the stories of the facts of her life. They testify very graphically to the doomed nature of Jane's heroic struggle to resist dollhood while accepting the terms of the doll's house. For the bondage of her sex was a bondage to men, not, as men liked to insist, a bondage to an essentially inferior, because female, nature. And that was a subject on which, living with a man for whom silence, like work, was the measure of moral worth, Jane Carlyle chose to be silent. What she chose not to say cannot, in the end, be known. But just as we strip much of the apparently secure meaning from what has been spoken – revealing the subjective behind the objective, the emotional need driving the intellectual pronouncement – so we can strip some of the mysteries of silence. Silence itself, of course, was a resource adopted in response to the stereotype of the chattering female. Also, the nagging female, the whining female, the romancing female, the complaining female. It was a way of being good-womanly rather than bad-womanly. In the early years of her marriage it was an optimistic silence; from the middle years onwards it became increasingly bitter and rigid. In 1858 she informed Thomas:

> Suppose, instead of putting myself in the omnibus the other day, and letting myself be carried in unbroken silence to Richmond and back again, I had sat at home writing to you all the thoughts that were in my head? But that I never would have done; not a hundredth part of the thoughts in my head have ever been or ever will be spoken or written – as long as I keep my senses at least.[20]

The fear of going mad was in part a fear of saying what she had learnt was unsayable. Sooner than speak out her thoughts, Jane bodied them forth in tumultuous illnesses. The fight that she agreed not to wage outside the doll's house took place inside her skin.

Silence was at the heart of Thomas Carlyle's philosophy – notwithstanding the fact that, as one friend remarked, he only loved it 'somewhat platonically'. 'SILENCE, SILENCE,' he thundered, 'in a thousand senses I proclaim the indispensible worth of Silence.'[21] And in a thousand sentences. Sara Coleridge was another person to observe that while Thomas Carlyle might bid his wife to be 'brief in narration', his own speaking style suffered from 'repetition, and the saying in a round-about, queer way, as if it were a novel announcement, what everybody knows'.[22] Jane was no more silent than Thomas was, but she was a woman burdened with knowledge she was determined not to speak. The more public her life became, the more stringently she imposed silence on herself. Her 'inward life', as she put it, was 'connected with outward *facts* on which I am bound to be silent'.[23] Relationships with women – friends, family, servants, 'celebrated females' – all took place under the shadow of the principal outward fact on which women generally agreed to be silent. Like Felicia Hemans, Jane Carlyle could not give full utterance to the truth about her married life. This had artistic as well as personal consequences; for both women, as artists, were compelled to explore their experience for its stores of truth, and both were compelled, as women, to repress much that was most significant. To criticize men was taboo. Further, it would inevitably rebound on the woman; as Felicia Hemans discovered, losing a man was the same as losing respectability. Criticism of men tended towards the godlessness of heartlessness. It was indecent. For a wife, it was unwomanly, if not by definition impossible, to tell the truth about unhappiness: for if such a woman placed the authority of her own experience at the centre of her expressive life, and said that she was unhappy when she had all the accoutrements of happiness – a husband, a home, a hearth – she proved herself no true woman. When Jane confided her deep marital disappointments to Giuseppe Mazzini in 1845, he rebuked her: 'Your life proves an empty thing, you say! Empty! Do not blaspheme.'[24]

Felicia Hemans grappled with this dilemma in *Records of Woman*. Jane Carlyle attempted to create a literary production out of the truth of her daily domestic life. She attempted to hold in balance two truths: the selfhood of unswerving individuality with the submission of an ideal wife. But these truths were no more compatible than were the social situations of women and men. Jane knew this. And she knew how damaging had been her life of submission to Thomas:

> It is sad and wrong to be so dependent for the life of my life on any human being as I am on you. . . . If I have to lead another life in any of the planets, I shall take precious good care not to hang myself round any man's neck, either as a locket or as a millstone![25]

The image of locket and millstone, ornament and weight, goes to the heart of feminist analysis. It did not lead Jane, however, towards other women articulating that analysis on a political level. She was antagonistic to 'isms' of every sort and certainly towards feminism in its public expression, placing herself in opposition to that represented by such women as the radical Frances Wright:

> If I were going 'at my age and with my cough' to take up a mission, it would be the reverse of Fanny Wright's. Instead of boiling up individuals into the *species*, I would draw a chalk circle round every individuality, and preach it to keep within *that*, and preserve and cultivate its identity at the expense of ever so much lost gilt lacker of other people's 'isms'.[26]

Jane looked for strength in individuality while at the same time subverting it. Her letters are dramatic monologues of daily submission. They operate most effectively, like much comedy, in the space between the ideal and the actual, in the contrast between effort and accomplishment, assumption and reality, the mythological and the prosaic. In making submission into drama, she seized the creative initiative, as Charlotte Cushman observed, out of the very embers of servility: the tea-table, daily domestic drudgery, dependence on a man who was at times pathologically unable to make up his mind (not a disability Jane suffered from). She used it to keep alight a vivid, inner-directed self. She was not always successful, but she was nevertheless responding rationally and creatively to a profoundly irrational situation. She rebelled against nothing, satirized everything. Thomas shared much of her satiric vision. Both felt themselves to be outsiders, and both, in literary terms, were at odds with mainstream culture. He was the leading member of her audience just as she was his first disciple. But whereas her artistic production was bound up with her domestic life, which included him, his artistic production, during their lives together, did not acknowledge dependency upon her. While she stayed inside the home, Thomas, from the early 1840s onwards, found himself invited into aristocratic circles in which he discovered a stimulus he was more than ready for. His 'trade of being a Genius' brought public recognition: he was sought out, spoken about, much admired. He might fulminate against the dusty folios in his study as she fulminated against a dusty house, but there was no disputing the fact that other people found a purpose in his work that they did not find in hers, and that he was revered for his productions and she was not.

Thomas Carlyle became infatuated with one particular aristocrat: Lady Harriet Baring, the wife of his friend Bingham Baring, and at first sight the finest fine lady of them all. Her husband's infatuation, and her own attempts to share in the blessings Lady Harriet had to bestow, were exceedingly painful for Jane. Lady Harriet admired Thomas for his work and took him away from it; she insisted he pay her long visits to the country or attend her soirees at Bath House in Piccadilly. Lady Harriet's wishes were always answered: 'her ladyship's will is become the law of this house! – even her *whims* are as imperative as the ten commandments!'[27] The relationship exposed Jane to gossip. She had to endure snide remarks from such people as Samuel Rogers, and be pitied or despised as a woman whose husband apparently preferred the company of another woman.[28] Her distress was real. Froude interpreted it as the understandable, if strictly unfounded, distress of a jealous, neglected wife, commenting that she had additionally to suffer the indignity of being admitted into the 'high regions' of aristocratic circles for her husband's sake not her own, since in those high regions 'wives of men of genius, like wives of bishops, do not take the social rank of their husbands'.[29] An entry in one of the few brief, surviving journals kept by Jane, beginning in October 1855, seems to confirm that she was jealous of Lady Harriet. The journal was started on the evening of 21 October, while Carlyle was out at Bath House, with the startling opening sentence: 'I remember Charles

132

Buller saying of the Duchess de Praslin's murder, "What could a poor fellow do with a wife who kept a journal but murder her?" ' The Duc de Praslin murdered his wife not because she kept a journal but because she had begun to resist his systematic rejection of her. Her journals, however, 'all about feelings', were seen by some as explanation enough for why the Duc should prefer the quiet company of an orderly governess. Jane's journal was not to be about feelings but about the 'fact of things'; however 'bleak and barren', she determined to stick with facts, and thus deny her husband any good reason to murder her. This was not easy to do:

October 22nd – I was cut short in my introduction last night by Mr. C's return from Bath House. That eternal Bath House. I wonder how many thousand miles Mr. C. has walked between here and there, putting it all together; setting up always another milestone betwixt himself and me. Oh, good gracious! when I first noticed that heavy yellow house without knowing, or caring to know, who it belonged to, how far I was from dreaming that through years and years I should carry every stone's weight of it on my heart. About feelings already! Well, I will not proceed, though the thoughts I had in my bed about all that were tragical enough to fill a page of thrilling interest for myself, and though, as George Sand has shrewdly remarked, 'rien ne soulage comme la rhetorique'.[30]

Though the feelings of jealousy and loneliness could not be denied, they were not the only factors at work. Jane's distress was also a philosophical perplexity. As the daughter of her father and the disciple of her husband, she placed a high value on work. As a woman who despised 'fine-ladyism' she sought to establish relationships with women that were based on something more solid than the 'strenuous idleness' of aristocratic life. Aristocratic life did not attract her. She noted its effects on Lady Harriet Baring herself, a woman of enormous intellectual gifts, whose wit and brilliance (and immense wealth) succeeded in drawing all the intellectual men of her time around her. At Bay House, the Baring's huge mansion in Hampshire, Jane had much leisure to puzzle over the leisured life of Lady Harriet, and try to understand what continued to baffle her: the attraction of such a woman for Thomas, a man who supposedly despised indolence and uselessness. She had no doubt that she preferred her own 'occupation and duties'; she had a feeling of urgency that derived from a sense of purpose stalled, even if others did not recognize that purpose. At Bay House, she was back in an intensified way in the life that Thomas had rescued her from:

Six weeks have I been doing absolutely nothing but playing at battledore and shuttlecock, chess, talking nonsense, and getting rid of a certain fraction of this mortal life as cleverly and uselessly as possible; nothing could exceed the sumptuosity and elegance of the whole thing, nor its uselessness!... This Lady Harriet Baring, whom we have just been staying with, is the very cleverest woman, out of sight, that I ever saw in my life (and I have

133

seen all our 'distinguished authoresses'); moreover, she is full of energy and sincerity, and has, I am sure, an excellent heart; yet so perverted has she been by the training and life-long humouring incident to her high position that I question if in her whole life she has done as much for her fellow creatures as my mother in one year, or whether she will ever break through the cobwebs she is entangled in, so as to be anything other than the most amusing and most graceful woman of her time.[31]

For all her brilliance, Lady Harriet settled for a part in life that was not much more than decorative. Jane had rejected the decorative in favour of the practical and useful; and given the chance to command men, she preferred to conduct a circle of carpenters and bricklayers than one of politicians and poets.

Lady Harriet Baring 'ruled half London' and was 'the most brilliant conversationalist of any woman in London'. Her houses were centres of the 'most glittering and sharp-tongued society in England'. Work of every kind, including intellectual work, was discouraged among the company that gathered constantly in crowds around the Barings. For all that Lady Harriet's circle was noted for their writings – they were known as 'Lady Harriet's printers' by disdainful rival hostesses – actual literary production took second place in the ambience of The Grange, Bay House, Bath House, or Addiscombe, to a version of conversation which reified the leisured existence of the aristocracy. Participants 'flitted from one topic to another, avoiding all discussion and all sincerity, playing at conversation as though they were dancing an intricate minuet'. Lady Harriet needed no books in her house because, as she explained, 'a few of my friends write and the rest never open a book: none *read*'. She said she liked idleness, her favourite image of which was 'an Indian god on a lotus leaf or a ploughboy on a gate'. And while enjoying the homage of men whose literary ambitions and abilities had carried them to the top of their profession, men like Thackeray, Tennyson, and Macaulay as well as her 'dear old Prophet Carlyle', she disavowed any personal literary ambition in words which were stunningly self-assured if not downright rude: 'I have not only never written a book, but I know nobody whose book I should *like* to have written.'[32]

What was Thomas Carlyle doing in such company? The question was given a cruel twist by the fact that, as gossiping contemporaries pointed out, Jane Carlyle and Lady Harriet were similar personalities. Each was the other's equal in wit, quickness, and sense, and each had a gift for dramatizing everyday incidents and making 'high comedy out of daily life'. They shared a sense of the ridiculous and a tart style of mockery. Jane reported on their similarity in another important area, very early in her acquaintance with Lady Harriet: 'I can see', she wrote, 'that the Lady has a genius for *ruling*; whilst I have a genius for – not being ruled!'[33] Aristocratic position and purse gave Lady Harriet the edge, however, and she exerted her genius over both Carlyles. Jane felt like 'a sort of animated, still wholly irresponsible carpet-bag, with Mr Carlyle's name on it', when she was summoned to stay, and she was not as grateful as others assumed she must be at being drawn through 'the Golden Gates of the Aristocratic Paradise such as it is'.[34]

Lady Harriet was a woman of remarkable independence and strength; Thomas Carlyle, his wife noted, '*never* by any chance refuses a wish of hers – the clever woman that she is!'[35] She for her part was soon running about like an upper servant meeting Lady Harriet's needs and not even having to be witty, for 'Lady Harriet *does* all the wit herself'.[36] Lady Harriet's wit and energy were in service to no one; she was 'brisk as a huntress'. She often took her own meals before the vast dinners she laid on for her guests so that, undistracted by need, she could orchestrate the conversation and participate in it with her full attention. She was powerful and she respected power. Like a queen, she ruled as born to it. She did not stoop to manipulation:

> a woman more perfectly regardless of *rank* I never happened to see. *Strength* is what she goes upon; a *weak* Prince of the blood she would treat with undisguised scorn, and would behave herself quite sisterly towards a *strong* street sweeper. In fact she is a *grand* woman every inch of her – and not a 'coquette' the least in the world – if all the men go out of their sober senses beside her how can she help *that*?[37]

She did not, in other words, seek to exert a sexual power over men. Indeed, her power was not recognizably womanly at all: it came from strength not weakness, and she had a habit of command that did not dress itself up as obedience. When she wanted any of her men to come and have dinner with her, she sent 'terse, clear and peremptory' little notes, 'rather like the commands of a sovereign than the easy communications of friendship'. Jane Carlyle's 'little notes', by contrast, were always carefully directed to charm, impress, or otherwise sway the recipient, especially when the recipient was male. Lady Harriet's friends were mostly male; there were few women in her inner circle for 'she much preferred the society of intelligent men'.

Lady Harriet revealed no sense of identification with other women. When she spoke of friendship she used the male pronoun and she meant men: 'Friendship has great advantages – you know a man so much better and can laugh at him so much more.' Evidently her charms were not passive and neither were they peaceful. She made fun of everyone. One victim of her rackety wit complained to Monckton Milnes, 'I do not mind being knocked down, but I can't stand being danced upon afterwards.'[38] Impatient and direct, she seems to have inspired metaphors of violence and battle; Jane observed that at least you always knew where you stood with her for she would 'blow you up with gunpowder rather than be bored with your company' if that company became tedious.[39] Above all, having surrounded herself with all the great talkers of an age of great talkers, Lady Harriet continued to assert herself in both talking and selective listening. Hers was not a self-effacing style of the hostess. And Thomas Carlyle acknowledged her leadership qualities. She was, he said, 'the greatest lady of rank I ever

135

saw, with the soul of a princess and captainess had there been any career possible for her but that fashionable one'.

Jane was astonished at the power Lady Harriet had over Thomas. At Bay House in 1847, she watched open-mouthed as Lady Harriet paid attention to her pet green parrot while her philosopher spoke to the air:

> and the parrot does not mind interrupting *him* when he is speaking – does not fear to *speak thro him* (as the phrase is) and her ladyship *listens to the parrot* – even when Carlyle is saying the most sensible things! By Heaven she is the *very cleverest woman* I ever saw or heard of.

Lady Harriet did more than listen to the parrot's words in preference to those of Carlyle. Jane continued: 'he meets with other contradictions which I cannot pretend to be sorry for – I cannot make out what Lady Harriet is after – but to look at her one would say she was systematically *playing my cards for me.*'[40]

But who was playing whose cards? For by 1847 Thomas Carlyle had had twenty years to domesticate a woman's sharp intelligence and wit, so that it no longer frightened him as it had done before they were married. He could enjoy Lady Harriet's power over him, indeed slavishly adore her, without feeling that he dared not love her. While his training made him more fitted for Lady Harriet's society, Jane's training, in wifely submissions and dependencies, weaknesses and obediences, made her less fitted. Lady Harriet went on strength, and strength was what Jane Carlyle, along with most of the other women whose company Lady Harriet found inferior to that of 'intelligent men', had agreed to endeavour to give up.

Lady Harriet did all the things which domestic ideology laid down as undesirable in women, and so far as Jane could see she was not punished for it. People said that she was ugly, but they did not say that she was improper, nor cast any slight upon her marriage to the indulgent and doting Bingham Baring. Aristocratic privilege accounted for much of her freedom, but not all; and Monckton Miles thought her 'strong individuality' had been too much even for her aristocratic associates. At first Jane thought that she could make a friend of Lady Harriet, but she soon learned that that was not a realistic hope. She continued to be fascinated by her because she eluded easy explanation: 'I profess never to this hour to have arrived at a complete understanding of her – but *that* I fancy is just a part of her fascination – the insoluble psychological puzzle which she is and bids fair to remain for me!'[41]

Trying to understand Lady Harriet was also about trying to understand the laws that governed a woman's life. Married to Thomas Carlyle, Jane tried to ground her life on a concept of work that had positive masculine valuation, even though the work she actually did was the ultimate feminine work: housework. Idleness, that 'feminine' characteristic, led to affectation and folly. But Lady Harriet, while indisputably indolent, was neither affected nor a fool. She operated with the freedom of a man in a man's world. Her cleverness, the quality in her which Jane returned to over and over again in her comments, was to be herself on her own terms. Taking Jane's comments on her as a whole, there is far less that suggests insecurity about Thomas Carlyle's feelings and the direction of his affections than there is about the impact of Lady Harriet on Jane Carlyle's own sense of self and fundamental purposes in life. When she tried to puzzle out the mystery of Lady Harriet, she did not only mean the mystery of that lady's charms for Thomas; she meant the mystery of Lady Harriet as a woman of intelligence who did not seek a more meaningful life for herself than that of aristocratic idleness. The purposeless suffocation of such a life, even lived as Lady Harriet lived it, threw into bright relief the purposes of her own.

> The more I see of aristocratic life, the more I wonder how people with the same system of nerves as oneself, and with the same human needs, can keep themselves alive in it – and *sane*! Lady Harriet especially, who is the woman of largest intellect I have ever seen – how *she* can reconcile herself to a life which is after all a mere dramatic representation, however successful, fills me with astonishment and *a certain* sorrow.... A *poor* woman has enough of serious occupations cut out for her by the nature of things – sometimes more than is good for her – and therein lies *her* grievance – we in our sphere have also something given us to *do* – how far it may suit our taste is another question and a secondary one – we see at least how our activity may be turned to account better or worse. But a great Lady – should she take a notion to wrap herself in a blanket and go to sleep like *Beauty* for a hundred years; what would stand still that needs go forwards? Only herself! And should she take the better notion to put away Great-Lady-things and lead a rational useful life, how is she to set about it? How extricate herself from the imposed *do-nothingism* of her *position*? As Lady Harriet herself once said to me, 'one would have to begin by quarrelling with all one's husband's relations and one's own'.[42]

Whatever else the middle-class domestic routines of Cheyne Row imposed, they did not impose do-nothingism. In non-stop work, Jane Carlyle found a way to turn her activity to account. Lady Harriet's life, lacking any impulse towards work, lacked, as far as Jane could see, real meaning; a state which was next door to insanity. Her own 'career of household activity' might be often enough 'anything but a pleasurable one!' but it was something she could call a career (knowing that others did not) and it was 'always open to talent'. She would not 'learn to go idle with dignity'. Escaping the idleness and grandeur of Lady Harriet's residencies, all of them 'magnificent to death', might mean going back to a bed that had been invaded by bugs or a chair that the worms had infested, but dealing with these homely crises with her own hands affirmed a self-worth that aristocratic magnificence undermined. Thomas Carlyle did not suffer the same threat to his sense of identity because the value of his work was not called into question by his presence in the glittering halls; rather, it was confirmed. Jane's purposes, which for her were central to a rational philosophy of life, tended to destablize her social position since they drew her towards the female life of a servant rather than the female life of a lady. The female life of a lady horrified her more than the female life of a servant. At The Grange, allocated a vast suite of rooms all with carved and vaulted ceilings, she felt not raised but lowered and ill at ease, identified with all the 'idle restless people under the same roof with me, whose idleness and restlessness is so contagious!'[43]

Jane Carlyle's 'human needs' included the need to work and the need for relationships that answered to the 'inward life' on which in public she was 'bound to be silent'. The individual most fitted to meet those needs was her own personal servant; the servant provided her with work as well as doing work for her, for a servant always had to be supervised. As Lady Harriet's guest, Jane worried about what was going on at home with a sort of yearning anxiety which sometimes found specific expression: 'I shall not be sorry to get back to the training of my maid-of-all-work, and the rehabilitation of my house.' All middle-class women of the nineteenth century spent a portion of their time on that 'most fearful item of our female existence': the finding, training, and supervising of servants.[44] For Jane Carlyle it assumed a momentous importance. Her relations with her servants could be intense. Her vivid descriptions of their quirks of speech, unexpected reactions, incompetencies, and heroisms are among the best known and most widely quoted parts of her letters. As a result she has come to be identified as the type of that unattractive creature: the middle-class lady complaining about the servants.

The relation of mistress and maid within the household is a subject on which any light that has fallen has fallen patchily. Of all subjects it is one in which class loyalties tend to inhibit full exploration; and, as usual, there is the practical fact that far more is known of what middle-class mistresses felt about their servants than about what servants felt about their mistresses. Jane's desire to develop a continuing relationship with one loyal maid foundered again and again. Her maids came and went with bewildering speed: thirty-four women were employed, trained, and dismissed or lost for one reason or another during the thirty-two years she lived at Cheyne Row. There were plenty of reasons why servants should have found conditions at Cheyne Row unsatisfactory; the maid-of-all-work was only too literally a maid of all work. Without other servant help, she had to do all the hard, heavy, dirty work that a tall and dusty London house demanded. She had to pump water daily, carry coals and water up and down flights of stairs, scour, clean, cook, and wash in an often dark basement kitchen (where she also slept – sometimes having to wait in the scullery alongside while the master finished his pipe of an evening); she had to sweep, sew, blacken grates, rub down furniture, and keep the whole house free of bugs. As well as all the dirty work she was expected to do the clean work: answering the door to callers, bringing in the tea things, serving at table, fetching books for Thomas Carlyle.

From the early 1840s onwards, the Carlyles, while not rich, were comfortably off. They could easily have afforded two or three servants to manage so much labour, but Mrs Carlyle always preferred to have one. One servant, working hard, kept at bay associations of feminine idleness: two servants created a separate empire. One servant, living in the house, experienced a daily life much like her own, subject to the same master, an ally in a shared endeavour. Together they worked to prevent the 'rushing down of an orderly house to chaos!' which, if it was allowed to occur, would drive the mistress's 'not too patient husband raving mad!' This identification of purpose, located in work, was a source of potential bonding. So, too, was the similarity in their relation to the master. In each other's company every day, in sickness and in health, the relationship between mistress and maid was inevitably intimate. Jane certainly looked for more from her maids than ordinary household services. When she was sick for example:

> My maid is very kind when I am laid up ... she does my bidding quietly and accurately, and when I am very bad she bends over me in my bed as if I were a little child, and rubs her cheek on mine – once I found it wet with tears – one might think one's maid's tears could do little for a tearing headache, but they do comfort a little.

Like a caring mother or nurse, the maid was expected to do emotional work. Mrs Carlyle lived in hopes of finding a servant 'whom it may be possible to, not only train into my ways, but attach to me!'[45] This dual role contained the possibility that through nurturing and emotional support, such as women sought in each other in a private world apart from men, the maid-of-all-work might cross class lines to become something more to the mistress than a mere servant. By a logic of reversal, a mistress who lived like a servant might inspire a servant to dream of equality with a mistress much as that servant might dream of marrying out of the servant class. Like the wife invited to seek power through obedience towards a husband, so the servant was invited to explore the possibilities of power in docility and sympathy. The longest lasting of the Carlyle's servants, Helen Mitchell, had the ability to turn the relationship around – in a way that Leonore Davidoff in her article, 'Mastered for life: servant and wife in Victorian and Edwardian England', describes as typical of some servants and a device on their part for maintaining dignity.[46] Helen Mitchell made herself appear the stronger, the one to whom the mistress looked for emotional support and practical under-standing of the world. Jane could not dismiss her, Helen said, because she would not be able to survive without her. Unfortunately, it was Helen who could not survive the strain of her life and she became an alcoholic. Her addiction to drink, unlike her mistress's addiction to morphia and opium, made her an outcast. The end came in 1849 when the Carlyles returned from a visit and Helen opened the door to them dead drunk. She looked, Jane wrote:

> like a stage ghost very ill got up; blood spurting from her lips, her face whitened with chalk from the kitchen floor, her dark gown ditto, and wearing a smile of idiotic self-complacency. I thought Mr C. was going to kick his foot through her, when she tumbled down at his touch. If she had been his wife he certainly would have killed her on the spot; but his maid-

139

of-all-work he felt could not be got rid of without his being hanged for her.[47]

Helen was not cast off without a great deal of pain, but she was cast off. Soon after, she tried to commit suicide. Dragged from the river, she survived a few months before she died. Her epitaph was perhaps spoken by a young woman from Scotland who succeeded her and was appalled at the quantity of labour she was expected to do. She declared, 'no one woman living could do my work'. Jane retorted that one woman had indeed been doing it for many years and received the reply: 'Oh yes, there are women that like to make slaves of themselves, and her you had was of that sort, but I will never slave myself for anybody's pleasure.' Needless to say, that young woman did not last long. There was no sympathetic weeping from her over her mistress's headaches; she was identified instead as the cause of a cold which laid Jane up in bed – 'caught by doing most of her work myself, and exposing myself after quite an unusual fashion' – and damned with the judgement that her character would 'lead her to the streets some day'. For just as a lady could only move downwards towards a servant, so a servant's fall took her out of the category of woman and down to the level of a prostitute.[48]

The demands Jane made on her servants mirrored the demands Thomas made on her. Work, in both cases, served as the visible embodiment of love as well as a route to positive feminine valuation. A life of willing service testified to love and loyalty; identity and fulfilment lay in slavish self-devotion. Fanny, for example, finding her mistress in 'desperate agony' on the sofa with colic and headache from the smell of new paint, 'when all else failed, fairly took to crying and sobbing over me'. Fanny was 'willing to fly over the moon for me, and always making light of her discomforts'.[49] Fanny's tears were more welcome than all Lady Harriet's cool self-possessed grandeur. They were more welcome too, as will be seen, than Geraldine Jewsbury's equally free-flowing testimonials to affection. Neither Lady Harriet nor Geraldine was bound by her tears, as Fanny was bound by service and Jane was bound in a marriage premised on service. There was a peculiar comfort in having another woman make light of her discomforts. And conversely, a woman who attended to her own comforts, which in a servant meant not making a slave of herself if she could help it, was a moral as well as a material irritant. Charlotte Southam, 'a jewel of a creature', only 15 years old, 'kind and attentive', 'a good, biddable, clever little creature', was employed in 1858 and became in a very short space of time 'far more like an adopted child than a London maid-of-all-work'. She had 'so much good sense and reflection in her, that she is quite as good to talk with as most of the fine ladies that come about me'. By 1860 she was given notice. The child was distraught at her dismissal and begged to be taken back. Her tears were gratifying once more; Mrs Carlyle observed, 'she really loves both of us passionately'. Charlotte could have found any number of places, but she thought of Cheyne Row as her home. Eventually she was taken back on, 'bursting with ecstasy as she ran up and down the house, taking possession, as it were, of her old work'. Charlotte was a clever enough child to mature, however, and in less than a year she turned the tables on her employers by giving notice. She wanted a larger establishment that would enable her to 'better herself'. Now it was Jane's turn to be distraught:

> Oh, child! child! you have no idea of the disappointment, the heart-sorrow you caused me! I had set so much love on you, and so much hope! So much permanent good was to come out of our chance-relation for both of us! And all ending in a mere vulgar commonplace disruption betwixt *Mistress* and *Maid*!⁵⁰

The fiction that a servant was part of the family was a manipulative device mystifying the true nature of the power relations that obtained. At the same time, servants could and did become, after years of close domestic intercourse, more like family than employees. The remarkably intimate relations that obtained between mistress and maid, the blurring of practical and emotional services, surely account for some of the heat in middle and upper-class women's reactions to their servants when relations broke down. The worth of servants, it was widely understood, reflected the worth of the mistress who managed them. The tension between management and need in an emotionally unfulfilled mistress could prove too much for the most willing servant.

Charlotte Southam's sensible career move, her positive action to improve her future prospects, was regarded as a betrayal of love. It also indicated the advantages the servant had over the mistress, for a servant could change masters in a way a wife could not. Jane was pained that Charlotte did not want to be like her, and begged her to come back, 'to be housemaid, and *valet*, and *lady's maid*, and *friend* and *little Daughter*'. Charlotte preferred her distance. The power to leave of her own accord was the only reliable power the servant possessed.

The family bonds Jane, as mistress, introduced were fragile and could be disrupted at any moment by the master's peremptory dismissal. In 1835 a housemaid whom Thomas described as 'a mutinous Irish savage' put the dinner plates on the table in an aggressive and noisy way. She was, Carlyle wrote, 'instantaneously dismissed by me ("To your room at once; wages tomorrow morning; disappear.")'⁵¹ In 1853 Fanny, 'The best comfort I ever had', was 'exploded' by him for reasons unknown, but probably because she became too friendly with some of the Irish workmen working on the house. Thomas Carlyle was fussy, irascible, extremely demanding, had an uncontrollable temper – 'I look forward to his dinner-time', his wife wrote, 'with a sort of panic, which the event for the most part justifies' – and was ignorant of the volume and nature of the work involved in running a house.⁵² Whatever emotional support Jane derived from the woman who worked with and for her could never form part of the reason for keeping them: for her own benefits were subordinated to those of her husband for whom the house was run. Trying to protect them involved her in further degrees of self-sacrifice:

I should not be at all afraid that after a few weeks my new maid would do well enough if it weren't for Mr Cs frightful impatience with any new servant untrained to his ways, which would drive a woman out of the house with her hair on end if allowed to act directly upon her! So that I have to stand between them, and imitate in a small humble way the Roman soldier who gathered his arms full of the enemy's spears, and received them all into his own breast. It is this which makes a change of servants, even when for the better, a terror to me in prospect, and an agony in realisation – for the time[53]

*

Francis Jeffrey, writing about Felicia Hemans in the *Edinburgh Review* of 1829, observed that women's 'proper and natural business' was 'the practical regulation of private life, in all its bearings, affections and concerns'.[54] A woman knee-deep in books as Felicia Hemans always was, was not a woman equipped to regulate the private life that went on within her house. No critic was so cruel as to point out the symbolic fitness of Mrs Hemans's last years, which were spent in wandering from one lodging house to the next in Ireland. Homeless, sick, and lonely, with one faithful servant in tow, she reaped the consequences of incompetence at woman's 'proper and natural business': domestic management.

Like her friend Francis Jeffrey, Jane Carlyle placed the business of domestic management above the business of writing in her own scale of values. By doing so, she found a way of placing the concrete and practical above the abstract and evanescent. The work of running a household was visible, daily work. Soot, dust, grime, untrained servants, and disordered drawers were practical realities. In taking hold of them, with sometimes desperate intensity, Jane attempted to hold on to something firm and true in a world where middle-class women especially, but men too, could feel themselves drawn increasingly towards the idle, the shifting, and the false. Paramount among the temptations to idleness and falsity for women were the many varieties of literature, offering as they did an escape from domesticity. Though privately she wrote letters and read novels, publicly Jane dissociated herself from both activities. In doing so, she was attempting to distance herself from the negative, feminine meanings attached to them. Novel reading, novel writing, and letter writing existed within, not outside, the young lady sphere Jane thanked Thomas for rescuing her from. They indicated leisure, not work. Leisure indicated the over-stimulation of female feelings to that point beyond reason and truth in which artificiality, affectation, hypocrisy, and triviality prevailed. Jane confronted the artificiality of female life on a practical rather than on a theoretical level: by engaging in household work rather than by writing a treatise. She took pleasure in disconcerting those who did not understand her theoretical position with its unusual practical application and awareness of class insecurities:

I am lamed in the first two fingers of my right hand: burnt them very bad –

'with sealing-wax of course?' a lady asked me. The 'of course' was a piece of fine-lady logic, which I met by the startling avowal: 'No, with the handle of a brass pan, in preserving cranberries.' And now I shall be regarded by that lady with a sort of sacred horror, as a woman who has handled a brass pan. For, being Granchild of a mechanic, she shudders '*of course*' at anyone who has the use of his (or her) hands, or at least uses them.[55]

So much for ladylike letter writing; ladylike art went the same way. The Carlyles' Chelsea neighbour, Mrs Hunt, Leigh Hunt's dramatically unhousetrained wife, told that Jane had been busy painting, assumed that she had been at work on a portrait. She was gleefully disabused: ' "Oh! no," I told her, "something of more importance – a large wardrobe".'[56]

In using her hands to paint wardrobes and make jam rather than to paint portraits or write ladylike letters – or to follow letter writing along its historical line of development and pen a novel – Jane Carlyle set her face against the prevailing cultural current of her time. She did so with full consciousness. Other women sent her their manuscripts. There was Katie Macready, 'in breathless expectation' of a letter from Mrs Carlyle:

> to tell her what I think of a bulky MS., on which, after the fashion of young ladies of the present day, she has been employing her leisure, instead of on a *sampler*; and there is Miss Anderton (a young Actress and a good girl as can be) expecting 'a few lines' about a sensible little 'Article' of hers, entitled *Thoughts on Actresses* in the *Englishwoman's Journal*, which she sent me yesterday. (What a mercy you were married a good many years ago! You could hardly have succeeded in finding a wife *now* who had not published a book or contributed to a Journal, or at least had a MS in progress!)[57]

Mrs Carlyle, for her part, had 'three pairs of socks in my workbasket in immediate need of darning', and recalled another excellent housewife of her acquaintance who had been untempted by the lure of fame or intellectual endeavour:

> When I first saw Mrs Somerville (of mathematical celebrity), I was much struck with her exact likeness to Mrs Gilbert Burns – minus the geniality – and plus the feathers in her head! and I remember remarking to my Husband, that after all Mrs Burns was far the cleverer woman of the two, inasmuch as to bring up *twelve* children, as these young Burnses were brought up, and keep up such a comfortable house as Grant's Braes, *all on eighty pounds a year*, was a much more intricate problem than the Reconcilement of the Physical Sciences![58]

Just as, for Thomas, houses and bridges were more obviously worthy of their maker than books, so, for Jane, wardrobes and pots of jam, running households and managing the internal economy involved, were a source of self-esteem in a way that writing could not be. They were womanly occupations that could be given masculine valuation at a time when literary production, traditionally perceived as male, was acquiring negative feminine valuation. The hard work of domestic life guarded and guided the female spirit through the human 'facts of things'. It tended towards truth and reality in an age when sentimentality, the 'twin-sister to Cant' in Thomas Carlyle's revealing words, attained cultural supremacy. Hard domestic work was real. Thomas might write, 'The thing that *is*, what can be so wonderful; what, especially to us that *are*, can have such significance? Study Reality ... search out deeper and deeper *its* quite endless mystery';[59] but his life gave him fewer opportunities to probe the wondrous mysteries of the real than Jane's life gave her. The real world of noisy neighbours, building contractors, tax commissioners, servants, visiting devotees, editors, publishers, and legal bodies of various kinds were his to complain about and hers to deal with.

The artistry she employed on these occasions, functioning as it did in the service of the real, was not 'feminine' artistry, even though it took the usual form of that most feminine of the literary genres: the letter. Writing an elegant letter was a fine-lady skill on a par with keeping the back straight. Letters (and journals) were also the traditional outlet for female emotions; apparently spontaneous, supposedly artless, informal, inconsequential, breathless, grammarless, and delightfully senseless, they depicted the essential woman. They served as appropriate depositories for those overflowing feelings women were expected to have and men were not expected to be burdened by. Letters allowed women's thoughts to run on from accidentally profound observations on the meaning of life to the contents of a wardrobe in a manner judged typically feminine because lacking in control. Jane Carlyle's letters, on the other hand, were highly controlled exercises with often very specific purposes to fulfil. While Lady Harriet was so sublimely self-assured that she could listen to a parrot when it spoke at the same time as Thomas Carlyle, Jane Carlyle used her literary ability to put down a parrot that was proving a pest. Such usefulness could, according to Carlylean doctrine, place her writings in a superior category even than the master's – though to suggest as much was an outrageous reversal that had to be clothed in irony:

Perhaps I am a genius too, as well as my husband? Indeed, I really begin to think so – especially since yesterday that I wrote down a parrot! which was driving us quite desperate with its screechings. Some new neighbours, that came a month or two ago, brought with them an accumulation of all the things to be guarded against in a London neighbourhood, viz. a pianoforte, a lap-dog, and a parrot. The two first can be borne with, as they carry on the glory within doors; but the parrot, since the fine weather, has been holding forth in the garden under our open windows. Yesterday it was more than usually obstreperous – so that Carlyle at last fairly sprang to his feet, declaring that he could 'neither think nor live'. Now it was absolutely necessary that he should do both. So forthwith, on the inspiration of conjugal sympathy, I wrote a note to the parrot's mistress (name unknown), and in five minutes after Pretty Polly was carried within, and is now screeching from some subterranean depth whence she is hardly audible. Now if you will please recollect that, at Comely Bank, I also wrote down an old maid's house dog and an only son's pet bantam-cock, you will admit, I think, that my writings have not been in vain.[60]

Letters with such very specific functions played no small part in Jane Carlyle's life. In her 'character of Lion's Wife' she had 'writing enough to do, by constraint, for disgusting even a Duchess of Orleans'.[61] It was work and it was duty. The grand phraseology – 'genius', 'my writings have not been in vain' – is contrasted with an unspoken narrative self: 'just a housewife'. This narrative self worked to question the values attached to his genius and her genius by unsettling assumptions about both: neither the trivialities of the housewife's activities nor the eternal verities hammered out by the husband remain secure. Language that can write down a parrot can also write down a husband. Language that succeeds, through the gigantism of caricature, in reducing to mockable proportions a figure whom a whole culture agreed to venerate, is utilitarian language indeed.

Jane Carlyle's writing characteristically sought ends which could be measured in practical terms and had strictly limited objectives. The same could not be said of Thomas Carlyle's writings. Even he did not know quite what he was doing with Cromwell or why he was doing Frederick the Great. As far as his wife was concerned, his writings and his position in the particular cultural milieu of the early Victorian period had a tendency to lead, paradoxically, towards the very things he fulminated against: idleness and affectation. Consider the following, from a letter by Jane to John Sterling in 1837:

let no woman who values peace of soul ever dream of marrying an author! ... this I observe to you in confidence; should I state such a sentiment openly, I might happen to get myself torn in pieces by the host of my husband's lady admirers, who already, I suspect, think me too happy in not knowing my happiness. You cannot fancy what way he is making with the fair intellects here! There is Harriet Martineau presents him with her ear-trumpet with a pretty blushing air of coquetry, which would almost convince me out of belief in her identity! And Mrs Pierce Butler bolts in upon his studies, out of the atmosphere as it were, in riding-habit, cap and whip (but no shadow of a horse, only a carriage, the whip I suppose being to whip the cushions with, for the purpose of keeping her hand in practice) – my inexperienced Scotch domestic remaining entirely in a nonplus whether she had let in 'a leddy or a gentleman'! And then there is a young American beauty – such a beauty! 'snow and rose bloom' throughout, not as to clothes merely, but complexion also, large and soft, and without one idea, you would say, to rub upon another! And this charming creature publicly declares herself his 'ardent admirer', and I heard her with my own ears call out quite passionately at parting with him, 'Oh, Mr Carlyle, I want to see you to talk a long long time about – "Sartor"'! 'Sartor', of all things in this world! What could such a young lady have got to say about 'Sartor', can you imagine? And Mrs Marsh, the moving authoress of the 'Old Man's Tales', reads 'Sartor' when she is ill in bed; from which one thing at least may be clearly inferred, that her illness is not of the head. In short, my dear friend, the singular author of 'Sartor', appears to me at this moment to be in a perilous position, inasmuch as (with the innocence of a sucking dove to outward appearance) he is leading honourable women, not a few, entirely off their feet. And who can say that he will keep his own? After all, in sober earnest, is it not curious that my husband's writings should be only completely understood and adequately appreciated by women and mad people? I do not know very well what to infer from the fact.[62]

Sharing a scorn for the vapidities of fine-lady life, the Carlyles also shared a scorn for the fashionable worship of genius such as Thomas Carlyle was deemed to embody. Once more, as in the days of Dugald Gilchrist and all the other misguided young men who came to court her, Mrs Carlyle retained her reason while those about her were losing theirs; only this time, the figures overwhelmed by inappropriate emotions were intellectual ladies and a leading philosopher. The narrative voice adopted in this account, while confessedly a woman and a wife, is a voice of great authority; a voice which reached out to claim its portion of male privilege, including the privilege of speaking on terms of easy familiarity with a cultivated and interesting man like John Sterling, her husband's friend. To set herself at a mocking distance from Thomas's female followers, Jane made use of conventional anti-woman prejudices, deploying familiar stereotypes: the confirmed spinster blushing and coquetting; the aggressive he-woman who looks more like a man; the beauty who must be empty-headed. The intellectual origins of the women's interest in Thomas Carlyle, as a thinker rather than as a man, and consequently *their* dignity as thinkers, are lost. Apart from the unknown American, the women Jane Carlyle cited were all writers of distinction: Mrs Pierce Butler being the actress Fanny Kemble, who had left her American husband after a fierce disagreement between them over her insistence on publishing an attack on his family's slave-owning connections. The women are presented, however, as physical beings only, their impulses reduced to uncontrollable sexual passion: ardour and passionateness, blushings and bed, whips and rubbings. That they were first and foremost working women, women who had an interest in Carlyle's thinking that derived from their own intellectual seriousness, does not form part of the comic description. That it could be so easily removed had much to do with the reluctance on everybody's part to consider women who wrote as women who worked.

Jane Carlyle's own writing retained, throughout her life, its close connection to the domestic work which was always given priority. Domestic labour helped shape the form in which she wrote – the private letter – as well as providing a good part of the subject matter. Like housework, that daily task of preventing an orderly house running to chaos, so letters, detailing the coming and going of every day, were a means of imposing order on events always tending towards chaos. Neither Jane nor Thomas was casual about letter writing. Between them they sustained a huge correspondence, and when apart expected to be in touch with each other – at length – daily. A missed letter could create panic and collapse. The daily letter was the assurance that all was in order in the emotional world; while its content might relate news of ordering the disorder of the domestic scene. For both the Carlyles, letter writing was both an extension of work and a respite from work: his work of writing found its way into his letters, as her work of housework provided a deal of hers. Letter writing was fitted in around the more serious work of the day. In a letter, perplexities, sorrows, exhaustions, hysterias, and despairs could be given a solidity, acquire a distance, that lent strength to the letter writer who was, for the greater part of the day, a book writer or housekeeper.

But letter writing had a different meaning for women, whether they were housekeepers or book writers, than it had for men. Passionate epistolatory female friendships were a recognized genre with a literary as well as a social history. In Rousseau's *La Nouvelle Heloise*, which Jane had read with enthusiasm as a young woman, the central emotional relationship is the one between the two women and it exists in their letters to each other. When Geraldine Jewsbury launched, after one or two brief meetings, into passionate epistolary declarations of love for Jane, she was obeying a literary impulse as well as an emotional one and Jane recognized it as such. Geraldine's lavish expressions of emotion were interpreted by Mrs Carlyle as bad writing rather than anything else, and resisted as she would resist a bad novel. She had, in any case, a horror of letters 'all about emotions' or 'all about feelings' – two expressions much in use in the Carlyle ménage to signal amused contempt. A glance at the *Collected Letters of Thomas and Jane Welsh Carlyle* will show at once that of the two, Thomas was far more at ease in expressing emotion and communicating feeling in a letter than Jane. Temperament contributed to this, but the facts of gender expectations and their embodiment in literary genres were also relevant. Jane Carlyle's dislike of letters 'all about feelings' reflected her unease with the debased currency of such speech between women. Women, defined as creatures of feeling not thought, proved their womanliness in letters 'all about feelings'. Claiming to feel a great deal was a way of claiming to be womanly. Confinement to the enclosed world of feeling was thus brought full circle, and in the airlessness of such life whatever truth there was in feeling was liable to convert into sentimentality. Women writers were faced with the fact that both letters and the novel, closely linked as they were, were associated with women and with the debasement of true feeling into sentimentality which was seen as woman's special contribution.

Jane Carlyle compared Lady Harriet Baring to 'our distinguished authoresses' not only in terms of her intellectual capacity – which she judged to exceed everyone's – but also in terms of her emotional restraint. The two were, in any case, almost synonymous: she was 'the only woman of genius I have found amongst all our pretenders to it' largely because she was not sentimental and she did not use her intellect to write. Similarly, Thomas placed Jane above 'all the

147

Sands and *Eliots* and "celebrated scribbling women" that have strutted over the world in my time' because, unlike them, she did not scribble for the public. In other words, she was not misled by false emotion into demeaning her intellect, or misled by a certain amount of intellect into exaggerated and debased emotion. Any woman who reached out to address the public had first to leap the hurdle of her assumed affectation. The phrase 'woman of genius' was well established by the 1840s as a pejorative term indicating a woman who demanded more attention than was good for her. Thomas Carlyle used it to describe his mother-in-law, a woman he had very little patience with, telling his wife: 'Your mother, my Dear, has narrowly missed being a woman of genius.'[63]

The curious thing about the stereotype of the woman writer was the degree to which it denied the qualities which were essential to the pursuit of the trade. Few books were written without hard work, some intellect, and some rational organizing of emotional experiences; but the stereotype of the woman writer depicted her as idle, foolish, and irrational. Thomas Carlyle, for instance, soon after settling in London in 1834, reported on the literary scene as follows:

> We have also seen several 'celebrated women' of the literary sort; but felt small longing to see more of them. The world indeed is wide enough for all ... meanwhile, if poor Mrs Feather-brain, Irrational All-for-Glory and Company are walking in the western quarter, we shall do it all the better by keeping ourselves in the eastern.[64]

Geraldine Jewsbury was no featherbrain, nor was she Irrational All-for-Glory; but casual readers of Carlyle biography might be forgiven for retaining just such an impression of her. They would learn that she was a 'flimsy tatter of a creature'; a 'most gossiping and romancing person'; a 'fluff of feathers'; an 'ill-natured old maid'. Geraldine herself would not have been surprised: she was 'used to people speaking of me with a sort of half-contemptuous smile'.[65] Some of that contempt was probably for her provincial origins, and much of it because she could never quite pull off a properly respectable, suitably restrained, female manner since her heart was not in it: 'after all', as she said, 'there is something in "respectability" that nobody can heartily sympathise with.'[66] Respectability was 'an antiseptic principle' that led away from 'human nature' rather than more deeply into its heart. In the controversy which followed the publication of Froude's biography of Thomas Carlyle and his memoir of Jane Carlyle, Geraldine provided a convenient scapegoat. She had furnished Froude with some of the anecdotes which placed Thomas Carlyle in a particularly bad light – suggestions that he was physically violent towards his wife, the hint that he was sexually impotent – and her capacity to tell the simple truth was easily called into question by referring to her occupation: she was a novelist; her brain teemed with 'romance' and 'half-formed plots and novels'; she was 'a sentimentalist'. Supporters of Thomas Carlyle (and of men's dignity generally) drew on stereotypes of the unmarried woman and the writer to discredit Geraldine. For G.M. Gould, whose emotions got the better of him in his psychoanalytic study of the Carlyles, *Biographic Clinics*, Geraldine Jewsbury was 'the ludicrous Geraldine':

> Witness this disappointed and prurient maiden lady rush to the unspeakable Froude and filling his ears with her idiotic psychosexual interpretation of a careless remark of Mrs Carlyle's early days. One may doubt if any such remark was ever made by her. Geraldine's fertile imagination needed no facts to build a whole world of misrepresentation upon.[67]

No more so, indeed, than men's imaginations needed any facts upon which to build a whole history of misrepresentation of women.

As a writer, too, Geraldine has been badly served by posterity. Her novels have long been out of print, her articles entombed in old volumes of the periodicals of the day, and even her role as a publisher's reader in the 1860s and 1870s, about which Jeanne Rosenmayer published an interesting article in 1973, seems to show her in a rather negative light. In 1935, when a sympathetic biography was published, the biographer, in her introduction, revealed the depth of hostility that still existed towards Geraldine Jewsbury. An unknown correspondent had taken the trouble to inform Susanne Howe that she 'had much better not write a life of Geraldine Jewsbury. She would be quite forgotten today but for her friendship with the Carlyles.' The note went on to add: 'Mrs Ireland's edition of her letters does all that need be done to preserve the memory of an entirely unimportant person.' When the book nevertheless appeared, reproof became reprimand. An anonymous reviewer for the *Times Literary Supplement* evidently agreed with Ms Howe's correspondent – might have been the same person? – and using the same language raged at the resuscitation of so '*entirely* unimportant' a person: she deserved no biography, she had 'made no lasting impression, socially, sociologically, or in literature'.[68]

Well, but she certainly managed to irritate, even beyond the grave. Jane Carlyle had a devoted following of men who loved her for her wit and warmth, her straightforwardness, and, not a little, her suffering, which, deriving as much of it did from the difficulties of living with her husband, was properly womanly; Geraldine's men had no such sense of security. She spattered her conversation and her books with such remarks as, 'All men are unreasonable – it is their normal state.' Her novels, as Edmund Mercer pointed out in 1898 in the *Manchester Quarterly*, were 'written for women and were mainly about women'.[69]

Other factors have worked against Geraldine. Her honourable actions in destroying Jane Carlyle's letters destroyed what was probably the best source for understanding the positive qualities the older woman found in her and which enabled her to write to her freely. More significant still was Geraldine's move to London in 1854. Living round the corner, there was no more need of letters to keep up communication. Jane Carlyle's journal of 1855–6 with its matter-of-fact, almost daily recording of outings with Geraldine, visits to other houses in Geraldine's company, Geraldine's presence amongst other guests at Cheyne Row, Geraldine's calls once and sometimes twice a day, make it clear that the two women were in each other's company constantly. Mrs Carlyle's excitement in 1854, when she told her Scottish friend Mrs Russell that 'the most intimate friend I have in the whole world ... has decided to come and live near me for good. ... It will be a real gain to have a woman I like, so near', had modulated by 1856 into an easy acceptance of Geraldine's presence as a part of daily life.[70] There is little about her in Jane's letters to other friends during this period. This paucity of comment is in marked contrast to the early days of the relationship, in the 1840s, when Jane's letters, especially those to the Welsh cousins, were full of Geraldine's doings and Geraldine's outrages. Even in the 1840s, that time of blistering sarcasms at the expense of this 'woman of genius', one has to remind oneself that Jane chose to spend a good deal of time with Geraldine, either at Manchester or at the Paulet's house at Seaforth. Seaforth became, for a few years at the latter part of that decade, 'a sort of house of refuge for me'; but Manchester was a better refuge still. The pain of her mother's death in 1842 made Scotland a country Jane Carlyle dared not enter for many years; Manchester and Liverpool between them provided substitute family homes. Geraldine's 'quiet kindness', her 'wise silent sympathy and unwearied assiduity', were beyond criticism in her own home. Geraldine was an efficient housekeeper, and her brother Frank no less willing than she to give hospitality to literary luminaries. They were 'strangers who have treated me like the dearest of sisters'. And they were like mothers:

> The stillness, the good order, the modest elegance of this bright little half-town, half-country house feels like a sort of cradle into which my good angel has laid me for a while to lie still and make believe to sleep.[71]

Visits to Manchester were not only about being cradled and rocked. In 1846, having meant to stay two days, Jane found herself taken on a round of visits to foundries, warehouses, factories, and mills that was so fascinating she stayed two weeks: 'day after day has passed for me in going up and down in "hoists" and thro forests of machinery.'[72] Like that indefatigable sightseer Dorothy Wordsworth, who stayed as Maria Jane Jewsbury's guest in 1828, Jane found the Jewsbury family, with their many connections among Manchester's industrial and trading families, as well as its literary and intellectual circles, ideal hosts. They were workers, not dilettantes. The men were in business; the women – both Maria Jane and Geraldine – ran households in which the mercantile principle had always dominated. Manchester, wreathed perpetually in smoke and pulsating with noise, stridently announced the pre-eminence of work. 'No person can for a moment mistake the character of the town,' according to one visitor; 'it is essentially a place of business, where pleasure is unknown as a pursuit, and amusements scarcely rank as secondary considerations.' The people of Manchester were marked by 'the look of thought and the step of haste'.[73] Dressing and undressing three times a day was not a feature of life in Geraldine's house and never had been: the women were as businesslike about their writing as the men were about trade. For Jane Carlyle, Manchester outlasted Liverpool as a place of refuge, not only because Jane's friendship with Geraldine outlasted her friendship with Elizabeth Paulet, but also because Manchester provided what neither Sea-forth nor Maryland St, the Liverpool home of Jane's Welsh cousins, provided: the restful ambience of businesslike and purposeful work. For a woman at war with womanly idleness, and ever at risk of being defined by its terms, that was no insignificant feature. Manchester might be smoggy, with an atmosphere 'so thick that one feels to put it aside with one's nose – oh, so thick, and damp, and dirty!' but its people, like the inventor Whitworth or the radical Samuel Bamford, were straightforward, unaffected, purpose-oriented. They were people who knew what they were about and were 'able and willing to give a straightforward account of it'. Whitworth might not be able to invent an epigram to save his life, but talking to him Jane Carlyle felt herself to be 'talking with a *real live man*, to my taste worth any number of the Wits "that go about"'. Just as the material annoyances of having workmen in the house could be borne because she found a satisfaction in supervising them far profounder than in 'talking *"wits"* in my white silk gown with feathers on my head, and *soirees* at Bath House, and all that sort of thing', so too the clamour of Manchester going about its business was a solace rather than an irritation. In 1851 Geraldine received the ultimate testi-monial, when Jane wrote to Thomas from Geraldine's house: 'I don't remember ever in my life before to have stayed a whole month in anybody's house without ever once wishing to be away: Geraldine says, "My dear, it is a fact that speaks volumes." '[74]

Facts that speak volumes, however, are not always the ones to receive closest attention. The Geraldine who lives most vividly in Jane's letters is the Geraldine of misdirected sentiment and excessive emotion, a Geraldine who was 'always . . . dropping hot tears on my hands' and declaring everlasting friendship out of her 'natural superabundance of emotion'. This Geraldine was drawn according to two prevailing stereotypes: that of the empty-headed 'fluff of feathers', the sexually and socially uncontrollable, circulating library female novelist; and that of the rabid, man-chasing spinster. What these stereotypes shared, and what together they reinforced, were a view of women generally and Geraldine in particular as emotionally untrustworthy, especially towards other women. Jane distrusted the vehemence of Geraldine's affection, not least because Geraldine was so unstopp-ably articulate in expressing and analysing, as well as enjoying, her feelings. She talked fast and emphatically and, when apart from Jane, she wrote 'prodigiously long letters, on such subjects as "the passion of *love* as it differs in Men from Women!!"' Geraldine's pleasure in sentimental excess, her vibrant abandonment to tears as well as laugher, were a form of self-possession as puzzling to Jane Carlyle as Lady Harriet Baring's very different, distinctly unemotional self-pos-session. More than once, Jane compared the two women. Lady Harriet, she observed,

rails at *sentiment* and never puts any into her *words*, but it peeps out often enough in her *actions*. She would not put an *affectionate* sentence in her letters for the world but she will put *violets* – leaves of the *flowers one likes* –

sometimes sends me envelopes by post containing nothing else!! What a contrast I often think betwixt that woman and Geraldine! the opposite poles of woman nature![75]

Geraldine spoke her love; Lady Harriet

> never says to anyone that she likes them – she goes upon *the silent system* as to all the thoughts of her *heart* – it is only the thoughts of her *head* which she gives one the benefit of – and so she has never *said* what one could call a *kind* word to *me* – but she proves by all her behaviour that she is rather fond of me – the mere fact of her having *kissed* me at parting and meeting again proves more affection for me than twenty reams of protestation from a Geraldine would do – for her Ladyship is *sincere* to death.[76]

Geraldine, on the other hand, was not; or so Jane Carlyle said. Geraldine, the professional woman of letters, was insincere in a way that Lady Harriet Baring, who never wrote a book, was not; her insincerity was part and parcel of her existence as a writer. It was 'her besetting weakness by nature – and her trade of Novelist has aggravated it – the *desire of feeling and producing violent emotions*'. As a sick room nurse, Geraldine, when asked for a glass of water,

> would spill the half of it by the way, and in compensation would *drop tears on my hand*, and assure me I was 'sure to die!' – and then fall to kissing me *wildly* (when I was perhaps in an interval of retching perfectly *hating* to be kissed) and bursting out into passionate sobs! (which of course did not prevent her from going out into company half an hour after, and being the life of it!)[77]

It was not so much the spilled water in the sick room that upset Jane Carlyle, as Geraldine's Jewsbury's capacity to go out and live her life in a way that suited her. Geraldine had begun by writing her way into Thomas Carlyle's good opinion. Like her sister before her, she wanted to sit at the feet of the master and grow, learning from the free ungendered exchange of intellect. She had a sense of her own purposes, partly derived from her unusual upbringing, and some familiarity with literary society. When she was first invited to stay with the Carlyles, in 1843, somewhat as a poor little provincial condescended to by those whose days of obscurity were behind them, her purposefulness of self was too strong for her hosts. Because she was not intimidated, she seemed brash; because she knew what she wanted, she seemed insincere. Like Maria Jane at Rydal Mount, Geraldine, having been invited by Thomas (though Jane took care not to reveal that the invitation originated from him), was faced with the task of finding a balance between that ambition and individuality which led her outwards – into argument, passion, strong language, intensity, and vigorous, determined action like going to stay with a well-known writer and his wife whom in real terms she personally knew hardly at all – and all their opposites which may be simply expressed as: appropriately decorous female behaviour.

Though Thomas Carlyle had not, like William Wordsworth, surrounded himself with a retinue of female dependents, he was no less buttressed by friends and family, none of whom appreciated Geraldine's intrusion. Geraldine, according to Jane, did 'no execution on either man woman or child here. No living soul takes to her – several, Mazzini, Elizabeth, Darwin testify a sort of *sacred horror* of her.'[78] The contrast between Geraldine's ability to take care of herself and the apparent insincerity of her speech was too much for Jane:

all the mornings she scribbles letters on her knees – and all the evenings she lies on the sofa and sleeps! I speak little with her – for her speech is so extremely insincere that I feel in our dialogues always as if we were acting in a play – and as we are not going to get either money or praise for it and not being myself an amateur of play-acting I prefer considerably good honest *silence*.[79]

In silence there was what in her opinion Geraldine lacked: some 'basis of truth'. The horrors Geraldine aroused amongst innocent literary people, émigré revolutionary figures, and sophisticated society types centred on her independence and her talk: not so much for its content as its quantity. Garnier, a 'wildly independent' German refugee friend of the Carlyles who later went mad, visiting one evening during Geraldine's first stay when all three occupants of the drawing room were stretched out fast asleep – Thomas having the previous day finished *Past and Present* and the women having spent the day visiting the Chinese exhibition – could not get over his astonishment at Geraldine. Jane described the scene and Geraldine's part in it:

Geraldine makes herself a bed with the *priedieu*-chair and a sofa cushion and the hearth rug – *every day* after dinner – and sleeps like a person under the influence of liquor – or drugs – a singular phasis of a young lady. Yesterday evening she was stretched out and sound as usual! – Into this enchanted looking room walked Garnier – considerably distracted. Singling out me to catechise he asked 'Why do you *tender* yourself in this way? or are you really not well?' Geraldine who had got on her end, and always bursts out of sleep into volubility – poured forth a torrent of words about 'the poor creature having been to that confounded Chinese exhibition, etc etc.' – but she was cut short by Garnier's uplifting his two hands, and saying to me with an affectation of dismay – 'Oh my goodness! how fast that lady does talk! it is quite impossible for me to follow her! Mrs Carlyle is she a relation of yours?' She pretended to be vastly amused – and vastly amused with the quizzing which he carried on the whole evening – but I believe she had her own private misgiving about it![80]

Altogether, Geraldine's first visit to the Carlyles, unlike her sister's first visit to the Wordsworths, was not a success as far as the hosts were concerned. She had been invited for two or three weeks and stayed, in spite of Jane's increasingly cold, indeed what she herself called 'repulsive', behaviour towards her, for five.

The visit coincided with the early days of Thomas Carlyle's involvement with Lady Harriet, and if he was not at Bath House in the evenings he contrived to be in his study. About Lady Harriet, as about everything else, Geraldine was forthright and outspoken: she was 'scandalized'. Her sympathy for Jane as a neglected wife flowed as freely as her tears. It was not a sympathy that was welcomed at that early stage.

Geraldine's ability to take care of herself, combined as it was with a tendency to talk about love and religion, and an appearance which was still youthful enough, at 30, to create a feeling of unease in drawing rooms, was interpreted in sexual ways. The 'sacred horror' was a sexual horror. She was unaccompanied, having neither mother nor master. Brimful of intellectual as well as emotional energy, her passionate engagement in discussion, her eagerness for experience, were understood as the indiscriminate desire to catch a man; that is to say, to offer herself sexually. The truth was, however, that Geraldine knew more thoroughly than most women how men and marriage signalled difficulties and danger for women and writing.

6

THE COMFORTS OF OTHERS

Why do women marry? God knows, unless it be that ... they do not find scope enough for their genius and qualities in an easy life.

Jane Carlyle[1]

I must do her the justice to recount that she uttered the terrible *'obey'*, with edifying distinctness.

Harriett Hughes[2]

Why did Maria Jane Jewsbury marry the Revd William K. Fletcher? By 1832 she had passed the all-important age of 30 which marked the divide between an unmarried woman and an old maid. She had experienced a life of freedom, autonomy, and achievement. No longer bound by her father's babies, she could travel the length of the country carrying letters of introduction to literary people, secure in the knowledge that her own fame as well as her association with leading literary figures would gain her entry to most of the circles that interested her. In the summer of 1830, for instance, she spent a few months in London and enjoyed herself so much that she made plans to leave the 'spiteful little town' of Manchester, of which she had grown weary 'beyond expression', and, as she told Dorothy Wordsworth,

> certainly (if all be well) settle there for some months next year – I can make more money with less labour – and I like London – and when tired of it, I can go to the country, which is a kind of featherbed for both body and mind!!!!!! ... I know in your heart you think my moral character done for but frankly I feel much improved by my Town life.[3]

Some of that feeling of improvement must have been associated with the significant fact that she had 'had more *literary* offers made me than I well know what to do with'. Working hard, receiving recognition, she was healthy and happy. Her days were filled with 'what suits me best – occupation, occupation from 7 in the morning till 9 at night'. Her father seems to have offered no opposition to the fact that both his daughters were fending for themselves in London. Geraldine, having had the benefit of London masters to polish up the education she had

155

received from the Misses Darby, possessed, in her sister's opinion, the 'capability of gaining a salary' and Maria Jane had begun to enquire amongst her contacts for a family with 'one or two *little* girls – this is my ambition for her – in a genteel, kind, *good* family'. Her only doubt was that Geraldine was 'too pretty and young' for some potential employers; but 'she draws now in a masterly style – dances – is a tolerable Italian and excellent French scholar'.

All this while, however, William Fletcher had been hanging around. Maria Jane had known him since at least 1826, for she mentioned him in a letter to Geraldine, urging secrecy on her as their father did not approve. He was clearly the model for Cecil in 'The History of an Enthusiast' – the young man with so 'dreadfully healthy' a mind that he could not contemplate the notion of taking a distinguished woman to wife. By the beginning of 1831 Fletcher had nevertheless proposed and been rejected. In March 1831, for reasons which are not easy to discover, Maria Jane tentatively took him back. She announced her astonishing news to Dora in a letter from which it is singularly difficult to form any impression at all of her fiancé:

And now, dear Dora, prepare for a surprise, and do not scream out about it, for it is a secret known to few – and not in a train to be proclaimed just yet. The tone of my late letters has been harassed and unhappy – *now* I may tell you the reason. I was called on to decide whether I would be married or not. I found it a harder matter than I expected – because I was not in love – but in a very morally prudential state of mind. My gentleman has not had very fine times of it, seeing that in the last three months he has been refused – recalled – and is now only accepted subject to a twelvemonths probation, and the fulfilment of certain conditions. He has my best wishes for his success – for in addition to having my judgment and esteem on his side, I am now free to own to *you* (not to him) that he has a growing interest in my affections, but the affections of a woman of thirty who has suffered as I have, are not so easily got hold of as those of unsuspecting and romantic seventeen. And who is he? Nobody you ever heard me mention – none of my flirts – none of my favorites – none of my shewy, talking, talked about appendages – nobody in London – nobody who paints, or (Thank Providence) who edits, or who says smart things, – but one who *was* a smoker, but flung away cigars long before he came and asked me to think about him – who *was* a sloven, but is trying his very best to be one no longer – and who has promised to make a sacrifice of his present tailor and take lessons in tying his cravat like a gentleman – one who in point of worth is gold; in point of mind silver; in point of manners iron – but in nothing pinchbeck – one who loves me as strong, rugged, yet noble natures only love when they break up under the influence of an emotion that they have never made a plaything of – one who wants a great deal of polishing and softening and mellowing, but gives promise of all I could ultimately love truly and lean upon safely – one, who, *if* he realise his own temporal prospects, and satisfy my moral requirements – I shall certainly feel bound in honour and inclination to marry, some time after his probation is ended...

But as my friend is only a good clergyman, and my father had set his heart on somebody very grand, forgetting that grand people do not take fancies to tradesmen's daughters – and as he had never contemplated the possibility of 'my daughter Jane' – arrived at thirty, thinking of settling and being maintained instead of having to maintain herself – he *has been* very angry, and *is now* very wretched – too wretched to be reasonable. He claims to be the judge of the kind of person to make me happy, and as I have gainsaid that, he takes refuge in lamenting how I can possibly think of leaving him – and the children – forgetting that the children have already had the best of me – and that Geraldine is nearly nineteen.

Thomas Jewsbury was not the only one to be unimpressed by Maria Jane's choice. Fletcher was, at the very least, mediocre by comparison with the woman who had begun, after some five years' acquaintance, to feel 'bound in honour and inclination' to marry him; Maria Jane's friends doubted that the marriage would come off. They did not believe she would want to give up her wandering habits: 'they doubt my power of ceasing to be ambitious, of being satisfied with a life of "homeborn happiness" '; nor did they believe

that I am so far advanced in goodness as to *prefer* the solid to the sparkling – but I *am* – *the world is too strong for me* – literary life poisons my moral being, at once by its blandishments and cares – 'Me this / Unchartered freedom tires'.

Maria Jane defended herself against the combined opposition of father and friends by reiterating that in making her decision, 'Reason led my feelings, not my feelings my Reason'. She was not, she repeated, 'in love'. In place of love she had, in the words of her letter to Dora, a 'very morally prudential frame of mind'. By this she seems to have meant: financially prudential. Though Fletcher had no private income, he was keen to take up a chaplaincy post abroad. Maria Jane favoured Italy, but when India seemed likely by November 1831, she was not discouraged: 'an East India Company's chaplaincy is a provision for life' and was 'not to be refused in these days'. Faced with the opportunity to hand on the care of father (and Geraldine, in 1831, was the same age Maria Jane had been when she became responsible for her father's household), given the chance to relax the pace of her own bread and butter writing, and offered the prospect of exciting travel, Maria Jane's reason told her to marry. In Fletcher, if he managed to get one of the chaplaincies he was hoping for, she had 'the palpable benefit of a certain and handsome income'. That was no small consideration. Maria Jane Jewsbury might have been supporting herself successfully, but she had ever in her mind the example of Mrs Hemans. Felicia Hemans's capacity to earn money had never failed her, and yet her life after 1828 was one of increasing loneliness, stress, and isolation which she herself attributed to the absence of male support and protection. Reduced to following her brother to Ireland in the hope of finding family and male protection – a move that could not on any account be considered a success – her reclusive habits were represented as vain and egotistical withdrawal in Dublin where the sociable Lady Morgan at that time reigned supreme. Her fate did not suggest that singleness in a woman could ever be an advantage, even when combined with worldly success.

Maria Jane's decision to marry William Fletcher was nevertheless fraught with doubt, and the eighteen months that elapsed between putting him on probation in March 1831 and the marriage in August 1832 were not happy months. Thomas Jewsbury was the problem Maria Jane spoke about. She dreaded receiving his letters and delayed going home in March because she did not have the strength to face him. But she was determined to make her own decision:

> If I alter my mind during the twelvemonth it shall be from personal reasons, and not because I am desired to do so. I do greatly wish, however, he would be reasonable – since I doubt my own power of resisting the wear and tear of miserable looks. *I am a coward.*

Those friends who would were urged to write to her father in support of William Fletcher; Dora, especially, was asked to ask *her* father to give his sanction to the engagement for his approval would carry much weight.

By August 1831 Maria Jane was sick in body and mind with 'a certain sickness of heart which says "of what use is it!" to everything that is not an absolute necessity'. Thomas Jewsbury, also ill – 'not merely ailing, but failing' – was persisting in his opposition to Fletcher. He refused to allow the young man into the house where Maria Jane might receive him 'in peace and quietness', and she was 'obliged to go elsewhere for the purpose of being visited by the man I am to spend my future life with. A pleasant look out for all parties.' All that winter she was depressed and ill. She hardly went out. It was uncertain whether Fletcher would get any of the posts he had been hoping for. In April 1832 Maria Jane went to stay with the Chorleys in Liverpool to recuperate after what she called 'half a year's imprisonment, and anxiety (yet continued) which wears one as water wears away a stone'. Her spirits were 'worn to the bone' – so much so, she admitted, that 'had I foreseen all that I must undergo, no man, and no man's merits, should have persuaded me to meditate what I have meditated'.

The problem she did not speak about, and which was potentially far more serious, was the crisis in her identity as a writer. In 1832 she wrote a long, despondent letter to Mrs Hemans, in which she looked back over her literary career, admitting that she had 'not been unsuccessful' but at the same time announcing her determination not to write another book for some years. She was disgusted with most of what she had written – 'I would gladly burn almost everything I ever wrote' – and still more disgusted with anything new she tried to write: 'I cannot write a line to please myself':

I have done nothing to live, and what I have yet done must pass away with a thousand other blossoms, the growth, the beauty, and oblivion of a day. The powers which I feel, and of which I have given promise, may mature, may stamp themselves in act; but the spirit of despondency is strong upon the future exile, and I fear they never will.

Facing the prospect of marriage, Maria Jane felt remorseful, dissatisfied with herself, haunted by 'a morbid state of feeling', and preoccupied by thoughts of death. Death had always been a favourite subject of conversation between herself and Mrs Hemans; now she told her:

In the best of everything I have done you will find one leading idea – Death; all thoughts, all images, all contrasts of thoughts and images, are derived from living much in the valley of that shadow; from having learned life rather in the vicissitudes of man than woman; from the mind being Hebraic.

Life, the new life she faced, made her want to lie down like a tired child and weep. She had no energy for it. All she could muster was 'timidity and sadness'.[4]

In this mood of crippling self-doubt and depression, Maria Jane Jewsbury married William K. Fletcher. The marriage took place on 1 August 1832 and was conducted by Harriett Hughes's husband. Geraldine was a bridesmaid. Thomas Jewsbury travelled to Wales for the wedding. Harriett Hughes wrote an account of the wedding for Dora, including the suggestive detail:

Our dear friend was much affected, (as indeed were we all,) during the ceremony, but not so much as to cause the slightest interruption or difficulty, and I must do her the justice to recount that she uttered the terrible *'obey'*, with edifying distinctness.

Exactly seven years earlier, on 1 August 1825, Maria Jane had signed and dated her initials beneath the last word of the afterword to *Phantasmagoria* and sent her first book out to the world. It is hard to believe that she chose her wedding date unthinkingly or unknowingly.

Eleven days after the wedding, after a gap of some six months, the fourth and final piece in the series, *On Modern Female Cultivation*, appeared in the *Athenaeum*. The first three had all appeared in February of that year. Sombre in tone, this last piece reflected the months of depression that had preceded the wedding and the uncertainty about her future role that had undermined Maria Jane's energies. Taking for her subject the grave question of what to do with educated women, Maria Jane represented such women as a social problem; the energies of an educated woman lacked adequate outlets, while authorship, the 'only accredited vent for a woman's intellect', although it removed the evil of empty days, brought far worse evils along with it. It was neither wisdom nor kindness, Maria Jane argued, much as she had argued in *Letters to the Young*, to encourage a clever girl to express herself in writing. It was far wiser to discourage her. Gifted women

159

needed to be restrained if problems were to be avoided; they needed not the 'spur' but the 'rein'. The female intellect was an inconvenience and a danger, leading to 'strange and troublesome' habits unless it was managed wisely. The key words throughout the article were: duty, influence, and management. The conclusion of the article was that the very best thing for a woman to be was a listener and a reader, rather than a talker and a writer. For the 'enjoyers of literature, in opposition to the producers', have 'all the good of cultivation and none of the evil'. Women who were happy were those women who were 'free from ambition' and interested in other people's minds rather than their own. They enjoyed 'collateral triumphs' not personal triumphs. The triumphs they shared were the triumphs, of course, of men:

> How few have been the distinguished men who have not acknowledged that their deepest obligations have, at some time or other, been to a wife, a sister, or, above all, a mother! Let the mind of every girl, especially of every girl of talent, be sedulously directed to this cheering view of female influence.

Girls should be taught that 'a passion for self-aggrandizement deteriorates mind, and alloys amiability'; that happiness may be found if literature is a 'garnish' to life, not its 'food', and if they value knowledge but 'never dream of celebrity'.[5]

The pain Maria Jane's celebrity had caused William Fletcher became, through wifely and womanly processes, Maria Jane's pain. His difficulties of adaptation to a life lived alongside a woman of high achievement and considerable experience, became her difficulties. Within her lay all the problem and all the solution. The transformation of Maria Jane Jewsbury into Mrs William K. Fletcher may be read in this fourth article on the subject of women's education. Refuge from the painful experience of personal celebrity was to be found in the ark of marriage; in the 'cheering view' of exercising influence over the undistinguished William Fletcher. Answering Anna Jameson, not many months earlier, Maria Jane had protested against the corruptions of womanly influence when it operated as a power behind the throne in the lives of such women as Madame de Pompadour and Catherine de Medici. Her argument then had been that women given power *as a right* did not use it badly; her argument in August 1832, couched in terms of anguished and earnest bewilderment before the undeniable reality of 'genius, mind, and attainments' in women rather resembling herself, was that such qualities were 'a snare, an anxiety, and a reproach'; consequently power did not come into it. They were to be controlled and regulated into non-existence. To whom were they a snare? To whom an anxiety? To whom a reproach? Since Fletcher's part could not be spoken, they could only begin and end in the woman.

After the wedding, the couple left immediately for London and within a matter of weeks, by late September, they had embarked for India. Maria Jane was excited by the prospect of travel, animated by the bustle that preceded it, full of anticipation of the novel sights that lay ahead, and only sorry that she could not 'carry with her half the books in the British Museum'. Once on board ship she began a journal, extracts from which were published in the *Athenaeum*.[6] She continued to write poetry. Her letters, from the middle of the ocean, from Madeira during a stopover, and from the 'biscuit-oven' of Bombay – 'alias brick-kiln, alias burning Babel, alias Pandemonium, alias everything hot, horrid, glaring, barren, dissonant, and detestable' – were lengthy and vivid and detailed. Travel writing was a leading commercial genre for women at the time, and it is plain that she had every intention of seeing her experiences into print, for all her declaration that nothing she did was good enough.

She did not like the Anglo-Indian community that she found herself amongst, and there is every likelihood that they were equally unenamoured of her. At Karnai, a port near Bombay, she found the social atmosphere 'entirely anti-pathetic'. There is a tale that she found an Indian child whose parents had died of cholera whom she adopted and cared for as her own – not an action calculated to endear her to the Anglo-Indians. Soon they were moved to Sholapore, where there was drought and famine, and on 8 June came an entry in her journal: an attack of 'demi-semi-cholera, only demi-semi'. When Fletcher became ill, too, the couple were given leave to return to Karnai where the climate was healthier. It was on the journey back to Karnai, at Poona, on 4 October 1833, that Maria Jane died.

*

Geraldine Jewsbury took over the reins of household government which her sister passed to her. Her daily life was not especially arduous, though her 'exacting' father had a liking for moving house regularly; and, as he aged, he was increasingly in need of care. Throughout the 1830s, the years of her twenties, she was a conscientious, dutiful daughter. So far as is known, she did not, like Maria Jane, trouble the local press with poetical efforts, nor sit up till three in the morning fine-tuning dreams. But she had in abundance Maria Jane's 'blended passion for knowledge and for truth'; and, having fewer obstacles than her sister, she was able to pursue that passion where it led. At some point, probably during the latter part of the 1830s, she experienced a profound depressive crisis, passing through an 'illness of body and mind. The former was of short duration, but the latter, at the time, was a more serious affair, as it seemed to threaten her interest in life.'[7]

In this crisis, doubts about religious doctrine came together with dissatisfaction with the limitations of woman's life, and she wrote to Thomas Carlyle.[8] She had been, she told him, brought up 'a strict *Calvinist* & amongst a set of people who conscientiously discouraged both *doubt* & *enquiry*'. Her sister had been 'very religious & held scepticism in horror & she discouraged with some sternness any attempt to doubt or question'.[9] Thomas Carlyle's appeal for Geraldine, as she acknowledged some ten years later in an essay in the *Westminster Review*, was that he was the first to say that it was possible to be 'religious of heart and sceptical of doctrine'; the first to declare 'that a sincere *doubt* was as much entitled to respect as a sincere *belief*'.[10]

It took a man's voice to say such things. When Geraldine put all her 'religious botherations' into fictional form in her first novel, *Zoe*, which appeared in 1845, the character who was given her religious doubts to express was not the principal woman, Zoe, but the leading man, Everhard. And yet, the whole 'truly pioneering effort', the first attempt to deal with the subject of religious doubt in a fictional form, was, as one critic has rightly observed, 'a kind of autobiography'.[11] *What* kind of autobiography is the question, however; for Geraldine's inability to speak plainly about dilemmas which 'seemed to threaten her interest in life' is as evident in *Zoe* as is her 'strength and independence of thought'. The difficulty she found herself in may be illustrated by the reaction of Bulwer Lytton. He read *Zoe* and was (like many men of the time) moved and impressed by it. 'At last', he wrote, 'an honest woman speaks out, right or wrong, to the world.' He predicted that she would be 'a great and startling writer'. Shortly afterwards he learned that she was unmarried and young (though not as young as he thought). He responded with revulsion:

> I cannot recover my amazement at one or two passages being written by a young lady of three and four and twenty. They would be striking in a woman ten years older and married, but what may be the simple result of experience after a certain age is in a younger person extremely distasteful to one's feelings as implying a monstrosity of development.[12]

Bulwer Lytton's queasiness was less for the content itself than for the association of that content in *his* mind with a young woman. His discomfort with his feelings, and the discomforts of the wider reading public, shaped and structured the form of the novel in significant ways. Though Geraldine may not have listened to Bulwer Lytton, she listened to Jane Carlyle who took it upon herself to represent the views of the respectable majority. Geraldine's development as a novelist was to be in the opposite direction to honest speaking out; she chose instead to develop the arts of camouflage. She was already well versed in the necessity for such skills:

> I had rather not have my name stuck to the thing. First, because there are many things said in it that I don't want to walk about amongst some of my reputable friends as being guilty of holding.... Another reason is, that I myself have a general sort of prejudice against women's novels, with very few exceptions. I mean, I would not on any account take up a woman's novel at a venture, unless I knew something about the writer.[13]

Even under the veil of fiction, fear only 'somewhat' departed from her mind, and she was only 'by comparison' free and natural and unconventional. That 'general sort of prejudice against women's novels', which Geraldine, characteristically frank, cheerfully admitted to, had to be anticipated in the text. Thus Geraldine's problems became Everhard's problems, her religious doubts became his – and they acquired a universal importance.

But the consequences of doubt as Geraldine described them, were noticeably female: Everhard falls into a state bordering on paralysis of the will, in which all

162

his efforts seem pointless because they have no 'adequate employment'. Given that 'it is the birthright of each man to have his powers of mind and body developed, and to have the means given him of becoming all that he has the capacity in him to become',[14] Everhard wants action. His inability to find it reflected the social realities of the female world rather than the male world. With 'his powers of mind expanded to their natural growth', he seeks a life's work worthy of them. His author informed her readers:

> it is the sense of intellectual effort, the striving to reconcile ourselves with an ill-understood task stretching before us day after day, that wears out the heart-life of man. If we once could discern what was required of us exactly to do, it is not the greatness of the task that would frighten us (for we are capable of immense drudgery of labour); but it is left to us to discover our own work, and set our hands to it as best we can, and this makes the weariness of life. We spend half our strength in beating the air, and we seldom have the satisfaction of feeling that we have wisely and adequately bestowed our labour; that which we ought to have done still remains undone, and we are devoured by unrest and vague remorse.[15]

Women readers of questioning mind but unaccredited vents for their intellects would have known what she was talking about.

Leaving the Church, Everhard first looks to social work among the poor to give him purposeful work for his energies. The Church, which had enclosed him like a home, had encouraged his 'passive, contemplative habits'; but out of it he was 'possessed by an energy like a devouring fire, – he panted for some obstacle against which to contend, to wrestle'. Everhard 'looked round earnestly to find some actual thing to do – an occupation in which he might spend his life. He was full of the energy of self-sacrifice.'[16] His descent into the lower depths of Wales satisfies neither his own needs nor the needs of the poor whom he attempts to enlighten, and Everhard follows instead a more intellectual trail. Like most thoughtful women and men of the early nineteenth century, he looked to Germany, 'the store-house of wisdom'. Touring Germany with a male companion, he found himself

> for the first time for many years entirely emancipated from the strain of a false position ... he was there amongst his brethren, dwelling as kings amongst each other, in a majestic simplicity of thought and speech. Everhard had never before been thrown amongst minds of a calibre equal to his own; now he lived in daily intercourse with men greater than himself, and in his own line. He felt his powers mature every day; and in the exercise of them he found rest and peace.[17]

During the German trip Everhard and the friend with whom he is travelling, a 'gifted and fiery-hearted man', have a discussion about fame. The friend urges Everhard to distinguish himself by writing a book and going back to England to launch it; by doing so he could teach others and at the same time ensure the immortality of his own name, for 'what is there in this world worth obtaining but fame?' Everhard prefers to stay where he is, learning rather than teaching, 'amongst greater minds than my own'. His friend tells him he is a fool:

> how can one work, strive, attain, as you call it without a motive? Reverence from one's fellows, honour and worship after one has passed away from this world, are the rewards assigned to him who labours to excel his fellows, and why, if I am willing to go through the labour, should I not enjoy the reward of my labour? You talk like a child; you say you are not ambitious and you say the truth, therefore you cannot understand what you are talking about; one throb of generous ambition, one kindling feeling of the god-like frensy, and you would throw your wisdom to the winds for ever; once braced and nerved for the struggle – gods! the thought is worth a life. Heroes are not made of such stuff as you are.[18]

Everhard distances himself from this version of the literary worker as Carlylean hero. He rather plaintively tells his friend, 'You look like an impersonation of Energy'; and the friend replies, 'Energy is the only deity a man ought to worship ... unless I struggle, I stagnate.'[19] Between men, this conversation does not quite ring true. The heroic exultation has been contextualized within a framework of female purposelessness. What is really being dramatized is the absence of heroic possibilities for women. Whatever spirit of heroism might lie within, social custom dictated that heroes were not made of the stuff of female bodies. The female literary worker had, like Everhard, to learn to do without the motives that might spur on her brother; the model she was invited to take for herself was not that of the Carlylean hero, but that of the Carlylean wife. Mary Mitford delineated it most clearly in 1851. The passage occurs as the preamble to recollections of Catherine Fanshawe in her *Recollections of a Literary Life*:

> It has always seemed to me that one of the happiest positions – let me say the very happiest position, that a woman of great talent can occupy in our high civilization, is that of living a beloved and distinguished member of the best literary society; enjoying, listening, admiring; repaying all that she receives by a keen and willing sympathy; cultivating to perfection the social faculty; but abstaining from the wider field of authorship, even while she throws out here and there such choice and chosen bits as prove that nothing but disinclination to enter the arena debars her from winning the prize. How much better to belong to the portion of the audience which gives fame to the actor – that class of readers to whom the writer looks for reputation – than to figure as actor or as author oneself!

This position, 'midway on the hill of fame', is the generically appropriate position for anybody born female. Women who choose it prove thereby their womanliness, for:

> besides its security, its happiness, and its wisdom, such a choice has always

appeared to me indicative of the very finest qualities, mental and moral: – feminine, modest, generous, pure. I look up to a woman, who, with powers to command the most brilliant literary success, contents herself with a warm and unenvying sympathy in the success of others.[20]

Pragmatism and idealism meet halfway up the hill of fame: the heroism of self-denial is worthier than the heroism of full self-development, but, just as importantly, by sitting only halfway up women could more easily run to the bottom if things got hot. The tension between her impulse to reach for the heights in her own properly female person, and a shrewd understanding of the dangers that lurked there, was played out in Geraldine's novels. Her decision to speak most densely on the subject through a male persona, in *Zoe*, suggests the extent to which the model of the wife – the silent listener enjoying the success of others – prevailed as the definitive female type.

Geraldine sent Everhard, not Zoe, off to Germany to enjoy the free, ungendered exchange of intellect. As an experience, all studious women had access to this through the agency of books – German studies symbolizing hard, masculine thought, while French was for frivolity; but to have shown a woman enjoying the benefits of such intercourse in her own person, one of the 'brethren', would have been a novel fiction indeed. This is not because women did not travel, study, and speak; increasingly, they did. But the conventions governing these experiences ensured that they were likely to be different for women, and they were certainly written about differently. Sara Coleridge recorded a 'very interesting' talk she had with Henry Taylor in 1847, in which Taylor spoke strongly about 'the unattractiveness of intellectual ladies to gentlemen', even 'intellectual' gentlemen, 'men of genius, men of learning and letters'. In the 1840s Sara was a familiar figure on the London literary scene, going about alone after her husband died, involving herself in literary matters, noted for her intellectuality and good sense. She often 'battled' with Carlyle, responding with independent judgement to topics he raised, often disagreeing, but observing: 'He is always smiling and good-natured when I contradict him, perhaps because he sees that I admire him all the while.'[21] Perhaps because she *didn't* admire Taylor, she didn't contradict him; or perhaps her inability to protest at his complacent rudeness towards her is one of those truths to be rescued from silence. She poured out her resentment in a private letter, insisting that 'intellectualism will not be abandoned by us to please the gentlemen', and enlarging on what she *would* have said if only she had dared:

> I could have said in reply, that while women are young, where there is a pretty face, it covers a multitude of sins, even intellectuality ... we that are no longer young pass into a new, old womanish, tough state of mind; to *please* them is not so much the aim as to set them to rights, lay down the law to them, convict them of their errors, pretences, superficialities etc etc in short, tell them a *bit of our mind*.[22]

The notion of telling men 'a bit of our mind', even as a tough old woman, was sheer fancy. Women whose feelings of provocation led them so far courted ostracism, as Sara well knew. By swallowing her words, Sara protected social opportunities that were important and nourishing to her, and which were privileges not rights. 'Things of the mind and intellect give me intense pleasure ... and they have gladdened me in another way, by bringing me into close communion with fine and deep minds.'[23]

Those 'fine and deep minds' belonged to women as well as men. But Sara Coleridge made a distinction between genius in women and men. Genius in women, she assured a correspondent, required no assertion of the self: 'Certainly all the women of first-rate genius that I know have been, and are, diffident, feminine, and submissive in habits and temper.'[24] Her judgement, based on observation, also reflected the ways in which she had learned to shape her own aspirations. She recognized and approved of women like herself who were 'brilliant and gifted, but quiet and unassuming'.[25] In order to claim the word 'genius' for women, Sara Coleridge was virtually forced to see only diffidence and submission because of the way the phrase 'woman of genius' was coming to be used. Women whose brilliance could not be denied, like Madame de Staël and George Sand, but who yet lived and spoke an assertive female self, were tumbling the hierarchies within which 'genius' and the cultural definition of femininity were situated. Their rejection of the values of diffidence and submission served to unsettle the word 'genius' rather than the word 'woman'. Genius implied an escape from control (indeed it licensed it) and was thus a dubious quality for a woman to exhibit. Those who possessed it were expected to find it a burden. Any woman who enjoyed her genius, and the fame it was likely to bring, could only be accounted for by removing the woman from the genius. Following one's genius to its highest expression was a defeminizing process, as the critic writing on George Sand in the *London Review* in 1864 made plain:

> The greatest female author living is certainly George Sand. How much has George Sand given up to gain her literary crown. She has simply abandoned the distinctive characteristics ... of her sex. She has gratified her genius by immolating to it her instincts and her nature.

At the same time, in what seems at first a contradiction, it could lead women to a deeper and more deadly level of their femininity:

> literary women amongst us would be horrified if they were told that George Sand was a type of themselves, she is a beacon that points out the rocks and shoals which literary women seldom reach, but in the direction of which most of them are sailing. Knowledge of life, with all its lights and shadows for a man, is part and a bitter part of his career. For a woman, it is the fruit from off a deadly tree.[26]

This was the language Maria Jane Jewsbury used. The public image of George Sand was an image Felicia Hemans – though utterly different in her personal and sexual conduct, and though she died before George Sand blazed on to the British literary scene with *Indiana* in 1837 – feared. The wreath of fame was a fiery crown for women to wear since it contained a power to burn its way right through womanliness: knowledge of life might lead a woman to take notice of her real experiences and reach her own conclusions instead of attending to those she was eternally hearing from men. The fact that women like Madame de Staël and George Sand asserted their right to sexual expression as well as intellectual and imaginative expression merely confirmed what was thoroughly well known: the female imagination, that volatile and highly erotic force, was not something any decent woman would choose to have too much to do with. Female writers working through female characters had to do double duty in disarming the reader if they were not to be damned.

*

Everhard's travels in Germany rendered in idealized, fictional form Geraldine's journey from obscurity, ambition, and despair in Manchester to 'the store-house of wisdom' that was Cheyne Row, London. By 1840, Geraldine was in a desperate condition. For ever afterwards, the depression of the years that immediately preceded her friendship with the Carlyles remained as a touchstone of personal horror, an experience of the lower depths which enabled her to sympathize with others in psychological distress, especially women. It was a time of hopelessness and nightmarish imprisonment, 'like being suddenly shut up, as one is in a nightmare, or a black cloud suddenly dropping down upon one'. The route she took out of the nightmare was a consciously non-female route, as she told Jane some years later: 'I endeavoured to drown my pain, not by inditing a "diary of an *ennuyee*" but by writing an essay on materialism.'[27] Geraldine's letters to Thomas Carlyle, written as a way out of depression, were a version of attempting to get her essay published.

They served their purposes. Carlyle was impressed by what he read. His notice of her, the letters which came from him at regular intervals throughout 1840, raised her self-esteem and did nothing but good for her credit locally. Given the recognition and potential opportunity his interest led her to expect, Geraldine's depression cleared. With such encouragement she was able to work with a sense of purpose. By 1840 her father was dying, she was approaching 30, she had had emotional involvements with men but none likely to lead to marriage, and she had not yet published a book. The contrast between her own progress and her sister's at the same age must have been a painful one. Emerging from the paralysis of depression, her refuge was work. It was to remain so all her life, and casual remarks like 'if I am long without writing, I get morbid and miserable', and 'I have fairly begun a new book ... and I shall now work like the Devil. I feel relieved as from a nightmare now my work lies straight ahead', recur frequently in her correspondence.[28]

Two years after writing to Carlyle, enough of *Zoe* had been written in collaboration with Elizabeth Paulet for the manuscript to be sent to Jane for her opinion – and to contribute to if she chose. Geraldine's attitude towards it was at once businesslike and detached: she might be writing her life story but she was also creating a product for the market. If the market demanded less of one shape and more of another she was willing to oblige. She knew what she wanted from Jane in this respect, and that was 'good, hard, professional, practical opinion'. Jane could give that herself and she had access to others, mostly men, who could give it. Geraldine explained:

> If my sister had lived she would have said all these things, and given me the 'drilling' necessary and taken all the dilettantism out of me. It must be done for everybody if they are to do any good, and I have nobody at my elbow to do it; therefore I am on the listen for practical, professional judgement, and thankful when I can get it.... I am glad to get a definite, practical opinion, not frittered away by civility, or the sort of gallantry (God save the mark!) that adulterates all the little bit of straightforward dealing women meet with from men, and is the reason they do so little that is really worth anything![29]

Taking the place of Maria Jane, Jane's voice was to be the motherly voice of duty rather than love, of a never-to-be-attained ideal, denying more often than she allowed and finding fault as a matter of course. This was what Geraldine had grown up on: 'I can do no sort of good on praise. I cannot work on it. I require pounding down with criticisms from people who know things better than myself.'[30]

One of the things Jane knew better was that a husband's claims came before those of a friend. Like Geraldine, Thomas had a trust in Jane's literary judgement, and in November 1842 he also had deposited a manuscript in her lap – 'about that old Abbot of St Edmunds Bury' – on which he wanted an opinion:

> and until I have *studied* that, which will be no light matter, I must abstain, for *decency's sake* from showing any curiosity about the other literary production in which I have only a *friend's* interest. My dear, tho' we are not trained here as in China, to 'the three-thousand punctualities' – we are always needing to look at our doings that we may not stumble over some nicety or other.[31]

When she finally came to read the early version of *Zoe*, Jane was impressed and terrified in equal measure: 'So much power of genius rushing so recklessly into unknown space!' She did not feel drawn to contribute, but she felt very urgently the need to pound Geraldine down with criticisms. Her cleverness was beyond doubt: she was 'a far more profound and daring speculator than even I had fancied her ... far too clever to do nothing in her day and generation'. But her indecency, albeit a '*scientific*' and '*essential*' indecency, was alarming. Jane made time to give them a 'full and faithful deliverance' of her views, a task which she found far from easy and which she dispatched with no little earnestness. The pounding did not have the effect she expected; Geraldine responded to it with levity, sending Jane in return 'a whole *pamphlet* of witty, devil-may-care objections to my objections'. Jane was not amused.[32]

The objections in question had to do with matters of propriety and of grammar: the convergence of propriety in life and on the page. On the subject of textual propriety, the grammatical decency of sentences, Geraldine assured Jane:

> your representation about 'stops' and 'capital letters' is telling upon me slowly. I have borrowed Blair's lectures, and I expect my sentences will soon be on more creditable principles of composition, and I have already felt respectability dawning on my soul from this contemplation of the Doctor's immaculate wig and well-balanced visage.

But on decency of behaviour, textual and other, she claimed to be helpless:

> Your criticism made me laugh till I was half-dead, for you little know all our strivings after decency. If you had seen the work as it was first schemed, you would have had something to complain of; indeed, it struck us that people might get scandalised. So there we have been softening it down, and doing our very best to make it proper-behaved, and fancied we had succeeded to a miracle. You don't know the trouble we have taken to see what would look decent at a distance. It is a clear case we have no vocation for propriety, as such.... However, my dear, there shall be a liberal distribution of spotted muslin! only, will you tell me where it is to be applied? It is no use 'leaving it to our own consciences'. Our sympathies are imperfect on that point.[33]

The poundings of *Letters to the Young* had given Geraldine an unusual strength. Nothing Jane said was new; indeed, her disapproval was probably a comfort since it established her more firmly in the motherly role Geraldine mostly looked for in her. She asked Jane to 'think of me as a child, to be taken care of and not be allowed to get into mischief'. Geraldine claimed to be ignorant of the ways of the world and dependent on Jane's better knowledge: 'I do not know what I would do if you were taken away from me! ... I should make all manner of mistakes, and get into scrapes innumerable without you, especially if I am to go about at all amongst people.' She even told her, 'I think of you as Catholics think of their saints, to keep them out of evil.' With Jane in place as an icon of respectability, absolutely firm and fast in her position, Geraldine's freer move-ments – her free thinking, free writing, free loving – could function within a secure frame. The point was not so much to respond to Jane's criticisms as to make sure that they would always be there.[34]

Jane's was the voice of conscience, which meant the voice of ideal womanliness. In this capacity, her suffering within her marriage was not a suffering Geraldine was moved to encourage her to escape; rather, she participated in nourishing the view which was to find full expression in Thomas Carlyle's *Reminiscences*, that her suffering was a form of ennoblement. By womanly suffering, Jane Carlyle was raised. Her marriage was admittedly awful in its effects on her; but Geraldine gained an idol thereby. Her most revealing response to Jane's misery was the suggestion that they should find happiness by going off alone to a cottage together, where Geraldine would replace Thomas as Jane's spouse: 'You should keep the house absolutely – keep the accounts, keep the money – and I would write; and you should make me work.'[35]

In fiction Geraldine's idealized vision of Jane may be seen in the curious figure, Miss Airlie, who appears in *The History of an Adopted Child*. In this children's story Geraldine dramatized her relationship with Jane as that of maid to mistress. Miss Airlie was a woman 'perfected through suffering'. She was a cripple, and had a heart 'filled with unknown treasures', and a 'capacity for deep and enduring attachment', but it was all 'thrown back upon herself'. Of Miss Airlie, we are told: 'It was not without a long and painful exercise of mind that she was enabled to accept her lot, and subdue herself.... But she did submit.' Miss Airlie found strength in 'the power of renunciation'. All of which her young maid adored:

> She became to me the type of a superior being and all my services were so many modes of expressing my hero worship. I believe if she had told me that putting my hand into the fire would have given her one moment's ease or comfort, I would have done so joyfully.[36]

This is Geraldine's authentic voice, recognizable from her letters to Jane and to Walter Mantell. Heroes and renunciation – *entsagen* – were central to Carlyle's philosophy; taken together, applied in the lives of women, they led to the elevation of sacrifice, submission, and endurance. Jane's heroism lay in accepting 'the stern moral' of her life's story, that 'the consequences of an action remain and must be endured to the end'. As Carlyle said, a man was 'made higher by doing reverence to what is really above him'; in the hierarchy of female values, a woman who was 'higher' than another woman was not a great commander or a great warrior, but the one who had pronounced more *entsagen* in her life. Loyalty and noble endurance on the fields of men's battles, such as captured Felicia Hemans's imagination and those of her readers; strength to bear the unbearable; a capacity to do without – these defined female heroism.

Having Jane Carlyle as a hero was not the most auspicious opening to a female literary career, and artistically speaking her influence was a narrowing one. It was mitigated, however, by the previous influence of Maria Jane. Both Janes pounded Geraldine with criticism of her behaviour in life and on the page, but there was an important difference, which had its origins in the fact that one was a professional writer and the other was not. The distance between what Maria Jane said and what she did was an open, observable distance. She understood the veil of fiction as a drapery that needed to be lifted if truth, in women's writing, was to be permitted or understood. Her movement was towards clarity and rationality, even if she had to approach it along the paths of accommodation. Jane Carlyle, on the other hand, having given the priority to marriage over a writing career, journeyed inexorably towards the shadows and half-lights of eternal accommodation to the irrationality of her own subordination. What she taught, in essence, was a fearfulness of truth she herself had had to learn. The spotted muslin had no other purpose than to hide. Geraldine had no vocation for decency, but a tremendous impulse towards survival: she learned to say what she had to say from behind swathes of spotted muslin. She learned to be cautious in her life about any actions whose stern consequences might have to be endured to the end. As Felicia Hemans served as a literary warning to her sister, so Jane Carlyle served Geraldine Jewsbury as a symbol of the way a woman's life could become a 'passionate kaleidoscope' whose shapes she had no power of her own to control.

Jane's response to Geraldine was determined (and over-determined) by her 'trade' and by the ambivalent feelings both she and Thomas Carlyle had about that trade. Operating on the principle that 'The less *passion* in the world the more *virtue* and *good digestion*!,'[37] she fired off screeds of good sense and decent repression whenever Geraldine's passions overreached the bounds of respectability on the page or in the parlour. Even thinking about passion could be a fault. When Geraldine contemplated the painter Gambardella in the light of passionate feeling and decided that he was too feeble to arouse any in her, Jane was shocked:

> It is bad enough to love *with passion* when one cannot help oneself – but to set about it, malice prepense, as a piece of the natural business of life, whenever a man presents himself – and without the slightest inspection of the probabilities of being bored in return – that does seem to me an exuberance of '*the social feeling*' which ought to be kept down by *cold pudding* or anything however disagreeable that is found to answer the purpose.[38]

Geraldine's 'scientific' approach to passion, her 'want of reserve . . . in the spiritual department', her tendency to write (and possibly do) things 'just *for fact's sake* . . . without a fig-leaf of conformity', jarred on Jane's sensibilities.[39] Thomas Carlyle's suggestion that Geraldine be invited to stay, in 1843, was as astonishing to Jane as if he had offered to entertain the high priestess of passion, George Sand herself. Passion, scientific or otherwise, was a threat in a household where sexual passion had given way – as all the circumstantial evidence seems to suggest – to hysterias and explosions of temper. Jane weighed Geraldine's intellectual liveliness, which was a stimulus she knew herself to be in need of, against the perilousness of inviting a young woman with such 'a born *spirit of intrigue*' in amongst a married pair. Her sexual insecurities probably accounted for some of the violence of her reaction to Geraldine during that over-long stay. Geraldine, she said, spent her time 'gazing' at Thomas (who referred to her as 'that dreadful young woman') and trying 'all sorts of seductions on him'. As for her intellect, that was brutally dismissed: 'Intellect! Carlyle made a grand mistake when he held this Geraldine up to me as something superlative – she is sharp as a meat-axe – but as narrow – there is no *breadth* of character in her and no basis of truth.'[40]

The seductions of Thomas were as nothing to Geraldine's attempted seductions of Jane, that '*cant* of sensibility' which led the older woman 'a devil of a life' when she had to endure its physical manifestations. By the end of five weeks the friendship was over as far as she was concerned. Geraldine's departure was a grim affair:

> She went yesterday according to programme – on her side, of course the parting was a dreadful business! – floods of tears – even a sort of mild hysterics – on our side of it was transacted with dry eyes, with a composure of soul impassive even for the claims of sympathy.[41]

But Geraldine wrote her way back into Jane's good graces; on paper, her peculiar combination of demonstrativeness and detachment seemed less like cant.[42] She was also always willing to be told that she was in the wrong. By February 1844 Jane had a revised version of *Zoe* in her hands: 'and by the powers it is a wonderful book! – Decidedly the cleverest Englishwoman's book I ever remember to have read!'[43] The reader for Chapman and Hall agreed, saying that it had 'taken hold of him with a grasp of iron'. Jane remarked, 'Think of little Geraldine having a grasp like *that* in her!' On the strength of such a favourable response, Chapman and Hall accepted the manuscript for publication. Jane, having personally gone to the office in the Strand to find out its fate, could not help making a very pertinent comparison: John Stuart Mill's first book, which he had spent ten years writing, and Thomas Carlyle's first book, *Sartor Resartus*, had had to 'hawk themselves about thro' all the *trade* before they could so much as get printed *free of cost*'.[44] Geraldine's terms were much more generous: she was to have half profits.

For the next year, Jane was to be closely involved with the development of *Zoe*. It is unlikely that she wrote any of it, but she read and criticized and advised rewriting. Certainly Geraldine looked to her for editorial and administrative help, much as her husband did. By August she was losing patience. She had had a visit from Geraldine's publisher who stayed 'for two hours – unmerciful human being; boring me about alterations to be made! I had better have written the book all over myself than have had so much intermediation to transact!'[45]

Geraldine's publisher, it soon became clear, had not actually read the manuscript. Once it was in print, but before it was released, he read it and, in Geraldine's words, '*nearly had a fit of apoplexy* he was so shocked! a work *he* had intended "to circulate in the bosom of families" was not fit to be read'.[46] He tried to persuade Geraldine to write something else. She refused. Thomas Carlyle intervened. Jane Carlyle was appealed to. The book was published and Jane received another visit from Chapman:

> Geraldine's publisher has just been here and said he would apply to *me* to *bail* him if he were taken up for bringing out Zoe! diverse individuals, among the rest Mrs C Hall (Geraldine's *kind friend*) having told him that it would do him no good as a publisher, that it was 'a most dangerous book *shaking the foundations* of all sound doctrine!' I engaged to bail him with *my head* against the book's having any serious consequences *of any sort*.[47]

Chapman's reader confessed to having overlooked the book's sins against good taste. As Geraldine remarked years later, '*I had thought I had been writing a Sermon* – well – sins against *good taste* are far more heavily visited than sins against morality.'[48]

*

Geraldine's sermon appealed to the morality of the moral and the immorality of the immoral. Its autobiographical theme, carried by both Everhard and Zoe, was that ever-popular one: the problem of genius and talent beyond the ordinary. Its central question: what should a woman do with her gifts and energies? Since, as J.M. Hartley points out in 'Geraldine Jewsbury and the problems of the woman novelist,' 'Femininity and genius are almost by definition irreconcilable', the subject could not be properly canvassed in Zoe's person alone.[49] The frustrations of Zoe's life could be shown; her dilemma could be demonstrated and analysed; a very great number of pertinent, witty, often caustic blows could be struck in the name of strong-minded womanhood; but in the end Zoe has to give up her strength and independence. In the real world of aspiring writers who seek readers, of young women hoping to make their way into literary society, there could be no hesitation about whether to choose textually to lose femininity or genius: one of them had to go and it was almost bound to be genius.

By showing Zoe, whose 'tropical organization and ... strong passions' (she is half-Greek) lead her to have two lovers at once – Everhard and Count Mirabeau – settling for a quiet life with neither of them, Geraldine depicted a woman whose strength had been bought by evasion. Wanting to reconcile passion, intellect, and femininity, Zoe learns in diverse ways that it is impossible: she lives out the rest of her life with a 'chastened spirit'. Her lack of fulfilment, her guilt, and her submission to a more dreary existence than she had dreamed of and known, are the measures of her womanliness. The waters of conformity close over Zoe; but the narrative bringing her to that point remains alive with open-ended questions and provocative, unwomanly interventions. For example, what is one to make of the statement, placed early in volume one, and rising from the conversational ether of Madame d'Aligre's salon in France? Does it provide the moral for the novel? Or is it just an example of clever talk? Madame d'Aligre tells a young man:

> Out of the million of women who are flattered by being told they possess genius, not one ever achieves a work that endures, or that obtains higher praise than of being something very clever for a woman. Scarce one has ever achieved any thing that, in a man, would be considered first rate. I do not belong to the sisterhood of 'women of genius' myself, so my testimony is disinterested. Look at history, which is a tolerable criterion. If ever, by an extraordinary combination of circumstances, a woman has, from her position, influenced her age and country, her name speedily becomes a historical doubt, and her actions fabulous. The name of a woman has never

173

authentically descended to posterity, unless preserved in the memory of some transcendent crime.[50]

Madame d'Aligre's piercing observations are quickly buried in a flurry of contributions to the discussion which neatly illustrate her point: they all blame women, locating woman's 'failure' in the inadequacies of the sex. Women are 'destitute both of patience and persistence', too busy displaying themselves, ineffectual, etc. Historical doubt, however, and posterity are not personal deficiencies; women do not choose either failure or obscurity.

Zoe avoids crime, transcendent or banal, but she does not avoid the psychological processes that lead women to be either blamed or lost. As a woman of 'strong, energetic character' ('her own energy was better than any theory ever invented') she has enough of the 'eccentricity' of those who 'chafe against the harmless conventionalities which are a law to their weaker or better broken-in companions' for her author to apologize for her.[51] Less directly, through irony and authorial comment of a sardonic kind, Geraldine apologizes for Zoe's lapse into self-blame in her relationship with the overpowering, egotistical, emotionally demanding Mirabeau. Searching her soul, Zoe finds nothing she has done that she would not do again, but she still made excuses for Mirabeau. That was not, as Geraldine pointed out, a compliment he would have returned:

> Men are much more magnanimous, and show their superior nature in nothing more than in that they never suffer their judgement to be impaired by any misgivings ... they are always equal to the effort of self-defence and justification. A true woman always blames herself, and it is a point on which her lover, to do him justice, never contradicts her.[52]

Maria Jane's precepts – 'in all disputes suppose yourself worthy of blame' – tested against the reality of a world in which, as Geraldine observed, 'when a woman steps beyond her own domestic circle, into whatever scene she goes she is the subject of a social fiction', revealed themselves as serving the interests of men.[53] While a true woman was blaming herself a true man was seizing the advantage.

Female strength and wholeness could only safely be achieved, according to Zoe, by separation from men. Zoe's stepdaughter Clotilde, after an unfortunate passion for a wastrel, enters a nunnery and over the years develops into a model of the composed, self-contained, mature, professional woman of inward strength that Geraldine herself became. As the abbess of her convent, Clotilde acquires a 'self-possession and gentle dignity' which takes the place of her 'former shrinking manner: the habit of directing the proceedings of others gave this, for though her sway was gentle, she was too conscientious not to be firm'.[54] Command and responsibility, along with repression of her own sexuality, remove Clotilde from the sphere of men's influence. Devoted to God, answering only to God and the women amongst whom she lives, Clotilde is free from the threat of men's manipulation of her through her feelings. Unlike Zoe, her strength, which comes from hard experience and the necessity to stand on her own feet, is not undermined by the need to be weak for a lover. Zoe loses Mirabeau in spite of her love for him because she puts the needs of her sick child before his (and, subsequently, because she will not entertain the thought of being his mistress). Clotilde is able to be a mother – to her nuns, to the little daughters of the man who caused her so much pain – without once doubting that her choices are the right ones. Glorified motherhood, within the walls of the nunnery, emerges as woman's highest good; the ultimate domestic scene and unsullied by any living male presence. Watching Clotilde preparing bandages for the hospital, Zoe exclaims, 'Oh that I were altogether such as you are! ... What good has my life done to myself or any one else? What profit has there been in all the intellect and beauty on which I so foolishly and vainly prided myself?' Clotilde tells her:

> all these gifts just seem wasted unless they are dedicated to the highest uses, not to our own glory. He who bestowed them, He alone can find due employment for them; He is the only being whom we may securely love, whom we may venture to serve with all our soul and strength. In Him alone can we safely put our whole trust.[55]

Coming from a woman whose emotional equilibrium was once destroyed by a man, heard by a woman whose men in different ways failed her, Clotilde's words carry a meaning that takes them beyond religious cliché. In praise of God, they also contain the disappointment of earthly experience of men. Trusting God is another way of trusting oneself; it is looking within for reassurance, preserving one's 'soul and strength', and finding, perhaps, a route round men's disabling influence towards the 'liberty and light' of full expression.

*

Maria Jane's old friend and colleague, Henry Chorley, reviewed *Zoe* in the *Athenaeum*. Half of his review took the form of a recollection of the elder Miss Jewsbury – 'one of our coadjutors in the long-past days of our struggle' – whose gifts as a journalist had remained known only to a few: 'the circumstances which made it then impossible for us to publicly speak of her merits as a writer, renders it only the more pleasing to recall them.' Chorley found similarities between *Zoe* and *The Three Histories*, 'imaginative and artistic resemblances ... traces of precept and direction, ... even ... modes of expression'; and having praised Maria Jane for her high intellectual gifts, and after optimistically declaring, 'There is no forgetting Miss Jewsbury, whenever the gifted women of England are brought under notice', he introduced his discussion of Geraldine's first book with: 'we could not look for a mere circulating-library novel from one bearing the name of our authoress.'

In the event, *Zoe* seems to have caused Chorley more pain than pleasure, though his loyalty to Maria Jane prevented him saying so outright. Its 'feverish apprehension of quiet pages', and Geraldine's 'tendency to fly at every game, which, though courageous, is indiscreet', as well as the over-numerous secondary characters and a tenuous story line, all tired him. His summing up was acute, however: 'Zoe contains matter enough to demand attention, and to indicate an original mind, though it may not ultimately prove the mind of a novelist.'[56] Presenting matter enough to demand attention was exactly what Geraldine had determined on and she succeeded. Zoe was 'unusually popular' according to Edmund Mercer, writing at the end of the century; it 'raised its author to the goddess-ship of the circulating libraries. Its arguments on religion were esteemed – by the average readers of the time – as unorthodox and even wicked', and consequently everyone wanted to read it. Impecunious residents of Manchester had more trouble than most in getting hold of a copy since it was put in a dark cupboard of the public library there, being 'calculated to injure the morals of the young men'.[57]

The book was talked about. Whether for good or ill was, as Jane knowingly observed, immaterial. Giuseppe Mazzini, considering it axiomatic that women wished to be loved whilst men wished to love, found Zoe a book that lacked 'womanness'; it was the book of 'a man'. Jane lent her copy far and wide:

> It is quite curious to see the horror excited in some people (and these the least moral) by Geraldine's book while the moralest people of my acquaintance either like it or are not at pains to abuse it. Even Miss Wilson to whom I dared to lend it – tho' she confessed to never having 'ventured on reading a line of George Sand in her life' brought it back to me with a certain equanimity – 'It is avowedly the book of an audacious esprit forte, and so of course you did not expect me to approve of it, nor do I, but I think it very clever and amusing' – voila tout! While old and young roués of the Reform Club almost go off into hysterics over – its indecency. The oddest thing of all is that Geraldine seems to me in the fair way of getting a Husband by it!!! – Robertson in a fit of distraction took to writing her letters of criticism about it which have led him already further than he thought – and she – has taken or is fast taking 'a fit' to him – and both I can perceive contemplate a lawful catastrophe. There is encouragement to young ladies to write improper books.[58]

Geraldine's reactions to the 'fuss and flurry' of emergence into publicity confirmed Jane's worst fears. Within weeks of the book's appearance, Jane had been drawn into a 'mess of Manchester diablerie' in which Geraldine, Frank Jewsbury, Robertson, and Elizabeth Paulet all whipped themselves up into what she considered an emotional frenzy of 'Minerva press nonsense' which overflowed in letters to Jane and which she calmed by the even-handed application of 'oil of vitriol'. She told the story to Babbie, observing that she was 'absolutely sick of the sight of paper and ink':

> A fortnight ago Robertson went off to see Geraldine who had already accepted him or to speak more accurately I believe offered herself to him on paper!! I had from the very starting of the correspondence warned them both against committing themselves, and declined so much as forming an

opinion as to the feasibleness of the match — so that I had no occasion to have been dragged into their mad doings as I have been.... A few days after Robertson's departure came a letter from Frank Jewsbury — entreating me to interfere to stop proceedings or at least to give recognisances as to Robertson — and every day since; I have had at least *two* letters on the subject from the several parties — yesterday there were four — two in the morning and ditto at night — this morning I have *three* and heaven knows what the evening post may bring. To all these letters from Frank — Geraldine — Robertson and Mrs Paulet — with whom Robertson now is — I answer as briefly as possible — in the spirit of Cassandra, telling them they are all mad....

Robertson — a very goodnatured somewhat chicken-hearted fellow has been *doing* the Mirabeau of Zoe, thinking I suppose that he could not make love to Geraldine more agreeably than after her own ideal of Love — Frank Jewsbury has suddenly revealed himself as a second Geraldine — full of 'madness' — 'ready to die' in fact reduced to such conditions by his sister's precipitate resolve as man never was before — Geraldine went off in great style as a Heroine of the first magnitude but ... has been looking of late days less like a Heroine than a bladder with the wind let out of it.[59]

Geraldine's conduct, in Jane's opinion, had been 'that of an arrant fool, tho she should have written not one but twenty clever books'. Jane's own writing was employed, once again, in the severely practical endeavour of levelling other people's emotions. Failing that, she turned gratefully to her sewing, producing 'covers for the large sofa, four pillows, the two easy chairs and one footstool!!', all in a 'reactionary movement' against the hysterias Geraldine's success had precipitated.

Jane's version of the story and of Geraldine's behaviour is the version that has come down to us. In it, Robertson is characterized along the lines of the hot-headed young blockheads who once courted Jane Welsh: he was a 'poor fellow' with 'a *constitutional* tendency of blood to the head which when anything *excites* him violently produces a sort of brain-fever'. Robertson was also one of Jane's men. He hovers in and out of her letters of the period, not a notable figure — he hung about 'like a physical malady' — but a steady enough part of the picture for her to feel, at some level, that he had been poached. Geraldine's failure to keep her head above the storms of rising passion, her failure to separate fiction from fact, her self-surrender to madness of every kind, were so many metaphorical ways for Jane to protest against Geraldine's difference which was, paradoxically, her self-command. The degree to which Geraldine took Robertson seriously as a lover is very much open to question. What is clear is how important it was for all the others in the affair, for their different reasons, that Geraldine should be regarded as hysterical and in need of control by others. The histrionics emanated as much from Cheyne Row as they did from Manchester; Geraldine's tone was not the hysterical tone that Jane's violent reactions to her might lead one to expect. Her tendency was towards understanding and acceptance. As usual, she recovered very quickly from the affair and a few months later passed through London on her way to Paris and called in on Jane. Jane's feelings of provocation had not yet subsided. On the way back from Paris, Geraldine tried again. This time she was more successful and Jane reported:

> I received her very coldly but there is no quarrelling with that creature! Before she had been in five minutes she sat down on the floor at my feet and untied my shoe-strings – 'What are you doing?' I asked – 'Why my dear I am merely going to rub your feet – you look starved – I am sure your feet have not got well rubbed since I did it myself last year!!' and all the two days she did not leave off rubbing my feet whether I would or no for a quarter of an hour together.[60]

For Jane, the months that followed the publication of *Zoe* were months of severe depression. She was 'in a sad way', feeling herself barely recognizable as 'something a few degrees above an *Idiot*'. Her intellectual and emotional security within her marriage were assailed by Lady Harriet, while Geraldine's success brought home her failure to make anything publicly recognized out of her own life. She hated, as Francis Espinasse recorded, 'to be thought of only as Mr Carlyle's wife'.[61] Geraldine's undisputed arrival on the literary scene as a woman of genius in her own right rubbed salt into the wound. Her celebrity brought her many new friends, women like Charlotte Cushman, the German feminist writer Fanny Lewald, and Eliza Ashurst with whom she was able to 'swear eternal friendship' in a manner that was arguably more profound than any she might have sworn with Robertson. Jane was jealous. The Ashursts she dismissed as a '*twaddly* family', but it was Geraldine's 'blaze of enthusiasm' for that forceful, self-possessed American actress who was a magnetic figure for more than one young woman, which really upset her:

> her letters have been filled with lyrics about this woman – till I could stand it no longer – and have written her such a screed of my mind as she never got before – and which will probably terminate our correspondence – at least till the finale of her friendship for Miss Cushman.[62]

As unmarried professional women, artists working in a man's world, Miss Cushman and Miss Jewsbury had much to say to each other and much that was mutually supportive to exchange. Charlotte Cushman's influence was an artistically enabling one for Geraldine in a way that Jane's was not; her gruelling experiences as an actress, supporting her family from a very young age, were to form the basis of Geraldine's portrait of Bianca – one of Charlotte's most famous roles – in *The Half Sisters*. It is most unlikely that Miss Cushman ever referred to Geraldine as the 'poor little authoress of a questionable *Zoe*' as Mrs Carlyle self-defensively did; she saw her rather as a woman of some importance on the literary scene, and a fellow female worker.[63]

Geraldine did not consider her friendships exclusive, nor did she think that a sworn friendship with one person devalued the friendship with another. She had a philosophical approach to what Jane regarded as insincerity or inconsistency:

> 'inconsistencies' as they are called, 'contradictions', 'incongruities' – all right themselves and find their peaceable unity and level if only we are true to ourselves at the *present* which is the only moment we have at our disposal.[64]

Being true to herself in the present meant moving with changing circumstances. *Zoe* changed Geraldine's life in the direction she had wanted it changed. It brought her professional and social opportunities. Not only could she approach Charlotte Cushman with full confidence in the dressing room when she was playing Manchester, but visitors to Manchester sought *her* out for 'an evening at Miss Jewsbury's'. The affair over Robertson apart, the transition from obscurity to some notoriety was managed with ease – not even Jane ever suggested that Geraldine's fame spoiled her. Elizabeth Barrett Browning, meeting Geraldine for the first time in 1851, was 'much taken' with her: commenting on the 'French sort of daring, half-audacious power' in her books, she added, 'but she herself is quiet and simple, and drew my heart out of me a good deal. I felt inclined to love her in our half hour's intercourse.' Being 'quiet and simple' in spite of being a woman of genius was, of course, learned behaviour, but the description suggests a deeper level of assurance. Geraldine was as well prepared for the part she played as any woman could have been.[65]

In 1847 she stayed a second time with the Carlyles. This time her name went before her. Monckton Milnes got up one of his breakfasts on her behalf, and Jane was drawn into 'a racket very foreign to my habits and tastes', as host and as chaperone. Conscious of her own contribution to the failure of Geraldine's first visit four years earlier, and conscious, too, of Geraldine's own calm and kind style of hospitality, which she had benefited from, Jane felt honour bound to accept all the many invitations that Geraldine's presence in town inspired. But her ambivalent feelings were made plain in a letter to her cousin Helen:

> on the strength of *Zoe* people whom I could hardly have intruded her upon before – were now quite glad to have her at their parties as a new specimen for their several *menageries*. Upon *my* honour I believe if a *Lady* had been tried for murder, so that she only escaped hanging or transportation; she would have a better chance of 'getting on' in society here than one of whom nothing had been *talked*. Geraldine was a much more lively and agreeable person in company, when I knew her first – before her book – than now – but there was hardly a house in London *then*, to which I could have used the freedom of taking her along with me – and now because she has put her cleverness into a *book* – above all a book accused of immorality (quite a new sort of distinction for a young Englishwoman) there is no house I visit at where people would not *thank* me for giving them a sight of her and an opportunity of *exhibiting* her to their friends. *She* feels no misgivings

179

about all this – she is *received* – *politely* – complimented on her book – and thinks the people are very kind, and it is all right. But I as her *Chaperon* have had considerable qualms I can tell you! Especially at Breakfast at Richard Milnes's the other morning ... I had to be responsible not only for myself but for Geraldine ... figure my consternation on finding ourselves in a room with eight men! and not one woman! ... – the situation would just have suited Lady Harriet, but me it was too *strong* for – obliged to make conversation with all these men brought to meet us – and obliged at the same time to keep an ear open to what Geraldine was saying to her next neighbour lest she should get on dangerous ground. *She* enjoyed herself immensely.[66]

Times had changed since 1830, when Geraldine was first led, by her sister, into London literary society, but one cannot help thinking that if Maria Jane had taken her to Milnes's breakfast, the fact that the company was all men would have mattered little. Geraldine's sublime self-possession did not arise from ignorance or immaturity as Jane's rather fussy assumption of responsibility seems to suggest. She was accustomed to talking (and smoking) on equal terms with men in her own home, where she would as often as not be the only woman present. She brought a broader experience to Milnes's table than Jane did, even though Jane, because married, wore the mantle of maturity. Like Lady Harriet, Geraldine was sufficient in herself. Like her sister, she resembled a liner rather than a skiff. Launching into the deep waters opened to her by her fame, she showed little inclination to be moored and not much natural aptitude for shame.

7

OF THE FEMALE PERSUASION

I was a human being before I was of the *female* persuasion.

Geraldine Jewsbury[1]

It is no good your getting up a theory about me. I was born to drive rules and theories to distraction and I want to beat yours to powder and then stamp upon it.

Geraldine Jewsbury[2]

Geraldine Jewsbury's friendship with Jane Carlyle began as a passionate love, continued in the hope of becoming a literary partnership, and developed into the caring attentions a daughter might pay a difficult, needy, much-loved mother. Jane's friendship with Geraldine began in doubt succeeded by revulsion, continued with some reluctance, and developed into a tolerance crossed by much impatience and some respect. The respect was always in danger of being undermined by envy. Having selected for herself the part of daughter, Geraldine was comfortable in the role. The same could not be said about Jane; she neither chose to be mother nor was comfortable in the part. Indeed, her own sense of unfinished business as a daughter, her feelings of guilt towards a mother with whom she had never been able to coexist peaceably and whose sudden death in 1842 she was still bitterly mourning in 1843 when Geraldine came to stay, led her rather to seek out substitute mothers herself. Mrs Buller, formerly Thomas Carlyle's employer when he was tutor to her two sons, was one such who found favour specifically because she treated Jane as a child of the family; Mrs Russell, her mother's friend and the last person to be with Mrs Welsh when she died – which Jane failed to be – was another. These older women provided an understanding comfort, the petting of women who had seen and understood a great deal. Mrs Russell, especially, became the person Jane wrote to most fully once she had managed, by 1849, to overcome her terror of returning to Scotland. Not only the friend and neighbour of her mother, but also herself the wife of a doctor, Mrs Russell was peculiarly suited to be the loving parent Jane had lost. However ill or depressed she was, Jane had faith that if she could get herself to Mrs Russell's

6. Geraldine Jewsbury (April 1855), reproduced by kind permission of The Rare Book and Manuscript Collection, Columbia University, USA.

she would find good care. Mrs Russell's sympathetic attentions brought back the lost comforts of the past. At her house Jane could take,

> a lifebath, as it were, in my quasi-natural air, in the scene of old affections, not all past and gone, but some still as alive and warm, thank God, as ever! and only the dearer for being mixed up with those that are dead and gone.[3]

Mrs Russell's 'lifebath' was one Jane felt immediate need of after spending a week at Ramsgate with Geraldine in 1862. Though not an unsuccessful trip, and accomplished at a time when relations between them had been severely strained since 1857, Jane returned to Cheyne Row feeling irritable. She was not entirely displeased that her husband was 'much more like a spoiled baby than other men' and needed her services. He had written to her every day while she was away, letters 'like the letter of a Babe in the Wood, who would be found buried with dead leaves by the robins if I didn't look to it'. The problem at the seaside resort was the familiar one of sleeplessness and noise, which 'seems to be the grand joy of life at Ramsgate'; but it was exacerbated by the fact that while Jane's nerves were fretted as usual, Geraldine, also as usual, 'sleeps like a top'. Nor was that Geraldine's only crime: the cocks, cats, dogs, barrel-organs, brass bands, female fiddlers, bagpipes, French horns, shrimp sellers, steeple clocks, drunkards, and babies, whose cacophony destroyed most of the good Ramsgate's sea air did Jane, all 'received an irritating finishing touch from the rapid, continuous scrape, scraping of Geraldine's pen (nothing more irritating, than to see "others" perfectly indifferent to what is driving oneself wild)'. Undaunted by noise and undeterred by Jane's complaints, Geraldine went blithely writing on. Her ability to keep going made Jane feel inadequate, weak, and depressed, and she turned to Mrs Russell for an affection uncompromised by worldly success or searching analysis:

> you have been in such depths yourself occasionally, and will have sympathy with me, instead of being contemptuous or angry, as your strong-minded, able-bodied women would be; and accordingly strong-minded, able-bodied women are my aversion, and I run out of the road of one as I would from a mad cow.[4]

It was hardly necessary for Jane to name Geraldine as the principal strong-minded, able-bodied woman she wanted to run out of the road of; and it was not long afterwards that their friendship broke apart again so absolutely that Geraldine did not expect it to be renewed as it had been so often in the past:

> She takes things into her head and believes them and nothing can alter her notions. I cannot blame myself altogether though I would gladly do so and take the whole of it if *that* would work any change, but I cannot renew her health and give her clear eye-sight and I can only feel that if I were in her position, domestic and physical, that *I* should be less reasonable and more disagreeable a great deal. The final *break* was so sudden, so entirely unlooked for that I might say of it as the maids say when they break a precious piece of china, 'Ma'am, I was holding it quite carefully when it *flew out of my hand*!' I could not have cared more for anyone than I have done for her, or have been more true.[5]

A year later Geraldine was back, making herself useful once more. But the anger and contempt Jane read in Geraldine's responses to her illnesses, and her own very obvious anger and contempt for Geraldine, were angers and contempts around the same source: broadly speaking, the question of the place of men in women's lives; and, its subsidiary, the kinds of work and the kinds of purposes women could seek for themselves. The continuous scraping of Geraldine's pen, year in, year out, had become intolerable to Jane long before they were confined together in rooms in Ramsgate.

Loving and observing Jane with all the intimacy of a daughter, Geraldine deferred to her greater age, wisdom, and knowledge, but at the same time seized 'the opportunity of working out in some degree' her ideas of Jane's character and life, much as she did with Lady Morgan. She had early concluded that Jane's physical condition was the direct result of her domestic situation. As a woman who had made it her business to observe other people's marriages, she watched and spoke with the annoying authority of the intellectual: thinking hard but never having actual experience of the matter in question. And although Jane liked to suggest that Geraldine would have married almost anyone who would have her, she must have known at some level that, for all her interest in men, Geraldine did not marry because she feared the effects of marriage on women, especially women like herself and Jane.

Geraldine's anger and contempt, which Jane perceived, arose from her essentially political conviction that marriage as it was constituted served men's interests at the expense of women. Caught between admiration of Jane's personal qualities and heroism, and horror at the destructive effects of her life, she attempted to reach some kind of resolution in her fictions. Jane's anger and contempt, partly envy of Geraldine, was also the anger of a woman whose story had been told by another without her permission. Geraldine's presumption in telling Jane's story, in different ways, was bad enough; she also, with the maddening superiority of the gifted child, printed her own solutions. Jane's impassioned defence of propriety, in *Zoe* and even more in *The Half Sisters*, as well as her cautionary hold on Geraldine at social gatherings, were not disinterested anxieties. They need to be understood as a fear of having her own identity revealed and finding her private life, in Geraldine's version, become an open book; for if Geraldine's real life emotions too closely resembled fictional ones, it was equally the case that her fictional debates could often be readily traced back to their sources, chief amongst which was the debate that extended for some twenty-five years between herself and Jane over the different womanly choices each of them had made.

In *Zoe*, for example, the figure of Mirabeau, a larger than life-size hero for his time, was drawn by a young woman who had been admitted into personal acquaintance with that larger than life-size hero for *his* time, Thomas Carlyle, whose vivid rendering of Mirabeau in *The French Revolution* probably formed the basis of Geraldine's imaginative knowledge of him. By placing Zoe in the position of being able to contemplate the possibility of becoming Mirabeau's life partner, Geraldine created a fictional version of Jane's situation. Using the device of a real historical figure, she cleverly intensified the fictional impression; Mirabeau's sudden appearance in volume three is hard to take seriously. But his presence enabled Geraldine to explore aspects of Jane's life as if it had been her own and to offer her own, very different, answer to the Mirabeau/Carlyle proposal – viz. that the adult female should give total submission and live in absolute servitude to the adult male, and that the larger the stage that adult male walked upon, the greater the degree of submission and servitude required of the female.

In *Zoe*, Geraldine made it plain that she rejected the validity of this demand. The basis of it – the greatness of the individual man – lost its substance when she showed Mirabeau as egotistical and selfish in his emotional demands. Although the dramatization and resolution of the issues are evasive, the meeting of Mirabeau and Zoe remains, in essence, the meeting of competing egotisms, male and female. Each has a large soul and large talents, but the male ego demands the submission of the female ego. By showing Zoe refusing to give up her own life in order to become a part of Mirabeau's life, Geraldine demonstrated to Jane her vision of the alternative path Jane might have taken. Representing Mirabeau much as Jane habitually represented Carlyle, as a man of inflexible will who could not be negotiated with but had to be given his own way, driven and destructive, she diminished him in stature just as the Carlyle she had read in his books was somewhat diminished for her by personal acquaintance and his wife's account of him. At the same time, and in order to disguise the fact that the drama was one of competing egotisms, she elevated Zoe to the higher spiritual plane of self-sacrificing motherhood. By these means she brought into question the justification others found in Jane's life – womanly sacrifice for a great man – ejected Mirabeau/Carlyle from first place in Zoe/Jane's affections, and, in the guise of the sick child, placed herself there.

There was not much risk that readers of *Zoe* would have thought Zoe was Mrs Carlyle – nor was she, any more than she was Geraldine. Less still would they have mistaken Mirabeau for Carlyle. But it is hard to believe that Jane and Thomas did not see something of themselves in these fictional creations, even if the recognition operated at an unconscious level to begin with. As an instinctively autobiographical writer himself (Carlyle's biographer, Fred Kaplan, observed that Carlyle was incapable of writing anything that was not autobiography), Carlyle was attuned to the way the rhythms of a lived life played through a fictional one; and Jane, no less of an autobiographer, had had many years of the best literary society in which to develop a sense of the inter-relatedness of the fictional and the real in art and life. And she was engaged in telling the story of her life in her own way, in her letters. The disparity between the social rewards of her writing and Geraldine's and Thomas's – all different forms of self-projection – was galling in itself. Whatever reasons were dominant, some explanation beyond propriety is called for to explain the vehemence with which both Carlyles turned on Geraldine when she produced a second three-volume novel within a few years of *Zoe*, though in Thomas's case it might be enough to point to her facility in writing and the ease of her rise to notoriety.

After the success of *Zoe*, Geraldine continued to look to Jane for editorial services and motherly guidance. She asked her to check over each chapter of *The Half Sisters* as it was completed, to allow her to dedicate the book to her, and to read the proofs. Though undoubtedly burdensome, this was no more burdensome than the demands she had made over *Zoe*. But by November 1847, when the proofs started arriving, Jane was driven to write to John Forster that she was in an embarrassing situation: she was caught between a promise made to a friend and a husband's embargo. She explained that she was 'bothered' about the proofs:

C. has got some furious objection to my meddling with them – even declares that I 'do not know bad grammar when I see it, any better than she does;' that 'if I had any faculty I might find better employment for it,' &c., &c. So, after having written to her that I would do what she wished, I must write again that I am not permitted.

I do think there is much truth in the Young German idea that marriage is a shockingly immoral institution, as well as what we have long known it for – an extremely disagreeable one.

Please countermand the proofs, for every one that comes occasions a row.[6]

In his fury, Thomas reached out for a traditional male stick, that of women's grammatical incompetence, and brought it down not on Geraldine's head alone but, with blatant absurdity, on that of his wife whose grammatical competence and submission to unbending rules were second to none. Jane resolved, even so, to be guided by her husband's 'authentic feelings in the matter', taking into account his dislike of being associated 'by even the slightest spider-thread, with what he calls "George Sandism and all that accursed sort of thing" '.[7] Such a stance conveniently obscured her own authentic feelings, which on the surface were feelings of straightforward moral disapproval:

This is worse than anything in *Zoe*, to my judgement, in fact perfectly disgusting for a young Englishwoman to write, – and from Chapman's point of view, quite 'unfit for circulation in families'. I would not have such stuff *dedicated to me* as she proposed, for any number of guineas. But I am done with counselling her, – her tendency towards the unmentionable is too strong for *me* to stay it.[8]

She did not want, she said, 'to promenade' herself as 'an "emancipated" woman'.[9] She objected to the presence in *The Half Sisters* of 'More *actresses*! more "hysteric seizures" more of "all that sort of thing" which played the deuce with her last book!'.[10]

Compared to George Sand, *The Half Sisters* is exceedingly mild stuff. Amidst all Jane's expostulations against Geraldine's lamentable lack of a sense of decency is an unexpected admission: it was not, after all, the 'questionability' of the novel which she regretted most but what she described as its 'total want of commonsense'.[11] Jane did not normally apply the criterion of common sense to sentimental novels. She read them for emotional comfort and sexual stimulus in an emotionally comfortless and sexually starved life. Nothing in Geraldine's books approached the 'questionability' of *Indiana*, for example, which boasts an extraordinarily intense focus on the woman as a desired body in a bedroom. *Indiana* positively pulsates with physicality. It was not for pages of common sense that Jane read George Sand, and it was something other than what is usually meant by common sense that was confirmed in Mrs Buller when Jane discovered, to her delight, that she, too, was a George Sand enthusiast.

However, the *want* of common sense did not appear to signify. What was the difference between Geraldine's pages and those of George Sand which made the 'want of commonsense' such a trial for Jane's nerves when she read Geraldine but did not disturb when she read George Sand? What kind of common sense did George Sand have that Geraldine lacked? If George Sand's novels, which appeared to be novels of revolt against the position of women in marriage, could offer the comforts of common sense as well as the more sensational comforts of vicarious sexual pleasure to an unhappily married woman, what kind of revolt did they encourage?

Leslie Rabine, in 'George Sand and the myth of femininity', argues very persuasively that George Sand's novels, while employing a rhetoric of rebellion, in fact encouraged conformity to the feminine stereotypes prevailing at the time. Far from being 'the voice of women when women were silent', she wrote when there was a strong independent women's movement in France, but instead of identifying herself with that movement, she ridiculed it. In place of the political vision of women working for an autonomous status for women, she purveyed the conventional view of woman as a being seen and thought by a series of men. The Sandian heroine had no self-consciousness because she existed through men's vision of her. Like Freud, as Rabine points out, Sand claimed to reject the traditional view of women, but also like Freud she in fact reproduced it: 'they each deny a female representation of origin and a female self-representation, which might challenge the male structure of origin and self.' In Sand and in Freud, woman

is prevented from forming any system of auto-representation of self regard, any system that would symbolize her own desires and sexual reality . . . an independent configuration of desire and of self would violate man's assurance of self-identity and even the concept of identity. . . . The woman must be looked at by the man, who sees her not as what she might be, but as lack and absence of what he is and has.[12]

Sand did not violate the prohibition against symbolizing female desire. Indiana herself is represented not as pursuing her own desires but as responding to men's desires for her. Feminine desire, in *Indiana*, is, according to this analysis, a masculine desire, the man's wish that the woman 'be someone *other than herself*, and that she correspond to his preconceived stereotype of femininity'. Most crucially of all, '*Indiana* encourages women to resign themselves to the established order and to live in a fantasy world instead of acting to alter their situation. . . . It does not simply reproduce the stereotypes but merges feminine aspirations for freedom into them.'[13]

The common sense in *Indiana* was George Sand's agreement to confirm all the conventional values of a society she appeared to condemn. Indiana herself is a superior woman because she offers herself to her lover not out of a desire for happiness or self-fulfilment but as a sacrifice. Geraldine's 'want of commonsense' would appear to have been her move towards a political vision of her own and Jane's situation. She was not content to represent women seen, thought, and desired by men, for she wished to be the hero of her own drama, the acting subject of her own life. It was not common sense in 1847 to suggest a political dimension to the situation of middle-class women, especially not within the confines of that middle-class art form, the novel. In *The Half Sisters*, the two heroines, Alice and Bianca, live out extreme versions of the lives chosen by Jane and Geraldine. Alice is the dutiful middle-class wife of a man who cannot respond to her emotional needs; Bianca a professional woman, single, earning a living and a place in society through the hard mastery of dramatic art. Fathered by the same man, subject to the same social laws that structure the feminine self, Alice and Bianca are sisters waiting to discover and act upon the knowledge of their kinship. Such an essentially political reading of the relationship between herself and Jane, suggesting as it does the family link between all women under patriarchy, was a more potent threat to Jane's peace of mind than volumes of George Sand. Geraldine's 'tendency towards the unmentionable' may not in fact have been her love of writing about actresses and hysteric seizures and the like, so much as her fundamentally critical view of Jane's life.

And there was another important influence on *The Half Sisters*: Charlotte Cushman. This remarkable actress had made her name on the basis of her 'manly', not her 'womanly', attributes. The newspapers never tired of pointing out her lack of beauty, heftiness of build, and gracelessness of movement. She played Romeo not Juliet, old women not young, had a deep voice and a determined chin, and she was successful. To Geraldine, Charlotte was the embodiment of 'protection and strength'.[14] For some years she kept up a correspondence with her that had in it much of the passion of her early correspondence with Jane. In Charlotte, Geraldine was able to contemplate the positive possibilities of a professional woman's life, and she set it against the negative example that Jane's life offered. Both were fictionalized in significant ways; and, in drawing on these living women, Geraldine left out a factor that was of great importance to both of them: their strong emotional relationships with other women.

Geraldine's move towards a political vision at the time of writing *The Half Sisters* was more than balanced, both in its pages and subsequently, by her move away from it. One of the most telling details about life for women in mid-nineteenth-century Britain was the fear that even assured and forthright middle-class women experienced at their own discontent and the channels it might lead them into. Women like Geraldine who had managed to achieve a position in male culture seem instinctively to have protected that position by distancing themselves from those middle-class women who, by the early 1850s, were beginning to organize together for specifically political change (as working-class women among the Owenites and Chartists had already been doing for some decades). Geraldine's loyalty to women as women deserted her when she described an 'emancipated lady' she observed at a reception:

> a great bow of ribbon at the back of her hair looked as if it had been stuck
> on by way of protest against the usages of society – if ever a bow of ribbon

looked indignant *that* did. She edits a newspaper about the Rights of Women, liberty & progress & so forth – Why cannot women make themselves into natural human beings without talking of it till they grow ugly? Nobody hinders them except their own absurd and bitter clatter & gossip about each other – Men don't hinder women half so much as women hinder each other & these emancipating women (all I have seen) look as though they had never cared for anybody more than themselves.[15]

This was written to a man. It is unlikely that she would have spoken in the same way when talking to Charlotte Cushman (though the fundamental point of view might not have been different) or when having tea with Frances Power Cobbe some years later. These women would have taken strength precisely from the intimations of political vision in Geraldine's novels and, in their responses and encouragement, provided those small communities of the mind which would have enabled it to develop. But Geraldine's first loyalty was to Jane, and back through Jane in a direct line of influence to Maria Jane. Though hard and painful, caring for others was the road of duty, the guarantee of social acceptability, and had been defined as a form of self-sacrifice. Caring for others, when applied to women, did not mean helping them take care of themselves: it meant helping them take care of others. Even in *The Half Sisters*, which tackled the woman question most directly through the subject of employment for women, the woman who works, Bianca, is shown as doing so rather for the sake of others than herself: first, to support an insane mother; second, to win the love of a scoundrel she unaccountably thinks is a good man. When personal satisfactions are admitted, they are the nun-like satisfactions of the surrendered self.

Like Geraldine and Jane, Bianca and Alice are very different personalities whose social roles intensify their differences. Geraldine heightened these differences further by making Alice dull, dreary, and decent, and giving to Bianca – who is half-Italian as Zoe was half-Greek – a Zoe-like exoticism. By doing so, and by offering, in Alice, a being entirely formed and moulded by the conventions of provincial femininity – passive, quiescent, and ultimately doomed – she successfully covered with spotted muslin Alice's origins in the life lived by Jane Carlyle. Simplifying Alice down to a type blurred the argument but was safer. It was safer on a personal level and also commercially; just as Jane Welsh could hardly have sold a novel about utterly imbecilic men and rational women, so Geraldine understood the demands of her market: the passive, vaguely unhappy, not very intelligent wife who merely needed a man to set her right (but who was likely to go wrong by going for the wrong man) did not disturb the order of things. One way or another, her gaze was directed towards men, she remained 'interior to a masculine desire'. Jane's very difference was that although a wife, and although agreeing to live out a passive role, she was not passive, nor stupid, nor wishing to be led; she contested the convenient implication that those characteristics, because socially enforced, were naturally occurring. But her fierce individuality had no place in Geraldine's fictional account.

Individuality exists only in the character whose social role led readers to expect it and therefore feel comfortable with it: Bianca, who is unmarried and an artist, and who, as a literary creation, harks back to Madame de Staël's Corinne. Bianca, an unusual woman, may lay claim to a different scale of values, is accorded greater freedoms, and negotiates (successfully) far more complex social ambiguities than ordinary Alice. Bianca's problems lie in the social world, in, very literally, her audience. As such they are material problems subject to observation, definition, discussion, and the possibility of agreed solutions. Alice's problems lie within, for Alice's problems exist within the walls of the home. Just as common sense did not consider the situation of middle-class women an appropriate subject for politics, so common sense in the 1840s did not view the home as a site for political analysis. In depicting the dire effects of Alice's marriage on her mental and emotional equilibrium, Geraldine carefully moderated her attack on the institution of marriage and the man Alice married. The theatre was safely identified as Bianca's problem – as well as providing her with an opportunity to develop her full self; but marriage, even though courtship and the attainment of marriage provided the staple of novelistic story telling, was explosive material. The most Geraldine dared do, by putting the married woman into her half-sisterly relation with the actress, was to suggest the commonality of interest between the two and to demonstrate which role, working actress or working wife, worked for the soul and which destroyed.

The problematic issue was the issue of self. While *The Half Sisters* is a novel about work, or rather about the benefits of purposeful work for middle-class women, it is only about work in the way that *Zoe* was about religion. Behind those themes beat the dangerous energies of the assertive female self, longing to lay claim to autonomy on its own female terms. Like Margaret Fuller, Geraldine Jewsbury could as well have said, 'I must die if I do not burst forth into genius or heroism.'[16] The hero is a self; the heroine, alas, was always liable to be or to become an appendage: Hamlet can exist without Ophelia, but not Ophelia without Hamlet. Geraldine's hero, Bianca, has her wings pinned in various ways throughout the novel to demonstrate that she is, in spite of everything, a heroine; and ultimately she moves through the experience of worthwhile work to end the novel married to a good man, thus ending up where Alice too literally ended, as the model female: a wife.

Bianca's husband, Lord Melton, is an achievement in every sense: aristocratic, urbanely feminist, intelligently philanthropic. His fictional perfections enabled Geraldine to represent as an ideal the very institution the bulk of her novel apparently denounces. At the same time, he is also a passive figure who reflects all Bianca's most deeply held convictions; marrying him, she does not have to give up her feminist point of view. Lord Melton can be seen in his relation to Bianca as the reverse of what Thomas Carlyle said should constitute marriage: she is not the beautiful reflex of him, but he is the beautiful reflex of her. Also, marrying into the aristocracy resembles becoming a genius in that it enables a woman to break free of the bonds of middle-class femininity. In that sense, genius and aristocratic marriage are interchangeable.

But Alice's marriage is a middle-class marriage, a sort of death-in-life, as is her upbringing. Alice has no special gifts, nothing strong enough to withstand the barrage of bad guidance she receives in the course of an ordinary English female growing up. She has 'fine qualities' but they are not distinct enough to defend her. And since 'wise guidance is precisely the blessing that seldomest falls to a woman's lot', Alice grows up 'ineffectual and incomplete'. The victim of a socially constructed femininity which renders her 'negative and useless', Alice is the model of what men – as Geraldine tartly observed – consider 'womanly perfection'.[17]

Alice's conditioning into weakness – womanly perfection – forms a substantial part of *The Half Sisters*. All her cultivation is directed towards gaining a husband, preferably a rich one, but even a man without wealth is enough to ensure a woman the basis of a social existence. Alice's attempts to improve her mind meet with determined opposition from her mother: she wants to read Sismondi, her mother orders her to 'make Fido a collar'. When she asks why she has to marry at all, she is told, 'For what else do women come into the world ... but to be good wives?' Being 'lucky enough' to be married is the best thing that can happen to a young girl for 'then she is something in the world'. In order to become something in the world, it is best for her to become as close to nothing as she can in herself. Alice's mother lectures her:

> if there is one thing I dislike to see in a young woman more than another, it is a love of singularity; indeed, it is the only impropriety a well-brought up young woman has it in her power to commit.... If a young woman allows herself to be different to other people, she throws herself out of the path marked by propriety, and has no guide but her own, giddy head ... no gentleman would *marry* a girl who set up to be remarkable.[18]

Being 'different' might include talking about love: 'men don't like it; it looks forward and impudent', Mrs Helmsby warns. Or, indeed, talking about anything at all: 'To manage the house well, and to see that the dinner was punctual and well appointed; to be very quiet, and not talk nonsense, or rather to talk very little of anything' were 'the principal qualities desired in wives and daughters'.[19]

As a mature and experienced woman, Mrs Helmsby spoke the observable truths of a woman's life. Her commitment to the values which inspired such truths was not philosophical but practical, a survival strategy. The life of an unmarried woman was unenviable: 'Poor, profitless, forlorn creatures they are, when they live single and get to be old.'[20] Calculation and manipulation were essential skills, and Mrs Helmsby, as a caring mother, endeavoured to instil them in her daughter: 'a young woman must never let her real sentiments appear; – the best of men are not to be trusted, they are our natural enemies, and always ready to take advantage of anything they see in their favour.'[21] Once Alice is matched for life with one of her 'natural enemies', the kindly industrialist, Bryant, she gains a deeper insight into these realities. She is taken to be introduced to Bryant's sister, Mrs Lauriston, the worldly-wise 'mistress of a handsome establishment' aptly named Matching Park. Mrs Lauriston, having gained her establishment through a 'good' match – to the miserable Mr Lauriston whose presence always bring with it 'the element of heavy silence', 'oppression', and not inconsiderable amounts of gloom – possesses a wisdom devoted to survival, which may or may not be termed cynicism. She tells Alice, even more emphatically than her mother, that a woman should never trust a man:

> never tell your husband ... anything which there is a chance he may not admire ... as men only see things in the light they are put to them, you must be very careful always to present your facts on the *right* side. How should I live with Mr Lauriston, who is reserved, suspicious, and *miserly*, to the last degree, unless I used great judgement with him?[22]

Mrs Lauriston's carefully chosen words make Alice feel extremely uncomfortable, as if she had 'eaten of the tree of knowledge and committed sin'. Mrs Lauriston tells her she is a child to think she might be able to confide freely and openly in her husband, given the nature of the marriage laws in England. Under the circumstances, manipulation and cunning were women's only resource: 'Men make their own laws; it is not our fault that they are suspicious, ungenerous, and selfish; if they choose to be such, we are obliged to take them as we find them, and make the best of them.'[23]

In Mrs Lauriston's company, Alice feels guilty. The older woman's words disturb her. Feeling tainted, she wants to be alone with her husband in their private world of bliss where Mrs Lauriston's words can have neither meaning nor power. Unfortunately for Alice, she soon discovers that her husband has unqualified admiration for his sister and entirely endorses her view of life and the relation of the sexes in marriage. Mrs Lauriston is to be Alice's model of the ideal wife. But Alice cannot find happiness in exercising her powers in deceit; her dominant mood is guilt; she is always sure she has done wrong, 'haunted by a dull sense of self-reproach' and 'divided against herself, weak, helpless and dissatisfied'. She has everything a woman could desire in the way of material possessions, but she feels 'shut up in prison; I can get to hear and see nothing that my heart cares for'. Feeling empty and useless, she suffers from the problem without a name: 'My whole life is one cloud, and I have a sense of responsibility which I can neither adequately discharge, nor deliver myself from. . . . I am of use to nobody.'[24]

The Half Sisters expounds the common-sense view that idleness breeds mischief – meaning, of course, sexual mischief – and it does so by exposing the moral deficiencies of women kept in ignorance of the real world and rendered entirely dependent on men for guidance. To a readership brought up on the conventional view that home was safe and the world dangerous, Geraldine offered a provocative reversal: it was the world, even the notoriously immoral world of the theatre, which led to moral safety; while the home, for all its goodness, led a well-intentioned woman to moral disaster. This was not an easy position to argue at a time when the tide was running strongly in the direction of home. Also, by making her heroine an actress rather than a writer (though it was clear that she was writing out of her own experience as a writer as well as from her knowledge of an actress's life), Geraldine chose a profession in which the work involved was more obviously visible and understood; but she chose the profession closest to prostitution in the public mind. Bianca's exposure to seaminess being extreme, the defence of her had to be pitched in extreme terms.

Alice, the respectable wife, succumbs to a sinful passion. Bianca, the actress, tempered in the furnace of a player's life, dealing with poverty, insecurity, isolation, lecherous managers, and inflamed admirers, knows how to look after herself: preserving her chastity before marrying into the aristocracy. Bianca's experiences lead her to develop a feminist analysis of woman's place in society. With the confidence of a woman who has earned her right to speak, and arguing from a knowledge of history, she tells Lady Vernon and Lord Melton that woman's position came about gradually and for reasons that need to be explored: 'language, as somebody said,' she explains, 'has been mystified for the use of women, and a whole set of elegant virtues has been invented for their special adornment.' As a consequence, women do not know what they are or what they can be. They are kept in 'a state of perpetual childishness'. Unmarried women in the middle classes, she goes on,

> spend their days in the same kind of trifling that slaves in the East amuse themselves with, till someone comes and puts them in a harem.... Days, months, years of perfect leisure run by ... at length they have all the vitality choked out of them. This is the true evil of the condition of women ... it is melancholy to see the blind, vague efforts women make to be useful; they do their various things, not as an imperative duty, but because they have 'plenty of time', and play at being Lady Bountifuls and lady patronesses to poor people, to get rid of their own weariness.[25]

Bianca, by contrast, has a purpose. In her life as an actress, she was:

> kept clear of ENNUI, which eats like a leprosy into the life of woman. I was leading a life of my own, and was able to acquire a full control over my own faculties: and I have always had a sense of freedom, of enjoyment of my existence.... I have had work to do, and I have done it. I have had a purpose, and have endeavoured to work it out.[26]

This is real life. Alice's existence, like that of most middle-class women, is 'a sort of fictitious existence'. They live as 'ornamental appendages'. Subject to 'rose-coloured' moralities, women without Bianca's advantages lacked those inner certainties which were the basis of principles which enabled them to 'stand against the stern reality of a strong temptation'. Looking to good men to guide them, such women were helpless when left alone with bad men.[27]

Alice falls when Conrad Percy, whom Bianca has loved and believed in, becomes enchanted with the angelic aura she projects. Having plumbed the depths of dissipation on the Continent, Conrad returns to England and finds himself 'perfectly entranced with admiration at the modesty of Englishwomen, and the prudent guard kept over them by English fathers'.[28] His senses aroused by Quakeresses and all 'delicate timidity', he recoils in disgust from Bianca. The number of stage kisses she has had bothers him. Her manners he now finds 'independent and unfeminine'. The truth is, he now observes, that 'a professional life ruins a woman as a woman'; it has 'unsexed' Bianca, for 'a public life must deteriorate women ... they lose all the beautiful ideal of their natures, all that is gentle, helpless, and confiding. The soft plastic virtues.' Conrad elaborates on this:

> The sort of woman I dream of for my wife, is, in all respects, the reverse of Bianca.... A rational, though inferior intelligence, to understand me and help me in my pursuits; clinging to me for help, looking to me for guidance; a gentle, graceful timidity keeping down all display of her talents, a sense of propriety keeping her from all eccentric originality, either of thought or deed, her purity and delicacy of mind keeping her from evil, rather as a matter of exquisite taste, than from any idea of the coarse realities of things, right and wrong.... There is something inexpressibly touching in a true woman's helplessness, her graceful prejudices and aversion to every thing that is too *prononcée*; she is the softened reflex of her husband's opinions – she does nothing too well. For the woman, whom alone I could love, would be too delicate to desire to attract admiration by her accomplishments; she would be religious, because she could not help it, but she would be alike removed from philosophic doubt or enthusiastic bigotry.... Quietly at anchor by her own fire-side, gentle, low-voiced, loving, confiding – such is MY ideal of a woman and a wife; and certainly a professional woman would not be likely to realise it.[29]

Lord Melton, with whom Conrad is having this manly chat, has to take a glass of wine to recover from 'such a vision of exquisite helplessness'. Conrad's vision of wifely perfection was an essentially middle-class vision; sophisticated aristocrats were interested neither in anchored wives nor in professional ones. Recognizing the depraved sensuality that lies behind Conrad's words, Lord Melton defends Bianca in the terms she herself, and Geraldine, would have used. The words he is given to speak echo Maria Jane's words in her early articles on women's education. He appeals to reason. He points to the interest men like Conrad have in keeping women ignorant: 'no higher motive is ever suggested to them than that of being agreeable to us'; women's charms and graces are therefore cultivated at the expense of real knowledge and real principle; the arbitrary tastes of men – which change over time – govern the training of women so that is is impossible to argue from history what women in their 'natural' state might be; and 'as to female virtue, that is legislated for on the score of its social convenience'. Lord Melton objects to 'the all-pervading sensualism which runs through the education and legislation men have provided for women'. Men's views have dictated standards which condemn energy and action, but, he insists – passionately intervening in Conrad's rhapsodic eulogy to winning helplessness – weakness, even in women, is '*not* grace'.[30]

Bianca has a grace that comes from strength. Far from being ruined by her profession, it is the making of her. She 'had a frank and decided manner of bearing herself and expressing her own opinions'. Conrad finds her capacity to 'meet a man's eye without blushing' a form of audaciousness, but Geraldine is at pains to ensure that the reader knows whose audaciousness is on trial. Bianca's very good friend, an old actor who knows the world and befriends her, warns her about Conrad: 'You will only break yourself against the ice-berg of his self-love.' He adds, for good measure: 'Why will women give in to a *grande passion*, and make themselves miserable; if they did but know it, there is not a man amongst us all who deserves it!'[31]

Conrad, a bad man, is bad for both women – he causes Bianca misery and is the direct cause of Alice's death from shame and guilt; but good men may not be much better. Alice's husband, Bryant, is well meaning, gentle, loving, but emotionally dim. Living in ignorance of his own emotions, he has no understanding of Alice's. He has a 'cold, passionless manner'. An industrialist, his mind is on the iron works of Silesia, and even his honeymoon is combined with a fact-finding tour of the mining districts of Wales. But Bryant is no cipher, and as a character has a more original function to fulfil in the text than has the unsavoury young rake, Conrad Percy. He is the type of the northern industrialist, the self-made, hard-working, no nonsense man of expanding manufacture. Bryant speaks up for the superior virtues of the industrial classes, who are also, in this book, the model of the industrious classes. Their virtues are seldom recognized – certainly not in books; and as Bryant explains, they do not possess the grace and charm, the plasticity, of the arts:

> real labour was never yet made to look beautiful.... We, who have to grapple with realities, grow stern and rude as the elements in which we work; we have to produce the substance out of which refinement, civilisation, the very country itself, have to come forth. It is not our fault if the fine arts, and the artists who produce them, seem small and trivial beside the immense interests with which we have to deal, and the materials with which we have to work.[32]

He has no desire to mix socially with 'authors, actors, artists, or professional people of any sort', for 'there is a want of stamina about them: they have no precision or business-like habits':

> This is an industrial country ... we have no real knowledge of art, no real instinct or genuine aspiration after it ... we ... do not feel drawn to the society of artists; we have nothing in common with them – we do not admire them; neither do we feel disposed to introduce to the society of our wives and daughters, a parcel of actors, artists, musicians and so forth, who

have little to lose, whose capital is all invested in themselves and their two hands.[33]

Women respond to artists, because the arts are a form of leisure and essentially feminine; they have nothing, in Bryant's view, to connect them with work. The rugged Bryant represents a masculine world of steel and iron; he possesses the qualities that can drive a road through a range of mountains, rather than those 'powers of pleasing' which, when Conrad employs them upon Alice, destroy her 'sobriety and balance of conduct'. Conrad is not an artist, but he hovers around the green room. He is a sort of false artist. The true artist in the novel, Bianca, by rising above temptation and enduring sorrows that would have broken a lesser person – her 'matriculation in humanity' – and by standing fast to principle, acquires the right to be as 'stern' and as 'rude' as her work demands. That is to say, to become as masculine as it is necessary to be to accomplish the masculine ends of work. Bianca's profession may be devoted to pleasing, but her commitment to work raises her above that, just as Thomas Carlyle's ruggedness evokes the steel and iron of a Bryant and separates him from the world of passive reading he was always in danger of being identified with.

Having said that, however, Geraldine quickly takes steps to restore Bianca to a properly feminine realm: the realm of religion. Being devoted to her art is 'a sacred necessity laid upon me, which I cannot help obeying'. Like Felicia Hemans and Maria Jane Jewsbury, Bianca's desire to work at an art of self-expression is justified in religious terms. It is for God, but the sacred necessity is also, significantly, to 'realise myself in my own way, or not at all'.[34] Bianca's way is to turn the theatre into a sort of nunnery, to purify it 'from the sensualism that has defaced it' through the sacredness of her own devotion to art. Living the life of a pure artist, she lives a 'calm, self-sustained existence, dedicated like that of a priestess, cold, strong, and pure'. This is Clotilde's life, one in which sexual passion and the vulnerabilities it engenders are thoroughly repressed. But Bianca 'needed some more human motive to sustain her'. Unwilling to remove herself from the world, morally upright and socially acceptable, Bianca faces the dilemma of a woman who has succeeded against great odds and made her own place in a society which, while accepting her, has not moved in accordance with her ideas or what she represents. The political potential of *The Half Sisters* comes to a dead end with Bianca's ability to root Conrad Percy out of her emotions and put high art there instead. Reluctant to develop the political dimension, Geraldine can only go back on her tracks, for she was too honest to leave Bianca coldly scaling the awesome heights of art; and not honest or brave enough to explore alternatives she knew about from her own life and from her intimate conversations with Charlotte Cushman. Marrying Lord Melton means the end of art. Lady Vernon 'requests' Bianca 'that she will not again appear on the stage, now that she belongs to us'. This curious formulation, agreeing to which makes Bianca 'a good child', emphasizes class over gender issues and is perhaps realistic – entering the aristocracy entailed even stronger prohibitions against putting one's wares about than getting married.[35] But it cannot obscure the circularity of the argument. Instead of a nun, Bianca becomes the wife of an aristocrat.

*

Much is made in *The Half Sisters*, directly and by implication, of the tendency of work to de-feminize. Conrad speaks his opposition to the 'dogmatic, harsh, self-sufficing' professional woman who, like a man with business to accomplish, 'strides and stalks through life'; from her 'contact with actual things, she is slightly masculine in her views ... she loves like a man.' Bianca, also, finds herself becoming depressed because she begins to be spoken to 'as if I were a man'. Enclosure in the rigid category of a female man is no better than enclosure in the category of a womanly woman. But the suggestion that women are deformed by work is not balanced by any exploration of the possibility that the definition of work might be expanded to include the work that women do. One significant way in which Alice does not resemble Jane Carlyle is that Alice does not work: neither Jane's work nor her writing formed part of the story Geraldine told about her. Alice's lack of work symbolically kills her at the same time as it defines her femininity.

Geraldine gives Bianca in marriage to Lord Melton on the grounds that they are equals in a world beyond work: they are both removed from the sphere of necessity and may both philosophically uphold a morality of self-realization. 'What is *life* in its very essence,' Lord Melton asks rhetorically, 'but the *power to struggle* ... to possess our souls entire, not to get them warped or crippled?'[36]

The power to struggle, like the power to work, is premised on endurance. In Lord Melton's meaning, the power to struggle is not a power to change anything, but a power of resistance; it is a struggle to retain personal authenticity. For middle-class women, this was a struggle that had to precede all other struggles, for the warping and crippling of women were central facts of middle-class mores. The struggle against warping and crippling was the struggle towards life. In moving towards life, women who struggled to possess their souls moved in the opposite direction to the womanly ideal. Even Geraldine, who was used to being at fault, experienced deep anxiety at the implications of this, for as an independent single woman the culture had no comfortable, properly defined place for her. The self she might be was not reflected back to her in the books she read. Her struggle to retain personal authenticity was a very real struggle to survive in a world where to be womanly and weak, without having a man to provide a front of protection, would have been to court catastrophe. Single women needed manly qualities to survive; they needed strength and independence in order to resist the warping and crippling effects of dependence which not only affected married women but had specific application, too, to single women. These began by being economic: single women might be 'obliged to receive house and shelter upon any terms'; and ended in being psychic: dependence in modern times was 'what slavery was of old ... it takes all manliness and quality of character out of whoever voluntarily submits to it'. For married women of the middle classes there was perhaps a compensatory elevation to the pedestal – in theory at least. Single women did not even have that.[37]

In *The Sorrows of Gentility* (1856), from which the above quotations are taken, Geraldine dramatized what might have been her own position if her work as a writer had not given her economic independence. Gertrude, having been brought up badly in the 'fine-lady' mould, makes a bad marriage and finds herself alone in the world with a baby to care for. That is when she learns 'practically what it was to be dependent'. She has to 'eat the bread of charity' from her sister-in-law's hand, and be grateful for 'small mercies of the most unpalatable kind'.[38] The lesson Gertrude learns, which is the reverse of the lessons she had grown up on, is that independent hard work is the route to happiness, while dreaming of fortune or even mere financial responsibility from men is the route to misery. But independence brought its own perils. Geraldine stated these explicitly in a letter to Jane of 1850, in which she reflected on a woman she knew:

> I think she is a good woman in herself. The only thing is, that, living on her own basis, she has got into a habit of taking care of herself, and making use of other people; that is the worst of women living in the world, and I don't know how they are to help it! I daresay I should get into the same sort of thing if I had to go about like men, and have nobody but myself to look to to help me ... it is a problem that bothers me – viz., that when women get to be energetic, strong characters, with literary reputations of their own, and live in the world, with business to attend to, they all do get in the habit of making use of people, and of taking care of themselves in a way that is startling! ... In short, whenever a woman gets to be a personage in any shape, it makes her hard and unwomanly in some point or other.[39]

The person Geraldine had to look to to help her at that time was her brother Frank, whose comforts she attended to and with whom she could go about much as if they were a married couple. But she also knew that in real life married women, too, needed manly qualities to survive; the negative vacuum of womanly perfection not only lead to sexual infidelities such as those her fictional Alice was destroyed by: weak women were at men's mercies in other ways. Geraldine told Jane of a woman she knew in Liverpool who was just about keeping herself from starving by painting miniatures, having left her husband, a 'brute' who had

> treated her infamously, spent all her money, beat her, and actually when he was in a worse temper than usual used to put her at the top of the stairs and roll her down all the way to the bottom.[40]

The continuum of womanly possibilities stretched from being hard and taking care of oneself – in the first instance through work – at one end, to being periodically rolled down a flight of stairs by one's husband at the other. Taking care of oneself was to move towards maleness, while being rolled down the stairs was the ultimate female posture; a posture in which, it will be agreed, there was little scope for heroism, even of the self-sacrificing kind.

198

Masculine qualities might mitigate female vulnerabilities. The extreme of men's power over women and women's submission to men's authority was inscribed in the marriage laws, and expressed in the brutality of violent husbands towards their wives. In *The Sorrows of Gentility* Gertrude's husband, the feckless Donnelly, is judged 'idle' and 'worthless' by comparison with Gertrude, but by the standards set by men he becomes 'not a bad husband'. This is because, though he neglects her and exploits her, he does not beat her. Lady Southend, Gertrude's 'true' mother in the novel – the woman who gives her sound advice about life – was the victim of a brutal husband. She tells Gertrude, 'I have worn my diamond bracelets to hide black flesh where he had pinched me.' She wore high-necked dresses 'to hide the marks of his brutality upon my shoulders'. One day, 'whilst my maid was dressing my hair, he came in like a madman, and, seizing the hot irons, scored them across both shoulders; the scars were ineffaceable'; another time, 'he seized me unawares and cut all the nails on one hand to the quick!' Lady Southend's response to all this was not to leave her husband, nor even to speak out against him: 'I appeared in public with him, and kept a serene and smiling face whilst he was uttering the most insulting language in a whisper.' In spite of this brutality, Lady Southend has not allowed herself, psychologically speaking, to be rolled down the stairs. Her inner resistance gives her power, a purely individual and limited one. By adopting the strategy of the serene and smiling front, she has personal power over her husband in the public arena even if she still has little defence against him privately: 'The world could not gossip about me or pity me, and my husband *feared* me when I looked at him and held my tongue!' Out of the distillation of her life's experience, she teaches Gertrude:

> Lay hold of the facts of things, even though it should be sharper than a sword. Accept your lot as it actually is – do not weakly try to make a compromise if it is miserable; say to yourself, it *is* miserable – and bear it … your strength will fail if you waste it in struggling to be *happy* into the bargain.[41]

The heroism is a heroism of endurance; no matter how bad the situation, how awful the husband, how unjust the demands made upon the woman, the greatness of a woman who had taken the vows of marriage, who had uttered 'the terrible "obey"', was perceived to lie in heroic fortitude. Lady Southend, being an aristocrat, was brisker and brusquer than the Miss Airlie who had been perfected by suffering, but like her she enunciates a noble ideal not an opposition; like her, too, she was the fictional outcome of Geraldine's attempt to reconcile herself to the realities of Jane's life as she saw them.

Thomas Carlyle's physical violence was potential rather than actual, but it formed the climate in which his wife lived. In 1853 Jane told Kate Sterling that she dared not leave the house in case she returned to find her husband in prison 'for having killed an Irish bricklayer because he had fallen through the ceiling. … It takes all my strength of mind to keep things from murder and utter insanity.'[42] Spiritually, the violence he did her manifested itself in sickness, hysteria, and despair; bleakness and loss characterized her middle years. Geraldine considered her life as Thomas Carlyle's wife a 'life laid waste', and Jane herself could hardly deny it. She warned Babbie:

> I may say to you of my own knowledge that the natural sadness of the latter part of one's life may be cruelly embittered by the reflection that one's best years, which might perhaps have produced something good have been suffered to run to waste, fertile only of tares and nettles![43]

As a young wife at Craigenputtock, she had known the importance of having a worthwhile sense of purpose and the relation of purpose to energy: 'With a goal before me I could leap six-bar gates.'[44] She had tried to make housework into that purpose, but housework, in the end, could not be made to be enough. Returning home from a visit, she had 'nothing to do but ray out darkness on all *my* human attempts at occupation or amusement'; looking ahead was like looking into 'unmitigated zero': 'I wish I could find some hard work I *could* do – and saw any sense in doing. If I do not soon it will be the worse for me. . . . All my talents seem to be going one after another.' Carlyle's violent engrossment in his work on Cromwell produced a domestic 'Reign of Terror', an atmosphere so sulphurous that 'it begins to look a stupidity rather than a heroism in me to stay till my life is crushed out in it'.[45]

Geraldine assured Jane that it was heroism not stupidity to let her life be crushed out by her marriage. The strength she helped restore was a strength to endure. In doing so, she was reduced to appealing to that Christian God neither woman professed to believe in, guiding Jane's steps around the hearth and towards the altar:

> The thing you intended for the best and noblest dedication of yourself has not borne the fruit you have reason to expect. Dear friend, do not let yourself be made bitter by this trial. Yield yourself up, and bow your head to Him who is the Father and Director of all. Don't worry yourself by thinking over all you might have been, if you can resign yourself into His hands ... accept as from His hands this humiliation of not having any visible, successful result of the great step of your life. . . . It is not with men you have to deal. Look away from human beings. You are in the hands of God, the Master of all, and it is to Him you submit. . . . Leave husband, friend, all alone, and resign your destiny to Him, and you will find your sorrows cease and your way made plain.[46]

If there was one thing that was clear in Jane's life, it was that her feelings of sorrow and confusion increased rather than decreased as the years went by. Her way became absurd rather than plain to her and she felt herself 'utterly worthless'. Her revolt against the validity of the life she led, was not spoken in a way that could be heard and built on by Geraldine any more than it was heard by Thomas Carlyle or any of their many friends. There was a persistent undertone of resistance, a refusal to give intellectual consent to the realities that made up her existence; but there was also what can only be described as a perverse determination to persist in the course she had chosen. Occasionally resistance broke out with main force. In 1859 a new young friend, Miss Barnes, told her that she was going to get married. Jane's reply was hardly conventional:

And you are actually going to get married! you! already! And you expect me to congratulate you!.... Frankly, my dear, I wish you all happiness.... But congratulation on such occasions seems to me a tempting of Providence. The triumphal-procession-air which, in our manners and customs, is given to marriage at the outset – that singing of Te Deum before the battle has begun – has, ever since I could reflect, struck me as somewhat senseless and somewhat impious. If ever one is to pray – if ever one is to feel grave and anxious – if ever one is to shrink from vain show and vain babble – surely it is just on the occasion of two human beings binding themselves to one another, for better and for worse, till death part them; just on that occasion which it is customary to celebrate only with rejoicings and congratulations, and *trousseaux*, and white ribbon! Good God!

Will you think me mad if I tell you that when I read your words, 'I am going to be married', I all but screamed? Positively, it took away my breath, as if I saw you in the act of taking a flying leap into infinite space. You had looked to me such a happy, happy little girl.[47]

Miss Barnes had a father who reminded Jane of her own father; the young woman's willingness to bind herself to a husband when she could have gone on living peacefully with her father seemed to Jane a form of madness. Childlike satisfactions were surer, if the father was there to give them. Thomas Carlyle succeeded in being neither father nor husband, and barely even a brother, while it was possible only for those beyond the walls of the home circle to consider him a sort of god.

Without a doubt, Geraldine had some investment in Jane's suffering, an investment which must have been among the evidences of insincerity which the years accumulated and for which Jane never ceased to berate her. Geraldine admitted, 'if you were happy, I don't think I should care for you half so much'. By noble suffering, Mrs Carlyle could become an idealized female heroine whose protective presence, as social being and icon, offered the reassurances of conventional feminity to a woman who strayed too near the borders of sexual unconventionality for her own peace of mind. At the same time, and ironically, it was Jane's very masculine qualities that attracted Geraldine to her, providing that 'protection and strength' she continued to feel the need of. If Jane displayed the masculine qualities, then Geraldine, in caring for her, could be sure that she herself was, in spite of everything – her work, her ability to be 'stern' and commit herself to self-imposed tasks – still feminine; for Jane had the feminine assurances of marriage within which she could be masculine, whereas Geraldine's femininity was daily placed at risk.

In pointing Jane towards the altar, Geraldine implied that a resource that had served her well would work equally well for Jane. Geraldine described her own experience of despair during the years when she had been locked at home in service to her father, with the bleak prospect of a life of maiden-aunt dependency stretching ahead. At that time, 'broken, helpless and prostrate', she had flung herself entirely on God. It was

> rest and healing, and everything one's shattered being needed. One gets hard again, and sets up for oneself. One has to come out of this mysterious sanctuary; but one comes out able to go on.[48]

That was the good side; Felicia Hemans might have said much the same thing. The bad side was that one then worried about one's ability to get hard and go on so well. Setting up for oneself was fraught with ambiguities and ambivalences. But in Geraldine's case, it gave her purposes which retained their meaning for her throughout her life.

The altar served another purpose: by elevating Jane to the status of a heroine verging on the saintly, Geraldine was perhaps able to soothe her own bruised sense of always being in second place to Thomas. She did not like it when Jane's improved health brought her back down to the drawing room to spend her evenings 'with *him* which may be more conjugal but it is much more grim than going into her own room and having *me* to keep her company'.[49] Her own relations with Carlyle, even so, were perfectly cordial to the very end of her life. She visited him while Jane was away – once, famously, was having tea with him while the servant, Mary, gave birth to an illegitimate baby in the awful confines of the china closet in the room behind. Neither of them knew about it and Jane only heard the story several months later.[50]

The facts of Geraldine's life as a writer did not have to be laid hold of, like sharp swords, in a spirit of grim rectitude. A sociable person, without husband or hearth, her solitary work brought her the affection and respect of a wide circle of friends. Like the Carlyles, she was taken up by the aristocracy; unlike Jane, she found no anguish in it. It was a satisfaction to be told by other women that her novels had helped them make sense of their own lives. Her writings provided a point of entry into intimacy as well as social acceptability. Lady Easthope, for example,

> showed me a little book into which she had copied some passages out of one of my books – and she told me that they had helped her and spoken more to her than anything she had met with for many years . . . it was worth something to have *any* fellow creature telling me that . . . she broke down the austere reserve she generally maintains and treated me like a friend or rather like one who would become so.[51]

Unlike Lady Harriet, the aristocratic women with whom Geraldine became associated often had literary projects they were keen to fulfil, and she put her editing skills to good use in advising them. Even if they were not themselves writers, the welcome they extended to her was extended to a writing woman:

when Geraldine went to stay with Lady Llanover or Lady Combermere, she went as nobody's luggage (though she certainly made herself useful in tending the sick and entertaining children), and manuscripts for Mr Blackett, the publisher, or books to review for the *Athenaeum* went with her. She was grateful to anybody who showed her kindness, though she could admit that 'as regards *society* I always feel more or less *like an Indian taking scalps*'. In London she kept up an active social life and defended her liking for going about at the parties of the great:

> first, I like to see things and people as a spectator at a play – it is part of my profession, 2. I generally amuse myself in a placid way ... and lastly and chiefly because I earned whatever success I may have without help from anybody – and if one has earned the right of putting the right foot before the left there is a value in it not its own.[52]

That value was one she never lost sight of. Quite apart from the difference of personality between Geraldine and Jane, the younger woman's more equable relations with others – of all social classes, from the aristocracy to the servants – owed something to her solid, observable, socially valid achievements which were cast in a form that enabled her to draw increasing credit from them as the years went by. Lady Easthope could copy passages from her book; Lady Harriet was unlikely to have made a note of Jane's witticisms. As Lady Harriet's own fate showed, a reputation for wit rarely extended beyond its own time and place.

Geraldine's acceptability, beginning in scandal, depended on her mastering the essentials of respectability in her fictions. This was to be the task to which she applied herself, and with Jane's help she achieved considerable success. The significant break occurred with *Marian Withers*, Geraldine's third novel, which appeared in book form in 1851. *Marian Withers* proved her, in Jane's opinion, to have learnt a great deal since the excesses of *Zoe* and *The Half Sisters*. There was 'no "George Sandism" in it at all. Indeed, Geraldine is in the fair way to become one of the most moral "Women of England".' Geraldine, it appeared, had 'made an immense progress in common-sense and common decency within the last year'.[53] There is no character in *Marian Withers* who at all resembles Jane Carlyle, though there are women with capabilities running to waste, like Mrs Arl, whom Jane recognized as a flagrant representation of Elizabeth Paulet.

Marian Withers is one of literature's might-have-beens. It was born less out of other books and more out of her own early life than Geraldine's first two books had dared be, and it was her attempt – emboldened, perhaps, by the successes of her neighbour Mrs Gaskell and by Dickens's popularity – to put industrial Manchester and her father's experiences, as well as her own knowledge of its ways, into her fiction. Mrs Arl figures in Marian's life much as Mrs Paulet had figured in Geraldine's, and the Carlylean rescuing angel who resolves Marian's perplexities with a gospel of work is a Mr Cunningham. Unlike Mrs Gaskell, Geraldine did not include Manchester's very poor in her picture; rather than the evils of industrialism, she was anxious to show the positive qualities to be found in those whose good luck combined with hard work to float them into the buoyant currents of upward social mobility.

The poverty and hardship that industrialism left in its wake are absent. More surprisingly, given Geraldine's record, even the attack on society for wasting women's good energies is a muted one, and it is taken less to men and those institutions, like marriage, which sustain the status quo than it is to women. Both blame of women and idealization of women are couched in more extreme terms in *Marian Withers* than in *Zoe* or *The Half Sisters*.

Suffering is accepted as an aspect of female life, and silence and forgetfulness prescribed as the best remedies. Work is an antidote to depression, but the nature of the work is unimportant: 'It is not by waiting for some great task that we honour our life; it is by doing the duties that every day and every hour brings forth.'[54] In an interesting subplot, a calculating young woman marries a debauched old roué in order to gain wealth and social standing. Hilda is so physically repelled by Glynton that she cannot bear to take even a teacup that he has handed to her, but as he is visibly decaying she hopes he will soon die. Glynton gets the better of Hilda by regaining his strength, living a wandering life on the Continent, and writing her out of his will. Thus suitably punished, Hilda learns where true womanly goodness lies and ends the novel a sadder, wiser, and nobler woman.

Women like Hilda who are prepared to play the game on worldly terms and be as cynical and corrupt as the men who desire them – Hilda knows that Glynton responds to the virginal so she poses for him in pure white – complicate the lives of women who wish to deal openly and equally with men. But apart from a few conversational asides, mostly from Lady Wollaston, to the effect that it would be better for both sexes if men would only be fair to women, the women themselves are blamed. Or if not blamed, at least shown as suffering the proper consequences of their own bad actions. One such bad action might be uttering the terrible word 'obey'. Lady Wollaston explains that few girls understand what marriage really means, and fewer still absorb the deep reality of its irrevocability:

> They are taught that no well-regulated young woman ought to think about love – that it is an idle fancy, if not a grave impropriety; and they are taught the necessity of making a good match – it is about the only thing they hear treated as a reality. Those who have any good, right, womanly feeling in their nature wake, when it is too late, to the knowledge of what they have bartered away. Believe me, that no man with the freedom and outgoing activity which is his birthright, can know or imagine what is endured by a woman shut up within herself, with no outlet for her feelings – nobody to whom she may, or indeed ought, to utter the thoughts that are perplexing her. Talk of despair! . . . To feel all that she might have been; to feel powers and faculties awakening within her, which might have made her life so rich in blessedness; and to have all thrown back to die within her heart; that is despair, if you like . . . if women sin, be very sure that they expiate bitterly![55]

Unfortunately they expiate their husband's sins as a consequence of their own bad judgements. Lady Wollaston's husband is unfaithful, but it is the foolish girl who is seduced by him and Lady Wollaston herself who take much of the blame. On the other hand, Lady Wollaston does not blame the girl but takes an interest in setting her straight about life before herself finding a freedom that marriage had never offered by doing social work in Ireland.

The novel is confused because it is the work of an unconventional and daring thinker who tried, and failed, to write a conventional book. It was impossible for Geraldine, writing about women, not to give way to anger and outrage at the many and varied ways in which their lives were cramped and their possibilities stifled. By directing that anger at some of her fictional females – like Hilda – and modifying it by understanding, she sought to bring the real situation of women before people's eyes in such a way that they would see the invidiousness of social structures that left women with no alternative but to sell themselves to the highest bidder. But apart from helping young women avoid such dangers, she did not have an alternative to offer. The expiation, endurance, fortitude, and willing or unwilling sacrifice of the female self were all directed towards goodness as defined by a society that was bad for women – as she continued to show even in her most respectable novels. By not marrying, she had saved herself from the worst of its evils, but her own solution was not one she offered to her readers. The satisfactions she had earned, being able to put one foot in front of the other and gain strength from so doing, rarely featured in her fictions. Harriet Martineau's 'busy, cheerful, satisfied, single women', amongst whom Geraldine could reasonably be classed, can only be found on her pages behind the walls of a nunnery.[56] Being single was not consistent with being respectable.

Equally, the lived self that gave Geraldine her deepest satisfactions will not be found in Jane's accounts of her. For all that Jane was so closely involved with Geraldine's literary projects, her vision of her as a writer did not develop beyond the grotesqueries of stereotype. In place of the working woman writer was a creature of fantasy – social fantasy. Geraldine was well aware of this, as she told Walter Mantell:

> We all mistake each other. I lived with Mrs Carlyle as clear and open without a thought of secrecy or concealment and she used often to startle me with the hideous and absurd dagguerotypes of what she thought me – and still worse of the sort of thing I was like to do – as *unlike* anything of my own consciousness as light from dark.[57]

Like the 'hideous and absurd dagguerotypes' Geraldine herself entertained of 'emancipating women', Jane's version of her fiction-writing friend reflected social fears. The social act of writing for a public demanded social controls: with the protectiveness of a mother, Jane worked to instil those controls in Geraldine. As far as Geraldine's fiction was concerned, she was successful; and the dullness of her later novels may be attributed to Geraldine's decision to maintain her friendship with Jane Carlyle – and her place in society on terms that Jane could identify with – in preference to a lonely place at the top of the mountain. She was tolerant of Jane's mistaken views of her, having, in any case, none of that absolute belief in truth which Froude was struck by on his first meeting Jane. Froude had concluded that 'one must speak truth only, and, if possible, think truth only, if one wished to be admitted into that house on terms of friendship.'[58] Geraldine did not try to copy the version of truth that ruled within the house, for though a 'broad basis of veracity' might be admirable, it could not always be assured:

> Ah, my dear love! is it not a deal harder to be true and to tell true than anybody believes till they try? You know that the manuscript of the 'Nouvelle Heloise', preserved in the museum, has hardly a blot or an erasure in it, whilst the MS of the 'Confessions', which profess to be gospel, is interlined, altered and cancelled from one end to the other.[59]

Neither fiction nor fact could be trusted to be what it asserted itself to be. Making Jane into a mother was a fiction. Geraldine knew that in real life she had grown out of her need of such a person: having had to fend for herself, more or less, since the age of 6, she might claim to miss her mother more every day, but she had certainly learned the more appropriate adult skill of mothering herself. She was not, in fact, waiting obediently to be told what to do. The contrast between her energetic willingness to run risks and put the past behind her, and Jane's caution and preoccupation with a lost golden world in which she was an adored only child, is striking. Both Jane and Thomas encouraged each other in a degree of filial piety and regret for their dead parents which was extreme even for Victorians. Like Casabianca, the boy on the burning deck who died while waiting for his dead father to give him permission to go, their version of heroism became ever more rooted in the securities of fidelity to parental injunction.

Making Jane into a sister was less of a fiction, but it was not a relationship Jane wholeheartedly welcomed. Her half-sisterly relation to Geraldine was scarred through with sibling rivalry; and more besides. Her experiences as a daughter and a wife had led her to put a negative value on femininity. The driving impulse of her life had always been to prove herself as good as any man; but proving herself the equal even of so great a man as Thomas Carlyle had not brought male privileges along with it. Geraldine had a vision of a future for women on the basis of a positive female self. Jane could not share it; she remained true to a genderless version of individuality that had only too painfully, in her own life, failed to bring her satisfactions. Her inability to formulate a direction for her life was a specifically female problem, as she knew, with its origins in the external social world:

> In these mere talking times, a poor woman knows not how to turn herself; especially if, like myself, she 'have a devil' always calling to her, 'March! March!' and bursting into infernal laughter when requested to be so good as to specify whither.[60]

But she would not look to external social change to resolve such problems. Refusing to seek solutions in 'isms' of any sort, she was driven to march off her frustrations in purposeless physical activity which brought her always, in a circular movement, back to the rigidities of an uncompromising and unforgiving self.

8

TELLING TRUTHS

I don't think I ever shall have luck with my lovers.... Other people find the world full of villains and rascals; for me it is full of respectable people.

Geraldine Jewsbury[1]

Geraldine's intellectual openness, her flexibility – 'I hate inflexible things of all kinds' – and her forgiving spirit, towards herself as well as others, were not qualities shared by the longest lasting of her lovers: Jane. In their quarrels, it was always Jane who had to be appeased. Geraldine would happily agree to be in the wrong but she would not agree to be cast off. It was, she said, 'utterly ... beyond your power to vex or estrange me permanently'. She would not be distanced by coldness and she would flatly refuse to accept outright rejection. She believed that even the worst wounds could heal. She demanded explanations for 'utterly, utterly unsatisfactory letters' when she felt herself 'very innocent' but suspected she had been judged and found wanting nevertheless. It was never her intention to lie down and die:

> there are two sides to every bargain, and I am not a subject for 'painless extinction'. I should first squeak for my life very sonorously, and try what moving speeches would do, and if they did not answer, I would wait patiently till the tide of things should bring us into right relation again.[2]

She recognized what Jane considered her faults: 'I sin against your notions of good taste very often, and that is quite enough to give you a distaste to me for the time being.'[3] She was not desperate and she could wait, as she often had to do, for Jane's displeasure to pass. But in 1857 her patience and loyalty were put to their severest test.

Geraldine's agreement to accept Thomas's prior claims on Jane were not reciprocated. The Roberston affair in 1845 indicated how passionately and personally – for all her protests to the contrary – Jane was inclined to involve herself in Geraldine's emotional dramas. She did not confine herself to reacting against Geraldine's conduct with men, as her anger over Charlotte Cushman showed, but there was certainly an additional venom when the potential lover was male. As a reflection of the emotional impoverishment of her own life this can be well understood, and Geraldine understood it in much that spirit. She recognized that Jane, having become more dependent on her since she moved to London, was quite as possessive as she herself had been in the early days when any other person occupied Jane's attention. But Geraldine's life had opened out as Jane's closed in – to illness and bitterness and the thirteen-year-long endurance of Thomas Carlyle's last major work, *Frederick the Great*. *Frederick* made him, in Geraldine's opinion, not just 'ill to live with' but 'as grim as Albert Durer's knight riding through the forest and dogged by Devils'. This 'indigestion of *Frederick the Great*' upset Jane as well as Thomas, and the 'bonds of Frederick' tied themselves as tightly round her as him: 'The stress and constant unfailing anxiety to keep *him* happy and comfortable is gradually wearing her out and the friction of her own nature makes it more difficult.'[4]

Jane had difficulty accepting the reality of Geraldine's sociable nature. Other friends were merely 'dissipation', a form of wilful abandonment of herself, the true friend. Once, having gone to stay with her friends the Hargreaves family, of Silwood Park, Geraldine accidentally bumped into Jane on the journey back:

I came away at eleven o'clock with Mrs Hargreaves to spend the day in London 'shopping' and doing errands. When the train came up some one called out 'Geraldine Geraldine!' with an emphasis of exasperation at what I suppose must have been my deafness to former appeals – it was from – Mrs Carlyle! I had left her nearly dead and quite unable to walk and there she stood at the window looking quite brilliant. Of course I scrambled into the coupé to her and Mrs H followed more deliberately – Mrs C had been down to East Hampstead to the Downshires and was now returning with a big bouquet of flowers half as large as herself – and the two days in the country had worked the miracle of bringing her back to life and apparent health.... After the first burst of enthusiasm had subsided we *all* wished ourselves elsewhere – respectively – when Mrs C hailed me she did not know I had a companion – My companion does not feel drawn to Mrs C, and moreover Mrs C liked *both* windows open, a thorough draught, and my companion was afraid of the rheumatism, and then the difficulty of making agreeable conversation – so it was no go at all. We at last settled ourselves. Mrs C shut her eyes and looked fatigued. I shut mine and tried to settle a refractory chapter – and Mrs H shut hers and settled her errands – and yet here were three women each of them with the capability of being – what shall I say? circumstances alter cases and we were all three stupid enough for prize ploughmen.

Geraldine felt 'guilty and awkward' at the time, but she also had a philosophic acceptance which enabled her to detach herself. What Jane felt was only too obvious.

The friction of Mrs Carlyle's nature could be borne with on a short rail journey when it came into conflict with the desires of another companion; but in 1857, after she had met Walter Mantell, Geraldine found herself having to make a choice. Jane was not prepared to share Geraldine with a love of this intensity, and their relationship, which had been at its strongest in the years immediately preceding Mantell's arrival, experienced its worst – and in some ways decisive, for things were never to be the same again – break.

The break came gradually. In the summer of 1857 Jane, on holiday in Scotland, received a letter from Geraldine in London that 'rasped me all over like a file'. It was an innocent enough letter, reassuring Jane that all was well at home, that Thomas was in better health than he had been while his wife was with him, and that the maid had been advised, by Geraldine, to take camomile tea. Jane replied to her husband: 'tell Ann, with my kind regards, that I particularly desire she will *not* take anything Miss Jewsbury prescribes; for *she* knows nothing whatever of Medicine, and would poison a cat if she had her way.' Shortly afterwards there came another 'disagreeable letter' from Geraldine, and a still more disagreeable reaction: 'I think she is growing into what is called an "ill-natured old maid", only that so long as Mr Mantell is to the fore, she has no idea of old-maidhood.'[5] Mr Mantell's arrival in Geraldine's life made her letters more 'disagreeable' than her belief in the medicinal properties of camomile. By January 1858 Jane told Mrs Russell that Geraldine had 'all but as good as gone out of my life!' She had not seen her since the beginning of the previous July and, unusually, even her letters had ceased.

> She has been making a considerable of a fool of herself, to speak plainly; and has got estranged from me utterly, for the time being; partly because her head has been pack-full of nonsense, and partly because I made no secret of that opinion. . . . Geraldine has one besetting weakness: she is never happy unless she has a *grande passion* on hand; and, as unmarried men take fright at her impulsive, demonstrative ways, her *grandes passions* for these thirty years have been all expended on *married* men, who felt themselves *safe*. And she too, always went quite safe thro' these romantic affairs, meaning really nothing but whirlwinds of *sentiment*, and the men too, meaning as little, – or less! But when I was in Scotland with you she made an intimacy with a Mr Mantell who had been ten years in Australia, unhappily not married, only *engaged*, or 'as good as engaged' to a young cousin of his own. For a long time it was an intimacy with 'the reciprocity all on one side'. But she went on writing him letters, inviting him to her house, flattering him (he is a proud, shy man), doing him all sorts of kindness, till he declared to his friends 'he couldn't help liking Miss Jewsbury, she was so extraordinarily kind to him!' He relied, I suppose, on his being some ten or twelve years younger than herself for security in accepting her kindness. I could not see her committing herself, as she did, and hear all her friends chattering about her 'assiduities for Mr Mantell' without testifying my displeasure; and, in proportion as she attached herself to *him*, she drew away from *me*, got pettish, suspicious, and mysterious. . . . But all that makes me so angry and what is worse disgusts me! It is making herself so small!

210

Openly making the craziest love to a man who, having £800 a year, may marry her at any moment (unless he is going to marry another, which doesn't make the case better!) and doesn't give any sign of intending to marry her! Gracious, what luck I had no daughters to guide![6]

Jane's anger was such that she refused to allow Geraldine to speak to her of Mantell at all. In essence, this was not new; she had usually shown an 'extreme indifference, not to say dislike to hearing of anybody I care about', and had even shown 'extreme rudeness' if introduced to them in person – as the episode with Mrs Hargreaves vividly demonstrates. But this was more serious. It hurt Geraldine deeply and conflicted with her own love of having things out once and for all. Jane would speak neither about their estrangement nor of 'the other friends I have made nor ... all that occupies me – she desires to know nothing ... she has chosen to have *reserve* instead of the entire *frankness* that used to be.' When Geraldine did not drop Mantell, and did not indicate that she was willing to speak and behave as if he were not a part of her life, Jane refused to see her. No invitations came from Cheyne Row and her attempts to make herself useful were spurned. Geraldine defended herself to Mantell:

if ever a human being *can* be faithful and entire of heart in their relation to another *I* have been, I am still to her. I am not suffering so much pain as she thinks she is giving me – that has at last worn itself out – but that rather gives one strength to bear and forbear. She has not alienated me but I can neither think nor say that she is *right* for she has got perverted in all her notions of me, so do not set this estrangement down compendiously as 'only a quarrel between two women who have been too great friends.' Our intimacy has subsisted since the early part of the year 1842. She is now trying, as I have seen her do in other cases, to *make* herself as indifferent and harsh as possible to *put* me out of her life and to exaggerate all my faults and *differences* of character. For it is the *differences* of nature that we tolerate less easily than faults. It is precisely the *right*, the necessity indeed, of entertaining other friends without being counted guilty of lèse friendship that we have split upon. She is far too proud to be conciliated. Indeed any act like dedicating my book to her would only bring down the contempt it would have earned and still more insolent treatment. If we are ever to be friends again we must stand on firm ground. I must be able to be *myself* and feel free to do all I think right, or in other words, that I have an *honest desire to do*. She knows from pretty long experience that my affection for her is not to be worn out, *but* though I never have and never should put any personal convenience or new people in competition with her claims as the oldest friend, I cannot live if I am to be shut up in a glass bottle and consent that all the rest of the world shall be all show and outside for me. It has come to my beloved 'laws of gravitation' – she can only have what she can hold, and second motives and amiable weakness can have no place.

I know that I am neither bitter nor unkind but I can do nothing in the matter.

For Walter Mantell himself, Jane and Thomas had nothing but liking and respect. Encouraging him to get to know them, Geraldine amply demonstrated the truth of her claim that she felt no bitterness. She reproved Mantell for his initially somewhat scornful response to Jane and was glad when he decided that he liked Mrs Carlyle after all:

> She is one of those who cannot be judged but must be accepted. She is a *heroine* and right or wrong makes a prescription for herself. If she is cruel sometimes and hard, at others she is more noble and generous than ninety-nine persons who need no repentance, and as to her *fascination*, I appeal to yourself!

Geraldine's generosity in her quarrels was in marked contrast to Jane's. Jane's way of praising Mantell, to his friend George Cooke, was to denigrate Geraldine:

> I liked Mr Mantell much when I saw him away out of the valley of the shadow of Geraldine. So did Mr C. like him: 'far too clever and *substantial* a man to be thrown away on a *flimsy tatter* of a creature like Geraldine Jewsbury', was his remark . . .[7]

To think and say such things at the beginning of a relationship, as Jane did in the 1840s, is one thing; but to be able to say them, and to a comparative stranger, after almost twenty years of intimacy and exchange suggests refusals of a very deep kind. Jane's refusal to hear about Mantell from Geraldine was a refusal to move and grow, not only in her relationship with Geraldine but within herself. To make sense of the difficulties Jane and Thomas had with Geraldine, one has, perhaps, to reverse the parts they allocated themselves in the drama: for the 'adult' Carlyles, substitute 'children', and for the 'child' Geraldine, substitute an 'adult'.

Jane was certainly wrong in saying that Walter Mantell meant little or nothing to Geraldine; he meant a great deal, quite as much as Jane had meant and with the important difference that he was not already married – even if his hopes were pitched elsewhere. Geraldine's passion for Mantell was the last attempt she made to establish an intimate relationship with a man, and to do so on the basis of her mature and fully realized self. Her part in the relationship is well documented in the many letters she wrote to him, and they provide extraordinary confirmation of the difficulty an experienced, intelligent, adult woman was likely to have if she attempted to initiate an emotional and/or sexual relationship with a man on the basis of those qualities. For what makes Geraldine's letters to Mantell so valuable is the fact that, for the most part, she refused to give up her pride in what she was and what she had achieved. However dear Mantell was to her, he was not dearer than the self she had resolved to be true to. If Jane Carlyle could not shake her firm grasp on that self, it was unlikely that Walter Mantell would; but he came very close.

Who was he? Jane was correct in saying that he was younger than Geraldine, but he was not as much younger as she chose to think: Geraldine was 44 when she met him and Mantell was 36 – hardly a very young man – and he might have been considered old enough to take responsibility for his own judgements about propriety and the possible meanings of an unmarried woman's interest in him. He was newly arrived in England, however, having spent sixteen years in New Zealand. Though an Englishman, England was strange to him. He felt uncouth in drawing-rooms. He was a scientist, explorer, administrator, and pioneer whose task latterly had been to persuade the Maoris to sign away their lands at ridiculously small cost to the government. To his credit, he took Maori culture seriously enough to learn the language and customs; and when he realized, during what had begun as a leave of absence in England in 1856, that the government had broken the principal promises he had made to the Maoris, he threw up his position and spent his time attempting to restore matters to what he considered a reasonably fair position. Of the British government he was bitterly critical. He considered Parliament nothing but a collection of public school bullies who hit subject peoples when they were down: England was 'a falling country' and it followed a 'narrow, nationalistic, exclusive line'. With views like that, there were few who agreed with him, and during his time in England he was unemployed, often depressed, usually disgruntled, and unable to see his future clearly. He was a man of strong principle, who had had experience of danger and authority in exotic parts, whose scope was narrowed by the genteel routines of mid-Victorian middle-class life, and who fretted at his inability to achieve 'name and fame and work to do'. Resentful that Labouchere, then Secretary for the Colonies, would not even see him let alone take notice of his protests, his energies began to dissipate into disillusion and self-pity. As Susanne Howe put it: 'Geraldine's outpouring of friendliness and confidence and her obvious respect and admiration, came at just the time when his self-esteem was low and he wanted reassurance.'[8]

Geraldine called Mantell 'Matara'. The word means chief. It was apparently the closest the Maoris could come to pronouncing his name, but nevertheless it still brought with it the consoling meanings of chieftainship: and Geraldine's use of it in her letters to Mantell has some of the rhythmic potency of Charlotte Brontë's use of 'Master' for Rochester in *Jane Eyre*. His name for her was 'Manu', meaning bird. Her pleasure in using the name 'Matara' for Mantell is obvious: she had found her chief. The philosophy she had learned and – with outbreaks of rebellion – tried to accept in coming to terms with her situation as a woman, was that all women needed the better strength of a man to guide them; and strong, intelligent women needed still stronger and more intelligent men. She had reconciled herself to the fact that such men were even rarer than strong, intelligent women, and even, as she bluntly told Mantell, that: 'as men are educated and brought up in this world I suppose *none* of them are *really worthy* of a Woman who has not been *warped* to suit the standard of men as they are.' But in Mantell she believed she had found a man who was worthy. Towards him she felt 'an instinct of obedience of feeling myself a woman beside you and looking up to you ... feeling you to have the *power* of governing'. She looked up to him 'as to a best self and expect you to keep me right when I go wrong – you are so much wiser than I am'.

All this was very fine and must have been pleasantly soothing. But just as Jane had detected insincerities in Geraldine's hero-worship, so too did Mantell. Geraldine's use of the word 'Matara' usually came at exactly those times when she was defending or trying to obscure her own tendencies to take charge and to know best. Her frequent apologies for failing to be as good as he deserved she should be were apologies for assertiveness. His need of her invited her projection of her whole self into his life: she listened sympathetically to his complaints, visited his mother – 'Matara you always make me wish to be so much better than I am – I will go and see your mother tomorrow' – gave him advice about his love for Calliope, the beautiful sister of Geraldine's Greek friend Stavros Dilberoglue, to whom she had introduced Mantell; tried to dissuade him from marrying another woman whom he did not love; and urged homeopathic medicine for his liver, and purposeful activity for his discontents. They met often and wrote long, detailed letters to each other every day. If, as Howe observes, Geraldine 'wrote herself out in these letters', what kind of a self did she write? What kind of a self will be found 'put down with completeness on paper' in the letters of a mature and passionate woman to a younger, disgruntled, less secure man? In professional terms and also to some extent emotionally, she had, after all, found herself while he, very evidently, had not.

It was, in the first place, a startlingly frank and honest self. She relayed without hesitation a rare comment of Jane's:

> Mrs C said 'You will have to weigh and consider every word you say to that man – to calculate the effect it will have on him.' I laughed and said 'he is precisely the one person I can speak out to – and I say just what comes into my head'. She said, 'Well, you will find it won't answer.' I still keep to my own instinct. I perhaps might have been able to please you more to make you think *me* something wiser and better if I had had more feminine artistic skill above all I should have been pleasanter but the faculty is not given to me ...

It was not a faculty she desired, for the rewards were not worth it. Unfortunately, Geraldine's assumption that Mantell appreciated her openness towards him in the same way that she regarded honesty and truth, as a broad general value, was over-optimistic. Her strong sense of identification with him – 'My life for a woman has been as hard as yours for a man and in some things not unlike it – this is the reason why we did not talk on the *outside* of things' – jarred on his sensitivities. Geraldine gave him advice out of her own experience, and it was only too painfully clear that her female experience was appropriate to his current circumstances. Like a middle-class young woman he was idling at home, restless, his capacities running to waste, becoming hypochondriac, raging against unseeeable, ungraspable opponents, and even thinking about marriage as a way out.

214

She knew that 'if one has to deal with men one humours them (God help us) one manages them, takes them with a knack of their humour', but nevertheless she gave Mantell exactly the advice she would have given a young, ambitious woman: she urged him to write a book. She had contacts with publishers; she reminded him that 'I cultivate newspaper editors and I could thereby *get said* in print anything you might wish to have set forth to the world'; she softened up Herbert Spencer and made an opening for Mantell to write a piece for the *Westminster Gazette*: 'it pays well, gives freedom of speech', and most of all:

> will do *you* good. A man of your faculties cannot remain fallow long, without suffering from a disquiet which is only unexpressed remorse and discontent of conscience. Matara I look up to you and take your judgement before my own in all [crossed out] *most* things – but what I am now saying I know from my own experience – a man who *can* is a man who *must* it is not *optional* whether he uses his faculties or no.

She could not help, under the circumstances, speaking from a greater knowledge which unbalanced the relation of master and pupil she obediently strove to maintain. She had dissected the problems of numerous fictional females in much the same terms; she was an authority on the subject of faculties left fallow; she knew too well the 'unexpressed remorse and discontent of conscience' that had eaten into Jane Carlyle for one. She also recognized his feelings, and his way of speaking, as a stage she had passed through and grown out of:

> ten years ago, the proud scornful bitterness with which you speak, would have had a most dangerous fascination, to say nothing that I should have spoken so. Or rather I *did* think and speak so and believed so – and I was a woman...

Being a woman meant that she did not have the advantages he had in being able to work off his frustrations and anger in strenuous activities like duck shooting:

> I had to sit still and be tempted of the Devil – to do many dark things, chiefly and most frequently – to cut my throat.... But that discouragement goes off and that horrible weariness, – I *know* that so much of all that comes from capacities that have not yet found their outlet and employment.

Blithely assuming that Mantell would see the parallels she saw between her life and his, and be grateful for the benefits of her wisdom, Geraldine continued to say whatever came into her head without calculating the effects. It did not answer. Mantell was furious. Her liberality with advice and devil-may-care dogmatisms led him to sulks and reproaches. She apologized for her 'preachments', for being, however hard she tried not to be, too 'trenchant'. She claimed that when she wrote about his situation she was really 'only working out my own ideas – not preaching':

> sometimes to *you* I have spoken positively – but that has always had reference

to something in my past life which would explain the *why* of the opinion – only dear Matara do not do me or yourself such injustice as to think I set myself up to teach or preach to *you*.

Such a prospect was unthinkable. But every time she spoke or wrote 'too vehemently', she veered towards it:

Please Matara don't think me *dogmatic* – but recollect that my employment has given me a certain positiveness of speech which I don't like to give into with you because you have worked things out more thoroughly than I have – whenever I speak or write opinions to you understand that they are put as *questions* – as asking you whether you see them so? – or how they strike you? – not as setting up my own options. Of course I don't pretend this holds good as a general rule because towards people whom I consider to have thought less on a matter than myself I fear I should make short work with them so don't give me credit for grace that I have not got.

Drawing on the connections she had made for herself, she spoke to her 'amiable' publisher, Mr Blackett, about the book on New Zealand which she felt sure Walter Mantell had it in him to write, and then wrote to Mantell a long letter telling him it was his 'duty' to produce such a book. Her presumption brought down a stream of reproaches. Mantell informed her that she 'would try the patience of God himself' – an interesting use of words – and though she knew more or less the sources of his displeasure, she begged to be told exactly what she had done wrong: 'if you will only tell me the *sort of way* in which I fail – I think I could do better.' She apologized:

When I think of that letter I wrote to you about your duty to write a book – It seems an impertinence that I wonder at, Of course it was 'well intended', that is the saving grace of all stupidity, but that it should have occurred to *me* to give advice to *you* – showed a want of knowledge which however I could not have – but also there was a want of insight which I *might* have had.

She discovered the weakening effect of being forever put in the wrong: 'If only you knew how quiveringly I fear doing or saying the slightest thing you would not like! It makes me seem so blind and so clumsy that I hate myself.' As a sign of her trust in his judgement and indication of lack of trust in her own, she invited him, as she had invited Jane, to edit her work, deferring to his opinions on matters of taste as well as grammar:

do not be sparing cut off all superfluities and redundant words and sentences – have no remorse – fancy it the work of a Colonial Secretary! and if someday you will give me some sage advices see if they will not be handsomely entreated – dear me *you* know Latin and Greek and everything else and I know nothing at all about those occult branches of humanity especially grammar and spelling. One thing please especially if any expression strikes you as being in bad taste – take it out – *leave nothing in you dislike*.

This was not enough to deflect criticism of her personality, however, and apologies continued to be the order of the day. He found a letter of hers 'abusive'. She agreed that he continued to be 'so good', while for her own part:

> Now that I look back I can see nothing but shortcomings, selfishness, egoism, hardness in all I have ever showed you – I *would* have been perfect if I could – the desire was there but the result is all flaws and utterly worthless.

The problem was that the humble tone, however genuine and however sincerely meant, was not a tone that Geraldine could sustain; cheerful self-assurance kept breaking through, bringing with it either direct criticism of Mantell or indirect criticism of him for being one of those irritating creatures, a man, whose nature it was to find pleasure 'in being tormenting and tiresome which is as good as meat drink work lodging and *smoking* to you'. Against the desire to be good beat the ever-insistent need to be true to a developed self. She was not unformed, not a blank page waiting to be written upon by a master hand; she had a firm hold on the pen. It was natural to her to speak out strongly and to insist on her point of view. She did not, for example, like to be denied:

> I hate 'No' and I fight it whenever I see it or hear it – it is a spectre that makes me mad.... You sent me a *No* that vexed me and made me feel as tho you had shut a door in my face.

And when she felt doors slamming in her face, she could not be silent about it no matter how much she might wish to be, or recognize that, strategically, silence might serve her purpose better. As she tried to explain everything, so she tried to explain her inconvenient compulsion to answer back:

> Now that I have honestly divided the blame by *first* giving it *all to you*; and then taking it *all to myself* there remains nothing not even one 'Basket of fragments to take up'. But if (I say this for my own comfort not for yours) I had held my tongue and consumed my grievance all to myself I should have been capable of feeling pained on the same score every time you vexed me (which as you are a man will of course be whenever you have the opportunity) so you see what a compound interest of annoyance I should have had. I *can* only be *myself* – tho it would be better for me if I were somebody else.

By the summer of 1858, Geraldine felt that her life was 'bound up with' Mantell's. She was grateful to him for letting her live in his life, a form of living which she would not exchange 'for any pleasure or comfort'. On the one hand she wanted to be a friend and companion to him as George Cooke was; on the other she felt bound to tell him: 'Matara a woman *cannot* be a friend like a man, we go closer and put more into it.' Mantell meanwhile was talking about returning to New Zealand. The thought of losing him kept Geraldine awake all night. She told him:

you are *always in my mind* ... if the entire love and kindness of one human being can be of any value to another – you have it from me. . . . I envy the very servant who waits on you – she is allowed to do for you what to me would be more of a proud and happy privilege than I could explain.

And still more explicitly:

Matara I feel to have a stake in you. I have invested a great deal in you – I have looked to you as a friend and companion I have looked up to you – I have tried to be better and stronger to deserve you – I care for you a great deal more than there is any need to express (not that you will care about that but naturally I do).

The thought that he might, after all, return to the other side of the world made her miserable: 'My life lies with you now I could sit down and cry':

come what will – do what you will – I am for you all that I have ever been able to be for you – I am not promising lightly or blindly I know what I am doing and all I mean – get any good you can out of me – I don't think there is any devil of egoism left in me as regards you.

The opening was not one he cared to take up. She went further:

I know I have no end of shortcomings and faults yet I know too that I am too good to be thrown aside for want of a little patience and shaping of me on your part. Dear Matara the last flush of youth and good looks has left me – but you don't know when one has ceased to be anything in one's own eyes *how much more* one has to give to those we care for!

Everything she did had,

some sort of reference to you I would melt down a year's life (no great gift) to give you one half hour's comfort or save you one hour's pain – you have taught me so many things and made me live *deeper* than I ever did before. Matara if I seem to speak of myself it is not to make you think of me as me – but because nothing but the *very best* that one can compass is good enough for you.

He told her she was 'to your faults a little blind/and to your virtues very kind'.

Before that summer was over, she had reconciled herself to getting 'pulled ... up sharp' by him whenever she 'indulged in the *expression* of feelings' and had apparently accepted that her love for him would not be returned in kind. Any humiliation this caused her was by no means enough to lead her to drop him, for even the 'worst fear to a woman (that of caring *more* than is asked or wished)' was one that she could outface:

It is thought weak and foolish for a woman to care – still more to *show* that she cares for a man who has not shown that he cares for her. But that is because they care *little* and not because they care *much*. If they care *nobly*

218

and *thoroughly* it is the same kind of heart service one pays to God Almighty Himself. The *more* one cares the less one *depends* on the return one receives.

The truest love is a heroic love; the most heroic love one that finds no reward. By modelling human love on higher love, a woman could translate a man into a God and by that means give herself the freedom to act rather than be acted upon. At any rate, by September 1858 the couple had temporarily reversed positions and Geraldine was on the offensive. She was feeling strong professionally. For her work with Lady Morgan she was to receive:

> 90 guineas for my labour – 45 to be paid down at once if I please – and all settled as pleasantly as possible. Blackett has paid me for the *Book* and when I took a cheque for £180 to the Bank I felt – like a woman of genius who had been *appreciated*!

She went to stay in the country, whither Mantell's letters followed her, but her mood had changed. She was not satisfied with giving all and receiving nothing except his lovetorn lamentations about other women in return:

> You take not the slightest interest in me or what concerns *me* – except just as I happen to amuse you. You taunt me for trying to mind my work tho' Heaven and my recording angel know it has not often hindered me where *you* are concerned. I am disappointed in you. You *know* that nothing which really interests or affects you would find me too occupied to attend to – you *know* that I give you myself . . . the heart of me. But Matara we give all *for* all – it is the law of necessity – no generosity. Your later letters since I came here which you accuse me of not answering point by point *were not real*. Also I am not likely to feel much patience at seeing you sit down to dream away your strength in a hopeless fantastic sentiment – when you ought to be – *Living* and *doing*.

When his reply proved 'ill-natured', she blasted him:

> Matara you are without exception the most tiresome perverse obstinate trying vexing obdurate unrepentant indifferent lazy deaf dumb stupid – adverb! I ever met with and that is *beaucoup* to say – that you may mend both your pen and your ways is the prayer of the patient individual who signs
>
> Manu

Perhaps he did mend his ways. By Christmas 1858 she had reason to believe that he loved her in the way she loved him, though her hints that they should marry had gone unacknowledged. As his plans to return to New Zealand became firmer, however, in 1859, he began to withdraw from her. His rejection made her ill:

> The doctor cannot imagine why I don't get better. I could tell him but it does not lie in his department – I cannot even heartily wish to get well –

only it is too ignominious to hang in the wind in this way neither quite alive nor quite dead.

Unable to eat, suffering from inflammations, knowing that he was busily preparing to go out of her life forever, she continued trying to be good: 'Matara I am *really* trying to be good and patient not to add to your plagues but it is *very dark*.' She begged him to come and see her:

> When you *can* come and have half an hour's rest and quiet and let me sit by you and rest my head on your knees *and put your strong hand over me and let me stay so*. I don't want to talk to you I only want to *feel you there*. There is getting less and less of me to look at every day so come whilst there is something left!

And at last, on 28 August 1859, she wrote him a letter in which she ceased trying to be good. She had decided to follow her desires wherever they led her. She had 'no sense of strength in myself or security against doing something that may bring shame and confusion ... upon me'. She was convinced that he had said that he returned her love. He denied it. The letter in which she proposed marriage to him is annotated at crucial points with Mantell's denials. But the most poignant thing about the letter is not so much his written refusals that make it into a dialogue (when did he write them – at the time, or much later?) as Geraldine's attempt to offer herself with all her accomplishments, much as a man might offer himself, as a desirable spouse, when it was precisely those accomplishments that had stood in the way of Mantell's comfort with her.

She confessed that she had contemplated proposing marriage to Cooke though she did not love him:

> I would have married *any*body who would have taken me out to New Zealand that I might be near you to watch over you and to be what I had always been for you – I would have gone great lengths to induce a man to go and to take me – When I knew you cared for me I felt how base I had been and I still feel very much humbled in my own esteem that I ever conceived such a notion.... When I knew you cared for me we stood on different grounds towards each other – *Why* are you trying to alienate me from you? to break my heart? to make me so wretched that if you had an enemy who had done you a grievous wrong I would pray you as a *human being* not to make him suffer as you have made me suffer...

Married to Cooke, she would have travelled out to New Zealand and spent the rest of her life watching over him like a mother. In a society which elevated women's servicing roles towards men, mothers, servants, and wives might all be much the same from a woman's point of view. She knew Mantell looked on her as spoiled goods, but she made one last attempt to win him:

> Matara I have had many hesitations before I knew clearly that I would or could belong to you – I am older than I know you would choose your wife

to be – but what young untrained girl could or would have the knowledge of life the forbearance the *discipline* of living with others that I have? – She would care more for herself than for you ['as you do Manu' – written in] then there was the disadvantage that in my past life there have been many things that would have been better not. I cannot alter anything in the past. I can only give you the *results* of what that past has made me – In outward position my present life is fortunate – I am independent – I can earn my own living and if I want more money I could get it – I have friends who are far better to me than I deserve – I have a good position I have a certain success in my profession. Matara I do not speak as boasting or valuing myself for these things but it is something to give you one who belongs to you should not be unaccredited in the world. If I could gain ten times as much worldly reputation or success I would do so because it would be so much more to give you.

She insisted that they were '*not merely* friends – we care for each other as *a man and a woman* – it is the highest and closest of human attachments which cannot be changed back into any other'. Given that, she claimed equal rights with him to determine the course of their relationship. Underlying her anger that he was 'flinging' her away, a more profound anger swelled: that he, and not she, had the right to make a choice:

You have told me that you love me ['untrue' – written in] – you have accepted the fact that I care for you ['submitted to' – written in], and yet you say 'I have made up my mind that if we belonged to each other we should be a miserable couple – I have *quite decided* that it shall not be – let me keep my *friend* and make somebody else wretched' – you say 'You do *not* know my temper and you are too *like me*' – If I do not know your temper it is not for want of descriptions from your friends! and some little experience from it of my own! but Matara, I know that *my* temper is *not* a bad one – ask anybody who has had to live with me – I protest against the imputation – with a bad temper (such as I have lived with) my own temper is under perfect control – tho I daresay with a very sweet tempered person I should be tyrannical enough – but *that* would not touch you – Matara – do you imagine that *anything* I could have had to endure from you as your wife with the *right* to endure it could have given me half the pain I have had to suffer since your return from Scotland? The utter blank despair – the days passing over like drops of lead – feeling the very *life* being slowly stamped out of me? But it is not of that I am now complaining, it is the *arbitrary injustice* of your behaviour – and the cruelty with which you have carried it out. *You have told me you love me* ['a nonsense' – written in] – not with friendship or brotherly love but as a man loves a woman whom he wishes to belong to him. When we stand thus face to face with each other is it just that you *alone* should have a voice in the fate of both of us? Is not my own happiness and welfare at stake in this matter? Am I a living woman

221

with a reasonable soul and human feelings? Or am I a piece of furniture that you decide on taking or leaving behind? You say, 'let me keep my friend'. Do you realise what it is you ask? You require my heart, my life, my devotion, my thoughts by day and by night to be slowly exhaled for you, and you – to give me a chance thought when you are in a fit of ennui or the spare moments after loitering over your breakfast or paring your nails or going to have your hair cut. Matara! Recollect that if I care for you, it is *you yourself* that have willed I should do so. Up to last Xmas were we not in a close intimacy, did I not know you and live in your life? *What* woman to whom you had thus shown yourself could have helped loving you to the full extent of her powers?

But Mantell's comment on the whole, written at the bottom of the last of eight sheets of closely packed writing, was that it was a 'most untruthful and unfair letter'.

From his perspective perhaps it was, but it was not untruthful or unfair from Geraldine's perspective. She believed in love and she believed she had found it. She believed in him, and was to go on writing to him as often as he allowed (he complained at first that she wrote to him too often) until she died. She told him before he sailed away to 'the great distance like death': 'Matara, I may be a fool, but I will with the grace of God *hold on by my eyelashes* to the faith I have in all I love.' Her truth was possibly not a truth he could properly appreciate. She was never much troubled by minor scruples: 'I try to lay hold of the *main truth* of any matter in hand and leave minor difficulties and doubts to settle themselves.' The main truth in Geraldine's life, then as it had always been, was the truth of an assertive and vigorous self. She knew that 'In this world we *cannot* act out clearly and perfectly our best thoughts and feelings', but she insisted that it was only by being true to the self, in whatever shapes it took, that worthwhile truths could emerge. Faced with a love that might evolve into marriage, she offered herself as a somebody to a man whose entire cultural conditioning led him to look for a nobody when he looked for a wife: to the statuesque and silent beauty of a Calliope, whose Greek family traditions ensured that she knew women existed to serve men in every conceivable capacity, who was there to be looked at (heads turned when she appeared in public) but who did not speak. What marriage demanded of women was an ability to give up rather than give; to become nothing so that they might be made into somethings by the husbands whose names they took. Geraldine knew Walter Mantell disliked her strengths because in a conversation which she did not find 'very agreeable', a friend of his had kindly told her so. Mantell, he explained:

never would marry a superior woman – he does not like them, he would choose to be Lord and Master and would only like a moderate intelligence to understand him at a distance and be a willing slave of the lamp.

Her strengths, her achievements, her substance, which in a man would have increased his eligibility, decreased hers. They were an obstacle; for *being taken* in marriage she was to *be given* a new identity, and she was too old and too assured (quite apart from the fact that she was not willing) to give up the one she had earned. Since we do not have many records of women proposing to men, we do not have a model against which to compare Geraldine's way of presenting herself. One can only observe that she squared up to Mantell as a man might, replete with her achievements, and it did not answer.

APPENDIX

A Farewell to the Muse

Not in envy, ire, or grief
Bid I now the Muse farewell;
'T is no childish fancy brief,
Lured away by newer spell;
As of earthly good the chief,
I have sought her long and well.

Not in anger; – inward joys
Have been mine, and meed of praise, –
Payment vast for idle toys,
Fleeting, unsubstantial lays;
Sandy columns wind destroys,
And that wind again can raise.

No, – nor yet in grief we part –
Never unto bard like me,
Gave the Muse a broken heart;
'T is to nobler votaries, she
Doth that awful gift impart –
Pledge of immortality!

Not in envy; – though around
Like the stars, a radiant throng,
In their several orbits found,
I behold the sons of song, –
Every brow with laurel bound,
And a few as giants strong.

Not in envy; – though I know
Neither wreath nor radiance mine;
I will yet pay homage low

Pilgrim-like, at every shrine;
Seek where buds and blossoms grow,
And for others garlands twine.

Never hath my Muse bereaved me,
Song hath lightened hours of pain;
Never Poet yet deceived me,
Truer friend I scarce could gain;
Ne'er among the things that grieved me,
Ranked the minstrel lute and strain.

Yet I bid the art adieu,
It may be, adieu for ever;
I abjure the syren too,
Vain, I own, my best endeavour;
Weak to grasp, though keen to view
Climbing alway – rising never.

Though I smite the rock of song,
At my stroke no stream will flow, –
At my spell no spirits strong
Bidden come, or mastered go;
Nor the world of passion throng
With its wild waves to and fro.

Farewell Muse! – vouchsafing never
But dim glance and veiled brow;
Farewell Lute! – a rude toy ever,
Broken, stringless, soon art thou;
Farewell Song! – thy last notes quiver, –
Muse, – Lute, – Music, – farewell now!

Maria Jane Jewsbury, The Poetical
Album, vol. 2, p. 330

NOTES

ABBREVIATIONS

CL   *The Collected Letters of Thomas and Jane Welsh Carlyle*, ed. Charles Richard Sanders and Kenneth J. Fielding, Duke–Edinburgh, 15 vols to date, Durham, NC: Duke University Press, 1970–.

Hux.   *Jane Welsh Carlyle, Letters to her Family 1839–63*, ed. Leonard Huxley, London: John Murray, 1924.

LM   *Letters and Memorials of Jane Welsh Carlyle*, ed. J.A. Froude, New York: Charles Scribner's Sons, 1883.

NLM   *New Letters and Memorials of Jane Welsh Carlyle*, ed. Alexander Carlyle, London and New York: John Lane, The Bodley Head, 1903.

Rem.   *Reminiscences*, Thomas Carlyle, with an Introduction by Ian Campbell, London: Dent & Sons, 1972.

PRINCIPAL MANUSCRIPT SOURCES CONSULTED

Dove Cottage papers: Maria Jane Jewsbury's letters to Dora Wordsworth.
Mantell papers: Geraldine Jewsbury's letters to Walter Mantell, available on microfiche. Alexander Turnbull Library, National Library of New Zealand.
Jewsbury papers: Maria Jane Jewsbury's letters to her family. John Rylands University Library of Manchester.
Hemans Collection and Nicholson papers: Liverpool Record Office, Liverpool City Libraries.

INTRODUCTION

1   CL, vol. 8, p. 246.
2   G.H. Lewes, 'A gentle hint to writing women', *The Leader*, 1850.
3   Hux., p. 336.
4   Rem., p. 138.
5   LM, vol. 2, p. 388; J.A. Froude, *Thomas Carlyle: A History of His Life in London 1834–1881*, London: Longmans, Green & Co., 1884, vol. 2, p. 324.
6   See: Waldo H. Dunn, *Froude and Carlyle: A Study of the Froude–Carlyle Controversy*, London: Longmans, Green & Co., 1930; also Introduction by James Crichton Browne to NLM. John Clubbe, in his Introduction to his abridged version of Froude's *Thomas Carlyle*, calls the Froude–Carlyle controversy 'one of the more sordid episodes in English literary history'. See John Clubbe, *Froude's Life of Carlyle*, London: John Murray, 1979, p. 51.

7   Ella Hepworth Dixon, *As I Knew Them: Sketches of People I Have Met on the Way*, London: Hutchinson & Co., 1930, p. 27.

8   Osbert Burdett, *The Two Carlyles*, London: Faber, 1930, pp. 65, 112.

9   See CL, vol. 2, pp. 265, 334; vol. 3, pp. 70, 395. It is only fair to add that these are all in very early volumes and that the most recent volumes to appear, which cover the early 1840s and include Geraldine Jewsbury, are free of such comments.

10   Mary Ellmann, *Thinking About Women*, London: Virago, 1979; Lillian Faderman, *Surpassing the Love of Men: Romantic Friendship and Love between Women from the Renaissance to the Present*, London: Junction Books, 1982; Sandra M. Gilbert and Susan Gubar, *The Madwoman in the Attic: The Woman Writer and the Nineteenth Century Literary Imagination*, New Haven: Yale University Press, 1979; Kate Millett, *Sexual Politics*, London: Virago, 1977; Ellen Moers, *Literary Women*, London: Women's Press, 1978; Elaine Showalter, *A Literature of Their Own: British Women Novelists from Brontë to Lessing*, London: Virago, 1978.

11   Virginia Woolf, 'Geraldine and Jane', *Collected Essays*, vol. 4, New York: Harcourt, Brace & World, 1967, pp. 27–39. Susanne Howe, *Geraldine Jewsbury, Her Life and Errors*, London: George Allen & Unwin, 1935; Faderman's account of the friendship is in *Surpassing the Love of Men*, pp. 164–6.

12   Geraldine Jewsbury's letters to Thomas Carlyle, from 6 April 1840 to 22 February 1841, a total of eight letters, are printed as an appendix in Jeanne Rosenmayer, 'Geraldine Jewsbury: Novelist and Publisher's Reader', University of London Ph.D. thesis, 1970.

13   CL, vol. 13, p. 50.

14   Geraldine Jewsbury, *Selections from the Letters of Geraldine E. Jewsbury to Jane Welsh Carlyle*, ed. Mrs Alexander Ireland, London: Longmans, Green & Co., 1892, p. 10.

15   ibid., p. 10.

16   ibid., pp. 20–1.

17   The main published source of information about Maria Jane Jewsbury is Eric Gillett, *Maria Jane Jewsbury: A Memoir*, Oxford: OUP, 1932, which includes a selection from her writings. See also Monica Fryckstedt, 'The hidden rill: the life and career of Maria Jane Jewsbury', *Bulletin of the John Rylands University Library of Manchester*, vol. 66, no. 2, Spring 1984, and vol. 67, no. 1, Autumn 1984.

18   Jane Williams, *Literary Women of England*, London: Saunders, Otley & Co., 1861, pp. 378–9.

19   Mrs L.B. Walford, *Twelve English Authoresses*, vol. 2, London: Longmans, Green & Co., 1892, pp. 86–7.

20   H.F. Chorley, *Memorials of Mrs Hemans*, London: Saunders & Otley, 1836, is one of the principal sources for her life, though this more outspoken observation is in Chorley's *Autobiography, Memoirs and Letters*, compiled by Henry G. Hewlett, London: Richard Bentley & Son, 1873, vol. 1, p. 129.

21   *The Infantile Pleasures of Willow-dale* is in the collection of Hemans and Nicholson papers in the Liverpool Record Office. Like Felicia's first publication, it was urged on by her mother whose precarious financial situation was the primary motive.

22   Jewsbury, *Letters*, pp. 425–7.

23   Mantell papers. This was how *men* were inclined to view Geraldine, as she explained to Walter Mantell; the full quotation is as follows (the Scot in question was not Thomas Carlyle): 'I have an irreconcilable incompatibility with Scotch*men*. He seemed to think me an amusing but ill regulated young woman who needed some sensible man to take care of her and *break* her which is men's usual idea of taking care of a woman *sensibly*!'

24   Jewsbury, *Letters*, p. 337.

1 CONTRARY TO CUSTOM

1   Geraldine Jewsbury, *Selections from the Letters of Geraldine E. Jewsbury to Jane Welsh Carlyle*, ed. Mrs Alexander Ireland, London: Longmans, Green & Co., 1892, p. 29.

2   Hannah More, 'Strictures on the modern system of female education,' *The Works of Hannah More*, New York: Harper & Brothers, 1838, vol. 1., p. 389.

3   Roland Barthes, 'Novels and children' in *Mythologies*, trans. Annette Lavers, New York: Hill & Wang, 1987, p. 51.

4   Jane Rendall, *The Origins of Modern Feminism*, Themes in Comparative History series, Basingstoke: Macmillan, 1985, p. 2.

5   Harriet Martineau, *Autobiography*, London: Virago, 1983, vol. 1, p. 400. See also Introduction by Gaby Weiner, p. xv.

6   See, especially, Gilbert and Gubar, *The Madwoman in the Attic*.

7   For the Barrett–Mitford correspondence, see *The Letters of Elizabeth Barrett Browning to Mary Russell Mitford*, ed. Meredith B. Raymond and Mary Rose Sullivan, Armstrong Browning Library of Baylor University, The Browning Institute, Wedgestone Press, and Wellesley College, 1983.

8   Lady Morgan's *Memoirs: Autobiography, Diaries and Correspondence*, ed. Hepworth Dixon and Geraldine Jewsbury, London: Richard Bentley, 1863, pp. 229–30.

9   Ruth Perry, *Women, Letters and the Novel*, New York: AMS Press, 1980, pp. 69–70.

10 For a good account of Lady Morgan, see Mary Campbell, *Lady Morgan, The Life and Times of Sydney Owenson*, London: Pandora Press, 1988; also Lionel Stevenson, *The Wild Irish Girl: The Life of Sydney Owenson, Lady Morgan (1776–1859)*, London: Chapman and Hall, 1936. Alison Adburgham, *Women in Print: Writing Women and Women's Magazines from the Restoration to the Accession of Victoria*, London: Allen & Unwin, 1972, includes Lady Morgan.

11 Lady Morgan's *Memoirs*, vol. 1, p. 212.

12 Showalter, *A Literature of their Own*, pp. 11–12.

13 George Eliot, 'Silly novels by lady novelists', *Westminster Review*, LXVI, 1856.

14 Showalter, *A Literature of their Own*, p. 18.

15 Eliot, 'Silly novels by lady novelists'.

16 Inga-Stina Ewbank, *Their Proper Sphere – A Study of the Bronte Sisters as Early-Victorian Female Novelists*, London: Edward Arnold, 1966. The whole of Ch. 1, 'The woman writer', forms relevant background to this chapter.

17 See Stevenson, *Wild Irish Girl*, p. 189.

18 See Campbell, *Lady Morgan*, pp. 231–2.

19 Mantell papers.

20 ibid.

21 Mrs S.C. Hall, *A Woman's Story*, London: Hurst & Blackett, 1857, vol. 3, pp. 41–2.

22 ibid., pp. 40–6.

23 Dove Cottage papers.

24 Mantell papers.

25 ibid., January 1858: 'I have just had a young woman here with a petition for me to sign "on the rights of married women over their own earnings". She was not pretty in the least and she did not look wise and she was abominably ill-dressed ... good-natured I say – but I ask *you* as a dispassionate individual belonging to our hereditary enslavers – whether *such* a person was the guardian angel one wd choose to entrust with one's petition to the foot of the Throne or the specimen one wd select to submit to the collective wisdom "of Parliament".... Of course I declined to sign my name but I took the trouble of talking as much sense to her as I cd summon up on the spur of the moment and wh. I spare you. The women who have taken upon themselves to speak up on behalf of the Women of England (all I have seen

of them) women with whom I shd entirely decline to have any acquaintance women whom I don't either like or admire and by no means my model of female excellence and I am not going to be mixed up with them.'

26 Jewsbury, *Letters*, pp. 347–9.

27 Mantell papers.

28 Jewsbury, *Letters*, p. 279.

29 Cheryl Walker, *The Nightingale's Burden: Women Poets and American Culture before 1900*, Bloomington: Indiana University Press, 1982, p. 26.

30 *Edinburgh Monthly Review*, vol. 3, no. xvi, April 1820, pp. 373–83.

31 H.F. Chorley, *Memorials of Mrs Hemans*, London: Saunders & Otley, 1836, pp. 138–9.

32 George Gilfillan, 'Female authors, no. 1 – Mrs Hemans', *Tait's Edinburgh Magazine*, ns 14, 1847, pp. 359–63.

33 *The Poetical Works of Felicia Dorothea Hemans*, Oxford: OUP, 1914, pp. 517, 404.

34 Harriett Hughes, *The Works of Mrs Hemans, with A Memoir of Her Life*, by her sister in 7 vols, Edinburgh: William Blackwood & Sons, London: Thomas Cadell, 1839. One other important source of information about Felicia Hemans is M.I. Leslie, 'Felicia Hemans: The Basis of a Biography', University of London Ph.D thesis, 1943. See also Cora Kaplan, *Salt and Bitter and Good: Three Centuries of English and American Women Poets*, New York and London: Paddington Press, 1975, pp. 93–123.

35 Barbara Welter, 'The cult of true womanhood: 1820–1860,' *American Quarterly*, vol. xviii, Summer 1966, pp. 151–74.

36 Hughes, *Works of Mrs Hemans*, vol. 1, p. 142.

37 *The Poetical Works of Wordsworth*, ed. Thomas Hutchinson, Oxford: OUP, 1904, p. 414: see footnote to the poem 'Liberty', written for Maria Jane Jewsbury: 'Her enthusiasm was ardent, her piety steadfast; and her great talents would have enabled her to be eminently useful in the difficult path of life to which she had been called. The opinion she entertained of her own performances ... was modest and humble, and, indeed, far below their merits; as is often the case with those who are making trial of their powers, with a hope to discover what they are best fitted for. In one quality, viz. quickness in the motions of her mind, she had, within the range of the Author's acquaintance, no equal.'

38 Maria Jane Jewsbury published the following titles: *Phantasmagoria or, Sketches of Life and Literature*, London: Hurst & Robinson, 1825; *Letters to the Young*, London: J. Hatchard & Son, 1828; *Lays of Leisure Hours*, London: J. Hatchard & Son, 1829; *The Three Histories*, London: F. Westley, 1830.

39 Chorley, *Memorials*, p. 314.

40 The *Athenaeum*, 5 May 1832, no. 236. All articles in *The Athenaeum* were anonymous, but a marked file exists which gives the names of contributors. Unfortunately, the file for 1832 does not exist. Thus, while it is possible to identify with certainty Maria Jane Jewsbury's contributions in 1830 and 1831, the same is not true of 1832. Monica Fryckstedt published Maria Jane's 1830 and 1831 listings in her article in the John Rylands Library Bulletin – see Introduction, note 17, above – but did not seek to speculate about possible attributions in 1832. It is known that the bulk of Maria Jane's contributions were made in 1831 and 1832. In 1831 her industry led her to write two, sometimes three pieces in a single edition, taking for her main subjects two identifiable areas: anything to do with women, and poetry. H.F. Chorley's obituary notice, which appeared on 21 June 1834, no. 347, p. 473, makes it plain that she continued to be a hard working member of the *Athenaeum* team until the last moment of her departure for India, as also does the fact that her ship's journal was published in December 1832, as soon as it arrived. It is probable, then, that

she wrote as regularly during 1832 as she had done in 1831, and reasonable to assume that her interests followed much the same course. Certainly, there seems to have been no rival on the staff of the *Athenaeum* for the post of spokesperson on women's issues. I have, therefore, with due caution, made an attempt to identify some pieces in 1832 which I am satisfied – on the basis of subject matter and style – were likely to have been written by Maria Jane Jewsbury. One series of pieces in particular, *On Modern Female Cultivation*, which appeared in February and August 1832, have formed an important part of my interpretation of Maria Jane Jewsbury's development, and the reader may wish to bear in mind that absolute proof of her authorship of those pieces can never be given.

41 Geraldine Jewsbury, *Zoe, The History of Two Lives*, London: Chapman and Hall, 1845, vol. 3, p. 4.
42 Jewsbury, *Letters*, p. 12.
43 Mantell papers.
44 Jewsbury, *Letters*, pp. 133, 136.
45 Hux., p. 208.
46 NLM, vol. 1, p. 144.
47 ibid., vol. 1, p. 64.
48 Richard Renton, *John Forster and his Friendships*, London: Chapman and Hall, 1912, p. 45.
49 Geraldine Jewsbury's third letter to Thomas Carlyle, see Jeanne Rosenmayer, 'Geraldine Jewsbury: Novelist and Publisher's Reader', University of London Ph.D. thesis, 1970, appendix.
50 Mrs S.C. Hall on 'Women's rights', quoted at length in Mr S.C. Hall's *Retrospect of a Long Life*, London: Richard Bentley & Son, 1883, pp. 438–42. Mrs S.C. Hall observed that she had 'no words to express the bitterness of my contempt for any woman who gives voice to her husband's faults. It is her duty to woo him from them within the sacred sanctuary of home – to entreat, to reason, to struggle against them heart and soul; but never to betray.'
51 CL, vol. 4, p. 70.
52 Rem., p. 67.
53 LM, vol. 2, p. 293.
54 Mary Smith, *The Autobiography of Mary Smith: Schoolmistress and Nonconformist. A Fragment of a Life*, London: Bemrose & Sons, 1892, pp. 256–7, 137, 122.

2 THE PRIDE OF LITERATURE

1 Maria Jane Jewsbury, *Phantasmagoria, or Sketches of Life and Literature*, London: Hurst, Robinson & Co., 1825, pp. 187–8.
2 Sara Coleridge, *Memoir and Letters of Sara Coleridge*, edited by her daughter, London: H.S. King & Co., 1873, p. 172.
3 Harriett Hughes, *The Works of Mrs Hemans, with A Memoir of Her Life*, by her sister in 7 vols, Edinburgh: William Blackwood & Sons, London: Thomas Cadell, 1839, p. 55.
4 H.F. Chorley, *Memorials of Mrs Hemans*, London: Saunders & Otley, 1836, p. 189.
5 Hughes, *Works of Mrs Hemans*, p. 93.
6 ibid., p. 74.
7 ibid., p. 73.
8 Anne Elwood, *Memoirs of the Literary Ladies of England*, London: Henry Colburn, 1843, vol. 2, pp. 232–3.
9 M.I. Leslie, 'Felicia Hemans: The Basis of a Biography', University of London Ph.D. thesis, 1943. See ch. 5.

10 Chorley, *Memorials*, p. 151.
11 Hughes, *Works of Mrs Hemans*, p. 170.
12 Chorley, *Memorials*, p. 188.
13 Hughes, *Works of Mrs Hemans*, p. 219.
14 Letter to Robert Graves, 26 July 1831, in Graves Collection, Alexandra College, Dublin. Quoted in Leslie, 'Felicia Hemans'.
15 Jane Williams, *Literary Women of England*, London: Saunders, Otley & Co., 1861, pp. 380–1; Chorley, *Memorials*, pp. 164–73.
16 *Letters of William and Dorothy Wordsworth, Part One, 1821–8*, ed. Alan G. Hill, Oxford: Clarendon Press, 1978, pp. 434–5; see also pp. 405, 427.
17 See 'First efforts in criticism', *Phantasmagoria*, pp. 8–18.
18 Dove Cottage papers.
19 Jewsbury papers.
20 Eric Gillett, *Maria Jane Jewsbury, A Memoir*, Oxford: OUP, 1932, pp. xvii–xviii.
21 See Williams, *Literary Women*, p. 380.
22 Jewsbury, *Phantasmagoria*, vol. 2, pp. 241–65.
23 ibid., vol. 1, pp. 55–73.
24 ibid.
25 ibid., vol. 2, pp. 115–29.
26 ibid., vol. 2, pp. 211–21.
27 ibid., vol. 1, pp. 189–98.
28 Mrs Ellis, *Christian Keepsake*, 1838, p. 35.
29 Jewsbury, *Phantasmagoria*, vol. 1, pp. 125–7, 187–8.
30 ibid., vol. 2, pp. 177–210.
31 *Letters of William and Dorothy Wordsworth, Part One, 1821–8*, pp. 342–3.
32 *Letters of Dora Wordsworth*, ed. Howard P. Vincent, Chicago: Packard & Co., 1944, pp. 53, 23–4. These are Dora's letters to Maria Jane, published in a limited edition of 450 copies.
33 Susan M. Levin, *Dorothy Wordsworth and Romanticism*, Rutgers University Press, 1987, pp. 3–4.
34 See *Letters of Dora Wordsworth*, Introduction, p. 10.
35 *The Letters of Sara Hutchinson, 1800–1835*, ed. Kathleen Coburn, London: Routledge & Kegan Paul, 1954, pp. 370–1.
36 Chorley, *Memorials*, p. 117.
37 *Letters of Sara Hutchinson*.
38 For a good introduction to Margaret Fuller and Thomas Carlyle's importance to her, see Susan Phinney Conrad, *Perish the Thought: Intellectual Women in Romantic America 1830–1860*, Oxford: OUP, 1976.
39 Hannah More, 'Strictures on the modern system of female education', ch. XVI, 'On the danger of an ill-directed sensibility', *The Works of Hannah More*, New York: Harper & Brothers, 1838, vol. 1.
40 Levin, *Dorothy Wordsworth*, p. 155.
41 ibid., p. 24.
42 Chorley, *Memorials*, p. 174.
43 Winifred Gerin, *Charlotte Brontë: The Evolution of Genius*, Oxford: Clarendon Press, 1967, p. 110.
44 Dove Cottage papers.
45 Hughes, *Works of Mrs Hemans*, p. 142.
46 See Gillett, *Maria Jane Jewsbury*, p. xxv.
47 See Appendix.
48 Dove Cottage papers.

3 DRAGOON KINDS OF WOMEN

1 Maria Jane Jewsbury, 'The History of an Enthusiast', *The Three Histories*, London: F. Westley, 1830, p. 25.
2 Dove Cottage papers.
3 Maria Jane Jewsbury, *Letters to the Young*, London: J. Hatchard & Son, 1828, advertisement on title page.
4 Ruth Perry, *Women, Letters and the Novel*, New York: AMS Press, 1980.
5 Anna Jameson, *Diary of an Ennuyee*, London: Henry Colburn, 1826. It was first published anonymously as *A Lady's Diary*, and Anna Jameson earned a Spanish guitar out of it; instantly successful, Colburn bought it for £50. The details are in Clara Thomas, *Love and Work Enough: The Life of Anna Jameson*, University of Toronto Press, 1967, a useful scholarly work marred by undercurrents of what seem to be disapproval of the subject.
6 Frances Ann Kemble, *Records of a Girlhood*, London: Richard Bentley & Son, 1878, pp. 124–7.
7 Jewsbury papers.
8 Jewsbury, *Letters to the Young*, Letter 8, pp. 81–2.
9 ibid., Letter 18, pp. 174–5; Letter 11, p. 113.
10 ibid., Letter 19, p. 194.
11 ibid., Letter 18, pp. 172–8; Letter 19, pp. 185–9.
12 Jewsbury papers.
13 Jewsbury, *Letters to the Young*, Letter 15, p. 161.
14 Francis Espinasse, *Lancashire Worthies*, London: Simpkin, Marshall & Co., 1877, pp. 323–39.
15 *The Letters of Sara Hutchinson, 1800–1835*, ed. Kathleen Coburn, London: Routledge & Kegan Paul, 1954, pp. 310, 370–1.
16 Jewsbury papers.
17 Harriett Hughes, *The Works of Mrs Hemans, with A Memoir of Her Life*, by her sister in 7 vols, Edinburgh: William Blackwood & Sons, London: Thomas Cadell, 1839, vol. 1, pp. 141–2.
18 Dove Cottage papers.
19 Felicia Hemans, *Records of Woman*, 1828. In the Oxford edition of *The Poetical Works of Felicia Dorothea Hemans*, Oxford: OUP, 1914, *Records of Woman* is on pp. 227–77.
20 Francis Jeffrey, 'Felicia Hemans', *Edinburgh Review*, vol. 50, Oct. 1829, pp. 32–47.
21 Jewsbury, 'The History of a Nonchalant', *The Three Histories*, pp. 187–9.
22 H.F. Chorley, *Memorials of Mrs Hemans*, London: Saunders & Otley, 1836, p. 222.
23 Jewsbury, 'The History of a Nonchalant', p. 193.
24 Jewsbury, 'The History of an Enthusiast', pp. 44–5.
25 ibid., pp. 141, 117, 124.
26 ibid., p. 134.
27 Maria Jane Jewsbury, *Lays of Leisure Hours*, London: J. Hatchard & Son, 1829, p. 180.
28 Jewsbury, 'The History of an Enthusiast', p. 151.
29 The *Athenaeum*, 12 February 1831, 'Original papers. Literary sketches No. 1. Felicia Hemans', pp. 104–5.
30 Eric Gillett, *Maria Jane Jewsbury: A Memoir*, Oxford: OUP, 1932, pp. xxlii–xlv.
31 The *Athenaeum*, 16 July 1831, 'Shelley's "Wandering Jew"', pp. 456–7; 11 June 1831, 'Poetry by the people', pp. 369–71.
32 ibid., 19 March 1831, pp. 180–1.
33 ibid., 28 May 1831, p. 337, reviewing *The Nature and Dignity of Christ*, by Joanna Baillie.

34 The *Athenaeum*, 5 May 1832, reviewing *Woman in her Social and Domestic Character*, by Mrs J. Sandford.
35 ibid., 12 November 1831, pp. 730–1.
36 ibid.
37 ibid., 4, 11, and 23 February 1832, pp. 79–80, 95–6, 129.
38 Mrs S.C. Hall, in S.C. Hall, *Retrospect of a Long Life*, London: Richard Bentley & Son, 1883, pp. 438–42.
39 L.E.L. died in mysterious circumstances after marrying and travelling to West Africa with her husband. See D.E. Enfield, *L.E.L.: A Mystery of the Thirties*, London: Hogarth Press, 1928.

4 DIFFICULTIES AND DANGER

1 CL, vol. 2, p. 273.
2 Mantell papers.
3 ibid.
4 *Selections from the Letters of Geraldine E. Jewsbury to Jane Welsh Carlyle*, ed. Mrs Alexander Ireland, London: Longmans, Green & Co., 1892, p. 76.
5 Harriett Hughes, *The Works of Mrs Hemans, with a Memoir of Her Life*, by her sister in 7 vols, Edinburgh: William Blackwood & Sons, London: Thomas Cadell, 1839, vol. 1, p. 300.
6 *The Poetical Works of Felicia Dorothea Hemans*, Oxford: OUP, 1914, pp. 632–9, 640–3, 647–50, 643–7.
7 *Charlotte Cushman: Her Letters and Memories of her Life*, ed. Emma Stebbins, Boston: Houghton, Osgood & Co., 1879, pp. 85, 84.
8 Rem., pp. 40, 95–101.
9 ibid., p. 51; CL, vol. 2, pp. 196–7.
10 CL, vol. 2, p. 304; CL, vol. 2, p. 143.
11 ibid., vol. 3, pp. 128–32.
12 ibid., vol. 2, pp. 247–8.
13 Judy Little, *Comedy and the Woman Writer*, Lincoln, University of Nebraska Press, 1983, pp. 19, 17.
14 CL, vol. 2, p. 198.
15 ibid., vol. 2, pp. 281–2.
16 ibid., vol. 3, p. 212.
17 ibid., vol. 3, p. 176.
18 ibid., vol. 3, p. 378.
19 ibid., vol. 2, p. 309.
20 ibid., vol. 2, p. 495.
21 ibid., vol. 2, p. 270.
22 ibid., vol. 3, p. 147.
23 ibid., vol. 3, p. 245.
24 ibid., vol. 2, pp. 196–7.
25 ibid., vol. 2, p. 262.
26 Rem., pp. 37–8.
27 J.A. Froude, *Thomas Carlyle: A History of His Life in London 1834–1881*, London: Longmans, Green & Co., 1884, vol. 1, p. 232.
28 Rem., p. 4.
29 CL, vol. 4, p. 152.
30 ibid., vol. 4, p. 188.
31 ibid., vol. 3, p. 301. Phyllis Rose (*Parallel Lives*, Harmondsworth: Penguin, 1985) discusses these letters. She describes them as belonging to the genre of

Bildungsroman – the novel of education – commenting: 'Carlyle had thought that if he worked hard to improve himself he might win Jane. That was not to be. His task instead was to educate Jane so that finally she would appreciate him. Without consciously setting out to do so, he trained his pupil so well, so transformed her values, that she was able to perceive him finally as the only fit object for her love' (p. 39). This is very misleading. All the action belongs to the man while the woman is the passive and helpless object of his will. It may serve as a warning that *Parallel Lives* as a whole fails to challenge the gender stereotyping so typical of writing about the Carlyles.

32 CL, vol. 15, p. 147.
33 Ellen Pollack, *The Poetics of Sexual Myth: Gender and Ideology in the Verse of Swift and Pope*, Chicago: University of Chicago Press, 1985, pp. 46–7. Although dealing with eighteenth-century texts, Pollack's book is remarkably suggestive about nineteenth-century issues to do with women as subjects of their own lives and objects serving men's needs.
34 Françoise Basch, *Relative Creatures*, trans. Anthony Rudolf, London: Allen Lane, 1974, p. 59.
35 Fred Kaplan, *Thomas Carlyle: A Biography*, Cambridge: CUP, 1983, p. 39.
36 Rem., p. 3.
37 LM, vol. 1, p. 14.
38 For a discussion of the impact of Carlyle's philosophy, see Walter Houghton, *The Victorian Frame of Mind, 1830–70*, New Haven: Yale University Press, 1957.
39 Mary Smith, *The Autobiography of Mary Smith: Schoolmistress and Nonconformist. A Fragment of a Life*, London: Bemrose & Sons, 1892.
40 *Jane Welsh Carlyle, A New Selection of her Letters*, ed. Trudy Bliss, London: Gollancz, 1950, includes the whole letter, pp. 256–8.

5 WORK

1 Flora Tristan, *The London Journal of Flora Tristan, 1842*, trans. Jean Hawkes, London: Virago, 1982, p. 258.
2 CL, vol. 1, p. 22.
3 ibid. vol. 6, p. 171.
4 LM, vol. 1, p. 213.
5 ibid., vol. 1, p. 234.
6 ibid., vol. 2, pp. 89–90; NLM, vol. 2, p. 161.
7 LM, vol. 1, pp. 243, 213.
8 NLM, vol. 2, p. 19.
9 Thea Holme, in *The Carlyles at Home*, London: OUP, 1965, has a good chapter on the rebuilding projects at Cheyne Row. See 'The soundproof study', pp. 77–98.
10 LM, vol. 1, p. 199.
11 NLM, vol. 2, p. 16.
12 ibid., vol. 2, p. 36.
13 Hux., p. 254. For a full account of Jane Carlyle and John Carlyle, see Mabel Davidson, 'The records of a broken friendship, *South Atlantic Quarterly*, XXIV, July 1925, pp. 278–92. It is worth observing that after Jane's death, Thomas and his brother found it impossible to live together.
14 CL, vol. 6, p. 410.
15 LM, vol. 2, p. 292.
16 ibid., vol. 2, p. 386.
17 NLM, vol. 1, p. 167.
18 CL, vol. 14, p. 134.

19 ibid., vol. 6, pp. 182–3.

20 LM, vol. 2, p. 112.

21 CL, vol. 10, p. 164; CL, vol. 13, p. 110.

22 Sara Coleridge, *Memoir and Letters of Sara Coleridge*, edited by her daughter, London: H.S. King & Co., 1873, p. 422. See also CL, vol. 7, p. 179: Jane to Thomas: 'Heaven help me to be what you have so often advised me to, *"brief in narration"*!'

23 Hux., p. 306.

24 In Lawrence and Elisabeth Hanson, *Necessary Evil: The Life of Jane Welsh Carlyle*, London: Constable, 1952, p. 336.

25 NLM, vol. 2, p. 18.

26 LM, vol. 1, p. 238.

27 Hux., p. 290.

28 Fred Kaplan, *Thomas Carlyle: A Biography*, Cambridge: CUP, 1983, p. 351. Dora Wordsworth's view of Samuel Rogers was that he was 'that Detested Dead Dandy . . . a selfish, conceited little toad'. Dove Cottage papers.

29 LM, vol. 2, p. 36.

30 ibid., vol. 2, pp. 37–8; for the astonishing and thought-provoking story of the Duchesse de Praslin, who was murdered in 1847, see Stanley Loomis, *A Crime of Passion*, London: Hodder & Stoughton, 1967.

31 LM, vol. 1, p. 268.

32 James Pope-Hennessy, *Monckton Milnes, The Years of Promise, 1809–51*, London: Constable, 1949, pp. 158–61. For additional material on Lady Harriet, see *Mrs Brookfield and her Circle*, ed. Charles and Frances Brookfield, Sir I. Pitman & Sons, London 1905; *Autobiography of Henry Taylor 1800–75*, n.p. 1885, vol. 1, pp. 309–11. Taylor felt Milnes had failed to capture the essence of Lady Harriet's charm. Iris Origo, 'The Carlyles and the Ashburtons: A Victorian friendship', *Cornhill Magazine*, no. 984, Autumn 1950, pp. 441–81, is a good introduction to the whole story.

33 NLM, vol. 1, p. 177.

34 ibid., vol. 2, p. 138; Hux., p. 258.

35 Hux., p. 222.

36 Ibid., p. 259.

37 ibid., p. 258.

38 Pope-Hennessy, *Monckton Milnes*, p. 160.

39 NLM, vol. 1, p. 185.

40 Hux., pp. 294, 297.

41 ibid., p. 268.

42 ibid., pp. 276–7.

43 ibid., p. 288.

44 NLM, vol. 1, p. 223; Hux., p. 104. Thea Holme gives a detailed account of the Carlyles and their servants, with a useful appendix listing the women employed between 1834 and 1866; see *The Carlyles at Home*.

45 LM, vol. 1, p. 88; LM, vol. 2, p. 73.

46 Leonore Davidoff, 'Mastered for life: servant and wife in Victorian and Edwardian England', *Journal of Social History*, 7, 1974, pp. 406–28.

47 LM, vol. 1, p. 321. See also *Carlyle Newsletter* (University of Edinburgh), no. 6, Spring 1985, pp. 106–26.

48 Hanson, *Necessary Evil*, p. 343.

49 Holme, *The Carlyles at Home*, p. 87.

50 Charlotte's full story is in Holme, ch. 11, pp. 162–84.

51 LM, vol. 1, p. 36.

52 ibid., vol. 2, p. 244.

53 NLM, vol. 2, p. 276.

54 Francis Jeffrey, 'Felicia Hemans', *Edinburgh Review*, vol. 50, Oct. 1829, pp. 32–47.
55 NLM, vol. 2, p. 163.
56 LM, vol. 1, p. 4.
57 NLM, vol. 2, p. 204.
58 ibid., pp. 205–6.
59 In 'The diamond necklace' (1837), *Critical and Miscellaneous Essays*, London: Chapman and Hall, 1899, vol. 3, p. 329.
60 LM, vol. 1, p. 85.
61 ibid., pp. 95–6.
62 ibid., p. 50.
63 See J.A. Froude, *Thomas Carlyle: A History of His Life in London 1834–1861*, London: Longmans, Green & Co., 1884, vol. 1, p. 11.
64 *Early Letters of Jane Welsh Carlyle*, ed. David Ritchie, London: Swan Sonnenschein & Co., 1889, p. 260.
65 *Selections from the Letters of Geraldine Jewsbury to Jane Welsh Carlyle*, ed. Mrs Alexander Ireland, London: Longmans, Green & Co., 1892, p. 181.
66 ibid.
67 G.M. Gould, *Biographic Clinics*, Philadelphia: P. Blakiston & Co., 1903, vol. 2, pp. 205–38.
68 See Introduction to Susanne Howe, *Geraldine Jewsbury, Her Life and Errors*, London: George Allen & Unwin, 1935; *Times Literary Supplement*, 18 July 1935, p. 461.
69 Edmund Mercer, *Manchester Quarterly*, vol. 17, 1898.
70 LM, vol. 2, p. 29.
71 ibid., vol. 1, pp. 271, 275; NLM, vol. 1, p. 203.
72 NLM, vol. 1, pp. 208–9.
73 Howe, *Geraldine Jewsbury*, p. 22.
74 LM, vol. 1, p. 405.
75 Hux., p. 378.
76 ibid., pp. 269–70.
77 NLM, vol. 2, pp. 126–7.
78 Hux., p. 90.
79 ibid., p. 89.
80 ibid., p. 93.

6 THE COMFORTS OF OTHERS

1 LM, vol. 1, p. 88.
2 Eric Gillett, *Maria Jane Jewsbury: A Memoir*, Oxford: OUP, 1932, p. lix. This forms part of Harriett Hughes's description of Maria Jane's wedding, written for Dora Wordsworth.
3 Dove Cottage papers. All subsequent quotations are from the same source unless otherwise indicated.
4 In Jane Williams, *Literary Women of England*, London: Saunders, Otley & Co., 1861, pp. 380–1.
5 *Athenaeum*, 11 August 1832, no. 250, p. 521.
6 ibid., 1 December 1832, no. 266, p. 777.
7 Edmund Mercer, *Manchester Quarterly*, October 1898.
8 Geraldine's letters to Carlyle are printed as an appendix to Jeanne Rosenmayer's Ph.D. thesis, 'Geraldine Jewsbury: Novelist and Publisher's Reader', University of London, 1970, pp. 49–65.
9 In her third letter, Geraldine ventured to ask if Carlyle had heard of her sister. He replied, 'Your dear sister's name was well known to me . . . I had gathered some

image of her as of a clear decisive rational woman.' CL, vol. 13, p. 296.

10   'Religious faith and modern scepticism', *Westminster Review*, vol. 52, Oct. 1849–Jan. 1850, p. 396.

11   Robert Lee Wolff, *Gains and Losses: Novels of Faith and Doubt in Victorian England*, London: John Murray, 1977, pp. 403–5.

12   Michael Sadleir, *Nineteenth Century Fiction, A Bibliographical Record*, London: Constable, 1951, vol. 1, p. 193.

13   Geraldine Jewsbury, *Selections of Letters from Geraldine E. Jewsbury to Jane Welsh Carlyle*, ed. Mrs Alexander Ireland, London: Longmans, Green & Co., 1892, pp. 158–9.

14   Geraldine Jewsbury, *Zoe, The History of Two Lives*, London: Chapman and Hall, 1845, vol. 2, pp. 264–5.

15   ibid., vol. 3, p. 29.

16   ibid., vol. 2, pp. 262–3.

17   ibid., vol. 3, pp. 23–4.

18   ibid., vol. 3, p. 26.

19   ibid., vol. 3, p. 27.

20   Mary Russell Mitford, *Recollections of a Literary Life*, London: Richard Bentley, 1851, pp. 143–4.

21   E.L. Griggs, *Coleridge Fille: A Biography of Sara Coleridge*, Oxford: OUP, 1940, p. 170.

22   Sara Coleridge, *Memoir and Letters of Sara Coleridge*, ed. by her daughter, London: H.S. King & Co., 1873, vol. 2, p. 70.

23   ibid., vol. 2, pp. 82–3.

24   ibid., vol. 2, p. 160.

25   Griggs, *Coleridge Fille*, p. 40.

26   'Literary women', *London Review*, 1864, p. 329.

27   Jewsbury, *Letters*, pp. 430, 104.

28   ibid., pp. 338, 280–1.

29   ibid., pp. 204–5.

30   ibid.

31   Hux., p. 57.

32   ibid., pp. 66, 82.

33   Jewsbury, *Letters*, pp. 145–6.

34   ibid.

35   ibid., p. 333.

36   Geraldine Jewsbury, *The History of an Adopted Child*, London: Grant & Griffith, 1852, pp. 347–52.

37   Hux., p. 61.

38   ibid.

39   ibid., p. 66.

40   ibid., pp. 97, 89.

41   ibid., p. 96.

42   Geraldine's hard work in finding employment for two young girls, Elizabeth and Juliet Mudie, whose cause Jane had taken up, was also significant.

43   Hux., p. 189.

44   ibid., p. 194.

45   ibid., p. 212.

46   In Guinevere Griest, *Mudie's Circulating Library*, Bloomington: Indiana University Press, 1970, p. 124.

47   Hux., p. 233.

48   Griest, p. 124.

49 J.M. Hartley, 'Geraldine Jewsbury and the problems of the woman novelist', *Women's Studies International Quarterly*, vol. 2, no. 2, 1979, pp. 137–53.
50 Jewsbury, *Zoe*, vol. 1, pp. 67–8.
51 ibid., vol. 1, pp. 260–1.
52 ibid., vol. 3, p. 207.
53 ibid., vol. 1, p. 260.
54 ibid., vol. 3, pp. 241–2.
55 ibid., vol. 3, pp. 256–7.
56 H.F. Chorley, *Athenaeum*, 1 Feb. 1845, no. 901, p. 114.
57 Sadleir, *Nineteenth Century Fiction*, p. 193.
58 Hux., pp. 235, 236.
59 ibid., pp. 238–9.
60 ibid., p. 243.
61 Francis Espinasse, *Literary Recollections and Sketches*, London: Hodder & Stoughton, 1893, p. 268. Espinasse noted also that the Carlyles had a tendency to talk over each other, and observed that it was better when they talked 'successively rather than simultaneously, but her husband did not always allow her that alternative' (p. 205).
62 Hux., p. 261.
63 Charlotte Cushman's life is fully documented in Joseph Leach, *Bright Particular Star: The Life & Times of Charlotte Cushman*, New Haven: Yale University Press, 1970.
64 Mantell papers.
65 Elizabeth Barrett Browning to Miss Mitford, October 1851, in *The Letters of Elizabeth Barrett Browning to Mary Russell Mitford*, ed. Meredith B. Raymond and Mary Rose Sullivan, Armstrong Browning Library of Baylor University, The Browning Institute, Wedgestone Press, and Wellesley College, 1983, vol. 3, p. 331.
66 Hux., p. 303.

7 OF THE FEMALE PERSUASION

1   Mantell papers.
2   Geraldine Jewsbury, *Selections from the Letters of Geraldine E. Jewsbury to Jane Welsh Carlyle*, ed. Mrs Alexander Ireland, London: Longmans, Green & Co., 1892, p. 191.
3   LM, vol. 2, p. 204.
4   The Ramsgate trip is related in LM, vol. 2, pp. 199–204.
5   Mantell papers.
6   LM, vol. 1, pp. 307–8.
7   ibid., vol. 1, p. 316.
8   NLM, vol. 1, p. 242.
9   LM, vol. 1, p. 317.
10 Lawrence and Elisabeth Hanson, *Necessary Evil: The Life of Jane Welsh Carlyle*, London: Constable, 1952, p. 359.
11 ibid.
12 See Leslie Rabine, 'George Sand and the myth of femininity', in Janet Todd (ed.), *Be Good, Sweet Maid*, New York: Holmes & Meier, 1981, p. 59.
13 ibid., p. 65.
14 Joseph Leach, *Bright Particular Star: The Life & Times of Charlotte Cushman*, New Haven: Yale University Press, 1970, pp. 165–7.
15 Mantell papers.
16 Margaret Fuller, *Memoirs of Margaret Fuller Ossoli*, London: Richard Bentley, 1852, vol. 2, p. 58.

17 Geraldine Jewsbury, *The Half Sisters, A Tale*, London: Chapman and Hall, 1848, vol. 1, pp. 60, 192.
18 ibid., vol. 1, p. 95.
19 ibid., vol. 1, p. 62.
20 ibid., vol. 1, p. 69.
21 ibid., vol. 1, pp. 98–9.
22 ibid., vol. 1, p. 116.
23 ibid., vol. 1, p. 117.
24 ibid., vol. 2, p. 103.
25 ibid., vol. 2, pp. 72–3.
26 ibid., vol. 2, p. 74.
27 ibid., vol. 2, p. 71.
28 ibid., vol. 1, pp. 274–5.
29 ibid., vol. 2, pp. 24–5.
30 ibid., vol. 2, pp. 26–32.
31 ibid., vol. 1, p. 263.
32 ibid., vol. 2, p. 97.
33 ibid., vol. 2, pp. 95–6.
34 ibid., vol. 1, pp. 205–6.
35 ibid., vol. 2, p. 292.
36 ibid., vol. 2, pp. 36–8.
37 Geraldine Jewsbury, *The Sorrows of Gentility*, London: Hurst & Blackett, 1856, vol. 2, pp. 46, 57.
38 ibid., vol. 2, p. 50.
39 Jewsbury, *Letters*, p. 367.
40 ibid., p. 129.
41 Jewsbury, *Sorrows of Gentility*, vol. 2, pp. 196–8.
42 Fred Kaplan, *Thomas Carlyle: A Biography*, Cambridge: CUP, 1983, p. 393.
43 Hux., p. 275.
44 CL, vol. 5, p. 423.
45 Hux., p. 282.
46 Jewsbury, *Letters*, p. 304.
47 LM, vol. 2, p. 142.
48 Jewsbury, *Letters*, p. 304.
49 Mantell papers.
50 Thea Holme, *The Carlyles at Home*, Oxford: OUP, 1965, pp. 177–80.
51 Mantell papers.
52 ibid.
53 NLM, vol. 2, p. 9.
54 Geraldine Jewsbury, *Marian Withers*, London: Colburn & Co., 1851, vol. 1, pp. 23–8.
55 ibid., vol. 3, pp. 34–5.
56 Harriet Martineau, *Autobiography*, London: Virago, 1983, vol. 1, p. 401.
57 Mantell papers.
58 J.A. Froude, *Thomas Carlyle: A History of His Life in London 1834–1881*, London: Longmans, Green & Co., 1884, vol. 1, p. 459.
59 Jewsbury, *Letters*, p. 197.
60 LM, vol. 1, p. 247.

8 TELLING TRUTHS

1 Geraldine Jewsbury, *Selections from the Letters of Geraldine E. Jewsbury to Jane Welsh Carlyle*, ed. Mrs Alexander Ireland, London: Longmans, Green & Co., 1892, p. 235.
2 ibid., pp. 242–3.
3 ibid., p. 244.
4 Mantell papers. All subsequent quotations are from this source unless otherwise indicated.
5 NLM, vol. 2, pp. 150–1, 155.
6 ibid., vol. 2, pp. 172–3.
7 ibid., vol. 2, p. 217.
8 See also Susanne Howe, *Geraldine Jewsbury, Her Life and Errors*, London: George Allen & Unwin, 1935, ch. 8, 'A proud, shy man', pp. 147–60. Howe draws very generously on the letters, and although her emphasis differs from mine the detail in her account will be of interest to those who wish to pursue the subject further.

FURTHER READING

The following is a brief selection of useful material not cited in the text.

Benstock, Shari (1987) *Feminist Issues in Literary Scholarship*, Bloomington: Indiana University Press.

Branca, Patricia (1975) *Silent Sisterhood: Middle Class Women in Victorian Homes*, London: Croom Helm.

Calder, Jenni (1976) *Women and Marriage in Victorian Fiction*, Oxford: OUP.

Davidoff, Leonore and Hall, Catherine (1987) *Family Fortunes: Men and Women of the English middle class 1780–1850*, London: Hutchinson.

Drew, Elizabeth (1928) *Jane Welsh and Jane Carlyle*, New York: Scribner & Sons.

Ecker, Gisela (ed.) (1985) *Feminist Aesthetics*, London: Women's Press.

Figes, Eva (1982) *Sex & Subterfuge: Women Writers to 1850*, London: Macmillan.

Foster, Shirley (1985) *Victorian Women's Fiction: Marriage, Freedom and the Individual*, Beckenham: Croom Helm.

Fox, Caroline (1882) *Memories of Old Friends: Extracts from the Journals and Letters of Caroline Fox, 1835–71* ed. Horace Plym, London: Smith, Elder & Co.

Fuller, Margaret (1971) *Woman in the Nineteenth Century*, Introduction by Bernard Rosenthal, New York: Norton and Co.

Gay, Peter (1984) *Education of the Senses: The Bourgeois Experience, Victoria to Freud*, Oxford: OUP.

George, Margaret (1970) *One Woman's 'Situation': A Study of Mary Wollstonecraft*, Evanston: University of Illinois Press.

Greene, Gayle and Kahn, Coppelia (1985) *Making a Difference: Feminist Literary Criticism*, London: Methuen.

Hardwick, Elizabeth (1973) *Seduction and Betrayal: Women and Literature*, New York: Random House.

Hayter, Alethea (1965) *A Sultry Month: Scenes of London Literary Life in 1846*, London: Faber & Faber.

Healey, Edna (1986) *Wives of Fame*, London: Sidgwick & Jackson.

Homans, Margaret (1980) *Women Writers and Poetic Identity*, Princeton: Princeton University Press.

Jacobus, Mary (ed.) (1979) *Women Writing and Writing about Women*, Beckenham: Croom Helm.

Jeffreys, Sheila (1985) *The Spinster and her Enemies*, London: Pandora Press.

Lefebure, Molly (1986) *The Bondage of Love: A Life of Mrs Samuel Taylor Coleridge*, London: Gollancz.

Marshall, Dorothy (1977) *Fanny Kemble*, London: Weidenfeld & Nicolson.

Miller, Jane (1986) *Women Writing about Men*, London: Virago.

Newton, Judith and Rosenfelt, Deborah (1985) *Feminist Criticism and Social Change: Sex, Class and Race in Literature and Culture*, London: Methuen.

Olsen, Tillie (1980) *Silences*, London: Virago.

Prochaska, F.K. (1980) *Women and Philanthropy in 19th Century England*, Oxford: Clarendon Press.

Robinson, Lillian (1978) *Sex, Class and Culture*, Bloomington: Indiana University Press.

Spacks, Patricia Meyer (1972) *The Female Imagination*, New York: Avon Books.

Spencer, Jane (1986) *The Rise of the Woman Novelist: From Aphra Behn to Jane Austen*, Oxford: Basil Blackwell.

Swindells, Julia (1985) *Victorian Writing and Working Women*, Cambridge: Polity Press.

Taylor, Barbara (1983) *Eve and the New Jerusalem: Socialism and Feminism in the Nineteenth Century*, London: Virago.

Woolf, Virginia (1975) *A Room of One's Own*, Harmondsworth: Penguin Modern Classics.

INDEX